Living Behind the Facade

Books by the author

Equine
The Natural Horse: Lessons from the Wild (1992, 2020)
Horse Owners Guide to Natural Hoof Care (1999)
Founder – Prevention and Cure the Natural Way (2001)
Guide To Booting Horses for Hoof Care Professionals (2002)
Paddock Paradise: A Guide to Natural Horse Boarding (2005)
The Natural Trim: Principles and Practice (2012)
The Healing Angle: Nature's Gateway to the Healing Field (2014)
Laminitis: An Equine Plague of Unconscionable Proportions (2016)
Training Manual: ISNHCP Natural Trim Training Program (2017)
the Hoof Balancer: A Unique Tool for Balancing Equine Hooves (2019)
The Natural Trim: Advanced Guidelines (2019)
The Natural Trim: Basic Guidelines (2019, 2022)
*Navicular Syndrome: Healing And Prevention Using the Principles and
    Practices of Natural Horse Care (2021)*
*A Closer Approximation of ☉ On the MATW Using An Infrared
    Thermometer With Laser Pointer Gun (2021)*

Other
The Canvas Tipi (1982)
*Guard Your Teeth: Why the Dental Industry Fails Us
    A Guide to Natural Dental Care (2018, 2022)*
Buckskin Tanner: A Guide to Natural Hide Tanning (2019)
*Cheyenne Tipi Notes (1903): Technical Insights Into 19th Century
    Plains Indian Bison Hide Tanning (2019)*
*Living Behind the Facade: Memoirs Of A Gay Man's Journey Through
    the 20th Century (2019) George Somers with Jaime Jackson*
Platform: A Humanitarian Model For An Egalitarian Society (2019)
Zoo Paradise: A New Model for Humane Zoological Gardens (2019)

Forthcoming
Horse Trek – Into the Mystic

Living Behind the Facade

Memoirs Of George Somers
A Gay Man's Journey
Through the 20th Century

Jaime Jackson

Natural World Publications

© 2023 Jaime Jackson

Book design: J. Jackson

ISBN 978-1-7333094-2-4

Natural World Publications
P.O. Box 1765
Harrison, AR 72602-1765

www.naturalworldpublications.com
jacksonaanhcp@gmail.com

"Straight people aren't normal,
they're just more common."
— J. Jackson

Contents

COMMENTARY by Jaime Jackson
PAGE 8

C1
THE FIRST YEARS   1914-1925
PAGE 17

2
MOVING TO AMERICA   1926-1930
PAGE 39

3
MOVING TO SAN DIEGO   1931-1932
PAGE 47

4
STARTING COLLEGE   1933-1934
PAGE 61

5
FATHER'S DEATH   1935-1936
PAGE 77

6
MOVING TO SAN FRANCISCO   1937-1941
PAGE 83

7
THE ARMY   1942-1943
PAGE 101

8
GOING TO EUROPE   1944-1945
PAGE 111

9
ON TO JAPAN   1945-1946
PAGE 143

10
RETURN TO SAN FRANCISCO   1946-1947
PAGE 159

11
MOVING TO MARIN COUNTY   1948-1954
PAGE 167

12
THE HOUSE IN LARKSPUR   1955-1965
PAGE 199

13
THE BUSH STREET HOUSE   1966-1968
PAGE 221

14
THE HOUSE IN OAKLAND   1969-PRESENT
PAGE 245

15
SPAIN AND MOROCCO   1972
PAGE 253

16
THE RIGHT ONE · THE TRAVEL BUG   1978
PAGE 267

17
BALI AND OTHER INDONESIAN PORTS OF CALL   1988, 1996
PAGE 291

18
RUSSIA   1992
PAGE 311

19
THE ARMY DOESN'T FORGET   1994, 1997
PAGE 325

20
RUSSIA, AGAIN?   1995
PAGE 331

21
TO RUSSIA WITH RICK   1997
PAGE 359

22
BORIS COMES TO AMERICA   1997
PAGE 393

23
TRIPPING THROUGH EASTERN EUROPE   1998
PAGE 403

24
PARTING THOUGHTS   2002, 2004
PAGE 431

§

POSTSCRIPT by Jaime Jackson
PAGE 438

GLOSSARY OF GAY TERMS
PAGE 441

IMAGE ATTRIBUTIONS
PAGE 444

ABOUT JAIME JACKSON
PAGE 445

COMMENTARY BY JAIME JACKSON

The reader deserves an explanation of how this biography came about. At the outset, neither the story teller, who is my uncle, nor I (his biographer and publisher) ever imagined a book. The "project" began as something else 26 years ago, when George was in his 83rd year. As I recall, it began with a simple query from me in a 1997 letter: "George, can you tell me anything about the Somers-Dominguez side of our family?" Somers was the paternal side of my mother's and Uncle George's family, Dominguez the maternal. At age 50, I was then I suspect like many my age, wanting to "know where I came from," having not really thought about it to the extent I should have in earlier years. But my own parents had deceased many years before, and George, it dawned on me, was one of the few surviving "elder" links to the family's past. Ironically, George was also a "terminal" branch in the Family Tree, for he was "gay."

George, as his story will reveal, and I had always been on good terms. I'm not judgmental towards gays or anyone else. Biologically, people are what they are, and we can accept it or, as I think of it, become bigoted. I have always abhorred bigotry, regardless of its target. George, from my early youth, had confided his homosexuality to me, and I never felt threatened by it like so many. Perhaps this was due to my familial love for and trust in George, or simply because I am secure in being a heterosexual. Or perhaps I just didn't care. My attitude at that age was, "So what?" Whatever the reason, I felt very comfortable in going to George to learn about our family tree, regardless of what other family members might have thought of him because he was gay. George readily accepted the challenge, and I eagerly awaited his genealogical report.

What I received from George in the mail, a rough typed out letter in an annoying cursive font, both stunned and disappointed me. What he had to say with Spartan brevity comprised less than two pages! I felt like I received but a trickle of what he actually knew about the family, except that there were fascinating Spanish and German origins coming down both sides of his ancestral tree. But a strange and ominous comment at the very end of his accounting piqued my interest: "This is not the story I wanted to tell."

I immediately fired back to George, "What story *did* you want to tell?"

A story about his life as a homosexual, of course, was what he really wanted to do. He felt he had an important story to tell, the truth of what it was like living much of his life "in the closet," behind a facade of an ersatz heterosexual identity, one superimposed upon him — like the mask on this book's cover — by the expectations of a dominant and homophobic society. I agreed to help him organize and record his memoirs.

As with the general void of genealogical data about our family tree, there was indeed much about George's gay life that had also remained a mystery to me. I knew vaguely that he had served in the military during WWII, attended U.C. Berkeley briefly in the 1930s, was employed for most of his working life as a display manager by several San Francisco department stores, and had always been gay. In fact, I was not entirely naive about "real" gay life since I had lived — as the only "straight" member — in his household of gay men for two years while I attended college in San Francisco, George's home at the time. And, no, the experience didn't "make me gay!" What I didn't know much about, was George's interpersonal relationships with members of our extended family. For example, how he perceived others attitudes in our family towards him for being gay, and, in the larger sense, what it meant for him to be gay in a straight, and often unfriendly, discriminatory and sometimes dangerous homophobic world. What I learned is that the socially impervious "closet" confining homosexuality can be as hard to penetrate from without, as it is to escape from within. George, understandably, simply didn't dwell on the subject of homosexuality, nor did I, while we lived together. We simply did our own thing.

But once the door to talking about his life was opened, I was as motivated to learn about it as much as George was eager to tell it. I then created a rather rough narrative format through which he could relate his story — to get it out, so to speak — while I, on the receiving side, would help to record it in hopes of satisfying my own curiosity about my extended family and George's obscure if not oblique gay lifestyle. Beyond this, with the possible exception of sharing a photocopied transcription with other family members, if they were interested (we didn't know if they would be at that point), there was no greater plan. We also agreed that if he was not comfortable going public with it, it would end there, or I could publish it well after he died. Further, we agreed to change the names of those gay men in his story who were still alive to protect their privacy.

Very roughly, that is, without my giving him much editorial input or a writer's template with which to help him organize his thoughts, we launched into the project. George was to give me a second draft. It arrived within a week, causing me to shudder, "What could he have possibly put together in such a short expanse of time?" And once more, to my dismay, George produced yet another "compressed" story, not 20 typed pages long. I chided him, "George, do you mean to tell me that your life story amounts to just 20 pages of double-spaced text?" He didn't find this amusing, but he also saw my point. He simply lacked a sense of what he should cover, and to what extent. I imposed upon him that we now create an outline of his life, a chronology. In the process of listening to him and reading his notes, I began to think like George, even put his words into text that would mimic him. That I could do this was critical as it turns out, because the first signs of Alzheimer's began to creep in to the project early on.

What came next was what I was hoping for: a fairly detailed, and very interesting accounting of his life (and our family's), from his earliest childhood recollections to the present. I relished it all. I also now realized as I gleaned its content, and contemplated his message, that we had the underpinnings for a great biography, to be published while he was alive or posthumously, his choice as explained above. I anticipated, but did not tell him so, that in the end he would decline to go public while he lived, particularly since his partner did not approve of the project from the get go. And more so because it might be asking too much for the man to go public after having been compelled to conceal his sexual orientation for most of his life. I'll explain what the outcome of this consternation was in my postscript.

As a comprehensive work on the inner life of a gay man, however, George's story still lacked sufficient breadth and depth. Moreover, it was evident that it was still written largely from a "closeted" gay perspective. How much pressure could I put on an 84 year old man — a year had now passed since the inception of our project — to "come out" and go beyond what might be his personal "comfort zone?" I decided to press him, and press him hard, even risking his alienation, for I personally believed in his avowed message, expressed in his final chapter, "To accept one another as fully human and that we can love the diversity of humankind as normal."

My plan now was to inspire George to go deeper into this story, to cast his life in the light of "Gay Liberation." But typical of George when confronted with an unexpected turn, as this was, he threw up a wall of protest.

"But what has Gay Liberation got to do with my life?" he struck back at me.

This was actually a bit of "denial" on his behalf, and the reader again deserves further background to understand why.

George, in the early 1960s, and nearing his 50th year, had attended in San Francisco the formation meetings of a new, perhaps the first, U.S. civil rights organization by and for homosexuals, SIR — San Francisco Society for Individual Rights. As a young teenager, I remember him proudly telling me about it at the time. But quickly, he moved furtively and deeply into the shadows of SIR, supportive, but staying clear of it publicly for fear that its increasingly vocal politics might cost him his job in San Francisco — if he were fingered as being a "queer" through association. Such was the terroristic and immobilizing power of the "facade" even at that late date. It would take waves of liberating changes in society — the Vietnam anti-war movement, the hippy generation, the famous gay Stonewall Inn riot in Greenwich Village (and other acts of resistance to police harassment and brutality), the convergence of hundreds of thousands of gays and lesbians in San Francisco, and perhaps his retirement too, to render George secure enough to "come out" and speak publicly about the injustices heaped upon homosexuals. Unquestionably, countless older gays and lesbians can identify with George's sense of vulnerability and the threat to his survival in that darker period of homosexual discrimination. And this is not to suggest that countless gays, including George until the day he died, and lesbians still do not cower in fear of losing their jobs, family rejection, their sense of personal security and safety, and their spiritual balance, in a society that to this day still toils ambivalently in its social conscience and in its laws towards the burgeoning homosexual imperative that will not be silenced.

Eventually, George agreed that we should meet vis-à-vis (I lived across the U.S. from him in Arkansas), to discuss how we might best bring our project to fruition: a story about a homosexual male who has always lived the gay life, much of it in the shadows, a full 90 years by the time the project was completed in 2004. To do it right, I believed that we should not impose stringent or artificial limits on the size and scope of his memoirs, so typical now of today's large publishing houses with their "formula" venues. While it would focus on one man's life, George's, we would cast it in the larger stream of gay liberation — the ultimate dream and hope of all homosexuals, gay and lesbian alike, not living in utter denial. This opened the door for George to speak more freely and expansively about his life, and his bio then grew quite organically from one hundred to the current near 500 pages. This seemed justified to me, because George's life has been a highly creative and interesting one deserving of the "shelf space" accorded other excellent works in the humanities. To me, it is an important seminal work. One I intended to take "out of the closet," with or without George on the planet as we had agreed upon.

§

Living Behind the Façade is an important work because it truly dispels many of the egregious myths about homosexuals which fuel America's widespread and persistent homophobia. It is clear to me that this bigotry exists, not because of homosexuality, but because of what ignorant people speciously *think* they know about it. What they know in the way of truth, in my opinion, is, sadly, very little. Time and again I have introduced close friends to George, and not one has ever come away with homophobic fear of or contempt for homosexuals as a result. To the contrary, they have learned to accept George for the well-rounded person that he is: talented, caring, intellectual, hardworking, spiritual, creative, and yes, successful too! Gayness, they have learned, detracts from none of these qualities that are coveted and appreciated by most human beings. Only misguided belief in the virulent bigotry of homophobiacs — whose ignorant and repulsive behavior may readily incur fear in the young, the timid, the unwitting, and the naïve — can lead otherwise decent people to an opposing perspective.

In "designing" the layout of George's book, I struggled constantly to bring its "gay" import into position for the reader to even see it. In fact, I am responsible for introducing the book's more revealing visuals: artistic nudes, gay parties, Gay Pride parade scenes, images of gay couples, and so forth. This took some doing on my part, as at the outset of our project, George, who is quite "private" like most homosexuals and heterosexuals, would never have allowed it. I also encouraged George to describe some of his sexual encounters — nothing too graphic, just enough to enlighten "straights" a little bit about gay courting, love, and sexuality. Contrary to what many may think, heterosexuals are often, so I've learned and am also amused by, quite curious about this facet of gay life "behind the façade."

So it may come as a surprise to the reader that George's book is not actually about homosexuality, but the life of a man who happens to be homosexual. The two, in this view, aren't necessarily synonymous. The homosexual no more funnels all thought and activity through his or her sexual orientation than does the heterosexual. Homophobiacs — who contend that all "queers" are, from morning till night, essentially mentally deranged, sex-obsessed and child molesters — would have us believe otherwise. Only such bigotry causes the homosexual to reflect, sometimes with guilt due to the façade, upon his or her sexuality as a "homosexual." Otherwise, it is given no thought at all from what I have observed first hand. Anymore, that is, than the heterosexual ponders his or her own sexuality. For example, I personally do not go around thinking to myself, that it is sad, or a joy, or a disgrace, or a fact, or whatever, that I am a heterosexual. Neither does the homosexual, except when confronted by the ignorance, virulence and insensitivities of the homophobic and his culture — not to mention society's historic legal incriminations against homosexuals. Hence, in George's story — and the reader is asked to contemplate this when reading it — I have had to highlight these unfortunate junctures between the façade and truth as homosexuals know it, and to intrude a little into George's private life, to remind us that the story being told has really little to do at all about homosexuality. Again, it is simply about the interesting and creative life of a man who just happens to be a homosexual.

Yet, *sex* seems to be the main bugaboo with straights concerning homosexuality. It is the "nucleus" of society's homophobia. The idea of having sex with one's own sex, like incest, is so abhorrent to homophobic heterosexuals that it is simply impossible to accept homosexuality as anything but willful immorality. I laugh at this personally, because I know from talking with George and other homosexuals, that they feel the same kind of repugnance at the suggestion of having sex with the opposite sex! So, really, no one has anything to worry about — providing we're not expecting or demanding that people have sex with persons for whom they have no sexual feelings or attraction, regardless of one's sexual orientation. That would be tantamount to rape, in my opinion. Yet, we hear and it is addressed in this book, it is the homophobic heterosexual's expectation for remedying "pathological" homosexuality through whatever means, from religious training to exorcism. The "devil," so they say, resides in the homosexual, and it must be removed to regain his God-given heterosexuality. It seems to me that homophobiacs generally are having a lot of trouble seeing past their own sexuality, and, therefore, cannot accept that homosexually is anything more than unnecessary promiscuity that the misguided heterosexual was drawn into.

Like most decent people, gay and straight alike, George views sex as a private matter, certainly not a public affair. He believes in the sanctity of commitment — yes, including in same-sex marriage! Although he confides to the reader that gays and lesbians are often (not always) more openly tolerant of infidelity, whereas straights tend (not always) to be more hypocritical and dishonest — spawning unrealistic expectations of human morality that, George argues, are reflected in today's staggering heterosexual divorce rate often the result of infidelity. I don't think this view is an invitation to immorality, as much as it is a realistic look at contemporary human sexual behavior regardless of one's sexual orientation.

Whatever the case, when we finally raise our heads out of the "sexual morass," we will find that the homosexual is not so different from his or her heterosexual counterpart, after all. Straight and gay alike, we are humans with the same social needs and issues. I fail to see any difference. Personally, I oppose the "islanding" of homosexuals, such as we see in San Francisco and other "gay Meccas." I believe their rightful "place" is within the "mainstream society" accepted like everyone else for who they are — including what they are biologically speaking — and right alongside their families, friends, neighbors, and fellow workers. I don't think social mores will have to be redefined to do this, because homosexuality has always been with us since the dawn of humanity — and it has never been the "trouble" or "scourge" that homophobiacs of Western Civilization would have the unwitting believe.

Perhaps the homophobic is him or herself in urgent need of counseling and psychotherapy. I suspect from their irrationality and arrogant heterosexism that their phobia is deep-seated in denial — anxiety and self-doubt concerning their own heterosexual identity. A victim of one's own self-hate, however misplaced. Many find their way to the religious pulpit to proselytize others to their hate, such is their insecurity. Most preach false doctrine, particularly in quoting the Biblical scripture. Christians may be surprised to know that Jesus never once mentions or castigates homosexuals in his admonitions against sinners. Given the Savior's example then, what reasonable person would be given to such extremes as to sit in virulent judgment of others? As a basically tolerant society, we've simply let some of these loud-mouthed troublemakers prey upon our own ignorance of human sexuality (and history) to jade the truth about perfectly natural sexual variation within our species. Gays are not out "to get us," "convert us," or "bring us down" *a la* "Sodom and Gomorrah" as the religious bitch-barkers rail at us from their mounts. As George relates in his story, "There are plenty of gays to meet our needs."

I am fully confident — and I am saying this as a "confirmed" heterosexual without a gay bone in his body! — that the human spirit can rise above the hatred and ill will, to turn things around. We are all reminded that every homosexual, with relatively few exceptions, was brought into the world by two loving heterosexuals. How can such love foster such denial and contempt? Certainly, it isn't God's work is it? As a naturalist, I think it's just part of what our species happens to be.

It's my hope, and my late uncle's, that *Living Behind the Façade* will help a little in the much needed transformation. Americans can help by imposing upon their State legislators to dismantle the "Gay Apartheid" laws of discrimination against homosexuals, but also women, minorities, and really all of its citizens by ratifying the Equal Rights Amendment (ERA) to the U.S. Constitution.

Jaime Jackson
August/2023

1
The First Years

1914 - 1925

"I sit on the end of a branch on the family tree that you can see elsewhere in the story. I will tell this story as honestly and sincerely as I can, because I am not ashamed of who or what I am. Being gay was not a decision I made at some point growing up." - GS

∫

Having succeeded in getting George to move beyond his 20 page bio, I asked him to start from the beginning, back in the Philippines where he and my mother, and his other siblings were all born. What came was all news to me, and the narrative that follows reflects my constant badgering him for details. I was struck by his prodigious memory in his 83rd year, and contemplated where all this might take us. - JJ

The First Years: 1914 – 1925

*H*ave you ever wondered just who your ancestors were and how your life evolved from theirs? It is only natural to be curious and as you age, you tend to reflect on the roles you have played in the lives of others, friends, lovers and family. I wonder sometimes how my actions have influenced and changed the way others have taken their paths in life.

In my own immediate family, sister Dorothy married and became part of the Moore family, while the next in line, Anita, became a Jackson. The youngest sister, Solita, never married. I, myself, never married in the usual way one tends to think of marriage. Being a gay man, I am not allowed that right in America except in the one state of the 50 (Vermont) and even there, it isn't more than a half-hearted civil act that is performed in an office.[1] So much for "Special Rights" that politicians say we are always demanding as our due.

I sit on the end of a branch on the family tree that you can see elsewhere in the story (*appended: "Somers Family Ancestral Tree"*). I will tell this story as honestly and sincerely as I can, because I am not ashamed of who or what I am. Being gay was not a decision I made at some point growing up. I simply, gradually, realized that my orientation was to be homosexual. Being gay is not a "choice" or a "preference" or a "lifestyle." Like being right-brained or left-brained, right-handed or left-handed, blue-eyed or brown-eyed — these are traits that are a fundamental part of a human being's make-up.

I will tell this story as honestly and sincerely as I can, because I am not ashamed of who or what I am.

Being gay was not a decision I made at some point growing up. I simply, gradually, realized that my orientation was to be homosexual. Being gay is not a "choice" or a "preference" or a "lifestyle."

---

[1] Same-sex marriage in the United States expanded from one state in 2004 to all fifty states in 2015 through various state court rulings, state legislation, direct popular votes, and federal court rulings. This occurred after George finished writing his book, and before I was able to publish it. However, to date, not all counties in the U.S. are willing to issue same-sex licenses. Officials of eight counties in Alabama and one county in Texas are still unwilling to issue licenses to same-sex couples, as of December 2018. Those wishing to marry in these counties must travel to another county to obtain a license. Further, opponents of gay rights seem determined to find ways to amend the Constitution to restrict marriages to heterosexual unions.

1 - The First Years

Does God favor people who have certain skin or hair color while rejecting other peoples? He isn't perceived that way by most of us, I think. Why would I have "chosen" to walk this most uncomfortable of paths and be perceived as an undesirable person unless I found it impossible to do anything else and still be true to myself?

In my span of years, I have seen Society change its view of the "Gay World" from one of abhorrence to one of toleration. It is much less difficult to be openly gay today than the 1920s when I was first becoming aware of my own direction. All this has happened through the work of some very brave individuals too numerous to name here in my own story. Their stories are well-documented elsewhere.* Fortunately for my gay brothers and sisters, it is much less of a stigma today as Society slowly changes its perception of homosexuality, just as women went through their struggle and the African-Americans had to fight their battles for equality. But even these fights still go on. Hollywood, that great molder of public morals and opinion, has recently acceded to show gay characters in a more favorable light — we see progress of sorts.

In the long span of Civilization, homosexuality has gone through many periods of acceptance and rejection. There are many references to the famous and infamous gays of history. Alexander the Great, Leonardo da Vinci, Plato, Michelangelo all belong in our gay ranks. There have been kings, warriors, poets, artists, writers and myriads of just plain people who lived their lives as gay men and women. Historians have often veiled the information available to please the heterosexual world, but today we are more likely to read the Truth about those of us living behind the facade.

§

To begin my own story, I went to a handsome complex of buildings that dominate the landscape not far from my home here in Oakland, California. This is the westernmost center of the Church of Jesus Christ of Latter Day Saints, more commonly referred to as the Mormon Church. A separate building houses the Family History Archives and there, in microfiche form, are the records of millions of families worldwide accessible to anyone who is interested. It is ironic for me to be helped to do this search for my grandparents and have the Mormon Church actually assisting me. Their stance on homosexuality tends to be very negative. I know that Mormons sometimes produce gay children but they would certainly never admit to

*FOR EXAMPLE, SEE THE GAY ALMANAC: COMPILED BY THE NATIONAL MUSEUM & ARCHIVE OF LESBIAN AND GAY HISTORY, 1996

such "aberrations". With the help of a kind Mormon volunteer, I was able to zero in on the files you see reproduced in the sidebar which were unmistakably my own history. I had come across such compelling information about a Christening certificate for my paternal grandfather in the year 1839 that I could feel certain that this was fact. Here I learned that his parents were almost certainly Catholic. So my great-grandfather now had a name, for the first time — Josephi Sommer and his wife was a Magdalena Flick. They had brought the 3 month old babe (my grandfather), named Georgius, to the parish church of St. Stephan in Landsheim, Pfalz, Bavern, Germany.

```
International Genealogical Index (R) - Main File - Version 4.01        Germany
                              INDIVIDUAL RECORD
04 MAY 2000                                                             Page 1
===============================================================================
NAME:  SOMMER, Georgius
SEX:   M
EVENT: Christening
       16 Mar 1839
       Sankt Stefanus Katholisch, Lambsheim, Pfalz, Bayern
FATHER: Josephi SOMMER
MOTHER: Magdalenae FLICK
===============================================================================
SOURCE INFORMATION
===============================================================================
Extracted birth and/or christening record for:
  St. Stefanus Katholisch, Lambsheim, Pfalz County, Bayern
Usually arranged chronologically by the birth/christening date.
Batch       Dates       Source Call No.  Type    Printout Call No. Type
-----------------------------------------------------------------------
C972341     1802-1875   367625           Film    NONE
```

The Christening certificates for my paternal grandfather in the year 1839 obtained from the Mormon Temple's family archives.

There the trail becomes obscured, and I don't have a clue as to the year Georgius left Germany with his wife, Anna to seek his fortune in America.* I would hazard the guess that this had to happen in those next 30 years, 1859-1890. Efforts to track immigrant records from ship's lists at Ellis Island, New York have led nowhere. Perhaps going to the island would be more fruitful. However, there were other ports of entry at that time along the Eastern coast.

We do know that Europe sent some 18 millions to America during the next periods of 1890 and 1920. In the census card I was able to find for the year 1900, you note that he was then 61, had anglicized his name to the more American version of George (SIDEBAR). This began a custom of including a George in every generation. Curiously, the county they chose to settle in was Sumner County. Did they choose it because closely resembled their name? The tombstones in the tiny town of Argonia, some 50 miles southeast of Wichita, Kansas have spelled the name as "Somers" on one stone but "Sommer" on the other. The census card comes up with a third spelling "Somrs". I have read that immigration authorities, in their rush to process endless lines of people at Ellis Island, simply

The Kansas census record listing my German grandmother, my father Robert, and a younger sister, Clara.

With the assistance of my nephew Jaime (who is also the publisher of this book), I have further researched this confluence in our Somer's Family Tree. Georgius was born near Frankfurt-on-the-Main and came to America – sans his bride – at age 18 (1857). Anna Kathryn Auer was born at Berne, Switzerland in 1845, coming to America (1859) as a young teenage girl to live with relatives in Washington, DC.

Georgius had arrived in America fully trained as a carpenter, working his trade in "various places." But these were turbulent times, and he soon joined the ranks of the Union Army for the War Between the States. He married Anna after the war

1 - The First Years

Jaime Jackson (my nephew) visits the old Argonia cemetery on a remote plain in Kansas. Georgius Somer's headstone is on the left, his wife Anna's on right. Jaime is holding a shaft with star, upon which is inscribed, G.A.R. (Grand Army of the Republic).

(September, 1865) in Washington. Later, they became pioneer farmers on the plains of Kansas, near present day Argonia. They had 12 children. Jaime visited Argonia in 1999, taking the photos of the farm seen in nearby pages, the gravestones above, and also the first Presbyterian Church in Argonia built by the elder Georgius.

Georgius died in 1912, according to the Argonia Clipper newspaper, "one of Argonia's most respected citizens and an old timer here." Anna followed in 1921, described in a latter paper, the Argonia Argosy, "as a fine Christian woman, a devoted wife, mother and grandmother, and a staunch friend."

changed names at their own discretion—usually to a version which they were more comfortable with. The census card also omits two of the children. My guess is that they were away at some other address and would appear on another census taking.

Farm families were large, of course, since many hands were needed to handle the chores. High infant mortality rates also had much to do with how many children were conceived. So the Somers family was comprised of — in the order of birth — George Jr., Robert (my father), Clara, Frances and Margaret. By the time my father had reached the age of 18 or 19, he must have had enough of farm life (OVERLEAF) and was anxious to see the world on his own. What better way to do this, for a penniless young farm boy, than to enlist in the Army. The Spanish-American War had been declared in 1898 and the papers were full of the adventures of young men going off to the Philippines to help subdue the "native" tribes. The Spanish had barely put up any resistance because they were so poorly manned in that far away land.

To save pride the Spanish garrison settled a face-saving plan with the American officers to fire off a few salvos which would give them the appearance of having put up a fight before giving up. Dad had enlisted in 1898 and, by 1899, was soon boarding a train for the West Coast's Army Presidio. He was heading out across the Pacific on a troopship with little idea of what lay in store for him. Little did he realize that it was to be for

(OVERLEAF)
THE SOMERS FARM
NEAR ARGONIA, KANSAS
IN RECENT YEARS

Argonia, Kansas — Somers old homestead today 125 Years later.

George and Anna Somers were among the first settlers to arrive in Argonia, Kansas in the early 1880's. George was a carpenter by trade, and he built Argonia's Presbyterian Church (*facing page*). The Somers became farmers, and the old family farm (*above*) — sold during the Great Depression by their son, my grandfather whom I never met, George Jr. — is still operational today. I went to find the farm in the early 2000s as part of our book project, and did after a bit of research at the county courthouse. When I arrived at its location, I found an older gentleman working the land on a small tractor. His father was the person who bought the farm from the Somers! He was also old enough to remember my grandfather, and, getting off the tractor, pointed to the location of the old farm house, "George Jr. was born in the corner bedroom right there." — J. Jackson

Leather Cover of Argonia's "official history," which I found in the Argonia Public Library.

Checking out old Presbyterian Church, as it was called in its earlier days — now a registered historical landmark in Argonia, Kansas. It was built by my great-grandfather, George Somers in 1885 shortly after the town was founded. — J. Jackson

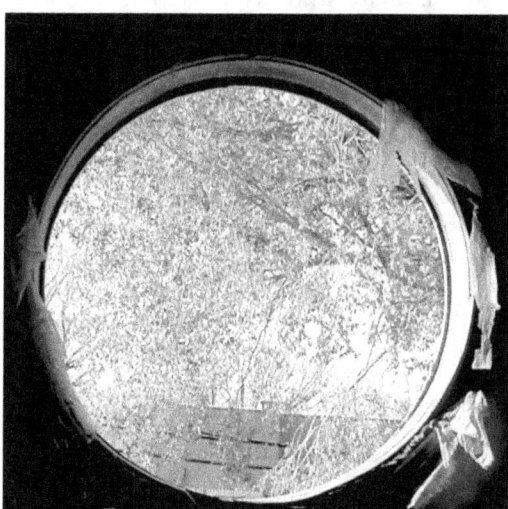

View through circular window from inside Presbyterian Church.

 Argonia's first Presbyterian Church still stands today, although in disrepair after 125 years of enduring blistering summers and harsh winters typical of the Great Plains. Built entirely by hand (there was no electricity yet), George Somers drew upon his carpentry trade learned in Germany to create an outwardly simple structure with a remarkably unique interior offering Old World charm: two great circular windows with stained glass, a 20 foot ceiling of lathed strips set at oblique angles, lush wall paper, hand carved banisters and joist braces, and a solid wooden floor with inlaid patterns. As the young town grew, the old church was sold, becoming a "morgue" during the 1930's, and later a storage building. It is now abandoned. — J. Jackson

the rest of his 53 years of life.

Back to a year earlier, in 1898, the American President, William McKinley was letting the world know that we were growing into our might as a new nation with great industrial power and a navy to back us up. Our sleek new battleships were patrolling the Atlantic seaboard and the islands of the Caribbean. One fateful night in Havana, Cuba's harbor, a visiting cruiser, the U.S.S. Maine, suddenly exploded, killing most of the crew aboard. Americans were outraged and we promptly declared war on Spain. The Hearst newspapers played up big stories, fueling much hate, and Colonel Teddy Roosevelt led the Rough Riders hurriedly into the Cuban hills with little preparation. The hasty plans were badly managed with inadequate supervision for the troops landing, who short on ammunition and with uniforms for winter wear, were not suitable for the hot climate. Spain had decrepit old warships in the Havana harbor which we made short work of them.

My father at San Francisco's Presidio just as he was embarking for army duty in the Philippines, in 1899.

Also in 1898, Commodore George Dewey received a secret cable on February 25th from the Assistant Secretary of Navy Roosevelt, ordering him to proceed to Hong Kong with his Asiatic squadron to prepare the attack on the Spanish warships moored in the Manila harbor. The ships were scuttled in the Bay and a peace protocol was signed on August 12 at Paris. Spain withdrew from Cuba, Puerto Rico, Guam and the Philippines on December 10 and we paid Spain some 20 million dollars for doing so. Some years later, San Francisco celebrated this lopsided victory by erecting a gigantic granite column in Union Square, topped by an angel carrying a laurel wreath. Colonel Roosevelt, himself, was immortalized by cuddly "teddy" bears.

The native people of the Philippines had expected the Americans to arrive as liberators from Spain. They learned soon enough that they were now under the rule of the United States. Although those living around the capital were docile, further a field in the outlying provinces were others in no mood to submit to a new master. On the southernmost island of Mindanao, feeling ran especially high against foreign rule. But the U.S. was determined to hang on to this colonial outpost, just as most European nations had their own territories in Africa and Asia.

This explains my mother's presence in the Philippines in 1898 and she and other Spanish citizens were now given the choice of remaining or returning to Spain. Many chose to stay and take their chance with the new regime. America was seen as a benign power. So my maternal grandmother and her teen daughter (my mother-to-be), made the momentous decision to stay – in Manila. The city had now been under Spanish rule for almost 350 years and had developed as a typical colonial capital much as Havana, Cuba had. Natives had built their "nipa" huts on stilts around the massive Spanish walled-city bordering the Pasig River. This medieval fortress city contained more than a 100 acres of well-built stone buildings including administration edifices, stores, churches and public parks. It was called *Intramuros* which translates to "between the walls." There was a great cathedral where I was later baptized. And the surrounding walls were so thick that you could have driven 3 autos abreast on its topside. An expansive moat encircled Intramuros and sentinel towers were set every 100 yards to alert the military from any attacks.

One of the Spanish gates into Manila's walled city, "Intramuros."

§

On arriving in the Islands, Dad saw little of Manila before he was rushed to the Island of Mindanao where guerillas were putting up resistance to American rule. Just south of Mindanao, lay the Islamic lands of Indonesia which were under the Dutch yoke. The Spanish had always referred to the Mindanao peoples as Moros which was the same name that they had given the Moors who had taken over the Spanish mainland until the year 1492. That year, of course, lives in history along with Ferdinand

and Isabella as a pivotal year for America.

The Moros of Mindanao were fierce warriors and thought nothing of taking heads as war trophies. This is where Dad was to see his first fighting. As I recall, Dad often talked later of being assigned to running motorcycles to the front lines. Sometimes, he was accompanied with another soldier riding in a "side-car" attached to the cycle. They traveled in pairs to assure that at least one of them got through. Telegraphed messages simply didn't work because lines were often cut by the enemy.

One fateful day, Dad got into the range of an enemy sniper and was shot in the shoulder. The wound bled profusely, and they turned back to the encampment where he was patched up and then shipped back to an Army hospital in Manila. His shattered shoulder bones were reinforced with Silver plating surrounding the place where the clavicle, humerus and shoulder blade all join together to make a workable moving point. However he was never again to have full use of that arm, at least without considerable pain.

The U.S. Army had little use for a soldier who couldn't lift a rifle to his

Notorious Bilibid prison in 1899, where dad served for a short time as a guard. Captured Moro insurgents were confined here; note the American military guardsmen.

1 - The First Years

shoulder and he was soon discharged. However, ex-servicemen who were in fair physical shape were being encouraged to stay in the islands and take on civilian jobs because the American government wanted an American presence to fill positions they could hardly give to Spanish or Filipino workers. Dad was soon hired as a prison guard at the huge facility called "Bilibid." Rebellious types were housed here since there was a strong chance of uprisings. But Dad found the work very unpleasant and tedious. He lasted a few months at most and simply quit in disgust with the filth and degrading conditions.

In his job-hunting status and without his own transportation, he found himself riding the city street-cars daily. One day, as the car came to a jolting stop, he found himself staring out the window at a very pretty young lady across the way. On her building, a sign said "Room to let." He could hardly believe himself, and had the presence of mind to hurriedly hop off and knock at the door. "Yes," said the girl, in hesitant English. Dad liked what he saw, paid an advance, and shortly moved into the house and into mother's life. He found her living with her mother but no father was present. My future grandmother was being courted by a recently arrived Texan named Frank Moffatt. With Dad's taking a room in the Dominguez household, both women were now being courted! As matters got more serious, there was even talk of a double-wedding. But it all seemed quite shocking for the times and the women decided to postpone the nuptials to a more proper Victorian time-table. Besides, Grandmother (to be) had only recently lost her Spanish husband who had been employed by a shipping line based in Spain.

§

Around this time, Dad learned that Singer was selling their machines in the Phillipines. In this undeveloped country, traveling salesmen were a real novelty, but Dad was anxious to get his foot in the door with a big company and he seemed to have the

(Above) Father as a civilian, working in Manila. *(Below)* Soledad Dominguez, 17 years, before she became my mother.

right stuff and was soon hired. Most American housewives in 1901 had a sewing machine in their home, since the concept of ready-to-wear clothing was only just beginning to be developed in the States. But Singer was already looking at foreign markets. Laborious hand-stitching was still the tradition in the Philippines and the Chinese seamstress or tailor was always called on to fashion the dresses and the "whites" worn by civilians in the tropics. Singer Sewing Machine Company of New York was operating their business in the Islands and was looking for Americans willing to travel through the provinces. Most likely sweatshops were the basic way this apparel was produced then, and today we know that Third World countries continue to be sources for this type of deplorable work force.

So dad's first trips were to be north of Manila up into the mountain provinces of Luzon and into the Bagio area where the Igorot people lived. There was little flat country here, and the villages cultivated rice terraces from the steep hillsides much as they do in Bali today. He had to learn to run a foot-powered machine or a table-top model and I chuckle at his becoming expert at this most feminine of household jobs. Of course, I never would have dared to bring this fact to his attention.

The Igorot people had little need of much clothing even though they were up in a mountain terrain. The men wore a breech-clout mainly and the women wrapped a skirt around themselves. Bare breasts were everywhere and I can imagine my father's acute embarrassment. A great photo, long lost, shows Dad standing in the center of a group of almost naked villagers. He stands there in his crisp "whites" trying to look business-like surrounded by all this brown skin. He actually sold some machines to the more affluent tribe members and we learned later that if a machine broke down, they would simply dismantle the thing and wear the wheels and gears as body ornaments!

The Singer people expected their employees to work steadily for a five-year period and then reward them with a six month vacation fully paid for.

A caricature from a Philippine newspaper of my father as a traveling salesman for Singer Sewing Machine Company of New York.

Bare breasts were everywhere and I can imagine my father's acute embarrassment. A great photo, long lost, shows Dad standing in the center of a group of almost naked villagers.

1 - The First Years

This included a trip back to the States with a wife and one child. For some reason I don't recall, he made the first trip home without mother and chose to take the long way around by going west across the Indian Ocean and into Egypt where he took the time to climb the Pyramids. Since he was traveling by sea, he didn't get to see Europe.

§

Dad must have married in that period — 1905-1910 — but we don't have a marriage certificate to authenticate it. I do know that there were two children born before my arrival. Neither of them survived, one being still-born and the other living a week. Mother tearfully showed me studio photographs of each of them in their tiny coffins. Thank God that this macabre fashion of photographing the dead is no longer fashionable. It was my first encounter with the concept of death and I was much puzzled by it.

The first house I remember as a child, was a huge, airy hacienda out in the suburbs, bordered by the Pasig River. Tropic breezes flowed through the rooms because we slid open window panels made of kapa shell. Even today, I see this lovely, transparent shell marketed in lighting catalogs as lampshades. The garden was a jungle of banyan trees and lush vines that harbored rhesus monkeys and green parrots. We children had a Chinese "amah" who attended strictly to our every whim. I was often warned of the danger of snakes we might encounter in the dense undergrowth. During the rainy season, the bordering river overflowed its banks annually and we had a lake instead of a garden area. You might see a dead water buffalo go drifting by on the current. Houses in the tropics were always two-storied because you could count on the ground level to be flooded. Our servants, who lived on that level, were allowed to come up and sleep on their mats in the hallways. It all makes me realize that this wasn't much different from what it was like to live in the American colonial Deep South just fifty years before this time.

We were one large extended family of eight people. Besides my imme-

Father, new manager of Singer's Manila store.

diate family comprising Dad, mother, and sister Dorothy, there were my grandparents—Mama Lola (Spanish for "granny"), her new husband Frank Moffatt. The three others were my aunt Tita Sanchez, her son Jose, nicknamed Paco, and Adolph Langenheim, who was a close friend of Dad's.

Langenheim had fled Germany shortly before the Great War (WWI) in Europe, possibly to evade the fighting. He was a fascinating man to me and I would follow him around like a puppy. I will never forget that he introduced me to my first piece of framed art depicting a nude male. It was an ingenious idea of a frame that showed a kilted Scotsman on one side and if you flipped the frame to its reverse, you saw the Scot minus his kilt! This fascinated me a great deal and I was always asking uncle Adolph to flip the frame over. It was my first encounter with the idea of sex. But there was another thing that happened at this time that makes me realize today that patterns begin to evolve early on for most of us. Sometimes, I would be hanging out the window and our Filipino gardener would decide to give himself a bath with the garden hose. I would watch, as he deftly squirted water over himself and kept one hand cupped over his genitals. He never showed anything and I was quite disappointed indeed!

Mother had a scary encounter one night, when on entering her bedroom at night, she went to her dressing table. In the dark, she was looking for a neck-ribbon to wear and picked up what she thought was a pretty green strip — only to have it come alive in her fingers! Her screams brought us all running to her side.

Myself at 7, with sister Dorothy, 3.

It was an ingenious idea of a frame that showed a kilted Scotsman on one side and if you flipped the frame to its reverse, you saw the Scot minus his kilt! This fascinated me a great deal and ... was my first encounter with the idea of sex.

A few years later, our immediate family-of-four, moved to our own house on Georgia Street. The American colony had taken over a lovely tree-lined area bordering Manila Bay. All the street names were changed to the names of American states. You may see bits of this house in nearby photos of the Somers girls and mother. I and my school buddies also found a marvelous place to hang out and play, a few blocks away. There, on the edge of the water, rose a great old ruin of a Spanish fort that must have dated back some 200 years. We would scamper through its passageways and up the great cannon ramps to the tops of the walls overlooking the Bay. Down below, floating placidly in the waters, were huge colonies of deadly, stinging

1 - The First Years

jelly-fish. And in the vast court-yard below, you could have encamped an entire regiment of soldiers. We fought battles here and also learned about one particular wall and why it was riddled with pock-marks. Traitors and spies were chained to its rough surface before being shot. But, all this was history from another time long, long ago and we were only kids playing our little games on sun-scorched afternoons.

The Somers' girls with mother at left, then Anita, Solita and Dorothy while living on Georgia St.

Our backyard, at Georgia Street, wasn't a garden at all but simply packed down earth with servants' quarters running along the back wall. Broken glass shards were imbedded into the cement that formed the top edge making it difficult for thieves to clamber over it. Dad began bringing home cardboard and wooden crates which we would turn into hiding places. We began lining up these boxes into neat little streets and buildings and soon an entire town evolved from our efforts. Even second stories were precariously added on. It was my first foray into architecture and I developed a fascination for building that still interests me.

One Christmas, my parents gave me a very special toy. Mother had found a miniature theatre from Spain that folded up for storage. You could hang scenery from its flyways and push little cutout actors in and out the stage. It came with four operas and famous plays that had complete scripts in booklets. One day, not too long ago, I opened a current magazine and saw the photo you see nearby which shows you the proscenium of this little theatre which I was so delighted to play with. It was with total amazement that I ran into this bit of my past some 70 years later. So many happy hours were spent on the floor, manipulating the actors around on the stage. From this childhood play, I acquired a deep love for stagecraft and I strongly suspect that it had a great influence on my choice of my life's direction as a window display designer.

The toy theater that sparked my love of show business.

Mother hadn't ignored my budding interest in the theatre and as she also loved opera, I found myself attending the performances of European touring companies. Manila was considered an important venue because of the huge Spanish audience already living there. As Dad had no interest in going to the theatre, I became her date for the evening quite often. Names like Caruso, Galli-Curci and the legendary ballet star Anna Pavlova, were discussed and praised by the two of us at the dinner table to Dad's amusement. But I need to admit that I wasn't unaware of the attractions of the new hero of the movie screen —"Tarzan of the Apes." I had been reading the Edgar Rice Burroughs novels and now I could see them come to life on the silver screen.

It was also decided that sister Dorothy and I would be taking dance lessons! I was totally humiliated at this idea. What would my school friends think I had turned into? We were to learn Spanish folk-dancing from a beautiful young Russian refugee who had just arrived from her country. Olga Dontsoff had fled the chaos and upheaval of the great Russian Revolution of 1917. She had crossed the enormous distances from St. Petersburg on the Trans-Siberian Railroad alone. She was a White Russian, the group that was loyal to the Czar and therefore the enemy of the new regime of Communist masters. To have stayed would have put her life in danger. She found herself finally in Shanghai, and took the extra step into the Philippines on a steamer, looking for work as a ballet teacher. We became some of her first students in Manila and I will never forget this lovely girl who had the courage to travel these distances across Siberia to end up in a totally foreign port like ours and find her niche in life. Olga was not only strikingly beautiful but a very patient soul who loved teaching children. We totally loved her and under her teaching, we became good enough to win first prize in a children's competition. We whirled through the intricate steps of the *Sevillana* and *Jota*, clacking our castanets in time to the folk music of the *Aragonesa*. Many an evening, my sister and I, when the folks had guests over for dinner, were the after-dinner entertainment. Television was still another 40 years in the future, of course.

Dancing at a competition, ages 8 and 4.

Still dancing away, now old professionals.

§

Several important events took place on the year of my birth worth mentioning. 1914 was a pivotal year in history. The Panama Canal finally linked the Atlantic ocean to the Pacific creating tremendous changes in commercial shipping routes. The assassination of the Austrian Archduke Ferdinand ignited World War I in Europe, and Africa continued its status as a possession of European powers. Henry Ford began producing his model-Ts on the first assembly lines and cocaine's use for medicinal purposes was banned. *Coca-Cola* owed its start to this most popular of drugs which today is in ill-repute.

In my own little world as a child, I was now to meet a mysterious, black monster, the piano. For some reason or another, it fascinated me and at the same time, was a formidable presence. As it turned out, Mozart didn't start spinning madly in his grave because he had nothing to fear from me. I proved to be a total disaster at the keyboard, and the distraught teacher was sent packing after the first few sessions. So much for culture at the age of ten!

Living in the Philippines, I was becoming aware that my skin color was quite a bit lighter than the natives I saw around me daily. Although my school-mates were the "right" color, meaning white, everyone else was nut-brown—with me in between. I began to worry that I was really a Filipino because I had been born in Manila and it really concerned me. I couldn't be proud of myself and I finally confronted Dad with the problem. He eventually came up with a metaphor that I could understand. One night, he explained it this way: "If a cat decides to have her litter of kittens in a nice, warm oven, that doesn't make them into cookies." I was so relieved to be assured of this dilemma — we were still living in a colonial time, of course, and I was reflecting on the bias for race that we are gradually tossing aside today.*

§

1921 had arrived and Dad was planning to take his six month vacation back in the States, and visit his siblings in California and Kansas. The trip started beautifully, I was very excited at the age of 6 to be on a great ocean liner. The Japanese were starting to build luxurious cruise ships to rival

*San Francisco Chronicle Staff Writer Benjamin Pimentel, recently wrote in his column, "Bush's Revisionist History": Many of the official justifications for colonizing the Philippines were openly racist. President William Howard Taft, who served as governor-general of the islands, called Filipinos "our little brown brothers".

those on the Atlantic. It was the NYK line which stands for Nippon Yusen Kaisha. I spent the first few days racing along all the decks and finding great places to hide. But as we neared the Japanese coastline, I began to slowdown because I was getting terrible stomach pains. The ship's doctor was of little help and I had to endure the discomfort until we could get to the American Hospital in Yokohama. Somehow, I had contracted intestinal worms! As to whether I had picked up these parasites on board the ship or at some restaurant I had been taken to, we never found out, of course. It was very important I receive the best medical care, so Mother and I let the others to go on to America, while we remained in Japan for some 6 months while I recuperated. She watched over me daily until I felt better. We then rejoined the family (Dad, and my oldest sister, Dorothy) on their return trip home.

I saw nothing of Japan except for the hospital gardens, sadly. I was so ashamed at my illness, that I never referred to it in my conversations from that time on. I was sure it was my fault to have had this most embarrassing disease. The tropics take a toll on those of us with delicate health.

Now Dad was growing more concerned with my next schooling. Should he keep me in Manila's mediocre schools for American children or be sent off to the States to live with his sisters in Kansas? His favorite, Francis, had moved to Wichita from the farm and had married. She offered to let me stay with her family if Dad would send money for my upkeep. I was turning eleven and it was time for the next big vacation. I was in turmoil. I wanted to stay in my family's bosom but I also wanted to live in America. There seemed to be little concern for my three sisters' schooling but then they would soon marry and would need little schooling: that was typical thinking in the 1920s, after all, women's Lib was still getting off to a rocky start on the East coast of America and was a faraway dream for women in the Philippines.

§

Let's go back now and connect the pieces to learn something about the Philippines and how it happened that my mother found herself living there at the turn of the 20th Century.

The earliest Paleolithic peoples who arrived in the Islands, some 250,000 years ago, must have walked there over land bridges that once connected the Islands to the Asian Continent. When the ice sheets melted, the seas rose and isolated them from the mainland. But these cave-dwelling tribes thrived on the bounty of the forests and surrounding seas. Other peoples began arriving by sail to make up the various ethnic groups that still inhabit isolated regions. Arab traders came, bringing the sophisticated cultures of China and India. Hindu divinities were introduced and Sanskrit words began appearing in the local dialects.

The Islamic peoples were beginning to dominate the islands when something dramatic happened. One morning in 1521, three great galleons bearing the flags of the Spanish crown arrived at the island of Samar. Portuguese-born Ferdinand Magellan and his starving crew had been at sea for almost two years when they sighted the emerald green shores. They believed they had finally stumbled into the long-sought and fabled Spice Islands that Columbus was searching for only 29 years earlier. They flung themselves on the beach in gratitude. They soon learned that the local chief was at war with another island chief and they agreed to sign a treaty in blood, to fight on his side. Magellan was making a fatal mistake because he had been ordered by his royal sponsor, King Charles of Spain to avoid any landings.

Chief Humabon went into battle against Chief Lapu-Lapu with Magellan's men at his side with their muskets. But Magellan had chosen the wrong side, and was slain by Lapu-Lapu's arrows. The remnants of Magellan's crew were driven away by a disgusted Humabon. They sailed away and for another fifty years no further attempts at landings took place. Then in 1565, Spanish ships landed and captured the ramshackle native town of Manila where they managed to establish a foothold. Miguel Lopez de Legazpi had secured the town and for the next 327 years, Spain ruled over the Islands, sending its diplomats via Mexico. At times, it almost became a lost cause but Spain needed to keep the trade lines to China open — it was a very lucrative business in precious metals, silks and spices. Also, the Spanish began building the famous Manila galleons of Philippine mahogany, which made an annual journey across the Pacific to Acapulco, Mexico, returning laden with gold, Franciscan friars and adventurers. Manila now started to become a wealthy colonial city linked to Europe through Mexico.

Britain entered the picture for a brief three years in 1762, when she occupied Manila and started controlling the trade between Madras, India and the Islands. Indian cotton and other goods began passing through Manila on its way to Mexico and, in return, bringing back silver, Chinese gold plate, pearls, animal hides, tobacco and horses destined for India.

But there was much wavering in the loyalties of various factions, and class struggles kept the Spanish busy quelling revolts during these 327 years of Spanish rule. Over 200 uprisings are recorded during this time by a people chafing under foreign domination. Emilio Aguinaldo, a native patriot who led one of the last revolts in 1899-1901, and this one against the Americans, is revered as one of the great heroes, along with Rizal, in Philippine history.

The British, at this time, had just finished the dredging of the Suez Canal, making the time-consuming trip around the continent of Africa, unnecessary and saving weeks of precious time. Spain joined other European nations in using this new route to the Orient, sending her merchant ships to her Philippine colony. And here we pick up the story again.

§

My Spanish grandfather, Señor Dominguez, was either a sea-captain or a merchant marine officer and he regularly sailed from Barcelona to Manila. He must have been entranced with the tropical air of Manila and its sophisticated society, because he moved his wife and young teenage daughter (my mother) to this far away capital with no fears. The two women had lived their lives in Madrid up until then. At some point during these trips he was making between Spain and the Islands, he died of some unknown cause, and the two ladies found themselves adrift in a foreign land. Americans to the rescue, of course, for grandmother was being courted by a newly arrived adventurer from Texas, the aforementioned Frank Moffatt. As a very young child, I remember him as a heavy-set man with rather bossy airs. He was definitely the patriarch of that extended family living in our riverside hacienda. He eventually became Manila's fire chief, as well as my step-grandfather.

2
Moving to America

1926 - 1930

"I was a miserable failure out on the baseball field. I found it embarrassing that I couldn't catch a ball as well as my friends. I was a "butter-fingers" to my fellow players. I secretly figured that it was an effeminate sign that I wasn't all male. This was a beginning in my self-questioning concerning my measuring up to other boys." - GS

∫

I sensed this is when the "façade" would begin to take shape in George's life. Foreseeing its significance, I encouraged him to speak openly and honestly about it. - JJ

MOVING TO AMERICA: 1926 - 1930

It was now 1926, and the much anticipated big vacation was at hand. This time, I promised my parents I would not get sick and have to remain behind in some hospital and miss seeing America. I was now eleven, Dorothy seven and the other two sisters, five and three. I had strange feelings to deal with, since I knew I would not be returning to the Islands with my family. It was a scary feeling and quite exciting at the same time. I simply did not know how to feel about it, so I decided not to think about it at all.

The Age of Air Travel was still in the future, of course. Lindbergh would be flying his tiny plane non-stop across the Atlantic the next year — 1927. New York-to-Paris in thirty-three and a half hours! Today that sounds like the plane was standing still! We had to be content with a more leisurely way of travel — via a great ocean liner and that was immensely exciting to a bunch of kids. The Japanese nation, in the 1920s, was entering the competition to create ocean-crossing luxury vessels to vie with the Atlantic fleets. The Titanic disaster in 1912, only fourteen years earlier, was still very fresh in everyone's minds. But we, of course, would be sailing through temperate waters. The entire trip, start to finish, would take up thirty days — Manila to San Francisco. Our first port-of-call after crossing the South China Sea was Hong Kong, the British Colony. That took up the first three days of sailing and we steamed into the steep-sided harbor with its bustling dozens of sampans and junks which are the home and business addresses of the Chinese tradesmen. Many of them spend their entire lives living on these colorful crafts and along the docks larger houseboats were serving as restaurants. We chose to stay across the Bay from Hong Kong at Kowloon which wasn't as expensive. I remember we hired coolie-powered rickshaws to jog us

The Age of Air Travel was still in the future, of course. Lindbergh would be flying his tiny plane non-stop across the Atlantic the next year—1927.

2 - Moving To America—1926

along the harbor's colorful boulevards and narrow streets. The street scenes reminded me vividly of Manila's downtown business areas since the Chinese are such a dominant presence in the Philippines. The Asians have always been a much more ambitious, businesswise people than the more easygoing Filipino.

After three days of seeing the sights, the ship was ready to sail again and we traveled north along China's coast to our next landfall — Shanghai. Here we indulged in another couple of days of being wheeled along in rickshaws, taking in the vistas and colorful markets. Then, it was off to Japan, a short crossing on the East China Sea to the bustling port of Yokohama. And then the next day, Nagasaki — but I remember nothing of these ports, perhaps all the dockside activity, and native population was beginning to blur in my mind. I know that I was dreaming of the big moment when we would see the California coastline through the portholes. The long stretch between Japan and Hawaii went by uneventfully and we children were more interested in racing about the decks, exploring the new levels and discovering new hiding places.

Finally, the American continent slowly materialized on the horizon and we eyed it intently to see if it was different from other coastlines. I must say, it appeared exactly as the others. We soon docked near the tall tower of the Ferry Building, San Francisco's earliest skyscraper, now dwarfed by buildings ten times taller. We went through customs next and then found Uncle George waiting for us in the reception areas. He seemed delighted to see us and I saw that he looked like an older version of my own father. Gathering up our luggage, we headed for another gate to board the ferry across the Bay to Berkeley. The great bridges that span the waters of the Bay were still in the dream state and for another eleven years, still unrealized concepts.

§

Uncle George had also fled the Kansas farm life but his was a less adventurous choice of careers.* He was employed at the Navy shipyards at Mare Island. He and his wife, Viola had bought a brown-shingled two-storied home at 1615 Bonita Avenue just a few blocks west of the University of California campus. He had a son enrolled there as well as a daughter. Five years later, I would be living there as part of the family. I immediately set out to explore my first American neighborhood and found that no one worried about floods here. Houses actually sat on the ground instead of stilts. The landscapes were not as lush green and more tailored. The Campus nearby, was intriguing, with a mix of architectural styles from Victorian to Classic Revival.

Uncle George's son was also named George and to avoid the confusion of too many Georges, he went by his middle name of Arthur. It seemed that every generation had to include at least one George. I was the fourth George.

I was so entranced with my first American city that I immediately asked Dad to leave me in Berkeley and skip the trip to his sister's home in Kansas. But he had other ideas for me and assured me that I would like Wichita even more. Was it because he wanted me to experience the Kansas landscape as he had when he was growing up on the farm?

So we soon boarded a transcontinental train, winding our way through the Rockies and down into the vast grasslands and wheat fields of the Central Great Plains. Wichita sits in the lower mid-section of Kansas with not a single hill to break the limitless horizon. I was very disappointed with my first glimpse of this city that was to be my home for the next five years. Of course, I had little to say in the choice of homes anyway and I would get through it somehow – but five years seemed like an eternity to my eleven-year-old mind. After a week of visiting with his sisters, Frances and Margaret, and showing off his Spanish wife and children, Dad bid me good-by. I stood on the front porch, stoically, not letting a single tear drop down my cheek. But inwardly, I was devastated. I resolved to get a calendar and start marking off the days, all 1,825 of them, before I would see the family again—it seemed like a gigantic task.

Dad bid me good-by. I stood on the front porch, stoically, not letting a single tear drop down my cheek. But inwardly, I was devastated.

§

Aunt Frances was a kind soul, very prim and proper and very concerned about the family's needs. She spent her days bustling about her house chasing the tiniest speck of dust and making sure we all ate the right things. Uncle Ed, a short, portly man, said little at all and he spent his working days at the local train-yards as a boiler-maker. He would come home all soot-stained and in need of a bath. We hardly ever spoke to each other and I compared him to my father and found him disappointing indeed. Of course, I was an additional source of income and so, I was accepted. I was glad that there were two children who were a little older than myself. Raymond, the older of the two was probably sixteen and so he looked down on me. He was not happy that I had been given his bedroom. He was relegated to a couch in the corner of the dining room. So I could expect no friendly relations with him. But his sister, Mildred, who was thirteen, became a close friend and confidant. She and I were assigned to clean-up the kitchen after meals and we would sit out on the front porch swing and trade stories about our school friends.

As I began my all-important American education, I didn't find it that much different from my earlier schools. I didn't have an accent to surmount, so I did fit in quite easily. I became interested in the school newspaper and got involved in the weekly production of it. I must have pleased the journalism teacher because I found myself as Editor-in-Chief in a short time. However, I was a miserable failure out on the baseball field. I found it embarrassing that I couldn't catch a ball as well as my friends. I was a "butter-fingers" to my fellow players. I secretly figured that it was an effeminate sign that I wasn't all male. This was a beginning in my self-questioning concerning my measuring up to other boys.

I was a miserable failure out on the baseball field. I found it embarrassing that I couldn't catch a ball as well as my friends. I was a "butter-fingers" to my fellow players. I secretly figured that it was an effeminate sign that I wasn't all male. This was a beginning in my self-questioning concerning my measuring up to other boys.

I'm front row center as editor of the high school newspaper.

Another troublesome change was in store for me — the Church. As my mother was a Catholic, I had been baptized a Catholic as well. Dad had absolutely no interest in religion. He had let my mother decide about the children's church going. I was to decide on my own as I grew up how I would connect to any religion. In the Philippines, I was used to going to Confession and Communion. The Masses I went to with Mother in Manila's great cathedral were elaborate rituals with much incense, priests in beautiful robes, Latin spoken in sing-song style. The music pouring out over us was awe-inspiring. In Kansas, the stark contrast was devastating. Now I sat in what looked more like a high school auditorium and stared at a minister in ordinary clothes. The magic rituals had vanished. I simply lost complete interest and it wasn't until recently that I chose to return to the Protestant faith to worship. More on that later in the story.

I began a new friendship with a boy my age who lived in the same block I lived on: Hubert Scroggin — I found the name very funny and teased him about it mercilessly. I would ask him if he was related to Scrooge from the Dickens' story. But I ended up calling him "Hube" much to his relief. We got into all the usual mischief typical of thirteen year olds and often spent the night at the other's house. I wonder why it is such a treat to stay-over at a friend's house and wrestle around half the night? Girls were still a mystery to us and I suppose we needed the physical contact. We found the wrestling around very satisfying and I was stimulated pitting my body innocently against his. It never turned sexual and we would have been disgusted perhaps to have it become anything more than horseplay. I have learned from friends that this was the way they learned about sex, but in my case, it never happened.

Myself with "Hube" Scroggin, my wrestling partner.

2 - Moving To America—1926

We were innocents.

The Hadlers — for that was my uncle's name — lived across the street from a neighborhood park where we hung out after school until we were called in for supper. My other aunt, Margaret lived down a block from our house at 121 Ellis, but we seldom saw much of her. She was rather snooty in manner and considered herself a society matron. I guess she had forgotten her humble beginnings as a farm girl and now thought herself a "pillar of society."

During summer vacations, I was lucky enough to land a job at a local drive-in malt-shop. I would dash out to the circle of cars outside with my clip-on tray. I would return shortly with hamburgers and frothy milkshakes. But I wasn't as popular a waiter as the teen-girls doing the same task. But girls on a date would prefer me to the flirty waitresses that they saw as a threat to their boy-friends.

But girls on a date would prefer me to the flirty waitresses that they saw as a threat to their boyfriends.

Sitting on the front steps of the Hadler's house at 145 Ellis, Wichita, Kansas.

The first winter a light sprinkle of snow descended, I was totally amazed at the stuff. I had never seen it before and even though it wasn't even an inch deep, I reveled in it. The world had turned pristinely white and cold.

Another summer, we kids were invited up to spend a two weeks on a farm in nearby Nebraska. We were beside ourselves with the excitement. What an adventure for we city-raised kids. We were driven north, passing endless miles of wheat-fields with an occasional grain silo or farmhouse to break the vista. On arriving, I met my first barnyard animals — the chickens, goats and cows. Later, I was horrified to see what happened to some of them while we were there. Farm boys thought nothing of chopping off heads when their mother ordered them to bring in a chicken for the dinner table. I had a hard time coping with this almost daily murder of the dear little creatures. I'm afraid I was thought of as a wimpy type. So be it.

Car-hopping beauties, note the antique car.

3

Moving to San Diego

1931 - 1932

"Suddenly, the impulse to touch this beautiful skin overwhelmed me. I simply rolled close to him and stretched my arm around him. What I was doing was so instinctual, that I couldn't have done anything else ... so began my introduction to my sexual self." - GS

∫

Obviously a sensitive subject, and George being a very private person, it took a bit of persuasion to get him to tell me when he first acted on his homosexuality. - JJ

Moving to San Diego: 1931 - 1932

The five long years of putting "X"s on the calendar had finally come to an end. Mother had always written regularly in Spanish and Dad was very conscientious about sending his checks for my upkeep. The one person I really would miss terribly was Mildred. She and I had grown very close because we had spent so many hours together. We shared secrets almost like a couple of schoolgirls, I realize now. But now it was time to leave and I said my good-byes to Hubert Scroggin and other school-friends. I boarded the train alone feeling very grown-up to be traveling some 2000 miles west to California. I was now sixteen and ready for whatever life would hand me next.

Our reunion took place at the family home at 1615 Bonita, Berkeley, Uncle George's brown shingle house. Although everyone was happy to see me and I to see them, there was a certain awkwardness to our talk. I had grown considerably and must have looked like a stranger to them. We covered our embarrassment with silly chatter and then someone proposed we go out to the backyard to take a photo of the reunited family (*facing page*). Dad took the picture as he hated being photographed. You see me standing at the rear. The line-up starts at the left with Mother, then Grandmother, Anita, Dorothy and the tomboy, Solita.

Uncle George and Aunt Vi had been carrying on a ridiculous feud for years. She refused to speak to him except through a third person. It had started at the dining table when Uncle George had inadvertently spilled a pot of very hot coffee on his son's lap and the boy leaped up howling with pain. He did suffer a severe burn and his mother berated the hapless father, Uncle George for causing the damage. It became a bitter argument and they stopped speaking to one another. It put a strain on having company around but we simply adapted to it as silly as it seemed. Recently, in 1999, I made a

3 - Moving to San Diego—1931

point of driving by the old house. It still stood there and I wiped away a tear to think of the seventy years that had passed since I had lived there.

My cousins, Ruth and Arthur, Uncle George's children were now going to the University which was a few minutes walk from the house. Arthur was nearing graduation and already had a job assured him at the Roos Brothers' Campus Shop on Telegraph Avenue. You will see later how important this was to my own career development. But for the moment, we were now saying our good-byes because we had plans to take the train down to San Diego to hunt for a new home.

Dad had heard how ideal the climate in Southern California was from friends in the Philippines. One particular close friend from army days, Colonel Parrott had already retired and moved to San Diego. He had a Filipino wife and two children and they were all good friends of our own family. Their letter had praised the climate, the city and its coastal beauty to the point that Dad thought we should seriously think of buying our home there. He was taking early retirement after the next five-year work period and he wanted to settle his family in California while he went back for the last time.

So we took the Coast train down to San Diego, skipping past Los Angeles which we were eager to see but decided that could wait. We were more than delighted with the city of San Diego and, after the initial visiting with the Parrott family, we immediately started house hunting. It was decided that we would move into the same neighborhood as our friends so that we could easily visit one another. I had decided I wanted to hunt on my own, while Dad and Mother drove around. In my walking around the surrounding blocks, I came upon a house I thought was perfect. After the others had not found anything that seemed quite right, they agreed that I had found what they were look-

My family returns from Manila, photographed at Uncle George's home in Berkeley. *(From left)* Mother, Grandmother (who later died at the hands of the Japanese during WWII), myself at 16, Anita, Dorothy and Solita.

ing for. It was the typical white stucco, red tile roofed Spanish style cottage that is so prevalent in Southern California. It had a large living room, three bedrooms, one and a half baths and a separate garage. We paid $11,500 for 1136 Madison Avenue. Today, in these inflationary times, that seems like a ridiculous price. You can't even buy a car for that price today but this was 1931 and California hadn't reached its full potential as a place to live. Throughout this story, I may mention what an item used to cost. For example, we would have paid five cents for that one-dollar candy bar you see on the shelf today.

On the La Jolla Cove beach with visiting cousin, Ray Hadler (*left*), and my sister Anita.

Mother was especially pleased with all the Spanish influence we saw everywhere around us. It made moving from Manila much more comforting. Names of the great Spanish explorers were used to name the parks and streets. And the beaches were La Jolla, Laguna and Mission Beach. Just south of us only sixteen miles lay the border town of Tijuana, although its rather unsavory character at the time was enough to limit our visits there. It was mainly, cheap souvenir shops, seedy bars and brothels.

Our house sat on a plateau running directly west towards the Pacific Ocean. A hundred feet to the north, the cliffs overlooking Mission Valley flanked us. When the Franciscan friars first arrived in California from Mexico, led by Father Junipero Serra, they erected their first mission here in this valley. It was to be the model for 30 more to come in the next century. Each was 30 miles apart as that was considered a good horseback day' ride apart. The San Diego Mission was 8 miles inland from the sea and situated near the river that ran dry most of the year except for the spring. I spent many happy hours along its riverbanks, as I will recount further along. But at the time I lived in San Diego, the old Mission was still a ruin, sitting there with its sun-baked adobe walls crumbling away and its terra cotta tiles scattered around the weed-infested graveyard. Today, of course, it is fully restored as are all the 30 other Missions stretching northwards up to Sonoma.

San Diego has much to boast about besides its great temperate climate. In the heart of the city, lies the magnificent Balboa Park and within the

3 - Moving to San Diego—1931

Park's vast acreage we had the world-famous Zoo. This was one of the first zoos to adopt the open plan with only a moat separating the animals from the visitors. Each enclosure was tailor made to those animals' natural environment. No iron bars or cages were allowed to be seen. The Park was conceived as the site of the Panama-Pacific Fair at the beginning of the 20th century. The people of San Diego were so enchanted by its beauty that they refused to tear it down when the fair was over. Its buildings were designed in the Spanish rococo style, which echoed Spain's most opulent architectural period. When the temporary stucco walls and ornamentation began to crumble after a couple of decades, San Diego's citizens voted to pay for the huge expense of rebuilding the entire complex in its original design. A visitor feels as if he is walking through an idealized Spanish city like Seville in a past century. A cathedral like building with an imposing bell tower dominates the central area. It now houses a museum to the Story of Early Man. All the other structures house various museums including a very beautiful mansion that shows important paintings and sculpture. I could spend pages praising this whole park, but it would never equal the experience of seeing it first hand.

One beautiful, balmy afternoon while I was enjoying a walk near the great, baroque bell-tower, I heard a scream and then next a sickening thud. A man had just leaped to his death from the tower's top levels. I didn't walk over to join the crowd that collected around the broken body. I mourned for the poor fellow that couldn't go on living in this lovely city by the sea. Was he that desperate?

My little clique of school buddies and I often took the late afternoon hours after coming home to race down the steep goat-paths carved into the cliffs just behind our homes along Madison Avenue. Our destination was always the great swimming hole we had found along the dry river's course. This was typical of most California's streams and even though the river would dry up or go underground, there would always be several pockets of water collecting along the way out to the sea. Coming down the cliffs, we would pass through Japanese owned truck farms that took up most of the valley floor. We always stole a carrot to munch on while we raced along the furrows in our hurry to reach the cool water. Nearby, as a backdrop, loomed the sad, ruins of the old mission, San Diego de Alcala. But we

Myself and Lewis, one of my best pals in front of the Madison Avenue house.

weren't much into history and our main concern was to rip off clothes and get into the cool water as fast as possible. It was great to shed off civilization, reverting to being primitive man and enjoying Nature. Just to be naked in the hot sun was a great joy. We got into playful splashing and tackling one another until we grew tired enough to lie back and let the sun's rays do their worst to our skins.

I began to notice that we had a visitor to our swimming hole. He always sat off to the side and merely watched us in our antics. I became curious enough about him one day to move over to his spot and start a conversation. He had a magnificent tan all over, with no white strips to mar the torso. He introduced himself as Al Brown, a librarian's assistant. He talked about the beauty of the Mission Valley and that there was a number of other swimming spots further inland. He ended by asking if I would be into exploring along the river with him on another day — say the coming Saturday when we could take a whole day? After agreeing to go with him, I returned to the other friends but for some reason or another, instinct perhaps, decided to keep the news of the invitation to myself. I was intrigued with his apparent maturity and reserved manners. Perhaps, I could learn something from this more grown-up guy who seemed friendly enough. We exchanged phone numbers as we got dressed later and agreed to meet the following Saturday to visit other swim spots he had discovered.

I met him at a crossroad in the Valley, and we hiked for a mile or so before turning off the road onto a small path that led us to a water hole. After walking along for a bit, we found one that seemed more to our liking. After a refreshing swim, we stretched out on the sandy banks, under some weeping willows and breathed in the wonderful smells of summertime.

I found myself admiring his great tan and his trim body. Suddenly, the impulse to touch this beautiful skin overwhelmed me. I simply rolled close to him and stretched my arm around him. What I was doing was so instinctual, that I couldn't have done anything else. There wasn't any feeling of shame and Al responded just as

Suddenly, the impulse to touch this beautiful skin overwhelmed me. I simply rolled close to him and stretched my arm around him. What I was doing was so instinctual, that I couldn't have done anything else ... so began my introduction to my sexual self.

3 - Moving to San Diego—1931

simply. The natural setting was so beautiful — lying there on this sandy beach and no prying eyes to deal with. And so began my introduction to my sexual self. But, somehow, when I returned to my house, I did feel guilt. Al called the next day to invite on another river hike but I made excuses for the time being. I had to think about what had happened. He did call again and I agreed to go that time and a number of other times through the summer. I was anxious to question him about what this all meant. I was very worried about myself but he began by telling of the great men and women of history that shared our sexual orientation. I was absolutely amazed at the names and almost refused to believe him. But Al worked in a local library and had access to much fact that I had never bothered with. He reeled off names like — Michelangelo, da Vinci, Plato and so many others that my head was buzzing. So I wasn't going to hell after all! If you are curious to know who is on this roll call, turn to the last pages of this book and be as surprised as I was. The list is well authenticated by world historians, and even contains the name of the only American president who never married and was called "Nance" behind his back.

My buddies and I began to get curious about *sex* and decided that since no one was going to talk to us about it, we would see what people did about it. We started creeping along the backs of houses at night and where we would see a bedroom light, we would peep in. Almost always, it was no more than someone reading in bed, but now and then we would hit pay dirt and see an amorous couple. We seemed to have no shame about these nightly forays into neighbors' gardens to learn about sex and no one was the wiser.

From my trips to see the art collections at the Balboa Park Museum, I had admired one particular sculptor that I learned lived in San Diego. He worked in granite and Native American Indians were his subjects. He gave them wonderfully muscular, compact bodies that I really felt drawn to see. Donald Hord's name was listed in the telephone book and I got up the nerve to call him and ask if I might stop by to visit his studio. He was gracious enough and said he would show me more work. Perhaps, he thought I was a potential customer. He gave me directions to his studio home, which was located along some marshy areas near the beaches. Since I didn't own a car, I hiked the distance down the Valley and found myself swimming across a creek to reach the house. I reached his dock and heaved myself up dripping wet to his amazement. He gave me some dry pants to wear while mine dried and I was shown around the workroom. I was in awe of the stunning work and the tools that it took to produce these fabulous figures. One of his largest pieces, which I had seen in a courtyard of a Spanish villa in Balboa Park, was of an Indian peasant woman sitting cross-legged in the center of a fountain. Water poured from a large pitcher she held in her lap.

I also became aware of another man who seemed much at home here at Donald's side. He was never identified as his partner, but I sensed they were very close friends. They had made a life for themselves in this wonderful studio home that spoke of their love of Nature and the Indian heritage. The walls were vertical planks, and the floor was made of terra cotta tiles. Huge native baskets held dried branches in the corners and Navajo tribal blankets hung from the walls. I was seeing my first artists' home and how two men could make a life together. I realized then that there was a chance that some day, I could have this all myself if I was lucky enough to find someone. I left them, later that afternoon, and although no mention was ever made of the nature of their relationship, I think we all knew what we were about and where I would need to go in life. I felt elated to see what the future could hold for me.

Mother spent these first years in her new home in San Diego, keeping everything super clean and spotless. She was learning how to cope with no servants when she learned how expensive they were here in the States. In the evenings, she sat at her baby grand piano and played light classical music, mostly Chopin. She never rose to concert-playing status, but played well enough to give me a life long love for the piano's emotional power. However, I still felt a barrier between us in expressing feelings. She seemed much more comfortable and confidential with her three daughters. The five-year separation had taken its toll, it seemed. Dad had always been an authority figure and one simply didn't get chummy with him although he showed particular affection for Dorothy, the eldest girl. The rest of us always felt a bit resentful of the attention he showed her on many occasions.

Although I wouldn't have called Mother frivolous, she didn't seem to be too concerned about her children's schooling or interests. She had done her maternal duty and brought four babies into the world for her husband to be proud of and now she would rest and play her beloved piano. I wonder sometimes how she would have reacted to the disturbing news that she had delivered a gay child, perhaps two, to her stern husband? I was too uncertain at this time, of my own sexual orientation, to have come to my parents with questions. And to make matters more vexing, the American Psychiatric Association still considered homosexuality a disease. A few more decades had to pass before they decided they had been hasty in condemning some ten per cent of Americans to this status of sick persons.

My mother in front of the Madison Avenue house in San Diego.

Dad was nearing the time for his return to his last five years of work for Singer in the Philippines before taking early retirement. As a father, he had spent little or no quality time with his sixteen-year-old son, away from his daughters (*sidebar*). And so one day, before his departure, he proposed that he and I would jump in the car and go fishing off an ocean pier. It would be good to have a chance, man to man, to talk about "male stuff." I had never gone fishing anywhere and was eager to go, of course. Perhaps, we would talk about college and my future, which had been ignored pretty much. I would finally get a chance to know him a bit before his next disappearance.

We found a bait shop further up the coastal highway past La Jolla, and we rented poles for the afternoon. Walking out to the end of a long wooden pier, the ocean stretched out to infinity and I was reminded of the great distance that had built up between us. How could I ever bring up and actually talk to him about these new feelings I had about myself?

I wonder sometimes how she would have reacted to the disturbing news that she had delivered a gay child, perhaps two, to her stern husband?

The Absent Father

My boyhood experience from age eleven on – of having no father present – cannot be blamed for my sexual orientation. As I think back to those early years in the Philippines before being sent to the U.S. for my schooling, I was already experiencing interest in the male body – I have described two instances in my story.

My lack of a father-son connection was not the reason for my development as a gay man, as some might also suggest. It was a genetic factor, to my thinking, that has made me gay. I did, however, feel a certain sense of betrayal in his sending me away to live with relatives I had never met before. At the age of eleven, I had no understanding of what this event meant except that I was being excluded from the family unit and it had repercussions for me. I was reassured by Father that it was for my education that it was necessary for me to live in the U.S. But I had mixed feelings about the decision then – and now.

It entailed a sacrifice in sending me away, and that hurt was hard for an eleven year-old to fully understand.

How could I ever bring up and actually talk to him about these new feelings I had about my self. What would it do to our fragile ties to one another and would I be cast aside once he knew I was gay?

What would it do to our fragile ties to one another and would I be cast aside once he knew I was gay?

So, instead, there were a lot of jokes, and I found I was laughing awkwardly, my voice pitched higher than normal. Dad mocked my voice and I froze in embarrassment. The afternoon turned frigid and I simply stopped talking. I couldn't wait to get away from him. I found it hard to be spontaneous in his presence from that time on. What a legacy to hand a developing youth who was in a critical time of self-identification. I grew sullen and unresponsive.

But Before Dad left for the Islands, he did call me aside and asked me to make a choice about my education for the next few years. I was almost through high school in San Diego. Did I want to start college at Berkeley or did I think I was serious enough about Art that I would want to go an art school in Los Angeles? I had been showing some talent in school but hadn't done anything at home to speak of. I spoke up in favor of art school and he thought on that for a brief moment. He decided for me, as it turned out, and I was to go to college. I wasn't to get a choice anyway! He reasoned that a general course with liberal arts major would give me a more rounded education; rather than a specialized direction. I did see the wisdom of this approach and it meant that if I weren't to be an artist, at least I would have a general education. Art could be my major in college anyway, I was assured. I would be living at Uncle George's and that would certainly be much less expensive than Los Angeles.

It was the summer of 1933, and I would be moving up to Berkeley to attend the University of California for the fall semester. But I had also been dreaming of one last adventure before seriously studying. There was much talk of the great Chicago World's Fair that summer and I was anxious to see it for myself. I had heard how spectacular it was going to be. There had to be some way I could get there but I had very little money saved. I couldn't expect much help from the folks, as they weren't keen on my going anyway.

Mother always shopped at a nearby grocer and she had grown to like a particular young clerk who always offered to help her to the car with her bags. His name turned out to be Johnny Slater and we were all to meet him,

Dad mocked my voice and I froze in embarrassment. The afternoon turned frigid and I simply stopped talking. What a legacy to hand a developing youth who was in a critical time of self-identification. I grew sullen and unresponsive.

3 - Moving to San Diego—1931

as he became a friend of the family. So when Johnny heard of my idea of getting to Chicago to see the Fair, he was quite enthusiastic about the idea and offered to go with me, reminding us that he used to live in Champaign-Urbana, which is 60 miles south of Chicago. He still had his girl friend living there and he would get a chance to see her again and rekindle the romance! What better incentive for making the trip and they could drive up to Chicago with me to see the Fair as well. We began plotting and planning in earnest.

I also had met a young marine, whose name I have since forgotten, but with whom I double-dated girls from school. I soon realized that he was my pal mainly for the fact that I was now driving and could borrow mother's car on a weekend night. He did some rather heavy necking with his dates in the back seat while my girl and I were much less physical in the front seat. Later, he asked me why I wasn't going all the way with my dates and wondered if I wasn't more interested in him than the girls we saw? I denied the whole idea, of course, I was attracted to him but refused to act on it. It was his suggestion when he heard of our plan to get to Chicago, to go dressed as marines on furlough. It was a bold idea and at first we scoffed at carrying it out. But, we needed to go as cheaply as possible and this way, we might get rides so much easier. After a week's worth of rejecting and accepting the plan, we told him to go ahead and get the uniforms. He was also able to get "on leave" papers to complete the deception. How he was going to achieve all this was none of our business, he said. That year, a number of highway robberies had caused drivers to be very reluctant to the idea of picking up hitchhikers. It seemed the only way we were going to make it on the cheap to Chicago was to hitchhike.

Within a week we had our uniforms and furlough papers and now began to feel uneasy about the ruse we would engage in. We started scanning the newspapers and found an ad to share a ride by helping in the driving. It was our destination and so we called the phone number and were accepted readily as relief drivers. There were six of us in an old vintage Cadillac that looked rather worse for the wear, but we felt committed now. We wore our uniforms brazenly and bid the family good-by as we turned eastward into Arizona. There were absolutely no provisions for eating or sleeping, but a couple of eighteen-year-olds could sleep anywhere—in the car or in a field. So the trip began and almost immediately we began to have engine trouble. No one in our little crew was an auto mechanic and we did nothing but make matters worse. We managed to drag ourselves to a couple of garages along the highway at the start of the trip but it became obvious that the repair work expenses shared were going to be more than we had anticipated. Johnny and I went into a huddle and decided we were going to cut loose from this money-eating monster and so we bid our traveling companions farewell. The local Greyhound Bus Depot was nearby and we bought tickets there for the rest of the trip. We reasoned we could borrow money from the girl friend's parents to cover the return trip once they saw the plight we were in. The bus trip was another day and a half of uneventful time spent peering out at flat plains and farm fields.

Johnnie Slater and girl friend, he hitch-hiked to Chicago with me in '33.

We arrived tired and needing baths but Johnny was in Seventh Heaven in seeing his sweetheart again. He could barely take time to look away from her and I became a bit jealous of the two lovebirds. It became apparent that he wasn't going to tear himself away from her to spend any time with me at the Fair. I did find one family member who was willing to make the short trip up to Chicago with me so that all wasn't lost. I even managed to talk someone else to go a second time, and we did all the pavilions and exhibits, the gardens and Art Deco buildings especially erected to dazzle the Fair-goers.

But our week's visit was up and we needed to get going. Johnny regretfully disentangled himself from his love's embrace and we hit the road once more. We put on our uniforms, her father took us out to the city limits and we were on our own. This time we were totally dependent on our thumbs to get us home again and we wondered how easy that was going to be?

To our chagrin, we discovered that cars were reluctant to pick us up even though we were obviously proud young Marines. I worried that real marine officers might come driving by and pick us up and quiz us as to our legitimacy. But this never happened. We spent countless hours watching autos go whizzing by as we sweated in our woolen uniforms. Our progress was agonizingly slow and only truck-drivers turned out to be our good Samaritans.

3 - Moving to San Diego—1931

Nights were spent off the highway, by crawling over farmers' fences. We had decided to lighten our packs by limiting ourselves to one army blanket. It grew surprisingly cold at night and we took to sleeping spoon-fashion to help keep warm. I found myself developing amazing self-control in this close contact with Johnny. He warned me jokingly not to get "fresh" with him — that he was being faithful to his love. But, I would venture that he enjoyed the warmth of a body against his back as much as I did.

Passing through Nebraska, we spent one very frustrating day standing across from a roadside motel without a single ride. The young manager, who had been noticing our ordeal, came over to chat with us and then offered to give us a free meal and a room for the night. We could barely believe this kind gesture from a total stranger and gratefully accepted his offer. We desperately needed baths and a real bed for the night. I told him that if he was ever in California, he could look me up by writing to my mother for my new address in Berkeley.

A couple of years later, our motel host, Randy, did actually turn up in San Francisco in time for a New Year's Eve celebration and I met him in the big city for a bit of bar-hopping. It got very late into the night and it became apparent I wasn't going to make it back to my home across the Bay, so I wound up in his hotel room. There was a double bed and soon after I climbed in, I felt hands reaching out for me. I reacted by jumping out of bed as fast as I could before I realized that I had nowhere I could go at that time of the night. So I tried to get comfortable in the hotel room armchair nearby. I was still so unsure of my real sexual identity that I couldn't accept the situation I was in. Randy was an attractive young man but that didn't mean anything to me. Nothing was said that night or the next morning and I left him standing there bemused by my denial of his approach.

We continued westward at a snail's pace, arriving finally at Denver late in the day. I had always known that Dad had a second cousin living in Denver. In fact, we were related to Harold Lloyd, the famous Hollywood comedian through this cousin.* While Dad had still been with us in San Diego, we had actually gone to visit the actor, who was

I found myself developing amazing self-control in this close contact with Johnny. He warned me jokingly not to get "fresh" with him — that he was being faithful to his love.

There was a double bed and soon after I climbed in, I felt hands reaching out for me. I reacted by jumping out of bed as fast as I could before I realized that I had nowhere I could go at that time of the night ... I was still so unsure of my real sexual identity that I couldn't accept the situation I was in.

gracious enough to invite us into his palatial mansion in the Hollywood hills. I was thrilled to meet him and also horrified to grasp his right hand, which was badly damaged from a freak bomb accident. He only had the thumb and forefinger left.* In his movies, he always hid this fact by wearing a flesh-colored glove on that hand but in reality, he preferred to be his natural self. After being shown the lovely, manicured gardens and view from the hilltop estate, we left and returned to our own humble home.

But back to our story now, I decided that I should call this cousin even though I barely knew her or her family, and let her know we were passing through. Perhaps she would put us up for the night. She answered the phone rather coldly, didn't seem to grasp who I was and shortly hung up. Of course, I could understand her anxiety about being hospitable to someone she barely knew. We could have been criminals trying to get a foothold into her house. Still, we were trying to conserve our rapidly dwindling wallets and couldn't really afford a hotel room. Sleeping on the streets of Denver didn't appeal to us either. I think it was Johnny who then suggested we go out to her house and sneak around to the rear to see if we could sleep on her garage roof if it wasn't too steep. It turned out to be flat and easily climbed so we spent the night there, under our single Army blanket. The next morning we climbed down and came around to the front door and rang her bell. I politely thanked her for her hospitality in letting us stay on her garage roof. She was taken aback by the news and then realized who I was. We refused to burden her further when she offered us coffee. Later, through the family grapevine, I heard that she was severely criticized for her lack of concern for the young travelers. Her husband did take us out to the western edge of the city to help start us on the last leg of the trip. Johnny and I now had to come to a parting of ways as he was taking a more southern route and I needed to take a more northern route towards Berkeley. I was truly sorry to see him go, as I had grown very fond of his wry humor and warm smile. The rest of the trip was so uneventful, that I will skip past it.

*Harold Lloyd's home, Green Acres' has 44 rooms, 26 bathrooms, 12 fountains, 12 gardens and is listed on the National Register of Historic Places. One of the 36 founders of the Academy of Motion Picture Arts and Sciences (AMPAS). A 1920 accident with a prop bomb which turned out not to be a prop, Lloyd lost the thumb and forefinger of his right hand. In subsequent films, he wore a glove and prosthetic device to hide it. (Source: www.imdb.com)

4
Starting College
1933 - 1934

"I still wasn't absolutely sure of my sexual identity and so I started dating a girl I had chatted with in one of my classes ... I was feeling torn to conform to what society expected of me and what my intuition told me was right for me." - GS

§

I was well aware by now that gay men, and probably lesbians too, create bogus marriages to armor up the Façade. This seemed like the perfect time to drag this out of George too: to let straight readers understand how homophobia also fortifies the Façade with emotional torment. - JJ

Starting College: 1933 - 1934

I arrived in Berkeley, famished and dirty, was welcomed into my new home and assigned to a cot on the sleeping porch on the second floor. I was to share it with another student as well. I learned that a former occupant of this room had gone on after college to a career in Hollywood. His name was Robert Young and he was a romantic male lead in many early movies and finished a distinguished career playing a doctor in several early television shows. He never came back to visit, so I didn't meet him, of course. I was too absorbed in beginning a new life as a college student to take much notice of my home environment. I signed up for as many art periods as I could possibly handle.

One of my favorite activities was the gym period and since everyone had to sign-up for some form of physical education, I chose wrestling, of course. I was teamed up with a sparring partner and learned that his name was Vallejo Wood. Val was a bit taller than I, blond and handsome in a Nordic way. We quickly became good friends, would meet later for coffee and running around the campus together. I don't think he ever had an idea of the fun it was for me to tussle with him on the mats. I had to be especially careful that he didn't notice the growing bulge in my gym shorts. The frustration was extreme but I couldn't quit now. It also reminded me of my bedside romps with Hube back in Wichita. It has crossed my mind since then that a lot of men must have discovered their true identities in this most sexually stimulating of sports. And what does this say about the avid macho types that hang out at big wrestling arenas taking in all the writhing, sweating, muscularity that is on display. Is this sublimation, a need to see male flesh being pummeled about for their covert enjoyment? I leave it to you to ponder.

It has crossed my mind since then that a lot of men must have discovered their true identities in this most sexually stimulating of sports.

4 - Starting College—1933

Anyway, as Val and I bonded more closely. He suggested that I move into his parents' home off campus. I had met them when I had been over for Sunday night suppers and they seemed to like me. Val's older brother had his own room but was willing to move in with his younger brother to accommodate me as a paying room and boarder. I really wasn't happy at my Uncle George's, what with his strained relationship with his wife, so I told them I planned to move. There was no objection to this and I was soon occupying a more comfortable room then a porch cot. Now I was seeing even more of Val and growing more frustrated. When the older brother discovered that neither Val nor I had ever been with a woman, he was amazed and decided he had to correct the problem. He used to go to a favorite house in Emeryville. He promptly gave Val the address and told us to go if we wanted to be called real men. Val insisted I go with him, of course and even though I was very nervous about such an evening, I could hardly refuse to go without raising suspicions. Besides, I really needed to prove to myself that I couldn't perform.

Emeryville, in those days, was a shabby backwater of tired old Victorian cottages and seedy storefronts that had been by-passed by people seeking more upscale neighborhoods. To live there was a sign that you were sitting on the bottom social rung. It was the perfect area for crime and prostitution.

We found the address with no trouble and walked up onto the front porch and rang the bell. I was ready to do an about-face then and there but stayed by Val who was almost as embarrassed as I was. An ordinary-looking housewife looked us over for a second before letting us in. Along a narrow hall, several girls in housecoats began lounging in front of doorways. It was obvious that we were to pick a girl and follow her into the room. Val chose immediately and disappeared, but I lingered a bit before selecting a partner and following her into the bedroom. I will spare you the details here, but let it be known that I was almost a complete disaster. My lady friend was all sympathy, assuring me that it was commonplace for a first-timer to fail at the starting gate. Not to worry she said, but she took the money anyway since I had used up ten minutes of her working night. I found myself out in the

Along a narrow hall, several girls in housecoats began lounging in front of doorways. It was obvious that we were to pick a girl and follow her into the room ... I will spare you the details here, but let it be known that I was almost a complete disaster.

Beneath Campanile Tower
U.C. Berkeley, 1933

4 - Starting College—1933

hallway again a few minutes before Val. He burst out of his room with a most excited look on his face. He could hardly wait to tell me everything. I, too, could barely wait to tell him how exciting it was for me. What else could I have said?

I still wasn't absolutely sure of my sexual identity and so I started dating a girl I had chatted with in one of my classes. Sally Searle was petite, charming and obviously interested. We seemed to have a rapport with each other, and besides studying together, we would go on long walks around the campus. One particular night, our stroll took us up into the hills behind the Greek Theatre. There was a lovers' lane up there that was much in use and we followed those paths for awhile. Then we came to a lovely vista of the campus below and a carpet of amber lights that spread itself out to the horizon. We began fondling each other and it became obvious to me that she was ready to go all the way with me. But try as I might, my heart wasn't in it — this wasn't me at all. I stopped before we unbuttoned any clothing. I was feeling torn to conform to what society expected of me and what my intuition told me was right for me. Sally sensed that something was wrong immediately and although a bit bewildered, she withdrew her attentions. We continued on down the hill and I saw her to her room and gave her a chaste little goodnight kiss. I wondered what she would think of me now. We did continue being friends but it never seemed the same again. I, reading the handwriting on the wall, never again tried seducing a girl friend.

The frustration of living so close to Val at his parents' home, was taking an emotional toll on me. The only way I could get intimate with him was to wrestle on the gym's mats. After a year of this, I made up my mind it was time to move on so that I could study without the distraction of seeing him around half-naked a lot of the time. I thought about the way people go on with their lives, denying who they really are or putting up false facades to get along with their mates regardless of whether they were heterosexual or homosexual. At this time, half of American marriages end up in the divorce courts. Whether this means we haven't the patience to

> *I still wasn't absolutely sure of my sexual identity and so I started dating a girl I had chatted with in one of my classes ... I was feeling torn to conform to what society expected of me and what my intuition told me was right for me.*

> *At this time, half of American marriages end up in the divorce courts. Whether this means we haven't the patience to live with each other's faults or we simply make commitments we don't really think through, I haven't the answer. I look back through my own personal history and see the number of times I have been sure I was making the right choice, only to regret it later.*

live with each other's faults or we simply make commitments we don't really think through, I haven't the answer. I look back through my own personal history and see the number of times I have been sure I was making the right choice, only to regret it later. I know that settling for an attractive face and body is probably the worst criteria for making a decision. I and most of us are apt to choose a partner this way. Wasn't it Shakespeare who said, "What fools these mortals be?"

I soon found myself hunting for new quarters and I wanted to live quietly alone this time. I found a rear cottage that had been divided into three studios. It was rented out to Cal students and was five minutes from Sather Gate, the main entry into the Campus center. The room was simple and the building had a certain rustic charm to it with morning glory vines almost completely covering its exterior. I was on Channing Way just half a block off of Telegraph Avenue, which is the main Business Street for the University's throngs of students. I was delighted and looked forward to my new life. At the front of the property, a huge old mansion had also been divided up into separate rentals for students. One wonders at the change in family size from the period (1900) when this home was built to house possibly a huge family. The student at the other end of my cottage was Music major and constantly played his classical records loudly. We were always being invited in to listen and I found myself beginning to appreciate the three "Bs"—Bach, Beethoven and Brahms. It was the beginning of my life-long love for the world's great music. I also favored the less cerebral composers like Tchaikovsky, Debussy and Ravel.

I finally got up the nerve to ask him point-blank, "Say, are you gay?" It startled him and he leaped up from the couch and indignantly denied it.

After study time, it was great to lie back and savor the gorgeous music in this little room. One of the other listeners was a student who lived in the big house in front. I had admired his trim, muscular build for some weeks and one night when our host was absent for a few moments, I finally got up the nerve to ask him point-blank, "Say, are you gay?" It startled him and he leaped up from the couch and indignantly denied it. I hastily assured him that he need not get upset since I, too, was gay. He calmed down considerably and we began to talk. I told him how inexperienced I was and that I would like to go to bed with him whenever he felt like it. We began a sexual relationship on the sly and I would sneak up to his attic studio room usually late night after study.

4 - Starting College—1933

It was touch and go because the house mother would lock doors at midnight and I didn't want to be left shivering outside. I managed to hold off my loneliness for the time being.

§

During summer vacations, I always managed to head home to San Diego for a few weeks. Mother and my three sisters were living quietly at the Spanish stucco cottage on Madison Street waiting for Dad to return and retire from his life-long connection with the Singer Company.

I discovered that my eldest sister, Dorothy, was dating a very attractive young man at this time and I, acting as the only present male in the Somers household, would have to pass judgment on him. He came by one night to take Dot out to the movies and I looked him over. Gay men like to kid around that they have developed a sixth sense for recognizing other gay men who are not effeminate types. We call this our "gaydar" and it comes to practical use in spotting our fellow members in a crowd. Perhaps it is the innate ability to perceive subtle body language tips or just plain intuition, I don't know. I became suspicious of his mannerisms and although I was new at making assumptions about people, I felt Dot might regret getting too involved with him. So after some hesitation, I pulled her aside one day and suggested she let him go. She was aghast at my verdict and demanded to know why I would say such a thing. I then stated that he was most probably "gay" and would never work out as a boy friend for her. She, of course had never heard the expression "gay" and wanted to know what it meant anyway. First, I told her I felt qualified to say that he was gay since I, myself was gay and could recognize others that were of my type. This double shock was almost too much for my dazed sister, but Dorothy has always been very cool and calm about anxiety-filled situations — something that seems to run in our family, it appears. She asked a lot of questions of me and I filled her in as best I could. What did the term "gay" mean anyway? This might be the right moment to tell you how it became the word used to label us:

In fact, the term "gay" really denotes homosexual men rather than lesbians who have favored their own term. In history, it was in the 17th Century that the word "gay," which had always connoted pleasurable things, began indicating a life of immoral pleasures. Later on, when applied to women in

Gay men like to kid around that they have developed a sixth sense for recognizing other gay men who are not effeminate types. We call this our "gaydar" and it comes to practical use in spotting our fellow members in a crowd.

Where does the word "Gay" come from?

the 19th Century, gay meant prostitute. By the early 1900s, homosexuals had appropriated the term as a camp word to refer not only to themselves, but also to promiscuity, flamboyance, and a lack of restraint. Since the 1940s, "gay" has been the preferred term used by homosexuals to refer to themselves. An enormous dictionary of slang has evolved to use as cover-ups or just to have fun with language. I will give you one of my favorites here, "Oh, he's a friend of Dorothy's." This refers to the Dorothy who is the little girl from Kansas who ends up in the kingdom of Oz. Gay men like to identify someone they are sure is gay by calling him a friend of Dorothy's. After all, gay men find themselves in a fantasyland, which exists in a hidden world. The comic part of all this for me, of course, was that this was my own sister's name!

Continuing, my "coming out" to Dorothy was an act of trust and I asked her to keep it to herself. I simply wasn't up to saying anything to Mother or writing to Dad about my new status in Society. It went no further than herself and she soon took my advice and broke off with her boy-friend. It was an act of faith for her but she trusted me implicitly. Several years later, I was having a drink in a San Francisco gay bar and who did I see sitting on a barstool but our ex-boyfriend from San Diego! We had a congenial chat about what had happened and he readily admitted that at that time he wasn't sure himself as to his orientation. He held no animosity towards me for having squashed his interest in my sister.

§

I had never met a family with two gay sons before and I wondered how often that rather unusual fact would develop in a family. I never again ran into that sort of family make-up.

But I was meeting other new friends in college classes after moving out of Valjean's family home. The most important of these new friends was Roger. He was a tall, slender, very immature-looking chap who was somewhat of a snob to most others. But he took a shine to me and we loved trading barbs about each other and we ridiculed anyone that didn't meet our standards of behavior. I was often invited to spend weekends just south of San Francisco at his mother's home. We called it the "Peninsula" then but now it is more famous as the birthplace of the computer industry and is called "Silicon Valley." Roger worshipped his mother, who was a navy widow. Amazingly, she also had another, slightly older son, Adam, who was also gay. I had never met a family with two gay sons before and I wondered how often that

4 - Starting College—1933

Mother at far right with my three sisters, and their boy friends at La Jolla Beach.

rather unusual fact would develop in a family. I never again ran into that sort of family make-up.

Adam lived in Hollywood, some 450 miles to the south, but he managed to come up to visit rather often. He was equally devoted to his mother who loved her two gay sons dearly and never tried to interfere in their lives. I was impressed with her total acceptance of her sons' identities and wondered if my own mother could handle the situation as well. She would never have grandchildren to dangle on her knees and I felt her unspoken thoughts on this sensitive matter. So this family was my first contact with a very sophisticated world that I had only read about. They had style and were trendsetters. I learned so much about famous society names from them. Names like Noel Coward, Cole Porter, George Gershwin, and Tennessee Williams were always being tossed around at the dinner table. It was comforting to know that we shared a sexual identity with these brilliant people. A whole new world was being opened up to me and I soaked it up like a sponge.

Adam's job in Hollywood was at Paramount Studios where he was employed as a set designer. He sat at a drafting table and turned out beautiful watercolor renderings of period rooms. These became working drawings that the construction crews would build into sets. I heard much about how gay the studios were. That if it

I learned so much about famous society names from them. Names like Noel Coward, Cole Porter, George Gershwin, and Tennessee Williams were always being tossed around at the dinner table. It was comforting to know that we shared a sexual identity with these brilliant people. A whole new world was being opened up to me and I soaked it up like a sponge.

weren't for the gay world, there would be no movies of any quality at all. I was eager to believe him, of course.

Ruth and her family had spent many years living in the Philippines because her husband had been a Navy officer. This created a special bond between us, of course. Besides recollecting old Manila, Roger and I were forever mimicking the problems that many Filipinos have in pronouncing their "F"s. In hindsight, it seems racist to think of, but we did avoid jesting in public about it. We would say, "Are you polks prom de Pilipines?," and double over in laughter at our accents. What can I say? We were young then and youth can be cruel.

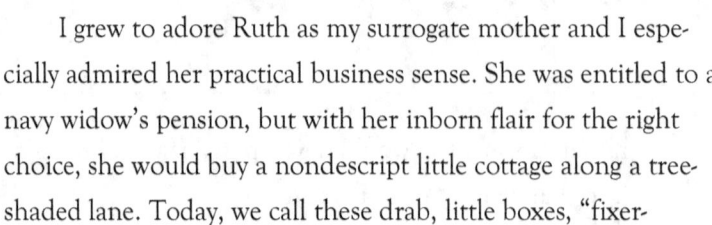
College buddy, Roger

I grew to adore Ruth as my surrogate mother and I especially admired her practical business sense. She was entitled to a navy widow's pension, but with her inborn flair for the right choice, she would buy a nondescript little cottage along a tree-shaded lane. Today, we call these drab, little boxes, "fixer-uppers." She would move in while transforming it into a little jewel of a place and her sons pitched in with minor carpentry and painting. She never failed to make a good profit and always had a roof over her head. Her series of house-fixings would have been attractive enough to appear in most decorator magazines.

Roger's gay brother Adam, visiting from Hollywood.

On weekends, sometimes, we would drive up to San Francisco to savor the black jazz clubs. We always made sure we had at least one girl friend or two with us to avoid being obvious. Along Fillmore Street, which was once the Harlem of the African American jazz scene in The City, we could duck into seedy night-clubs. Often, we would be the only whites in these dimly lit, smoky rooms where we could savor the great sounds that sent us into dreamy reverie. Drugs were not part of all this enjoyment. It was a more innocent time for us then.

Drugs were not part of all this enjoyment. It was a more innocent time for us then.

A few years later, after the college years, I still kept in touch with Roger who had moved to Chicago to pursue a career with Foote, Cone and Belding. They were a very successful advertising agency. Roger started hobnobbing with Chicago society and married into an important family. He eventually gave up working since there was a good deal of family money. His way of dealing with his life is not that unusual and I know that other gay men have chosen to marry into money and live a double life quite happily. Roger and his new family decided to buy a lovely old farmstead in Connecticut that dated back to the first settlers. The nearby town had a most appropriate name, "Gay Hill," and that was funny to me. I spent one vacation later, visiting them and the nearby seaport named Old Mystic where there were wonderful old ships and a fabulous collection of carved figureheads that adorned sailing ships. And then even later, Roger and his family bought a villa on Nassau, which lies out off the Atlantic Coast. I was always invited to come visit them in the next dozen years but I never made it there.

§

Although I am making no attempt to delve into African-American gay history here in my story, I think it is important to refer to the 1920-1935 period which is now called the Harlem Renaissance. Central to this significant time was the emergence of some prominent writers, artists and musicians, including Count Cullen, Claude McKay, Langston Hughes, Bessie Smith, Ma Rainey, Alain Locke, Bruce Nugent, Bayard Rustin and Ethel Waters. James Baldwin, the fiery gay author was to come along a bit later. There are no racial groups that don't have a certain percentage of gays within their populations. In fact, the American Indian tribes often revered their gays as shamans, dream interpreters, artisans, entertainers, and matchmakers.

§

But, of course, it wasn't all play in those college days and I put in plenty of time studying. As an Art major, I was enrolled in several art classes and attended lectures on world art history. My favorite studio teacher was Margaret Peterson who always arrived for her painting class wearing a smart cocktail suit. We were impressed with her ability to stay spotless while supervising messy, paint-smeared students. Her great passion was Russian icon painters and many of us began to paint in that style to please her. This wasn't her intention at all and she would get quite upset with the imitation icon paintings that proliferated in that class.

I also had another great teacher, Chuiro Obata, from whom I learned of the great contribution that Japan had made to the world of Art. I began a

His way of dealing with his life is not that unusual and I know that other gay men have chosen to marry into money and live a double life quite happily.

Julio, our Spanish professor was a rather pompous, gay gent who was apt to throw little cocktail parties for his favorite male students at his elegant, off-campus apartment. I admired his taste in furnishings and art but I also made sure, at the end of the evening, not to be the last one out the door!

love affair with Oriental Art that continues through today. In my living room hangs a large six-fold screen in black and white depicting a mountain landscape. I bought it when I could ill afford to pay for it but I sensed that it was a once-in-a-lifetime opportunity. I wheedled the oriental antique shop owner into selling it to me on the installment plan. $35 a month for ten months and finally it was all mine.

I had signed up for a Spanish language class which was rather unfair of me since I already knew the language but I didn't really know the grammatical rules and so this was my chance to learn why words were constructed and placed in certain orders. I had always instinctually spoken Spanish with no idea why I spoke the way I did. Julio, our Spanish professor was a rather pompous, gay gent who was apt to throw little cocktail parties for his favorite male students at his elegant, off-campus apartment. I admired his taste in furnishings and art but I also made sure, at the end of the evening, not to be the last one out the door!

§

One of the most interesting events that took place during these college years was the huge Beaux Artes Ball, called the "Parillia." It was held annually in San Francisco and was sponsored by all the art and architecture schools and related organizations in the Bay Area. I was able to go to three of these raucous, freewheeling affairs staged in the cavernous Civic Center Auditorium which now is called the Bill Graham Auditorium. This venue sits in the Civic Center complex dominated by the City Hall, all designed in the Classic Revival Style.

The U.C. University Art Department chose me to design and construct our entry. It was the custom for each participating school to devise some spectacular entry and to parade across the vast floor to the stage end where the monarchs sat receiving their subjects' offerings. There was always a theme to these affairs, and one year it was pre-Columbian Mexico, another year it was Egyptian. The year I was involved as a designer, it was the South Seas, which we would work around for the unifying theme. I began exploring through books at the library for suitable ideas. I decided on having a procession of scantily clad natives of some imaginary island, entering the hall carrying a litter, which would be crowned with two sacrificial maidens. They

THE BEAUX ARTS PAGEANT
MYSELF IN THE CLOSEST TO CENTER SPOT

THE BEAUX ARTS PAGEANT
MYSELF STANDING BETWEEN TWO WOMAN ON THE RIGHT

would be seated back-to-back and hold, on their heads, a tray. This held the giant Sacred Peach, which they would present to the royal pair. I also wanted the mythological monkey god, Hanuman to be frolicking about the natives as they wound their way up to the throne. A color scheme of pinks and purples seemed exotic enough to me. At each of the corners of the litter, I planned to fasten a huge tropical flower whose stamens were actually incense sticks which we lighted just as we came onto the floor. This proved to be a wise choice when we discovered that no other entry had used the sense of smell to intrigue the audience. We were a sensation, with our two barebreasted maidens on top of the litter and helmet-crowned warriors dancing alongside. The Polynesian royal couple sat on their thrones, framed by a gigantic smoking volcano. At the climax of the evening revelry, a live sacrificial maiden was tossed into the fiery maw of this volcano.

But no more Artists' Balls were staged after this Polynesian Year because of the "action" up in the balcony areas. It seemed that some revelers had decided that this was an opportunity to go "all the way" with the voluptuous nature of the evening. The police were called in to arrest a few couples. The newspapers the next day were having a field day, trumpeting the wicked ways of the Revels. When I think of what goes on during the New Orleans Mardi Gras in these times, it all seemed so innocent in the 1930s.

§

In more prosaic areas, my cousin Art had moved up the corporate ladder and was now the manager of the Roos Brothers' Campus Shop just outside Sather Gate. Often, on my way back to my studio room, I would stop in to chat with him and ask about Uncle George and his family. Coming out the entry, I would notice the large display windows with their stylized wooden mannequins in the women's section and the stiff men's suit forms in the adjoining windows. I would think to myself — I could do that, it looked simple and creative — and I would be doing street theater. It all made sense to me as I would be ending Dad's concern that I choose a career that would support me and that would still be in an artistic field.

Today, the role of display windows is much less important to a store, but in the 30s, it was considered to be an important tool to attract customers. It is hard to come up with statistics to evaluate the attraction value of store windows but there is much greater emphasis on "in store displays" at this time.

I mulled over the idea of working in the windows and finally talked it over with cousin Art who seemed interested all right but said he simply could not add another paid worker to his staff. Actually, he didn't even have anyone working a full day at the campus shop because the main store in San Francisco would send over a woman to do the changes in the women's windows. A journeyman came to do the male side. Art didn't even have the right to hire anyone. I asked if I might learn the ropes without pay — no one would know that I worked for free. It was a highly unorthodox idea and he would be sticking his neck out but he agreed to let me come in and "audit the display classes." In today's business world, with the strength of the unions, no one could possibly get away with this notion, but this was the 30s. No one raised an eyebrow, and it was assumed I was on the payroll; I started showing up half day a week to learn all the tricks. I was much more interested in the women's side since it permitted a more free approach.

Marge Kinney and me at Roos Brothers.

To her thinking, all the good-looking men were always gay and the rest were already married.

A young woman, Marge Kinney, would arrive from the City across the Bay, where she worked in Display; I would always be there to assist her in the weekly changes. She was apt to swear like a stevedore at her troop of mannequins when they resisted getting dressed but she and I got along splendidly. We became great friends and I listened to her go on about the dearth of good husband material. To her thinking, all the good-looking men were always gay and the rest were already married. She was feeling the years slipping by as she was in her 30s and still looking for a husband. I sympathized with her since I had no one myself yet — but then I was only in my early 20s.

This then was to be my life career direction, as a display designer and I stayed with it for the rest of my working life with few regrets.

5
Father's Death
1935 - 1936

"I wept for the father I had known so briefly as a child and now would never get to know." - GS

§

Fathers not accepting their gay sons, seems to be a common thread in the gay community. So, with no empathy or expression of love for his son, George's father went to his death bequeathing this lifelong emotional scar for George to live with. - JJ

STARTING COLLEGE: 1935 - 1936

Christmas of 1935 arrived and I headed down to San Diego for my two weeks of winter vacation from college. I would be with my sisters and mother with no study, exams or lectures to worry about briefly. We planned a festive supper for just ourselves on Christmas Eve. As we sat down to enjoy turkey with all the good things that go with it, the phone rang. We figured it was friends calling to wish us a happy holiday, but instead it was Western Union with a telegram from the Philippines. A mixed sense of joy and dread swept across the table. The voice asked if we wished the message read out or sent by mail? "Yes, yes — read it out now," Mother said, thinking it would be Dad wishing us a Christmas greeting. Instead, it was a wire from a Manila hospital stating that Mr. Robert Somers had been admitted with a serious kidney infection!

Our holiday mood was instantly changed to one of gloom. Supper was forgotten as we thought about Dad lying in a hospital bed with none of his immediate family there to care for him. Then another phone call an hour later asked if we wanted this message read? We dreaded this one but had to know what was happening to Dad. He had died in the short interval between calls from malignant kidney stones—acute hemorrhagic nephritis — as the death certificate later revealed. He was then 50 and had been troubled by chronic nephritis for years but had chosen not to tell us. We were all devastated and in tears. I wept for the father I had known so briefly as a child and now would never get to know. All of us went to our beds that night in grief and I doubt that anyone slept thinking of Dad lying there thousands of miles to the west and there was nothing we could do. The

On the beach with sisters Anita and Dorothy during my Christmas vacation from college. Days later "our holiday mood was instantly changed to one of gloom."

I wept for the father I had known so briefly as a child and now would never get to know.

5 - Father's Death—1935

next day we sent a wire with instructions to the hospital to allow the Singer Company to handle the burial and funeral. We felt terrible that we couldn't afford the trip to Manila and it would take a month at best to get there. There were still my grandparents and Adolph Langenheim, my godfather, who could be present for us at the services.

And so, shortly after that sad day, we sat down at the dining table to assess our futures. There would be a small Army pension and some insurance funds for Mother. She had already done some sewing on her machine for neighbor women-friends and now planned to increase this work. With a very careful juggling of money, I could continue in college if I could find a way to add to my support. I vowed to find a way. It was going to be my third year and I hated to give up now. If she could send the rent money, I would take care of

My beloved sister, Anita, whom I photographed on a school vacation.

Mother, around the time of dad's death, proud in her Spanish dress.

the food question. When I got back to Berkeley, I didn't go back to Uncle George's for help because I had left them a year earlier to go live at Val's and I now felt some guilt about that. I did go to the college employment agency and they offered me work as a waiter at a nearby sorority. This would provide me with meals at least, so I had the basics covered. Very little was left for spending money but I determined I should tighten the belt severely. No time for play now and my education was the important thing to get nailed down. It was rather ironic that I had the ideal job for a typical male student at college — easy access to sorority girls — but absolutely no interest in them! It was the perfect solution for the "House Mother" for she never had to concern herself with the kitchen help showing unwanted interest in her young charges.

§

Classes, the new job as display apprentice, hashing at the sorority and study time filled my days and nights and the pressure to get everything under control was having its effect on me. I wasn't sleeping well

with worrying whether I could handle it all. I would lie awake thinking why I was doing all this anyway? I could just quit at the end of the semester and, since I was now being offered a paying job at their main store in San Francisco, why stay in school? It was the lifeline I was looking for and I accepted. A diploma wasn't going to make an impression in this particular line of work, anyway.

But, there was one last memorable experience waiting for me in college. I was lucky enough to be chosen to design and supervise construction of a parade float for the celebration of the completion of the two great Bay Area bridges in 1937. The Golden Gate Bridge now would link San Francisco to Marin County to the north and the other bridge running eastward would link the City to Oakland and a dozen other burgeoning communities around it. The era of the ferryboats had come to an end and I felt sad that we would see little of this wonderful way of travel. I would miss the smell, fresh air and great vistas of the surrounding hills and cities of our Bay. The ferryboats were being sold off to other cities like Portland, Seattle and

(Continued on page 82)

SKETCH OF MY FLOAT FOR THE SAN FRANCISCO MARKET ST. PARADE CELEBRATING
THE OPENING OF OUR GOLDEN GATE AND OAKLAND BRIDGES, 1937

(Continued from page 80)

Vancouver. Ironically, today with the horrific traffic congestion we have to endure, people are clamoring and getting a few of the old ferries back in service.

When the Oakland Bridge was first in operation, it carried a rail line on its lower deck called the "Key System" but oil and automakers interests soon had it removed to add another auto lane in its place. The ensuing congestion over the next decades led to cries for a new rail line and at a cost of billions, we voted for an underwater tube that we call BART (Bay Area Rapid Transit). What a fantastic waste of taxpayer money for a rail line we already had and had scrapped!

Battleship U.S.S. California passes under the incomplete deck of the Golden Gate Bridge in 1936.

I now began to think of what I could do to make that gigantic truck bed into an artistic statement pertinent to the two bridge openings. After some day-dreaming that I always find necessary before starting any project, I decided on this concept: On the thirty-foot length of the truck bed, I would have a giant of the sea god, Neptune reclining in San Francisco Bay and a model of the Golden Gate Bridge would span over his body. He would be in the act of relinquishing his trident to the genius of Man in conquering him with the bridges. For sex appeal, I wanted six lovely mermaids sitting around the perimeters, flashing their iridescent fishtails at the crowds. I got an enthusiastic response from the Parade committee and my final weeks became a frantic beehive of activity as I tried to juggle my regular schedule with this added responsibility. I began to feel like a mother hen trying to keep track of her scurrying chicks. The huge figure of Neptune would easily have been 25 feet tall if he had decided to get up for a stretch and he was conceived in a Cubist Style as I was under the spell of Picasso at that time. Someone else handled the costuming of the coed mermaids and we decided they should be blowing soapy bubbles that would add to the watery ambience. Amazingly, I never got around to photographing this creation but I have included close by, a sketch of its general look. I felt very good about the "ohs" and "ahs" I got from the sidewalk throngs.

6
Moving to San Francisco
1937 - 1941

"San Francisco became known as a most tolerant city to live in ... gay men have flocked here for some 150 years." - GS

§

I was surprised to learn from George that SF had been a gay mecca from this early on - certainly widely known as such since the 1960s. - GS

Moving to San Francisco: 1937 - 1941

And so, I left Berkeley and college studies at the end of my junior year. Much as I knew that I would miss my school-friends and the Art Department, the excitement of going across the Bay to live in the big city was a thrilling challenge. I was now entirely on my own and must earn my living without anyone's help. I was twenty-three now and a bit apprehensive about striking out in this new direction.

I decided to look for rooms in the Bay-bordered area of San Francisco known as North Beach that was, and still is, the most colorful section of the City. It was the site of the first settlement (1836) around Portsmouth Square and had been the home of the Italian fishermen. The main street, Columbus Avenue, was a colorful mix of cheap restaurants, bars, bakeries and coffee shops. I reveled in the atmosphere, which somehow made me think of what a European city must be like. I knew that Jack London had walked these streets and shipped out to foreign shores to write his adventure stories. There were numerous others who had made names for themselves as well. Perhaps, Jack Kerouac is one of the most-recognized of them but he came along in the fifties.

I loved wandering through this most European section of the City. Along its northern flank, rose a steep hill that was once crowned with a semaphore hut where a signalman would announce the arrival of sailing ships. This was a very important event for early San Franciscans. They depended on these vessels which had sailed completely around South America's treacherous waters to come to California bearing precious cargoes, like books, tools, and food delicacies. The Hill took its name, Telegraph Hill, from this all-important signalman who set the town abuzz with hope and excitement. Letters from families back East were the most precious items, of course.

6 - Moving to San Francisco—1937

Then in the early thirties, a huge memorial tower was placed where the modest little semaphore flagpole had stood. A Victorian eccentric named Lillie Coit, who had inherited her husband's gold-mining fortune decided to leave a sizable amount to erecting a monument to the firemen of San Francisco. Her particular brand of madness was to chase fires and San Francisco seemed to always be burning somewhere in its limits. She became famous for appearing at every fire and supplying the sweating men with liquor. She was also known to visit the City's night spots attired as a man! After her death, a committee took a couple of decades to decide what sort of monument to erect and after much indecision, came up with the rather phallic tower supposed to represent the nozzle of a fire hose. It has always amused me to think how unwittingly this tower does homage to her passion for her gallant firemen!

Lillie Coit's memorial to San Francisco's firemen.

The history books tell us that the first settlement was called Yerba Buena before it was named San Francisco to honor the patron saint by which it is known today. The lusty Tent City grew at an unbelievable rate once gold was found in the Sierra foothills. Thousands of young men were suddenly without women. At first, before the prostitutes began arriving to set up their "houses of ill repute," men, hard-pressed (sorry for the pun) for human contact, sometimes got drunk enough to go to bed with each other. At Saturday night dances at saloons, it was quite common for some men to be designated the female partner by the fact that he would wear a colored handkerchief on his arm. And one wonders who these men might have been in

Montgomery St., my first home in San Francisco after college.

A group of my gay friends and me visiting the 1937 World's Fair on Treasure Island.

reality. I doubt that anyone objected to the arrangement and from then to this day, San Francisco became known as a most tolerant city to live in. Necessity bred the diversity that is a hallmark of this colorful city. Gay men have flocked here for some 150 years. World War II was especially effective in bringing in an enormous influx of men who had no appetite to return to their old hometowns where they had to hide their true natures. I was already a citizen of the Bay Area and felt more at home here than anywhere else I had been.

San Francisco became known as a most tolerant city to live in ... gay men have flocked here for some 150 years.

§

In looking around North Beach, I soon found a small two-room apartment, up a few steps on the very steep block of Montgomery Street that crosses Broadway. This was a very raucous, nightclub district and Finocchio's, the world-famous drag-show nightclub was only a half block down Broadway. It was the destination for tourist crowds seeking the thrills of seeing how the wicked city lived. I am sure that they imagined that all gay men always dressed in women's clothes and led dissolute lives in back alleys. How totally wrong they were in their thinking, but I had no plans to open their

6 - Moving to San Francisco—1937

eyes to the truth. I hadn't the money or the interest in the cross-dressing entertainers at Finocchio's, but I did take some visiting friends from out-of-town there a couple of times. It was considered the place to visit when in gay "old Frisco." Pacific Street, a block away had always been a bordello address for early visitors and it was just beginning to become a fairly respectable business address when I arrived on the scene in the late thirties. Jackson Square, another block east, was fortunate in being spared the devastation of the 1906 fire and earthquake. Its handsome, Victorian business buildings, which filled two blocks bordering Montgomery St., were just beginning to attract the decorator and design business. They soon got to work and did a magnificent job of restoring these beautiful old buildings to their original state. It's worth the time to visit this pristine little section to see how San Francisco looked prior to the catastrophic quake of '06.

I am sure that they imagined that all gay men always dressed in women's clothes and led dissolute lives in back alleys. How totally wrong they were in their thinking, but I had no plans to open their eyes to the truth.

Another world-famous club nearby on the corner of Broadway and Columbus was "The Condor," featuring America's first topless act: Carol Doda, she of the gargantuan breasts! She was noted for descending onto the club's tiny stage riding a baby grand piano, naked. I believe that this was a first time ever show gimmick for America and the place was jam-packed every night of the week with raunchy males. I never bothered to go, of course, and I needed to conserve my tiny salary.

My new digs consisting of two bare rooms, set me back $16 a month out of my monthly paycheck of $64. Today, in the year 2003, that seems a ridiculously improbable sum but in 1937 that was not too bad a starting salary. How amazing that seems to anyone today when gas for your car can cost almost $2 a gallon. And this was also the year that President Franklin Roosevelt cajoled Congress into enacting the Social Security Act. It all began in 1937 and I, for one, am very thankful that it was accepted as a part of our working lives.

Since I couldn't afford a car yet, I always walked to work down Columbus Avenue past Vesuvio's Bar and the City Light's Bookstore. These famous hangouts bordered an alley street later named after its most famous denizen, Jack Kerouac and his gay buddy, Allen Ginsberg. Allen became famous for his Beat Generation poem, "Howl." Poets were a dime a dozen in North Beach bistros at that time.

The gay men and women of the late 30s had few places that they could hang out in, but the most famous one was the Black Cat on Montgomery Street, just below Broadway in an old brick building from the Victorian era. It still had its handsome, ornate back bar with much carving and carpenter's fretwork intact. The police allowed it to stay open because it was a good source of pay-offs. They also kept the straight world content by doing token raids every so often. I never saw anyone hauled away in paddy wagons and both sides seem to be able to live with each other. I would stop in on weekends to have a cold beer and to watch a ribald, effeminate entertainer who would be helped up onto a table to give us a hilarious version of operatic arias off key. He often made the whole thing even funnier by donning a moth-eaten wig topped by a fake rose. His greatest hit was the "Habanera" from the opera Carmen. We would applaud him wildly for more and more. Jose was later crowned the Dowager Empress of San Francisco. In Victorian times, the City had its Emperor Norton, a man who was probably driven mad by financial losses during the Gold Rush period. He wound up on the streets proclaiming himself Emperor of San Francisco. He roamed about in a mildewed naval uniform and when he walked into saloons, was hailed with cheers. He always got free drinks and often invited everyone to "drinks on the house." Bartenders loved his crazy antics as he always attracted a crowd. We, in this later generation, only wished the two could have held court as a royal pair!

There were probably no more than three or four strictly gay bars in San Francisco at this time. Of course, there were many that had a mixed clientele. For instance, the best hotel in the city, the St. Francis, had the Oak Room, a step off the main lobby, which was very discreetly gay. You rarely saw a woman in these very proper, handsome oak-paneled quarters. The police generally kept out of this bar, but the others paid a price to stay open. Cops felt it was their duty to charge into these establishments, even though no laws were being broken, and bawl out, "This is a raid!" A few token patrons were hustled out to the wagon. It was certainly safer for the police to go after harmless gays than to go after the real criminals down in the Tenderloin District, where prostitutes and drugs were easily found.

This was what it was like some 32 years before the world famous eve-

6 - Moving to San Francisco—1937

> *It is a little known fact that, for all Stonewall Inn has come to represent to homosexuals as an important milestone in Gay Liberation, the event was actually preceded by other lesser known acts of public gay resistance to police brutality. Two occurred in San Francisco over 3 years before Stonewall. Black Sheets Magazine recently wrote an editorial about them, citing their significance:
>
> "To raise funds for the fledgling organization [SIR— Society for Individual Rights, America's first gay rights organization based in San Francisco], [organizers in 1964] planned a New Year's Eve party for the gay community. In an era when the police arrested citizens and revoked liquor licenses for same-sex touching of the most innocent sort, holding a public gay dance was tantamount to a confrontation.
>
> "On the night of the dance, dozens of uniformed officers stalked California Hall, with police cars and paddy wagons parked in front. Police photographers took pictures of each of the 600 guests in a blatant attempt at harassment. Two days later, the ministers held a press conference condemning the police. They accused the police of 'deliberate harassment and bad faith' and charged officers with intimidation, broken promises, and obvious hostility. The police had overplayed their hand. ACLU lawyers, angered by the incident, took the case to trial. According to the Chronicle, 'complaining officers sat with mouths agape' as the judge ordered the jury to return a verdict in favor of the gays. The [organizers] validated the charges of police harassment in a way that the words of a homosexual individual did not.
>
> "In August 1966, a Tenderloin cafeteria became the site of a showdown between gays and police. Compton's, at the corner of Turk and Taylor, was frequented by hustlers and queens, One night, a policeman grabbed at one of the queens, and rather than tolerating the harassment, she threw her coffee in his face. Fighting erupted as angry young gays broke out the windows, threw dishes and trays at the officers, and burned down a nearby newsstand. The next day, drag queens were barred from the cafeteria, and a picket line sprang up. That night, protesters smashed the premises' newly installed plate-glass windows.
>
> "Thus, almost three years before Stonewall, San Francisco's gay militancy was born."

ning of Friday, June 27, 1969 when gays finally decided to fight back at the New York City bar called the Stonewall Inn.* For three nights, the "fems" and their more masculine brothers threw bottles and trash at the raiding officers. They lit fires in trashcans along Greenwich Village streets and in general, caused havoc. Today, in 45 American cities in the month of June mainly, this history-making event is celebrated. In San Francisco, the crowds watching the Gay Pride March along Market Street are numbered in the five hundred thousands.

§

But I am getting ahead of my story here, and so we return to 1937 and my first three or four years at Roos Brothers store on the corner of Market and Stockton. I was teamed with my friend, Marge Kinney and mainly worked in the women's windows. Since the corner was in the center of town, there was very heavy foot-traffic. It took some time before I got used to people gawking at me as I hoisted "naked ladies" onto my shoulders and exchanged them with others from nearby windows.

§

It is strange to think back to those years when I was getting into the display business, a madman, named Hitler was launching his blitzkrieg armies across the face of Europe with practically no opposition. Everyone was wondering how soon America would come to the rescue again as we had in 1914, the year of my birth. It had only been 23 years earlier that the same nations had tried to annihilate each other in the First World War — little had been learned, it seemed. We knew that it would take a direct incident aimed at the U.S. for the country to galvanize itself into action. Where or how that would happen was on everyone's minds. With our ships plowing across the Atlantic to supply England with armaments, that was already starting to happen, but hadn't lit the fuse yet. A more dramatic incident like the blowing up of the battleship, the Maine, in Havana's harbor in 1898, could be the catalyst. We waited for it to happen.

Adolph Hitler

It is strange to think back to those years when I was getting into the display business, a madman, named Hitler was launching his blitzkrieg armies across the face of Europe with practically no opposition.

Meanwhile, I was now unhappy with the noise level I had to put up with living in the nightclub area on Broadway. I could barely get a decent night's sleep with all the carousing, drunken crowds wandering around my street. My front door reeked of urine and spilled beer. I didn't know what to expect next.

Mother had written to say she had befriended another young grocery clerk who was talking about his desire to move to San Francisco to find a better job. His name was David Roach and he hailed from a small town, Lubbock, Texas. I was to later learn he was as straight as an arrow.

If I was to upgrade my living situation, I needed to share whatever I wound up with, so I told Mother to tell David to come up for a look-see visit and, if we seemed to be congenial, he could stay. I hunted the streets of Telegraph Hill and soon found a little block long street on the northern flanks, which gave one a direct view of Alcatraz, the famous prison island. This was once the home of Al Capone. This gent was once the most notorious criminal of the Prohibition Era. The new digs on Filbert Street weren't really any bigger than the two-rooms that I was leaving on Montgomery,

6 - Moving to San Francisco—1937

but it was blissfully quiet. It had small rooms arranged in what is known as a "railroad flat." You walked through each room in a straight line to get to the back porch. The nicest feature was a small front porch where you could soak in the sun and watch the sails on the Bay.

So Dave arrived shortly after I had moved in and he turned out to be the good-looking, clean-cut American Youth we often see in clothing advertisements for Calvin Klein or Ralph Lauren. Naturally, I was pleased but I wondered how he would react to the fact that I had only one twin-bed size couch that I had in the living room? He said that he could handle it even if it would be a bit tight. My worry was whether I could handle it. Imagine the average man having to sleep on a small bed every night with the likes of — say, Marilyn Monroe? David hadn't a clue about my sexual identity and I decided he would not learn it, as least not for awhile until we were better friends. We slept in tandem fashion, skin touching skin for the next six months. We kept our boxer shorts on. I was in seventh heaven, but only at the gates of the kingdom. I think he needed the close proximity of another body as much as I did. It occurred to me that he had probably slept with his two brothers as a child and didn't see it as unnatural to be in the same bed with another male.

I wondered how he would react to the fact that I had only one twin-bed size couch in the living room? He said that he could handle it even if it would be a bit tight. My worry was whether I could handle it.

Peering from my "railroad flat" on Filbert Street.

David was soon writing home to Texas, and describing the pleasures of living in San Francisco. The older brothers, Sam and Erskine, the youngest were now eager to come out to the Coast and seek better jobs. I had to decide if I could share an apartment with three brothers and a wife! Sam was married. I came to a decision after a bit of soul-searching. I would be the minority in a group of five individuals. We would need to find a larger apartment. But I decided that if the brothers were as congenial and easy to relate to as David, I would have no problem. I had to keep in mind that these were Texas country folk who had never experienced big city living.

The Texan brothers, Erskine and David, my straight roommates.

Erskine, the youngest, arrived first and he proved to be as handsome as his brother David with blonde hair that was almost white. It wasn't out of a bottle either, to my amazement. We started hunting in earnest for a new address and it didn't take long before we found a suitable flat on North Point Street. It had ample bedroom space so that I would have my own room, while the two brothers would share another bedroom. When Sam and his wife were to arrive, they would occupy another bedroom for themselves. I liked the building itself, which was two-storied and was at one time, a working class Victorian with none of the fancy carpenter's fretwork that decorates so many Victorians in San Francisco. We were directly across the street from a handsome 1878 complex of brick buildings that were once the Ghirardelli Chocolate Factory. At the time that I lived nearby, it was boarded up and the City was deciding whether to raze the entire block it occupied. An enterprising developer with wonderful foresight decided to turn it into a shopping mall by adding one more building in the same brick style. It was renovated a few years later and proved to be the forerunner of a trend to save old Victorian business buildings by adding modern conveniences that were artfully buried in their walls.

Across the lower street below Ghirardelli, there was another interesting structure called Aquatic Park and this had its own small bay suitable for sailing small craft. The Maritime Building was shaped like a grounded ship with Art Moderne styling. It housed a handsome collection of sailing ships' figureheads and ship models, plus huge anchors, capstans and all the other gear needed to sail a vessel. There were many old photographs of early San Francisco during the gold rush Era and I spent countless hours taking in all this evidence of this fascinating past.

Although we were blocked from having a bay view because of the

6 - Moving to San Francisco—1937

The Ghirardelli Square today, home to the Ghirardelli Chocolate Factory that blocked my view of the Bay back in 1937.

Ghirardelli buildings, I had a two-minute walk down to the Bay shore, and I started thinking how much fun it would be to be able to sail the Bay. Shortly after I started thinking this way, lo and behold, I heard of a man who was moving out of town and had a kayak he had to sell. I had never sailed before but it didn't stop me from buying the fourteen-foot craft. It was a hybrid contraption that was used as a regular kayak with paddles, or could be converted to a sailing boat as a South Seas skiff by attaching outrigger pontoons, sail and rudder. I was totally enthralled with the boat and spent many happy hours sailing out into the choppy waters of the Bay on weekends. It was easy to carry on my shoulders as it weighed little, being made up of aluminum framing and airplane fabric. I named it the "Molani" – which means the "ridge of heaven" in Hawaiian. When I wanted to use it as a sailboat, I needed help in carrying the other components down the hill to the shore.

So, it was I and three brothers and one wife for awhile and even though we all got along very well, I began to feel inhibited. As I sometimes would bring home a gay friend to share my bed, it always seemed awkward to have to do the introductions the next morning. The Roach family had learned of my identity soon enough but had easily adapted to it. I was surprised at how well they accepted me, perhaps because I didn't have any feminine manners. But I missed not having spectacular views of the Bay even though this usually meant paying considerable more in rent.

I heard from a friend that there was a vacancy on the top of Telegraph

I was surprised at how well they accepted me, perhaps because I didn't have any feminine manners.

Sailing on the first "Molani" at Aquatic Park with friend Bill Simpson.

Hill, a highly desirable area much sought after. The old building was a stone's throw from the giant Tower that Lillie Coit had funded in memory of the valiant firemen of old San Francisco. The apartment's bay window looked out on the curving drive that ascends to the plaza in front of the tower with its huge statue of Christopher Columbus. The rear windows of my flat looked out over the panorama of the City's financial district with its growing collection of high rise towers. We had access to the roof-deck which had been where 1900 tenants had hung their laundry lines but we went up to get ourselves tanned.

It was decided that Erskine would move with me. He wasn't concerned about my sexual identity in the least, and I welcomed the split in paying the rent as he had found employment. We were sunning ourselves on the roof-deck one weekend afternoon when we learned of the beginning of World War Two. But it took another few years until the Japanese bombed Pearl Harbor and we had our catalyst for the American entry into the conflict.

One evening, as I sat in a downtown gay bar on Stockton Street, I chatted with a suave young New Yorker who had just arrived in town and hadn't made any friends yet. His name was Dean and he had been sent out from the W. & J. Sloane store in Manhattan that dealt with home furnishings. The San Francisco branch on Sutter

We were sunning ourselves on the roof-deck one weekend afternoon when we learned of the beginning of World War Two. But it took another few years until the Japanese bombed Pearl Harbor and we had our catalyst for the American entry into the conflict.

6 - Moving to San Francisco—1937

Street's 200 block was an imposing four-story building but had been rather neglected as a stylish place to shop. It needed some drastic attention from its New York parent. Dean was the boy friend of the New York advertising manager and he had been promoted to be the new advertising manager for the San Francisco store. He had a lot of enthusiasm for bringing the staid old establishment up to New York levels. He and I talked until the bar closed and I learned that one of the first things he wanted to do was to replace the current display man who he considered too dull to achieve the new look he wanted for the store. The man had no vision and the windows reflected his lack of it. Was I interested in trying for the job? We walked back to his small apartment in a Pine Street high-rise and we had more drinks and talked of what he planned to do to update the stodgy old store.

Myself in my Telegraph Hill apartment, 1940.

I wound up staying the night and we began seeing a lot of each other. I had never been a friend of anyone from New York and I was quite impressed with his sophistication. But his drinking was prodigious and I soon learned I couldn't keep up the level of his intake. He was convinced I would make a much better man to implement the display ideas he had envisioned for the store. As I was involved with him, it meant I had succumbed to the infamous "couch-casting" methods of Hollywood — I couldn't pass up this marvelous opportunity to advance myself so spectacularly. I accepted the offer and promptly gave notice at Roos Brothers. However, we decided it didn't make sense to continue the affair for fear of repercussions from other store executives. I also learned that Dean had not given up on his New York partner, so there would be no long-term commitments possible. The boy friend would be coming out to the Coast to inspect the new setup and I didn't want to be suspect.

And I had a lot of learning to do since I had my training in the clothing end of Display and now this was Home Furnishings and not the cheap end of it either. I thanked my lucky stars that I had paid attention to Ruth and her two gay sons who were so clever with home decorating. Although I felt over my head, I was determined to make it all work. I started reading all the decorating books and magazines I could lay my hands on. I learned to distinguish Chippendale from Sheraton, Colonial from Victorian and not make a fool of myself.

The brand new Display Manager at W. & J. Sloane Home Furnishings, San Francisco.

The handsome old iron façade of the Sloane Store housed a collection of expensive period furniture priced for the wealthiest Pacific Heights matrons. We carried the finest furniture in town and at this time the fabulous Jackson Square area had not been resurrected. Nor was there anything yet down in the SOMA district (South of Market). It was a very stagnant period for home decorating and if a wealthy woman wanted the best things, she went directly to New York or had a decorator come out to the coast to do her house. But he would find little to work with here except what we had to offer. We had a couple of experts in our house staff, but they were not on the level of New York decorators.

I had the use of a couple of grunts that moved furniture onto hand trucks, and I could get them to handle the big items when I was changing a window. My main task was to change the look of the four large sidewalk-fronting windows that tempted the passerby into coming in to see the interior. Two of these sidewalk windows were so large that I could treat them as complete living rooms or any other room of a typical upscale home. I grew to relish the task of making up these settings and tried to do a little more than just setting the rooms by adding little touches like a couple of magazines or books lying on a couch or perhaps, a drink half-finished on the cocktail table. In a bedroom setup, I would drape pajamas across the bedspread or leave a letter lying on the night table. I hadn't seen anyone else trying for this touch of realism and I was pleased with the compliments I was getting from management.

The third week of my new job at Sloane's proved to be a worrisome time as I learned I would be handling a very important promotion. Already for weeks, the movie-going public had been excited about the imminent release of the film, "Gone with the Wind," the story of Southerners during

6 - Moving to San Francisco—1937

the Civil War of 1861-1865. There was as much anticipation then as the recent stir over the "Titanic" movie which was one of the most expensive movies ever made after "Cleopatra." The publicity people at the studios had contacted the Advertising staff at Sloane's to see if we wanted to do a tie-in with the opening of the movie in San Francisco. Of course, we were very interested. The studio was willing to loan us certain pieces of furniture from the sets including the famous green velvet draperies that Scarlet uses to make herself a ball gown. This act of hers dramatizes the poverty she is then suffering because of the ruin of the plantation she had owned. It would certainly be of interest to the women who shopped in the City. And for months beforehand, Clark Gable had everyone guessing as to whether he would take the lead role. It seemed he was not happy working under a director who was rumored to be gay and usually gave female leads the best camera angles. They gave in to him; it seems they hired a new director: Gable's daring remark, "Frankly, my dear, I don't give a God Damn," was the first time those words had ever gotten past the censor.

I was told to develop the look of all four windows as an ante-bellum home of the pre-Civil War period. This was some 35 years before the conflict and calls for a much simpler style of furniture than the Victorian period. I started thumbing through books for ideas and the studios trucked up the pieces they were willing to loan. I filled in the rest from our own collections. On the day the windows were unveiled, the newspapers carried a huge ad advising the public to watch the arrival of costumed actors in horse-drawn coaches. There were dozens of photographers on the sidewalks as the hoop-skirted ladies descended from their carriages and entered the store heading directly into the windows to enjoy "high tea." The concept of live people in store windows always excited pedestrians and this was no exception. The sidewalks were mobbed and the store was filled with people who had never thought of coming in before. A black butler was pouring the tea and I now think back to how that politically incorrect that idea was then. We would be in trouble today, it's for certain.

One of my friends during this time was Bruce. He was employed by the House of Prime Rib on Van Ness. His job was to greet you as you came into the restaurant. He knew I was unattached so he started regaling me with stories about this dashing Air Force sergeant that he had met recently and

Clark Gable had everyone guessing as to whether he would take the lead role. It seemed he was not happy working under a director who was rumored to be gay and usually gave female leads the best camera angles.

The sumptuous "Gone With The Wind" windows, my first job at Sloane's.

couldn't get to first base with. Would I like to meet him myself since he was getting nowhere with his attentions? He arranged a blind date for the two of us and since we would meet at the restaurant and only have supper, it would be simple to cancel out the rest of the evening if necessary. I was introduced to Steve a couple of nights later and we hit it off beautifully from the first night. Bruce wasn't exaggerating one bit when he described Steve's Irish good looks and physique. He was stationed just south of San Francisco at Moffet Field and so he started coming up on week-end passes to spend the time with me. I couldn't have been happier and for the next seven years, he

Steve, near my Telegraph Hill apartment, 1942.

Steve, as an Air Force pilot just before WWII.

was my first real love.

However, dark clouds were gathering as Hitler kept up his relentless marching over Europe's nations. We wondered how much longer we would be on the sidelines, and Churchill was pleading with Roosevelt to get involved as soon as possible. Steve and I spent much time discussing what we should do ourselves. He was already in the Air Force, of course. It was the premise of most draft-age men that enlisting was a better way to go than wait 'til your number was called up. Your employers would see that you were not sitting back and appearing timid. Eventually, you would be called up anyway, unless you declared yourself a conscientious objector, or worse — stated that you were a homosexual. I had no intention of jeopardizing my employment record with this black mark. So, one day, I showed up at the recruitment offices and was signed in. It was a very uncertain time and I needed to stop waiting for the axe to fall. I hated the idea of leaving Steve but it seemed that our relationship was going to be put on hold shortly anyway. He had been hearing rumors about his own departure. I also heard that bosses looked more favorably on enlistees and they would get preference in getting their jobs back on their return — that is, *if* you made it back.

Japan made it all much simpler to decide then, when she launched her infamous raid on Pearl Harbor on December 7, 1941. We were stunned by the audacity of the act, and war was immediately declared. We

I was introduced to Steve a couple of nights later and we hit it off beautifully from the first night ... I couldn't have been happier and for the next seven years, he was my first real love.

now had our modern version of the sinking of the Maine in Havana's harbor! America was at war with the Axis, which included Germany, Italy and Japan.

7
The Army
1942 - 1943

"I was swept up with all the hysteria and outrage of what had just happened in Hawaii. A lot of young men were signing up for the armed forces ... I wondered what they would prove about me? That I was unfit to serve, a flaming homosexual, a hopeless case?" - GS

§

George never brought up his time in the Army during WWII that I can recall. Except once when I was drafted into the Army in late 1967, when he encouraged me to serve my time for the country. George, as it turns out, was a patriot. And here begins that story, and not without the continuing saga of the Façade. - JJ

The Army: 1942 – 1943

I was swept up with all the hysteria and outrage of what had just happened in Hawaii. A lot of young men were signing up for the armed forces. My own physical defect, poor eyesight, meant that neither the Navy nor the Air force was an option — but the Army would take anyone that could breathe. We had been told that it took seven men to keep one infantryman equipped to fight. The materiel needs alone were staggering, so there was a decent chance that I wouldn't actually do any combat, at least only in an emergency. I knew that I might end up servicing trucks, helping build bridges, roads, or in communications. I couldn't imagine myself actually killing another person. I had always had trouble even killing a mouse.

Much later in life, I recall a Sergeant Matlovich being discharged from the Army for being gay. Later, his gravestone read, "I was given a medal for killing two men, a discharge for loving one." [SIDEBAR]

The first thing that happened to me was boarding a bus while still in civvies to report for induction and processing at Fort Ord, Monterey.* The Army dearly loves mountains of paperwork and it would take three days to make me into a G.I. This gave me a chance to call Steve and tell him where I had gone. Since he was only forty miles north at Moffet Field, he got permission to hitch down to my camp and we spent a few hours together. I had no idea where I would end up. So we wandered off to the western edge of the Base, sat on a high sand dune bluff facing out over the blue expanse of the Pacific Ocean. We wondered if we would ever see each other again. What came next?

Tomb of gay veteran, Sgt. Leonard Matlovich, U.S. Congressional Cemetery.

Where I was sent myself in January of 1968. — J. Jackson

Describing himself as an army brat, Leonard Matlovich was born the son of a career Air Force man at a base hospital on July 6, 1943, in Savannah, Georgia. He died of AIDS on Jun. 22, 1988, San Francisco. Technical Sergeant, US Air Force, Veteran of the Vietnam War. A proud, gay veteran, he challenged the US Air Force policy on automatically discharging homosexual service members as "unfit for military service." His most famous quote: "They gave me a medal for killing two men, and a discharge for loving one." In 1975, T/Sgt Matlovich, a decorated veteran of the Vietnam War with 15 years of service, openly announced his sexual preference, and challenged the US Air Forces' policy of automatically discharging homosexuals. The Air Force

102

7 - The Army—1942

> *I wondered what they would prove about me? That I was unfit to serve, a flaming homosexual, a hopeless case?*

promptly discharged him anyway. In 1980, he successfully sued the Air Force for reinstatement, and the court ordered the Air Force to allow him to rejoin the Air Force. However, he settled for a one time payment of $160,000 from the Air Force, and did not retire. The case ruling allowed homosexuals to remain in the military as long as they abstained from any form of sexual activity and kept 'in the closet.' Later, he lived in San Francisco, California, and became active in the Gay Rights movement. His court case was made into a TV-Movie "Sergeant Matlovich vs. the US Air Force" and was telecast on 21 August 1978. Burial: Congressional Cemetery, Washington District Of Columbia, USA

A couple of days of being issued uniforms, getting used to new surroundings and in general, just waiting — something the army loves to have you do for hours on end — and I was hustled onto a train along with a hundred other strangers. Our destination was the East Coast, some 3,300 miles of track. Again, like the train ride I made at the age of eleven, I was headed over the Rockies, across the vast plains, but this time I was going to end up in an unknown area. It was exciting and disturbing at the same time. I have always preferred knowing what I was about to get into. Not that I don't relish adventure, but it is my nature to have a good bit of control over my personal destiny. I was a helpless pawn now in the clutches of a vast machine cranking out G.I.s (Government Issue) and I felt so powerless.

The train's track ended just short of the Atlantic shore at a huge facility called the Aberdeen Proving Grounds. I wondered what they would prove about me? That I was unfit to serve, a flaming homosexual, a hopeless case? We were 30 miles north of Baltimore and most probably another 150 miles further south lay Washington, D.C. Aberdeen was a huge complex of training facilities for the Ordnance Corps. They are the folks who keep the soldier supplied with the equipment he needs to keep fighting. Mostly, it had to do with artillery guns, anything you could aim and fire. The grounds were vast tracts of forest and open fields that were used for testing weapons. We were also expected to go on overnight marches, bivouacs and endless drilling. We were going to be toughened up for a much more primitive way of life ahead. We had no idea of where we would be going, but it would certainly be Europe. Since the Grounds bordered onto Chesapeake Bay, we could already savor the watery expanse that we would sooner or later be carried across to meet Herr Hitler.

Outside the barracks, Aberdeen Proving Grounds, 1943.

§

Aberdeen was to be my home for the next eighteen months and I shared my Spartan bedroom with sixty other men I had never met before. The lack of privacy was unnerving to say the least. When I walked into the latrine, I had a choice of twelve toilet seats with no walls between them. I could sit and chat with another man a few inches away. But I got used to that as I got used to a lot of other little things I would have cringed about in civilian life. The showering in a large room with no private stalls wasn't too disconcerting as I had gone to gyms in San Francisco and college gyms where naked men usually surrounded me anyway. I had to chuckle to myself, wondering how a straight man would react to showering with a dozen naked girls slavering soap onto their bodies, would they have handled it? But that was my cross to bear, and I bore it as bravely as I could! I never got into the interminable poker games and beer-guzzling that seemed to keep everyone else in a stupor. No one seemed concerned anyway as to how I spent my loafing moments, which weren't that ample either. I spent a good deal of time reading about the War in the Recreation Room, and just chatting with other lonely soldiers.

I was writing to Steve often and he told me that he could actually be at Aberdeen himself if he were to enroll in the Officers' Training Corps. He was able to choose this option and before many weeks had passed, we found ourselves in the same camp, which seemed like a miracle. Although he was at Aberdeen, we were not able to see one another except for a brief fifteen minutes directly after the evening meal. We would rush through our supper in different mess halls several blocks apart, then run to a chosen spot where we would spend a few minutes in conversation before we had to hurry back for roll call. But on weekends, we had the entire two days to dash into Baltimore, rent a motel room and let go. This routine went on for eight weeks before he finally had to admit he couldn't keep up with the classes. He was failing the Course, and would be shipped back to California and be assigned to overseas duty. We were desolate about this turn of events and when he said good-bye this time, we really thought it would be the last time that we would see each other.

To distract myself from the misery I now felt, I sought out a new friend I could pal around with. Everybody seemed to be forming bonds with one or two others, so it didn't seem unusual to buddy with someone else. I had

I had to chuckle to myself, wondering how a straight man would react to showering with a dozen naked girls slavering soap onto their bodies, would they have handled it? But that was my cross to bear, and I bore it as bravely as I could!

7 - The Army—1942

been aware of a chap from Chicago named Ray Kunce. He had been given a choice of serving a jail sentence for stealing a car, or to enlist in the Army. Ray had a very funny sense of humor, kept me laughing a lot, and was certainly my physical type — well-built, brown-hair, mischievous eyes and smile. I liked the fact that he wasn't always yapping about getting "laid," which seemed to be everyone else's ("straight" guys) big problem. In the course of idle talk about how to spend our brief leisure time, we discovered we both liked to fool around with carpentry. The Bay was a short distance away — easy walking for us — and we decided we would talk our officers into letting us build a small sailboat to use on the Bay. We got our permission and immediately went to work in the well-stocked carpentry shop. Within a month, we had duplicated the same kayak-sailboat that I had owned in San Francisco a few years back. This one was also named the "Molani". I was surprised that I could remember the lines and dimensions of the first boat that well. For the launching, we invited some of the barracks buddies we had been friendly with and a case of beer was brought down to the shore for the launching. So in the following weeks of the summer months, we had a way of forgetting the endless drilling, and marching long hikes through Maryland forests. Life was considerably better when we could glide out on Chesapeake Bay with a six-pack for ballast. I didn't miss Steve as much with this new distraction.

My closest friend, Ray Kunce, registering the "G.I. Blues."

I learned that my old college mate, Roger was stationed now in nearby Washington, which was easily reached with a short train ride. Roger had teamed up with a high-ranking naval officer that he had met in California, and when he enlisted in the Navy, he was sent to Washington for duty as an ensign. The two lovers had the good fortune to lease a small

Lounging on the Molani in Chesapeake Bay, 1943.

house in Georgetown, which had seen earlier times as slave quarters. The building had gone through a lot of restoration and improvement by the time I visited and stayed for a weekend or two. It was a joy to see Roger again and we did our "Pilipino accent" routine for his partner's amusement.

But, I suppose I had it a bit too soft and it was bound to get grittier and so it did. I had been at Aberdeen some eighteen months and I had met a small circle of gay soldiers by using my built-in "gaydar." This, as I mentioned previously, is the instinctual sense that another man is gay because of his body language, or his vocabulary. It doesn't always work, of course, and I would not make assumptions until I was very sure of a person's interests. The soldiers I met this way would always go into Baltimore for a night's carousing. A few sailors we managed to meet at Baltimore bars joined us to form a clandestine circle of friends and bedmates.

I had been at Aberdeen some eighteen months and I had met a small circle of gay soldiers by using my built-in "gaydar" ... A few sailors we managed to meet at Baltimore bars joined us to form a clandestine circle of friends and bedmates.

§

We now had orders to move to a more specialized training camp and this was to be in Texas. The very top northeastern corner of that huge state where Arkansas and Texas bordered each other. Texarkana was the town's

7 - The Army—1942

name, of course and there couldn't have been a more forlorn spot on earth. A sad, poverty-stricken bunch of shacks was all there was to see. We were ten miles out from the town limits and seldom made the trip since there was nothing of interest there. We now learned what our role in the Army would be. We were to be specialists in the Art of Tire Repair! I had to laugh when I thought about it, how did the Army brass decide I would excel in this profession? I had never looked at a truck tire as an art object in my life and had never expected to confront one ever except in its usual lowly position on a vehicle.

> *We now learned what our role in the Army would be. We were to be specialists in the Art of Tire Repair!*

The training buildings housed big, clunky tire treading machines that would be used to familiarize us with the process of affixing new rubber to worn-out tires. We were told that the life expectancy of a tire on war-torn roads in Europe was short indeed and that we were an important link in keeping materiel moving up to the battlefronts. I was quite depressed at the thought of spending months heaving tires on and off these big monster machines. But, as it turned out, I never had to. I don't know who pulled strings or whether some officer had glanced at my previous work file, but I was assigned to the offices. Perhaps, the company commander had seen that I had listed "Art" as my primary vocation, and so I was put to work painting street and road signs for the Base. I was also put to use doing graphs, and lettering folders — anything that remotely resembled a draftsman's duties. I was even doing cartoons for the company newspaper and did a mural for the recreation room. It was a map of the whole base with little G.I.s running about the landscape.*

The endless marching and drilling only intensified and I didn't escape that activity, of course. We were out on overnight bivouacs, dug fox-holes,

Relaxing after a day's stint at marching.

480th Ordnance Company (*Memoirs*)

7 - The Army—1942

1st Platoon, 480th Ordnance, Fort Runnels, Texas. My unit just before we were shipped out to the European theater of war, October 24th, 1944.*

ran the obstacle courses and dragged our weary asses back to the barracks only to repeat it all over again the next day. Everyone lost those pudgy, soft waistlines that are the trademark of most civilians. We all looked a lot better for it, of course.

Something rather ironic happened one day that bears repeating here. I was summoned to the company captain's office and I broke into a sweat fearing the worst. Had someone detected my interest in my fellow soldiers and decided to rat on me? No one was ever called into the Inner Sanctum unless he had committed a crime. Captain Harris ordered me to be "at ease" and to sit. Could I keep the information I was to hear to myself only? In a quavering voice, I swore to say nothing to anyone and wondered what I could possibly have done. Then I learned that I was to become a secret agent for the company. Others would also be assigned but I would never know who they were. I was to be the "ears and eyes" of the security officer and report any subversive gossip or action I came across in my relations with the troops. How on earth had anyone decided to choose me for this duty? Didn't they realize that I was probably the first person to be concerned about since I

I was summoned to the company captain's office and I broke into sweat fearing the worst. Had someone detected my interest in my fellow soldiers and decided to rat on me?

*For several years after the war, my artwork could still be seen in the old Fort Runnels library at the Military Detachment Training Center, where you see us in formation on the facing page. In the early 1960s, the Training Center was demolished, and Fort Runnels was absorbed into the current Red River Army Depot. Only a few old cement foundation pieces are left today, quiet and largely unnoticed reminders of the once vast training facility where tens of thousands of troops prepared for war.

could be blackmailed to reveal tire-treading secrets! In some perverse way, I was flattered because I realized that no one had any suspicion of my sexual identity. I did agree to be their stool pigeon and so for the rest of my stay in Texas, I looked and listened for traitorous remarks but outside of the usual bitching of the lack of women, nothing turned up to report.

But one day, I got word that I had a visitor awaiting me in the offices, and I was blown away to find David Roach, now Captain Roach standing tall in his best uniform and grinning like a Cheshire cat. I got permission to absent myself from the Base for a few hours and David and I drove out to a nearby lake to sit and talk about our new lives in the Army. It was such bliss to talk to an old friend that I had been so close to in the past. I complimented him on how dashing he looked as an officer and warned him he would have to be sure to protect himself from the attentions of ladies who would melt at his new looks. He laughed.

8
Going to Europe
1944 - 1945

"I will never forget the anxious hours spent that sleepless night, as I waited for a German paratrooper to sneak up behind me with his wire garrote to twist around my neck." - GS

∫

All of this was news to me. But his story is what sparked my interest in WWII and the history that surrounded it leading into the present in ways that had escaped me and that have come to shape my thinking about war, imperialism, and the military-industrial complex. - JJ

Going to Europe: 1944 - 1945

A year of this idyllic life went in a leisurely fashion and it became obvious to us that the monster, Hitler, could only be defeated if we confronted him with our wrenches and tire irons. The Normandy Beach landings had taken place and the bloodshed and horror of all those men dying was on our minds. We learned that we were going across the Pond to follow in behind the advancing front pushing the Germans back toward their own country. Although we had learned to use carbines and had roughed around in the Texas scrub country, we didn't look forward to the winter weather we would encounter in France. Our mission was to find a secure village somewhere behind the lines where we could set up our machinery and start repairing the thousands of worn tires being yanked off the trucks rolling back from the front.

We loaded up our gear, boarded a train for New York City and simply headed for the docks instead of being regaled by the temptations of the Big Apple. Well, we hardly expected to get to see anything anyway and I had made one week-end trip up to NYC while at Aberdeen and had gotten laid so who was I to complain? Still, it would have been nice to have another glimpse of this most fascinating of cities. We boarded our troop ship immediately, steaming out past the giant Lady who sneaked a good-bye kiss in our direction. "When would we see her again or would we?" I thought. Most of us hung out on the open decks a lot, feeling safer there than down below. Although the chances of being torpedoed by a German submarine were somewhat slim because it was late in the War, it hadn't ceased to happen and we were grateful that we had a Navy escort to watch over our convoy of a dozen ships. We simply denied ourselves the talk about what could happen and got into interminable poker games until we pulled into Southampton, England.

The Normandy Beach landings had taken place and the bloodshed and horror of all those men dying was on our minds.

8 - Going to Europe—1944

Although this port is close to London, we saw nothing of the city except for a bevy of U.S.O. girls standing on the dock ready with cheery smiles and hot tea for us. We only got a dozen words out before we were hustled into trucks bound for who knows where. The Army rarely tells you where you are going for fear you might leak it to a spy.

We were heading northwest into Lancashire, which faces over to Ireland, but we were seeing this lovely bit of England during a grim time. We didn't see any bomb damage because this wasn't an industrial area. Blackpool, a seaside resort town was simply boarded up and looked deserted. We drove our convoy of trucks a little further inland to the small town of Ulverston and just past its limits; we finally braked in the courtyard of a baronial residence. The huge brick mansion had been requisitioned by the American Army for the duration of the war as a holding station for arriving troops. It was formerly the residence of a wealthy coalmine owner who had moved to a much smaller home as his patriotic duty. The dark, foreboding walls covered in dense growth of vines reminded me later of the Edward Gorey cartoons that I used to see in New Yorker Magazine. These cartoon characters were always depicted in the faded grandeur of these opulent palaces that the English could barely afford to maintain any longer. The roof sprouted what seemed like a forest of forlorn chimneys and the grounds surrounding the main building were in a state of neglect but still impressed one with their classical Greek statuary and urns. I was simply awe-struck to be staying at a millionaire's home if only for a fortnight. The interminable card games resumed, but I found it more fun to go for walks around the country roads past the gatehouse. What a grand way to live, if only for two weeks!

The brick "castle" at Ulverston, England.

§

Soon, we were hustled off to waiting trucks and boarding small steamers for the short ride across the English Channel. I was very conscious of the terrible price that others had paid a brief five months earlier to make this same crossing. We were lucky to be support troops and the guns along the opposite shoreline would be silent now instead of hurling death at us.

It was night, a cold blustery November night, as we disembarked at Honfleur, a small fishing village on the French coast near Dunkerque. We were immediately hustled onto a convoy of waiting trucks and on our way to the train yards. The infamous cattle cars called "40 & 8s" were waiting for us. European armies called them that since they were meant to haul 40 men or 8 horses. When Hitler was rounding up the Jews of Europe, he crammed twice that many souls into its bare slatted walls with a bucket tossed into a corner for a toilet. I shuddered to think what misery these cattle-cars had contained in the recent past. We, at least, were allowed to build small fires in metal drums to ward off the biting cold. Each of the train-cars was allotted a couple of bales of straw, the fire drum with a pipe extending out the sliding door and a toilet bucket. We each had our own G.I. blanket and a few feet of space to stretch out on the straw. No one had any idea how long this train ride would go on or where we were heading.

For three days and nights, we shunted from one set of tracks to another, fitfully slamming to a stop, then jerking ahead for a few feet before stopping again. If they had wanted to think up the ultimate torture device, this should have rated amongst the cleverest. We weren't being physically abused, but the uncertainty, the waiting was quite agonizing. We had a very low priority on the right of way, so that a troop train passing through always got us shunted off to a sidetrack. Finally we were at our most northern station, Namur, Belgium and here we simply reversed our direction and headed back on the same tracks. We later learned that Army brass was uncertain as to where we would set-up our tire repair facility, and so we were on hold, riding the rails while they made up their minds for our ultimate destination. But the most devastating news of all, which we only learned a couple of weeks later, was that a stray German buzz bomb had dropped on the same tracks that we had sat on in Namur — only

The infamous cattle cars called "40 & 8s" were waiting for us. European armies called them that since they were meant to haul 40 men or 8 horses. When Hitler was rounding up the Jews of Europe, he crammed twice that many souls into its bare slatted walls with a bucket tossed into a corner for a toilet. I shuddered to think what misery these cattle-cars had contained in the recent past.

Riding a "40 x 8" to Namur, Belgium, December, 1945. One of my many sketches depicting our lives as soldiers.

two or three hours after we had pulled out and headed south again! We silently thanked the Lord for sparing our lives in the first few days of our French visit.

But the most devastating news of all, which we only learned a couple of weeks later, was that a stray German buzz bomb had dropped on the same tracks that we had sat on in Namur—only two or three hours after we had pulled out and headed south again!

Finally, we were allowed to get off the cattle-cars, in the middle of a bitterly cold, drizzling rain and the trucks hauled us off to a muddy field a few miles from the tracks. It was dangerous, of course to set up camp near rail lines. We were told to spread our tarps in the thick, oozing mud, and pitch our small pup tents over the tarp. This was our first home in France. The mud had turned to a sort of slush that was almost a sort of snow. It was every two men to a tent and we made the best of the miserable situation we found ourselves in. We huddled together for warmth and comfort.

Dawn revealed the muddy landscape and our disconsolate men trying to joke about our sad surroundings. Our company officers had been assigned a jeep and they started canvassing the surrounding terrain for a better bivouac spot. Luckily, a neighboring farmer was cajoled into letting us use his huge brick barn as our next home. It was amply filled with bales of sweet hay. This was really heaven and so for the next few nights, I paired off, just as everyone else did, with a friend to sleep spoon-fashion again. I had managed to keep a small camera with me and I did some picture snapping around the nearby village. I don't think we spotted any farm folk about and I suppose they were as fearful of us as they had been of the German soldiers a few months earlier.

Some of the company men became restless and started exploring the countryside, but we were told to stay close by because we might be ordered to move on to our final set-up spot. The hundred or so of our company were getting anxious to bring our wandering to a close.

One of those evenings, which I will never forget, started out innocently enough. The supply sergeant had managed to borrow a truck from the officers and he was asking his buddies if they wanted to go on a little spin around the nearby village. It was just growing dark and at the last minute, I heard about the joy ride and asked to be included. There were twelve of us aboard, with nine riding in the truck bed. As we jolted along the terribly rutted muddy road, we passed a young farm girl and the driver slowed up and backed up to where she stood. A few words were exchanged, mostly signing

8 - Going to Europe—1944

because no one really knew more than a dozen French words. But the gist of it was that some bargain had been struck. We all piled out of the truck and then I learned what they had in mind. Somebody pulled a dozen straws out of the adjacent field and cut them at various lengths to pass out to the twelve horny soldiers. I was dismayed at the predicament I found myself in, but to refuse to go along with the plan would have given me away. I felt enormous sympathy for the farm girl but my own situation was just as critical to my future in the company. How could I avoid the spot I was now enmeshed in? I wished I had never asked to come along. As we started drawing straws to see what order we would go in, I grew very nervous. But, through some strange quirk of fate, I found that I had the shortest straw of anyone. This meant that I would go last. I had time to think of a way out of my dilemma. As the men started entering the back of the truck singly, I decided on a course of action, which seemed sensible at the moment. The men stood around out on the road, telling ribald jokes and kidding each other about their prowess in bed while I remained apart and silent. Finally, it was my turn to get in the truck with the girl, whom we couldn't see as she was lying on the straw inside. I had to do something now, and as I was urged to get going, I simply refused. I mumbled that I couldn't see myself going in after eleven others had just entered her. It was simply too abhorrent. No one seemed bothered by my refusal, and perhaps there was a bit of shame involved. She was handed some francs and left standing there in the road forlornly. I sat there in the truck with the others, in shame and disgust. It was never brought up in conversation afterwards.

§

Another short train journey in the same 40 & 8s, across the northeast corner of France in the Champagne Department, brought us to a tiny village named Betheniville. It was the 18th of December, a week before Christmas and it was snowing lightly. The great forests of the Ardennes were a mere 25 miles north of our position, and two days earlier, the German General Von Rundstedt had launched a desperate drive to split the American armies in two and drive us back to the English Channel ports. A great battle – the famous "Battle of the Bulge"– was raging at Bastogne not too far away, but since we weren't

We passed a young farm girl and the driver slowed up and backed up to where she stood ... then I learned what they had in mind ... I sat there in the truck with the others, in shame and disgust ... it was never brought up in conversation afterwards.

The German General Von Runstedt had launched a desperate drive to split the American armies in two and drive us back to the English Channel ports. A great battle was raging at Bastogne not too far away.

infantry, we weren't getting much news about our own vulnerability.* We were to stay ready to move out at a moment's notice. Our brothers-in-arms at the front lines were enduring a hell we were exempted from experiencing.

§

Before continuing, I feel compelled to comment on another story that readers may not be aware of. This concerns the incarceration and murder of thousands of homosexuals during Hitler's reign of terror. The sidebar on the facing page, and the images on subsequent pages, certainly do not do justice to this tragic but important story. However, I've provided links below to internet sites which provide a more complete picture for those who are interested in learning more. — JJ

THE ORIGIN OF GAY AND LESBIAN SYMBOLS
WWW.SWADE.NET

HISTORY OF THE GAY MALE AND LESBIAN EXPERIENCE DURING WORLD WAR II
WWW.PINK-TRIANGLE.ORG

HOLOCAUST LEARNING CENTER
WWW.USHMM.ORG

§

Our town, Betheniville, was northeast of Reims, which was a handsome, medieval city. This is where Joan of Arc came to crown the Dauphin of France in the year 1429, as Charles the Seventh. This took place in the great cathedral of Reims. And I was lucky enough to visit this impressive pile of stones on more than one occasion during the next six months.

The countryside around Betheniville had been fought over for centuries by neighboring countries, yet it still was the home of the famous grapes that produced the champagne known the world over. I hadn't realized that the name meant the district in which the grapes grew. I subsequently got to ride a bicycle over these lovely country lanes and by-roads. But while we took over the town's main buildings for our needs, we saw little of the townspeople, as they were no doubt fearful of our intentions. The thou-

(Continued on page 123)

Popular name in World War II for the German counterattack in the Ardennes, Dec., 1944-Jan., 1945. It is also known as the Battle of the Ardennes. On Dec. 16, 1944, a strong German force, commanded by Marshal von Rundstedt, broke the thinly held American front in the Belgian Ardennes sector. Taking advantage of the foggy weather and of the total surprise of the Allies, the Germans penetrated deep into Belgium, creating a dent, or "bulge," in the Allied lines and threatening to break through to the N. Belgian plain and seize Antwerp. An American force held out at Bastogne, even though surrounded and outnumbered. The U.S. 1st and 9th armies, temporarily under Field Marshal Montgomery, attacked the German salient from the north, while the U.S. 3d Army under General George Patton attacked it from the south. Improved flying weather (after Dec. 24) facilitated Allied counterattacks. By Jan. 16, 1945, the German forces were destroyed or routed, but not without some 77,000 Allied casualties.

Symbol of the SS-Totenkopfverbande Nazi SS Deaths Head Organization

The Plight of Gays and Lesbians In Nazi Germany

Like other G.I.s serving in the European Theater of War before V-Day, George was unaware that Hitler had been murdering staggering numbers – 20 to 25 millions – of Jews, Communists, Socialists, gypsies, Seventh Day Adventists, the mentally and physically challenged, and other "undesirables" in the eyes of the Nazis – including homosexuals. Only in recent years have gay activists begun to unravel and relate the true and terrible story of the "Gay Holocaust".

A cumulative estimated 220,000 gays and lesbians died along with Jews, gypsies, and members of the Nazi resistance from the beginnings of the rise of Nazi power, in the concentration camps of Hitler's Nazi Germany and during the aftermath of the war. 10 to 15,000 mostly male homosexuals were worked to death or brutally tortured and murdered. Concentration camp prisoners were identified by a set of colored triangles. Gay men in Nazi death camps guarded by the notorious SS-Totenkopfverbande (Deaths Head Organization responsible for exterminating Hitler's "undesirables") were required to wear Pink Triangles, (with one tip pointed down), on their uniforms to identify them for special abuse. The Pink Triangle is now used as a gay identification symbol as well as a reminder of oppression. The pink triangle is a symbol of the phrase "Never Forget, Never Again." The pink triangle, inverted, was also adopted by ACT-UP (AIDS Coalition to Unleash Power) as their symbol for "an active fight back rather than a passive resignation to fate".

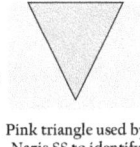

Pink triangle used by Nazis SS to identify Male homosexuals in concentration camps

The Black Triangle was used to identify "socially unacceptable" women, according to the Nazis. Lesbians were included in this classification. Now, Lesbians have reclaimed the Black Triangle as their symbol in defiance of repression and discrimination as Gay men have reclaimed the Pink Triangle. When Allied troops freed the other survivors of the camps, the Gay and Lesbian prisoners were taken by U. S. Army personnel from concentration camps to allied prisons. Since the 1940's, the pink and black triangles have become the most recognizable and powerful symbols for gay people and the oppression they have faced throughout Western History.

Black triangle used by Nazis SS to identify "socially unacceptable" women, including Lesbians, in concentration camps

[Note: material for this commentary researched and edited by Jaime Jackson.]

Prisoners of Sachsenhausen concentration camp.

White circle marks location of black triangle badge worn by prisoner at Ravensbrück, the only all-female Nazi concentration camp.

(OVERLEAF)
NAZI PERSECUTION OF
HOMOSEXUALS FROM
1933 TO 1945

 ## NAZI PERSECUTION OF HOMOSEXUALS, 1933-1945

Cover of the September 1931 issue of The Island, a magazine for homosexuals, edited by Martin Radzuweit. Although illegal, homosexuality was generally tolerated in pre-Nazi Germany, particularly in urban areas. Some 30 literary, cultural, and political journals for homosexual readers appeared during the Weimar era.

Operating room in Barrack R1 of Sick-Bay in Sachsenhausen Concentration Camp. After November 1942, concentration camp commandants were authorized to order the castration of prisoners in unspecified, 'special cases,' thus permitting the compulsory castration of incarcerated homosexuals.

8 - Going to Europe—1944

Prisoners at forced labor in the Mauthausen concentration camp. Beginning in 1943, homosexuals were among those in Concentration Camps who were killed in an SS-sponsored "Extermination Through Work" program.

"The windows had a centimeter of ice on them. Anyone found with his underclothes on in bed, or his hand under his blanket—there were checks almost every night—was taken outside and had several bowls of water poured over him before being left standing outside for a good hour. Only a few people survived this treatment. The least result was bronchitis, and it was rare for any gay person taken into the sickbay to come out alive. We who wore the pink triangle were prioritized for medical experiments, and these generally ended in death. For my part, therefore, I took every care I could not to offend against the regulations." Heinz Heger

The magnificent medieval Cathedral at Reims, where Joan of Arc crowned the King of France.

8 - Going to Europe—1944

(Continued from page 118)

sand or so villagers kept to themselves and hid their women in their homes away from sight as much as possible.

We had arrived tired and dirty and no one seemed to welcome us except the mayor of the town. The Hotel de Ville, where he had a small office, was the city hall and we found suitable for our quarters just as the German Army had a few months earlier. Most of us bedded down in the enormous attic since the hotel rooms were requisitioned by the officers and non-com staff.

In fact, our arrival that week couldn't have been worse timed because on Christmas Eve we were informed that our location was so precarious — it was thought that the advancing German tank forces might overrun our position — that we might need to evacuate at any minute. On our 7th day at Bethenivile, Captain Harris, our commanding officer, gave us orders to evacuate. Three men were detailed to stay behind to guard some vital supplies while the rest of us piled into our trucks and headed further back away from the shifting battle lines twenty-five miles to the west. At a place called Bazancourt, a main supply dump area, we left the trucks and were placed in a cordon around a vehicle park set in a wooded area for camouflage. G2 reports were alerting us that the German High Command was planning to drop a company of paratroopers into this vehicle park to grab the trucks they desperately needed. Like all the rest of the Company, I was to take a post around the perimeter of the wooded area and keep my eye open for suspicious movement. I had my small carbine for my protection. I will never forget the anxious hours spent that sleepless night, as I waited for a German paratrooper to sneak up behind me with his wire garrote to twist around my neck. This silent way of killing a man would not alert any nearby guard. We were to plaster ourselves against trees or stone walls to hamper their actions. You might wonder what a bunch of very unseasoned troops were doing in being assigned to this duty. We were told that there simply weren't enough infantry troops in the vicinity to do the guard duty, so we were given the job. No one slept a wink that dreadful night, a Christmas Eve, as we waited for the Germans to arrive. But they never came, even though a few overly tense Americans fired off a few rounds at what

We found suitable for our quarters just as the German Army had a few months earlier ... our arrival that week couldn't have been worse timed because on Christmas Eve we were informed that our location was so precarious that we might need to evacuate at any minute.

I will never forget the anxious hours spent that sleepless night, as I waited for a German paratrooper to sneak up behind me with his wire garrote to twist around my neck.

looked like shadowy figures. The second night of this nerve-wracking duty was hardly more bearable but then we were told we could return to Betheniville and we could relax again. The French came out of their hiding, bearing bottles of champagne, cognac and red wine to celebrate our escape from harm and to toast Christmas. *Again, I was aware of the fact that it was a fateful date for me and would be in the future.*

§

We started to make our lives more comfortable by looking for brooms, utensils, mattresses and anything like household goods. The bulk of the company remained in the hotel and was assigned to either rooms or at least, spaces in the attic. I was lucky enough to be quartered in a small stone cottage a block away down the street and across from a huge concrete factory that we were going to rehabilitate as our workshops. I shared the cottage with other office staff, as they wanted us to keep together.

The French had originally used the concrete factory as a textile mill and cloth manufacturing plant. When the Germans came in and took over the area, they turned the entire building into a glider construction operation. They were planning to invade England by sending hundreds of these towed craft holding their men to landings across the Channel. It was obvious that most wouldn't even survive the trip into England with her anti-aircraft guns, but Hitler wasn't concerned about losing a few thousand more boys. And he was growing more desperate the last few months of the War. Of course, the glider invasion never happened and you read nothing of this foolhardy idea in the history books.

Stone cottage where I lived while in Betheniville, France, 1944.

Our immediate job was to transform the cleared halls into a workable tire repair facility. To our great surprise, we discovered that we had acquired a company of German prisoners who were to be our forced laborers at any jobs we required to have performed. We could put them to tasks inside or outside the factory as we saw a need. We also had been assigned a smaller group of Polish soldiers who had only recently been the prisoners of the Germans. They now had the satisfaction of turning the tables, and become the masters of the German prisoners. I wondered what they would have done if we weren't around to keep them from savaging the Germans now in their care. The Polish people had suffered enormously at the hands of both the Germans and the Russians in the recent fighting around their towns and villages.

The German glider factory we revamped for tire repair at Betheniville.

The Polish guards who kept our German prisoners under control.

To our great surprise, we discovered that we had acquired a company of German prisoners who were to be our forced laborers at any jobs we required to have performed.

So now, our Company found itself in a new role as supervisors and instructors in the Art of Reconstituting a Tire. The Germans were immediately shown by sign language and what English they might know, what we wanted done either inside the factory or outside in the bitter cold landscape. Since I seemed to be destined for office work, I was to keep production records for all the machines. As I have noted before perhaps, the Army keeps meticulous files of anything it might possibly want to review later. I soon enough got very bored with this repetitious task of adding columns of numbers. As worn tires began arriving by the truckload, I had to keep an inventory of their status. After the first few weeks of this job that no one wanted, and I seemed to be stuck with, I had a bright idea. Why not

A sea of worn out tires waiting to be reborn as retreads.

have some flunky to do the adding machine routine? I would still be in charge and responsible, but not so bored.

Every morning, the German prisoners were assembled in neat rows outside in the slushy snow to be assigned to various work details. Some were assigned to work outside in the wintry weather, breaking up the glider components into smaller sections for hauling away. Or they might be digging trenches in case we had to defend our positions. A more fortunate group got to come inside into the cavernous hall to learn to run the retread machines. They would need to be closely supervised so that no sabotage activity could be contemplated.

One morning, I went outside when it was time to pick men to work on various details. I had to wait while the other soldiers picked their work squads and then I had my choice of any left over prisoners. I could barely see whom I was picking since the Germans were bundled up in their winter overcoats, with mufflers covering their cheeks up to the eyes. All one could see was a pair of hard, resentful eyes staring back at you.

It was announced in German that I was looking for someone to work inside with me and instantly, every prisoner's hand shot up. Since I could barely make-out who I was getting, I simply pointed to the nearest person and he followed me into the office corner I had staked out as mine. In first speaking to him, I told him to shed his overcoat

The German prisoner stockade at Betheniville. The "Battle of the Bulge" raged not far away from where I took this photograph.

and as I said the words, I went through the physical action. From then on, I used this method as well as using the little French I already knew. I learned his name was Gunter Wotzka. That seemed curious enough since it was a Polish name but it would be very difficult to delve into the reason he had ended up with such a name. As he cast off his outer gear, he appeared more vulnerable and young, most probably in his early 20s, and quite good-looking. He was my height – 5 foot, 8 inches – with straight brown hair and gray eyes. He was eager to get started and kept thanking me for bringing him inside from the cold. I thought of the fact he was supposed to be my bitter enemy and that in a different circumstance, I would be aiming a rifle at his heart. What an amazing world we inhabit were the role of the dice puts one in a reversed position. Not more than two or three weeks ago, I had been expecting a wire noose to be slipped around my neck by an enemy paratrooper!

I began showing Gunter what I wanted done with the figures and found him adept at the additions. We weren't given an adding machine, so it was all done in a most arduous way. I indicated I wanted him back each day and he was happy to oblige. As the only German prisoner working in the office, he was a novelty but was left to himself. It was standard practice to not fraternize with the prison inmates, but since I had to talk to Gunter to explain what was needed, I seemed to be excluded from this rule.*

Gunter Wotzka, my personal German prisoner helper, outside his "home."

I learned that Gunter had only just started working as a messenger boy for a Berlin insurance company before he was conscripted to serve in the German Army. He wasn't in the least happy about it, but since every available male was being called up for duty, he could hardly refuse the authorities.

I told him of my own German grandparents who had long ago left the mother country to seek their fortunes in America and he envied me wistfully. As we sat at our makeshift desk, we sat so close that our knees often rubbed together, and neither of us pulled away it seemed. I wondered if he was as starved for even that small gesture of human contact as I was. Nothing ever came of it but I knew that he needed the touch as much as I did.

Another duty I had been assigned was the maintaining of a map of France and Germany. It was tacked up near the door into the office and every day I was given the latest news on the fighting fronts. With this information, I would place pushpins along the lines indicated to me. My German could hardly wait to get over to see what changes had taken place with his

Headquarters, Communications Zone, European Theater of Operations, U.S. Army

"You and other American and Allied soldiers are steadily forcing the Germans back into their country. As a member of the greatest combat force in history, you are destroying the visible products of Nazism. But we must do more. We must also destroy its very roots.

"We Americans have a kindly feeling in our hearts for other people, for we, perhaps more than any other nation, believe in the inherent decency of man. Now you must be required to exclude a nation which once was a friend — Germany — men, women and children... Until they have proven themselves entitled to respect as a people and as a nation, we cannot accord them comradeship, faith or honor."

John C.H. Lee
Lt. General, USA
Commanding
(excerpt from "Special Orders for American-German Relations")

8 - Going to Europe—1944

own armies. He was invariably disappointed with the beating his country was now enduring as Hitler's panzers were slowly being pushed back towards Berlin. But Gunter was also aware that it wouldn't be long before he would be a free man again, even though he would be returning to a devastated homeland. His fellow prisoners besieged him nightly on his return to the prison barracks for any news, as he was their only reliable source of dependable news. But it was hard for them to accept the reality of the news and they insisted that we were deliberately falsifying the battle positions just to discourage them. I kept hearing the words "propaganda, it's propaganda!" What could I say to make him believe the truth? We talked about how wonderful it would be to visit Paris — which neither of us had really seen yet and Gunter assured me that he would find his way there as soon as he was free again. But I brought up the fact that he would be most unwelcome there if he ever made it to Paris. We made a pact that we would keep in touch with each other after we were no longer enemies. He would get to Paris and would send a photo of himself with French signs behind himself to prove he had made it there. And he did make it a reality, as you can see from the photo included here. Gunter took up

I learned that Gunter had only just started working as a messenger boy for a Berlin insurance company before he was conscripted to serve in the German Army ... I told him of my own German grandparents who had long ago left the mother country to seek their fortunes in America and he envied me wistfully.

My friend Gunter made it to Paris after the war, but was never heard from again.

news photography for a living for awhile after his release from prison camp, wrote for a couple of years, fell in love, married a pretty fraulein and was never heard from again.

§

Captain Harris had grown concerned about company morale and decided to have the office personnel print a small newssheet on the mimeograph machine. We stirred up interest in the endeavor by holding a contest for its name. Everyone got in the act and we had dozens of names to choose from. The most popular of them was the title, "SNOW JOB." Roget's Thesaurus explains it this way for those of us who haven't come across this bit of Americana: coaxing, wheedling, sweet talk, and soft soap. We soldiers were always using this sort of inducement to get out of odious duty, so it seemed very appropriate to name the rag with this title. I was the first victim of a snow job when I was cajoled into being the staff-artist, cartoonist for the paper. About this, I will quote here from our Company's "memory book," *Memoirs of the 480th Ordnance Tire Repair Company*, published after the War when most of us had returned to civilian life:

> But the key man in the whole affair, of course, was our artist and illustrator, George Somers. The hit the "SNOW JOB" made with the men was due, in large part, to the humorous and down-to-earth drawings, which accompanied practically every story ever written for it. Especially memorable was the sketch George drew showing one of our sergeants creeping along the road from Pontfaverger to Betheniville, all worn-out and tired from a rough night with Paula.

And then, another time I was sweet-talked into redecorating the hotel's lobby, which had been turned into our recreation room. I tried to give it a cheerier look with fresh paint and new curtains to rid it of the wartime drab and gloom that was so prevalent everywhere around us.

§

A French civilian contractor had been hired to rewire the factory building since the retreating German Army had methodically ripped out and left with the existing electrical wiring systems. Monsieur Naylor was our contractor and we wondered why he had an English name since he barely spoke the language. But it had something to do with his English father settling in France, of course. His working team was son, Yves and another young man whom we knew as Andreas, the Spaniard. Yves was unusually handsome and

Captain Harris playing peek-a-boo with large and small tires. To help boost the Company's morale, he had the men create a fun newsletter. I was to be the staff-artist and cartoonist.

A Cover drawing for my Army Company's memory book, *Memoirs of the 480th Ordnance Tire Repair Company.*

could have earned a living as a fashion model, Andreas was quite plain but the two were close friends and worked as a team. Since Yves spoke no English, Andreas spoke French and English and I spoke English and Spanish, we began a hilarious friendship, which continued up until the time our company left the town. I would see them often after work hours for a small glass of wine and we would chat about our lives although I never gave them a hint of my true nature. They were much too polite to get nosy anyway. They roomed together in Reims, but I never felt they were anymore than simply two working partners. We did spend weekends together, when they were able to round up three bikes and we could take short jaunts around the countryside. What now looked like lovely landscapes, tree-lined lanes bordering farmers' fields, had been the battlefields of World War One. Twenty-seven years earlier, this same landscape had been the scene of carnage and total destruction. We visited a number of imposing stone monuments to the war's victims. Was mankind to ever learn to live with his brothers in my lifetime? I had been born at the beginning of the First World War, in 1914, and here I was, involved in another world war in 1945. I saw the military cemeteries of the Marne and the Ardennes and speculated if the present war would soon send tanks rolling through these graveyards. It was a grim thought to be thinking on such a lovely day.

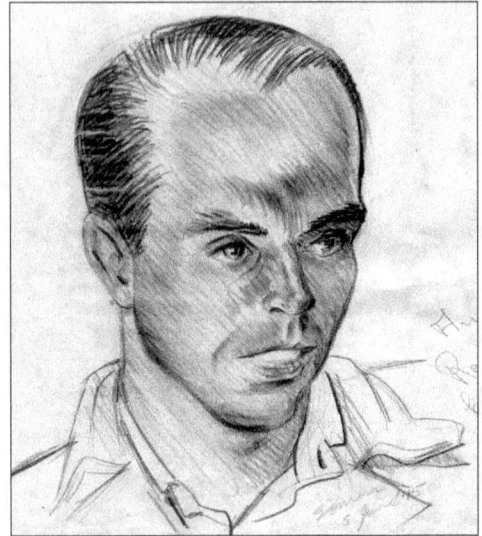

Yves, one of the French electricians contracted to rewire our Company's new "factory" at Betheniville, which had been stripped by the retreating Germans.

Andreas, Yve's Spanish co-worker at the Betheniville tire repair facility, standing before a WWI Memorial.

I grew to cherish my brief moments with these great comrades. A Frenchman, a Spaniard and an American in a crazy mix-up of languages. It reminded me so much of my childhood, speaking to parents who preferred to use their native languages. Before I finally left Betheniville, I got around to making a pencil portrait of Yves and another of Andreas. I

8 - Going to Europe—1944

had kept a box of colored pencils in my duffel bag from the start and had done sketches of a number of other friends along the way.

On a couple of occasions, I was able to wangle duty on truck trips going into Paris to look for missing equipment that had been sent to the wrong train-yard. On the way across the city, we would rumble past the fabulous Louvre Museum and I would have this almost overpowering urge to hop out of the truck's rear. But I also had heard that this incredibly rich storehouse of the world's greatest art was off-limits to everyone, including the French themselves at this time. I wondered if the Nazis had ransacked its treasures from the walls. It was heart-breaking to think about, but we knew that Field Marshall Goering who headed Germany's Air Force was busily accumulating hundreds of masterpieces for his private villas. War booty is nothing new to the victors.

§

Spring of 1945 finally arrived accompanied by the blooming of lilacs and fluffy pink clouds of cherry trees. The slushy ground gave way to new grass shoots and we welcomed the warmer weather. In the first week of May, the German lines had dropped clear back to Berlin. I reflected that fact on my map studded with push-pins. It was a popular spot for American soldiers and German prisoners to gather at. There was a wary sense of politeness between the two groups, with the Germans always inching away when an American came over to have a look. The dejection of the prisoners was apparent but they also had to look forward to being released from their imprisonment. They would be

Chick Hiken, editor of the "Snow Job", and I take a lunch break from the office.

(Continued on page 137)

I Pose with Our Company's Non-coms in Paris after the Liberation of France.

My sketch of a Paris café encounter.

We led a parade through the streets ending up in front of the stone obelisk honoring the fallen soldiers from World War One. I am standing t just left of rear/center with hands clasped behind my back.

8 - Going to Europe—1944

The office guys at Betheniville. I am at far left, kneeling in front row; Gunter, "begrudgingly by now accepted as part of our team," is immediately to my left.

(Continued from page 133)
homeward bound but what awaited them there was anyone's guess. I almost felt sorry for the poor bastards, how could all this mess have come to be and ruined so many lives? We, at least, were going home to towns untouched by the War's cannons. After we heard the news that the Russian Army had been allowed to enter Berlin first and that Hitler had shot his mistress after a brief wedding ceremony and then killed himself, we knew the War was finally over.

The world was going wild with joy now and our little French village started breaking out bottles of wine hoarded for this occasion. They celebrated for a week and we led a parade through the streets ending up in front of the stone obelisk honoring the fallen soldiers from World War One *(facing page)*. I bid Yves and Andreas a sad good-bye. The next day, our last one, the entire office staff gathered for a group photo and I asked if they would allow Gunter to be in it as well. He was grudgingly accepted by now as a member of the team and you see him next to me in the nearby photo of the occasion. Gunter did promise to write to me in America and he even sent along a small record of his voice, which I still keep in my albums.

We packed up all our gear, spent a couple of weeks crating the machines and boarded a train for Paris for one final fling of drinking and carousing. The next day, with everyone accounted for, we were on another train heading south down the Rhone Valley — 800 miles of track, which was to put us in the sun drenched fields of Provence, Van Gogh country. We hung out the train windows taking in all the beauty of the French countryside. It was little disturbed by the recent war and we passed endless miles of orchards, wheat fields and stone villages and cities that called for my camera's eye. I felt terribly frustrated that I couldn't hop off to paint or shoot this passing panorama. It took four days to get to our destination and we were a merry bunch to see because we soon expected to be boarding a ship for the good old U.S. of A, as we fondly called it. Coming into the train-yards at Marseilles, the southern terminal of the line, we were now seeing ships sitting in the Mediterranean. How soon would we be hustled aboard one of them? But the trucks we boarded were headed away from the docks and began traveling westward and inland.

After a couple of jolting hours in the back of the trucks, we came to a field just outside of the town of Arles. As an artist, I was well aware of the importance of this town in the Vincent Van Gogh story and I was thrilled to actually be in the countryside he had made so famous. I hoped to see it all. He had lived here for some months before ending up in an insane asylum. As you may know, he painted his blazing landscapes later and ended by shooting himself fatally one afternoon after completing a painting of a cornfield swarming with hideous black crows. It had all happened 55 years ago and now he was starting to become a famous artist. Vincent had sold only one painting while he lived, traded others for food and canvas, his brother Theo being his main support.

Is this a career move anyone in his or her right mind would have made? I wondered if I could do any better or if I even had the talent and the energy to devote my life to the thankless task. I felt then as I do now, that I didn't have the enor-

After a couple of jolting hours in the back of the trucks, we came to a field just outside of the town of Arles. As an artist, I was well aware of the importance of this town in the Vincent Van Gogh story and I was thrilled to actually be in the countryside he had made so famous.

Vincent Van Gogh, a self-portrait.

My sketch of our creekside camp outside Arles.

mous compulsion to keep making art for a world that really doesn't care much. What's one more artist anyway?

However, I was determined to walk around the town and fields and savor the beauty that Van Gogh saw here in commonplace scenes. The company was to settle in a farmer's field along a creek and immediately began erecting a tent city. Everyone got into interminable card games and beer appeared to help drive off the boredom of waiting until we were assigned to a ship. The air was steaming hot and on one occasion as I stood in a chow line, I actually keeled over in a dead faint, the first time I had ever passed out from heat prostration.

Card games were not my thing, and I found a couple of other men who were more interested in checking out the town of Arles. I took along my colored pencils and managed to make quick sketches of the streets and squares. I hunted around looking for a Van Gogh Museum, but discovered the townspeople barely knew of his fame. There were some poor cheap reproductions tacked to a hotel dining-room wall. That was it, to my amazement. Had the French hidden any Van Goghs they might have owned in fear of what the Germans might carry off? No one could inform me and so I chose to seek out other sights. There was a Roman past here, well-documented by a smaller version of the massive Roman Colosseum. The people of Arles still used their arena for bullfights but, like the Portuguese, they never allowed their bulls to end up dead. I wasn't able to see a fight as they were cancelled during this post-war period. There was also a beautiful medieval church with a cloistered garden next to it that I enjoyed spending an afternoon in

On other occasions, we trucked along the coast to stop at a lovely little town called Martigues, that bordered the Sea and was so quaint that it seemed like some Hollywood set. I bought a number of postcards here to recall its canals and boats. It even had a reputation as a poor man's Venice. But our main destination was Marseilles, which had always had a wicked reputation. Being a seaport, it was a haven for all the sailors of the Mediterranean. There were dozens of dives and brothels in its narrow, teaming streets. I didn't have the nerve to enter any of them since we had heard horror stories of people being knocked out and divested of anything of value they might have. We stuck to the safer sights like doing the zoo and climbing the steep steps leading up to a great church sitting on the city's outskirts. This cathedral, named Notre Dame du la Garde was topped by a figure of the Virgin Mary and was so tall that

(ACROSS) ONE OF MY SKETCHES OF AN OUTDOOR CONCERT IN ARLES. AS AN ARTIST, I WAS WELL AWARE OF THE IMPORTANCE OF THIS TOWN IN THE VINCENT VAN GOGH STORY AND I WAS THRILLED TO ACTUALLY BE IN THE COUNTRYSIDE HE HAD MADE SO FAMOUS.

(*Left*) War damaged Notre Dame du la Garde. A grand church so tall that ships could see the statue before they could sight land. — G.S. (*Right*) Rehabilitated Notre Dame du la Garde today. George took the photograph at left a year after the liberation of Marseille. The German army had taken over the church as a defensive position. Declining to use artillery or air power to unseat the Germans for fear of completely destroying the church, a French Algerian rifle company stormed the hill and took it the hard way. — J. Jackson

At Marseilles, we stuck to the safer sights including climbing the steep steps leading up to a great church sitting on the city's outskirts, Notre Dame du la Garde.

ships could see the statue before they could sight land. It 's a shame that the church was built some time after all the wrangling about the earth's curvature.

While wandering about the city, which dated back to the Roman Era (and was then called Massalia), we ran into a strange little man who was dressed in a Russian soldier's uniform. He seemed lost and couldn't speak English or French but we could see that he was starving. We handed him some francs, took his photo and walked on wondering what had happened to him and how he had wandered so far from his country. Had he stowed away on some Black Sea cargo ship?

Our month long "holiday" in beautiful Provence had come to its end; we folded our tents and boarded the trucks for a short hop to Marseilles. This time we expected to arrive in the U.S. and freedom beckoned temptingly. I had really had enough of living like a gypsy in temporary situations, but truthfully, it had been quite exciting not knowing what was coming next. I even thought it would be great to live in France — I savored the look of France, its charm and picturesque scenery. The only complaint I could make was that I wasn't free to go where I pleased and time constraints made it all seem like I was glancing through some picture postcards that I would stick back on the store rack.

I had really had enough of living like a gypsy in temporary situations, but truthfully, it had been quite exciting not knowing what was coming next.

9
On to Japan
1945 - 1946

"Hiroshima had instantly disappeared as a living city in a blinding flash. [Truman] then sent another bomb hurtling down on a second Japanese city, Nagasaki. We were stunned by the news and began arguing amongst ourselves about the morality of the action." - GS

§

George and his company had been a support unit during the Ardenne offensive. If that wasn't enough, after the German's capitulated, his unit was sent off to Japan, George giving us a first hand account of the devastation they encountered as they landed on the Japanese mainland. - JJ

On to Japan: 1945 - 1946

> *I passed the time chatting with the chaplain's assistant. This job was usually handed to a soldier who had a more sensitive side. I strongly suspected that it went to gay soldiers and several of my fellow soldiers were of the same opinion, but it wasn't denigrated at all.*

Soon after boarding our new transport, we were steaming along the French coast to the right and then the Spanish mainland appeared in a soft haze and then disappeared entirely. The boys took up where they had left off in their card games. I passed the time chatting with the chaplain's assistant. This job was usually handed to a soldier who had a more sensitive side. I strongly suspected that it went to gay soldiers and several of my fellow soldiers were of the same opinion, but it wasn't denigrated at all. I liked the attractive youth who was holding that job on the ship, even though we never got to the point of discussing gay subject matter. It was enough to simply be on friendly, chatty terms with a secret brother after all these months.

We were now passing through the Straits of Gibraltar, and I recalled that the ancient people of this area called this narrowing neck of land and sea, the Pillars of Hercules and the ocean beyond was considered the edges of the known world. If one ventured much farther, there was a strong possibility that you would simply fall off the rim and hurtle through limitless space. For us, however, it was a much more relaxing crossing this time as we didn't have to worry about the lurking German submarines that had been a threat when we came across the Big Pond six months or so earlier.

We seemed to be veering southwards according to the compass, and speculation was running high. As usual, the Army doesn't want to overload one with all that burden of information, so they tell you nothing. Perhaps, even the ship's captain didn't know what course to steer, until he himself was notified! So, where were we headed, everyone was asking? Well, one might guess it was into the Caribbean Sea and its necklace of palm studded islands. Were we going to languish on some pristinely white

9 - On to Japan—1945

Rare photos of Nagasaki nuclear blasts.

Hiroshima had instantly disappeared as a living city in a blinding flash. He then sent another bomb hurtling down on a second Japanese city, Nagasaki. We were stunned by the news and began arguing amongst ourselves about the morality of the action.

stretch of beach for a week or two? We didn't stop in anywhere, just continued westward and were soon carefully threading our way through that marvel of engineering, the Panama Canal. Again, no stopping here and we began guessing games and placing bets as to whether we were headed to Los Angeles or San Francisco. I hoped it would be the southern port, because I knew that Steve was living in Long Beach at his parents' home at this time. We had kept in touch through all the preceding months. The Army postal system was extremely efficient and I had been alerted that Steve was now a civilian and waiting for my own discharge.

Now we were literally holding our collective breath as we headed out into the vast expanse of the Pacific. Would we head north now along the Mexican Coast and California or would it be more duty in some unknown land? All our speculating came to an end two days later with a devastating announcement from the ship's radio. President Truman had just ordered the dropping of the first atom bomb on a civilian target in Japan.* Hiroshima had instantly disappeared as a living city in a blinding flash. We were stunned by the news and began arguing amongst ourselves about the morality of the action. Half of us thought it was merited since it would significantly shorten the war. The other half thought it was a blot on our national honor. We were now no better than the Japanese attack on Pearl Harbor. I was torn between the two opinions, as I abhor the taking of lives for any reason, yet I wanted the War to come to its conclusion soon. I knew all about the toll of human life that became necessary to win beachheads and

*The atomic bomb named "Little Boy" was dropped on Hiroshima by the Enola Gay, a Boeing B-29 bomber, at 8:15 in the morning of August 6, 1945. Over 70,000 civilians died instantly, another 70,000 within 5 years, and 60,000 more by 1990 due to the long term effects of radiation poisoning. This wasn't the end of the horror, however. At 11:02 a.m., on August 9, 1945, the American B-29 bomber, Bock's Car left Tinian carrying Fat Man, a plutonium implosion-type bomb, headed for Nagasaki. The primary target was the Kokura Arsenal, but upon reaching the target, they found that it was covered by a heavy ground haze and smoke. Pilot Charles Sweeney turned to the secondary target of the Mitsubishi Torpedo Plant at Nagasaki. Of the 286,00 people living in Nagasaki at the time of the blast, 74,000 were killed and another 75,000 sustained severe injuries. Many more died later from the after effects of radiation poisoning. At the end of the Second World War Japan's large industrial groups were dismantled by order of the Allied powers and Mitsubishi Heavy Industries was split into three regional companies, each with an involvement in motor vehicle development known today.

(OVERLEAF)
SKETCHES: "LIFE ABOARD A TROOPSHIP COULD BE VERY BORING."

(Continued on page 148)

(*Above, across*) The troopship newsletter for which I added my cartoons.

Our G.I.s killing time on the troopship decks. Life aboard a troopship could be very boring.

9 - On to Japan—1945

the horror of street-by-street fighting that would lie ahead. I reluctantly sided with the half that thought our president had made the right decision. I still wept for the thousands who had been blown up instantly and the hundreds of survivors who walked around with their flesh hanging in shreds. The U.S. bomber plane that delivered the lethal blow was named the "Enola Gay" and the irony of that name was not lost on me. Truman sent another bomb hurtling down on a second Japanese city, Nagasaki soon afterwards and Japan capitulated. The War was over for everyone and we might be heading homewards.

But someone had other ideas for us, it seemed. We continued westward across the blue expanse and a week later we were pulling into a harbor in New Guinea, which is the large island directly north of Australia. New Hollandia was not our real destination and we weren't allowed on the beach there. It was a refueling stop only; tractors, huge stacks of oil drums and all the myriad supplies needed to conduct a war, ravaged the strip of tropical landscape we could see. It was Nature stripped of all its beauty — ugly beyond belief but essential to our needs. The raw red earth of the shoreline and the wrecked war machines spoke eloquently of the destruction this island had recently endured.

We were on our way within 24 hours, with our new supply of oil, as we headed north into the Philippine Archipelago. There are some seven thousand islands included in the Philippines, some of them no larger than a city block. I was very excited by this turn of events since I hardly expected to return to the place of my birth. I assumed we would pull into some provincial port before long and we would have another vacation, this time in the tropics. The scuttlebutt got around that only three men would be disembarking and that it would be at Manila, the capital city. I soon discovered that my name wasn't on that list and I was very upset at the news. I made a beeline for our company captain's cabin and faced him with the problem I had with his decision. It was apparent that he had no idea that I was born right here at our next port of call, Manila. Obviously, he had no reason to consult any records in deciding who was to go ashore and he was happy to change the list for me. I brought up the fact that

9 - On to Japan—1945

I was familiar with the city's street layout and could be of great help in getting about. We were being loaned a jeep to do our search for our tire repair crates, which had traveled on another ship for some reason or another.

Of course, I hadn't seen Manila since the age of eleven when I left to go to school in Kansas. I had no idea if I would recognize landmarks amongst all the rubble of bombed buildings everywhere. But enough remained for me to give directions to our driver. We wound our way past all the devastation, and with help from people on the streets; we managed to make our way. We got to the docks, found our crates and with a few spare hours available to us, I asked the driver if he would do me a special favor. I wanted to get to the cemetery where I had been told I would find my father's grave. He agreed to take me and we then searched the grounds for the marker. It turned out to be a simple concrete slab about twelve by twenty four inches with his name and dates inscribed on its face. There was nothing else, of course. I took a hurried picture and we rushed away. I was strangely unmoved by the bit of business, almost without any emotion. My father had become an abstract concept, not a living, breathing being.

There was one more thing I wanted to see, and I begged for a quick run into the ancient walled city of Intramuros, which forms the center of Manila. Since it was on the way to the docks, they agreed to a two-minute detour through its cleared streets. I had been baptized here at the great cathedral as a Catholic infant. The huge dome had collapsed into a pile of rubble and we didn't stop. As we drove out through one of the ornate gates, we passed a grisly reminder of the recent fighting—a Japanese soldier's body squashed flat as a pancake by an army bulldozer. It looked much like a paper-doll cutout of a man and I turned away once I knew what I had seen.

§

My last task I didn't even dare to bring up to my two partners, as it was obvious we had to get back on the ship very quickly. I had wanted to find some kind of office for war records so that I could find some information on my grandparents, my mother's people. My mother had lost all contact with

One of my many sketches of the war: a bombed-out Manila in the ancient Intramuros district.

them once the Japanese had taken control of the islands. We had known that the civilian populations had been herded into camps enclosed by barbed wire. I knew that Santo Tomas University on the outskirts of Manila had been turned into a vast concentration camp and the chances were that they had been sent there to languish until the War was over. Much later, back in California, we learned that all older Caucasians past working age, had really gone there but since they were fed minimal rations, mostly a bit of rice and soup, that the chances of their survival were hopeless. The Japanese authorities did not record the deaths that resulted from this slow slide into oblivion. They wanted no incriminating records left to document these hundreds of needless deaths. My family never heard anything more of them — Mama Lola had vanished.

§

Our jeep rushed us back to the docks where we learned that our troop transport had just steamed away an hour earlier. The story seemed to be that the docking space was needed for new ship arrivals. We were stranded now but still, there were inquiries to be made from the port authorities. We learned that the boat was heading up the western coast of Luzon which was the island we were on. It was scheduled to drop anchor at Lingayen Bay but there was no dock there since it had been destroyed in

9 - On to Japan—1945

the bombings. This area had been the scene of American landings recently as we retook the Islands. Now, with our borrowed jeep, we drove north through the rice fields to the village on the bay . . . but in talking to an American company commander there, we were told that no ship had just arrived that matched the numbers on our ship. We were disconsolate and, against our better judgment, decided to keep moving. We had heard that some companies had headed up into the mountains behind us to the east. This was the Bagio Province where Dad had first sold his sewing machines as a young man. I was curious to see it for myself and so we kept driving. After an hour of torturous roads that were barely wide enough for our jeep, we pulled into Bagio. Pine forests here surrounded us — totally unexpected, since we were supposed to be in the tropics. But we were too worried about our absence from the company to enjoy ourselves much. We found no sign of them here either after asking around and we turned around and headed back down the treacherous roads to the fishing village at Lingayen. We were paralleling the train tracks some of the way and, at one point, we passed a series of open cattle cars crammed with Japanese troops in dirty, tattered uniforms. They were being brought down to return to their homeland. We had often been told that a Japanese soldier would commit suicide before surrendering, but these woebegone remnants of His Imperial Majesty's Army only looked thankful to be alive. Some even gave us a tentative smile as they flew past us down the tracks.

We passed a series of open cattle cars crammed with Japanese troops in dirty, tattered uniforms ... they were being brought down to return to their homeland.

As soon as we were back at the village of Lingayen, we headed to the company headquarters and finally recognized some faces. No reprimands were issued, everyone was glad to see us back and we almost felt like conquering heroes. Now we could relax on the palm studded beaches and try for a bit of tan. Oily wastes from the tankers anchored nearby fouled the waters of the Bay. Anyone making the mistake of getting in the water was soon covered in black goo that was nasty to get rid of. So much for ideas of a Hawaiian Holiday. Also, we now got the news that we were most probably headed up to Japan to become occu-

Jaunty G.I.s in the Philippines.

Sketch of a marketplace at Balungao, one of several villages my Army unit passed through during the liberation of the Philippines.

pation troops. We groaned at the thought of more duty but who were we to choose our destinies? We were simply "G.I Joes" ready to fill any duty assigned to us. The Army had by now set up a system where you accumulated points from the number of months one had already served. When you reached a certain level of points, you were discharged. We all began to feel better, knowing we had only two or three more months to get through.

§

Back on our ship again, we headed north for the short voyage to the Japanese mainland. Arriving at Kobe's huge industrial docks, we were surprised to see so little damage. However, in passing through the nearby cities of Kobe and Osaka, there was nothing but charred skeletons of buildings, the devastation was almost total. Here and there, we could see makeshift hovels were the people were making do with temporary shelter. It was a grim sight to experience, yet we felt that they had started the conflict and now was payback time. Of course, we also knew that the average Japanese had little to say about getting into this horrible conflict to begin with. How it was ever explained to them that they must take on the American giant will remain a mystery to most of us.

We were heading into a suburb halfway between Kobe and Osaka

In passing through the nearby cities of Kobe and Osaka, there was nothing but charred skeletons of buildings, the devastation was almost total.

9 - On to Japan—1945

where the devastation was minimal. The U.S. Army occupation authorities had assigned us to a tennis club for well-to-do Japanese families. It was the Nishnomiya district and no bombs had fallen here, the buildings were in good condition and we moved into the large spacious quarters adjoining an exhibition stadium for tennis matches. The few civilians we could see from our windows seemed intent on hurrying by and ignoring us. I could almost feel the resentment they harbored for us, but they were always in complete control of their feelings. Some workers had been hired to tend to the cooking and housekeeping duties and we started to live like honored guests. Still, everyone was apprehensive about exploring the neighboring areas. We had no idea of what could happen so most of us simply hung about the club grounds rather than risk our necks. In fact, the Japanese workers were very servile, almost groveling at our feet and we realized that they had always taken this attitude toward the Conqueror. We were looked on almost as gods for we had proven our superiority in battle.

The company commander soon advised me that I would be kept busy putting together a small sign shop. While most of the company would be sent out to guard army depots, I would be in charge of producing road signs. Since all existing highway and street signs were in Japanese, we had a huge backlog of requests for English signs to help other companies find their way around the adjacent areas. So, just as in Texas, I was a sign-painter once more. Actually, I rather relished the work since it would fill the waiting days before my discharge, which turned out to be no more than a month away.

The company was billeted in the spacious clubhouse, an American style building and I was told to use the dressing rooms in the exhibition stadium to set up my sign shop. I was given two fellow soldiers as my working assistants and three Japanese were hired to do the menial tasks. We started immediately to make the road signs to identify crossroads and main streets of the local areas. Merle Murphy, one of my two soldier assistants hadn't a clue about sign making, nor did anyone else but it didn't matter. I said that neatness counted more than experience and within a week, we were cranking out fairly decent sign work. Merle had been an acquaintance up until now and he proved to be a good friend as he kept us all in good humor with his dry wit and crazy stories. Today he lives three hours south of me, at Carmel,

> *In fact, the Japanese workers were very servile, almost groveling at our feet and we realized that they had always taken this attitude toward the Conqueror. We were looked on almost as gods for we had proven our superiority in battle.*

Myself and sign shop workers at Nishnimiya, Japan 3 Japanese bordered by 3 G.I.s.

which is one of the most beautiful resort areas of California. Monterey, California's first capital under the Spanish period is next door to this lovely coastline resort. Now and then, I have gone down to visit with Merle and he's always sure to haul out the mementoes and stories of the 480th Tire Company. He has become a collector of Nazi war trophies like the swastika flags, bayonets, guns, helmets — you name it. He had insisted I take back a bolo, a sort of bushwhacking short sword I had left behind in the Philippines since I had no interest in war memorabilia. Merle was very proud of the fact that he could still squeeze into his old uniform if he held in his breath.

§

But I digress here . . . back to the Japan scene . . . the Tire Company was never set up to function and the crates remained at the dock warehouse. The Tire Company was merged with several other companies now to form the Kobe Ordnance Service Center whose primary mission was to receive, store and service all ordnance equipment of units that were now being deactivated. So it turned out that we were spread all over the local areas and time was allowed for sight-seeing although there was a certain sense of uneasiness in ever going out to see anything because we felt unwelcome. However, we felt the confinement in our off-duty time and some of us did go exploring, snapping pictures of the devastation and ruin of entire neighborhoods. It wasn't the sort of scenery one feels good about and we were the reason it looked this grim. Small children, probably unaware of our being Americans, would cluster around me when I attempted to sketch, making it difficult to see what was in front of me, but I felt heartened that they, at least, were unaware of our connection to their homeland.

§

9 - On to Japan—1945

One particularly sunny, warm afternoon, I asked Chick Hiken, who was a good friend and was very clever with words, if he wanted to stroll with me. No one ever went out alone since it could prove to be dangerous. Chick, after the War, was to head up a group of ex-G.I.s that compiled the 124 page "memory book" mentioned in the previous chapter, telling the story of our experiences in the Army. I was asked to illustrate this book and I painted some dozen pieces for it including the end-papers, which depicted the two hemispheres of the world and our circumnavigation of both theaters of war. It is rather singular that a company like ours got to experience both Europe and Asia. The slim volume was privately published in an edition of 150 copies for distribution to the families of the company. And I could mention here that the feeling of comradeship was strong enough that some forty years later, the former buddies decided to hold annual re-unions at each other cities. I was asked to come to them, and I did attend two of them but always felt awkward about the fact that I didn't have a wife in tow.

Riding a stone lion in bomb-devastated Kobe.

It is rather singular that a company like ours got to experience both Europe and Asia. And I could mention here that the feeling of comradeship was strong enough that some forty years later, the former buddies decided to hold annual re-unions ... I did attend two of them but always felt awkward about the fact that I didn't have a wife in tow.

§

Back in Japan, on that lovely fall day in November, Chick and I headed for the massive, concrete breakwater that held the sea in control. A very pleasant-looking Japanese gentleman in his forties was standing there looking out to sea and as we passed him, he greeted us in English. As we chatted with him, we learned that he, like so many Japanese men, had come to the U.S. for schooling in his teen years. He deplored what had happened to our two countries. He said he had never felt it was the consensus of opinion of his countrymen to fight the war that had just devastated his country. He didn't seem bitter about the ruin it had brought, perhaps because his own home had been spared miraculously. He also felt that his Emperor should have headed south to the oil-rich lands south

At a park in Osaka, still intact after the U.S. aerial bombings.

His polite family, who barely concealed their astonishment to find enemy soldiers in their modest home, greeted us.

of the Philippines, which made up the Malaysian nation. The Dutch had once exploited this area as well. He felt that America would have been less concerned in that enterprise, but I didn't hear him mention what he would do about the Philippines being in the path of this conquest.

As the talk seemed to be drawing to a close, he asked us if we cared to visit his home, which he said was only a few blocks away. I don't really know why we should have trusted him at all, and especially on such short notice. We could have been walking into a trap of some sort, but trusting souls that we were, we followed him home. His was one of the few neighborhoods that had been spared by the bombers and it seemed odd to come into neatly fenced, intact dwellings. It was a typical house of seasoned grayish-brown wood planking walls that slid back to reveal rice paper filled panels called shojis. The immaculate garden had dwarf pine trees and sculptured rocks artfully arranged around stone paths. His polite family, who barely concealed their astonishment to find enemy soldiers in their modest home, greeted us. They were reassured by Papasan that we meant no harm to them. Although no one except the father could speak a word of English, we did a lot of sign language back and forth. We remembered to remove our big, clumsy boots as we crossed into the immaculate straw tatami floor pads that smelled faintly of new-mown grass. We were almost immediately served a green tea at a foot-high table while we tried to get comfortable at sitting at this level. We learned that the two pre-teen

Kobe, Japan.

girls and the teen son were all studying English in their schools and were most anxious to try out their level of skills on us. It was rather hilarious and certainly broke the ice for us all. It was all accompanied with much giggling from the women. There seemed to be no wife, but a petite grandmother seemed to be the matriarch of the house. It all seemed to be a stage-set for "Madame Butterfly," the famous Puccini opera, and we were to play the American officer who takes on a Japanese bride only to toss her aside like a doll. But, of course, there were two of us and I certainly wasn't interested in a romantic relationship. But we did promise to return soon and next time we would bring some canned goods. It was obvious that they were severely rationed, had been living mainly on rice and what fish they could catch themselves. So we returned the following weekend with the foodstuff and I also brought my sketchpad and colored pencils to do quick portraits of the girls. We were somewhat puzzled about where to hang the finished and framed art since the walls all seemed to slid back and forth, but we ended up hanging them from the top of the wall where it joined the ceiling.

The Hayasaki family, for that was their family name, wanted to repay us for the food we had brought and the portraits and they gave us a number of

But we did promise to return soon and next time we would bring some canned goods. It was obvious that they were severely rationed, had been living mainly on rice and what fish they could catch themselves. So we returned the following weekend with the foodstuff and I also brought my sketchpad and colored pencils to do quick portraits of the girls.

> This rice paper volume of erotic illustrations is placed under the pillow of newly-weds on their first night together to instruct them on the mysteries of Sex. I was much amused by the depictions of the idealized couples in their passionate embraces.

quite beautiful gifts which I still treasure. I was given a red lacquer stationery box, a samurai sword, another short dagger-like sword, two cast iron figurines, a kendo fencing uniform, a wooden shrine encasing a golden Buddha and lastly, a pillow book of colored wood-cuts. This rice paper volume of erotic illustrations is placed under the pillow of newly-weds on their first night together to instruct them on the mysteries of Sex. I was much amused by the depictions of the idealized couples in their passionate embraces. Years later, I was foolish enough to sell this unique pornographic treasure to a collector who kept hounding me to sell it to him at a handsome price.

§

All the men in my Company now had a new pastime and that was to figure out how many more days before we could head back to the States. We were being discharged according to a rotation system based on the number of days served since entering the Army. I reckoned that I had enough time served; in fact, had I been called then to receive my discharge papers, I would have totaled three years, nine months and five days! I was given authority to get on a ship within a couple of days and, as in so many other significant dates in my life calendar, it happened to be Christmas Eve. Why would this date always signal some important event in my life — such as my father's death, my mother's fatal accident, the terrifying night on guard duty in France, the possibility of a German paratrooper strangling me in the night during the Battle of the Bulge? But at least this Christmas Eve I was getting on a homeward bound ship to America.

The Hayasaki girls with my pastel portraits of them and their grandmother.

10
Return to San Francisco
1946 - 1947

"We were part of a huge migration of gays and lesbians who had passed through San Francisco on their way to the Pacific Islands and the lucky ones who had actually been allowed to come back in one piece." - GS

∫

Strangely, George's narrative of the war and its aftermath goes silent upon his return to the states. Here he mentions gays and lesbians who served in and survived the war heading to new lives in SF. - JJ

RETURN TO SAN FRANCISCO: 1946 - 1947

*T*hrough all this traveling, thanks to a very efficient Army Postal Service, I had never lost contact with Steve. He had been stationed in the South Pacific although he couldn't tell me where because of security concerns. But he had not been in great danger, since he wasn't a fighting soldier. He had spent his days in the bakery, cooking up pies for the officers and enlisted men. I thought this was hilarious.

Steve was discharged three or four months ahead of me and was relaxing at his parents' home in Long Beach, California. That is the town just inland from the San Pedro harbor where I was due to go for my final moments of army life. It seemed like it was planned that way, but it wasn't at all. My ship crossed the Pacific safely, docked at San Francisco but I chose to remain with her until we anchored at San Pedro. Steve had learned of my arrival time from a phone call I had made from San Francisco and he was waiting for me on the dock. We embraced, weeping tears of joy, not caring who might not approve of the sight of two grown men slobbering over each other. Besides, we knew that these reunions were taking place everywhere at this time and who would begrudge his neighbor the emotion of seeing his beloved for the first time in years?

We immediately drove to his home in Long Beach where I met the parents who had heard of Steve's best friend for some weeks already. I was totally accepted on face value and I know that they either had no idea of the true nature of our relationship or simply chose to ignore the issue. They also knew that we had no intention of staying around but that within a week, we would leave and head for San Francisco where we could feel more at home. We were part of a huge migration of gays and lesbians who had passed through San Francisco on their way to the Pacific Is-

We were part of a huge migration of gays and lesbians who had passed through San Francisco on their way to the Pacific Islands and the lucky ones who had actually been allowed to come back in one piece.

We embraced, weeping tears of joy, not caring who might not approve of the sight of two grown men slobbering over each other.

(ACROSS)
MY FIRST LOVE,
STEVE, IN THE FIRST
WEEKS OF OUR
PARTNERSHIP

160

10 - Return to San Francisco—1946

lands and the lucky ones who had actually been allowed to come back in one piece.

As soon as we came to the City, (everyone in the Bay Area knows that that refers to San Francisco rather than to any other of the dozen smaller communities that encircle the Bay) we put in a call to Bruce, our mutual friend who had originally introduced us to each other. He was delighted to see that we were still a pair and that he had been the reason for our relationship. Bruce was living on Macondray Lane, which later became famous as the setting for Armistead Maupin's "Tales of the City". First it was serialized in the S.F. Chronicle as a convoluted tale of gays and straights dealing with each other and their loves. Then it was turned into a movie, which made it even better known and accepted. It managed to breakdown most of the barriers that still befuddled straights, making San Francisco the most liberal city in America after New York City.

But this delightful one block-long path through the woods on Russian Hill was still a secret to most San Franciscans and we relished the feeling of being out in the country while only steps from the steep climb up to the summit. It still is one of the most desirable nooks that anyone could possibly want to live in while in San Francisco. And Bruce had been making plans to spend his vacation in Los Angeles at this time, so he was glad to have somebody housesit for him. Our arrival time was perfect for him and for us. We promptly moved in to his cozy apartment and he left us in this romantic hideaway for thirty days! But we

Armistead Maupin's "Tales of the City" was serialized in the S.F. Chronicle as a convoluted tale of gays and straights dealing with each other and their loves. It managed to breakdown most of the barriers that still befuddled straights, making San Francisco the most liberal city in America after New York City.

(Left)
Macondray Lane, where Steve and I lived just after the war. It was to be an inspiration for Barbary Lane in Armistead Maupin's "28 Barbary Lane: Tales of the City."

(Facing page, Top) View of S.F. Bay from Macondray Lane entrance.

(Facing page, Below) The entry at 72 Macondray Lane.

10 - Return to San Francisco—1946

were well aware that all good things seem to come to their end sooner or later, and we began searching for a place of our own before his return.

In the search through North Beach, which had been my neighborhood before the War, I came across a very hidden passageway that was advertised in a sidewalk window on Jones Street. The address was 2222 Jones and you walked down a planked boardwalk to the rear of the post-Victorian building to get to its entry. Because

the building sat on a steep hill, what might have seemed to be a basement was actually another story above the ground. It had a view out over the whole panorama of North Beach with St. Peter & Paul's cathedral framed in the windows. The Chinese landlord was pleased with us and we promptly moved in without a stick of furniture. With the landlord's permission, I got busy with new tools and turned the two and a half rooms into a larger one-room studio. The kitchen wall now had a new bar-counter that separated it from the dining room. The living room couch was actually our bed and I did some excavating to double the size of the small bathroom. I was so elated with the outcome of all this work that I got a professional photographer friend to come over and shoot some pictures of it. I subsequently sent the shots along to Sunset Magazine and was amazed to see them printed a few months later in an article on how-to transform your basement into a stylish apartment.

§

Of course, I got my old job back at Sloane's home furnishings but Ross was no longer there, he had moved back to New York and I had been told that I would have to share managerial duties with the man who had replaced me while I was away in the Army. He and I didn't see things in the same way, there were disputes and I decided to look around for another job. I visited my old employers at Roos/Atkins (it had added on a new partner and a new name) they seemed pleased to see me and immediately hired me as Assistant Display Manager and Designer. I was much better placed now, with an increase in pay as well.

Steve had hunted around in the Financial District and had landed some type of desk job which I could never figure out but he seemed happy enough working with reams of typed pages. I would have gone crazy doing this sort of work as I hated being desk-bound. He and I started having our own little circle of friends as I noticed we really had different tastes in life. He even started dating a young Italian that I thought had a very juvenile outlook on life. This guy, Peter, was the public relations promoter of a group of rock musicians. I had never been a particularly jealous sort in my life and I accepted the fact that Steve wanted to play around. I had seen it coming to this for some time and as long as he was open about it, I could go along with it. In fact, I began to see my own friends as well, those that I found more interested in my own interests.

The entry at 222 Jones St. at the end of a long passageway.

Steve and I started having our own little circle of friends ... he even started dating a young Italian ... I had never been a particularly jealous sort in my life and I accepted the fact that Steve wanted to play around. I had seen it coming to this for some time and as long as he was open about it, I could go along with it.

(FACING PAGE)
THE SUNSET
MAGAZINE ARTICLE
ABOUT MY JONES
STREET APARTMENT

1948

From door, only clothes rack, chest of drawers, and ceiling high screen are visible

Space savers

IN REMODELING these small living quarters, it was found necessary to combine bathroom and dressing room. Designer George Somers used screens to good effect. The cloth and reed screen used here is hard to find, but split bamboo or tied reed may be substituted with satisfactory results. Wood framing screen makes useful towel rack. Prefabricated shower is masked ceiling-high by one wall.

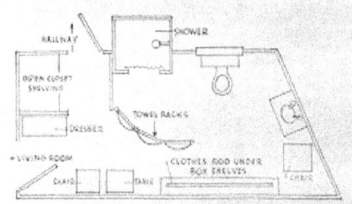

View from living area into dining-kitchen. Bookcases built into space formerly occupied by two doors. Partition between rooms removed, leaving trellis as semi-division

Remodeling ideas

Kitchen work counter screens utilities of the kitchen from dining, living rooms. Storage below work surface. Indirect light above counter

Copper strips placed at top, middle, bottom of screen. Screen nailed to uprights

SUNSET

11
Moving to Marin County

1948 - 1954

"Down at the Beach, we had our own special area where male couples would set-up their umbrellas and blankets." - GS

§

George settles into what is a near bohemian lifestyle along the northern edge of San Francisco Bay, connects with other gay men and lays the groundwork for a new life. - JJ

MOVING TO MARIN COUNTY: 1948 – 1954

Steve and I had decided to buy a Buick convertible together before the "playing the field" period had started. I still didn't think we had reached the end of our relationship, but I was spending more time going on sketching trips on my own. I would take the Buick out and drive across the magnificent Golden Gate bridge and search for lovely views of the Bay and the panorama of San Francisco's storied hills. They are dazzlingly white against the azure of the Bay. I felt so fortunate to be living here even though our love was fading away. It is important to hold back some part of yourself to salvage in case you are left. I didn't want our relationship to end, but I knew that there was little I cold do if both of us weren't whole-heartedly involved. I suppose I have always been a fatalist — it was bound to end and I knew it. I accepted the fact that our outlook on life was simply too different for any permanence to develop. It had been seven years since we had met and almost four yeas of that had been spent in different parts of the world. Steve and I had really never had a chance to know one another. The letters that had come had given only a partial picture of the reality of living together.

As I scanned the beautiful vistas of Marin County, I wished I could live here some day, never realizing that it was about to happen for me. Sausalito, Tiburon, Belvedere, and San Rafael, China Camp — it all seemed so desirable. I carried my sketchpad to all these places but wondered how I could possibly capture the beautiful light and color that surrounded me. I tried anyway.

On one of these jaunts along the shores of the Bay, I made a very fortunate contact. I was in Tiburon on a Saturday afternoon with my sketchpad

I felt so fortunate to be living here even though our love was fading away. It is important to hold back some part of yourself to salvage in case you are left. I didn't want our relationship to end, but I knew that there was little I cold do if both of us weren't whole-heartedly involved.

11 - Moving to Marin County—1948

and I stopped to sketch a seaside cottage that sat on pilings out over the Bay. A short gangway reached it and it appeared to have once been the forecastle of a sailing ship. The porthole windows and paneling gave hints of its past on the high seas. I was so intrigued with capturing its lines that I didn't notice a vintage roadster pulling up to the curb. A young couple got out and I noticed how far along she was in her pregnancy. They seemed entranced that I was sketching their home. After a brief conversation on the sidewalk, they suggested I come inside to see the place and have a refreshing drink on their deck. I didn't wait for a second of time and as I finished the sketch in watercolors, I rang the ship's bell, which hung by the cabin door. I was intrigued with the nautical look they had given the place but the most beautiful thing was the superb vista of the shimmering-white city, San Francisco, in the distance. Baghdad-by-the-Bay was what it had been named by the world-famous columnist, Herb Caen. Everyone read his gossip column before any other part of the morning news.

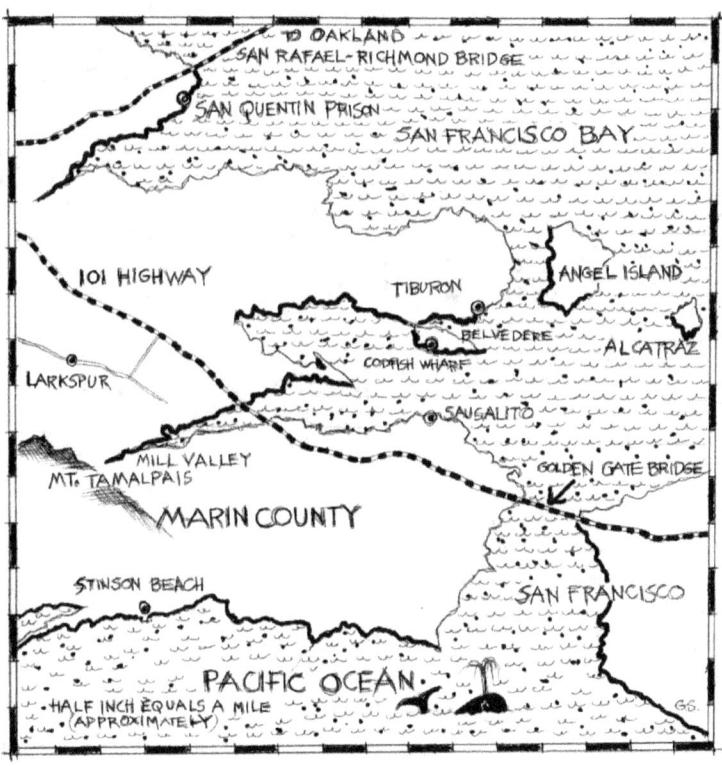

We sat in the balmy sunshine, soaking in the smells and sounds of the beauty surrounding us with a gin-n-tonic in hand. It was really heaven and I wondered if I could ever live like this myself – no, it was a dream. As we got better acquainted, I learned that they were the younger generation of the Allen Family. This far-sighted clan had bought up much of the hillside land and shores of the neighboring island called Belvedere – generations back, that is, when land was considerably cheaper. Belvedere originally was connected to the village of Tiburon by a shallow lagoon that allowed one to wade across to the shacks built on its flanks. Later on, in the 1870s, a dike was built across its northern edge and the seawater was allowed to form a deeper lake or lagoon. A roadway was

stretched over the dam and the island became much more accessible to homebuilders. The vistas from this enchanted spot were so sought after that the well-to-do families of San Francisco started to buy land on its flanks and erect weekend homes facing either Sausalito or in the southern direction to the City. To say you had a place on Belvedere implied you had "arrived socially." One either sailed in one's own yacht or was invited over for the weekend at the grand homes clinging to the steep slopes of this most lovely island. I imagined that the whole scene could have been the Amalfi, Positano Coast along the Italian coastline.

The Codfish Wharf, a quick sketch done on the waters of Richardson's Bay.

The Allen's now asked me if I was interested in renting a studio apartment they had on the western slopes, which faced Sausalito. As an artist, surely I would like the vistas from there, they reasoned. So, intrigued, I asked to see it right then. We jumped into their roadster and within five minutes, we were parked along a forested roadway that circled around the island. We clambered down a precipitous goat-path leading to a most unexpected scene. Below us, some two hundred feet, lay a long wooden derelict of a wharf with two buildings on it. Most of the dock's surface was clear of any equipment because it had been the area used for huge drying racks.

§

The Codfish Wharf was now a ghost of its former self. In its prosperous days, it had been the base for a thriving industry with three-mast sailing ships docking here with their holds brimming over with tons of cod. They had fished up along the Alaskan Coast and brought their catch here to this wharf for processing. They were left in huge salt tanks and then allowed out on the dock's drying racks. The larger of the two buildings was called the Tank-house because its main floor held a dozen redwood-sided tanks

11 - Moving to Marin County—1948

that were some eight-by-eight feet in size. From 1875 to 1925, this was a busy scene, with several scores of workers unloading ships and handling the codfish catch as it arrived. I tried to imagine what it must have been like but it was impossible. The Italians of North Beach counted on getting their supply of "Bacalau" from here. Salted cod was a staple of their diet and when one remembers that refrigeration hadn't been developed yet, it makes sense. Salting foods was a way of preserving them against rot.

The Japanese fishing fleets began to fish the same waters of the Alaskan coast and with their lower wage scales for their workers, they were able to undercut the American fishermen. By 1925, the Codfish Wharf could no longer compete with the cheaper prices the Japanese would sell for and the Wharf simply closed down. The real estate entrepreneurs now moved in and that is where the Allen's came in. They were able to buy up much of the western flanks facing on Richardson's Bay with Sausalito across the water. It was a very smart investment and the Allen's prospered as they sold off tracts of land through the 30s, 40s and the 50s when I was lucky enough to wander into the scene.

§

I was shown into the Tank-house, past the brine vats and up a ship's gangplank, which led to a loft arrangement. It was subdivided into two sections, each with its own entrance. A writer already occupied one half but the northern half was empty and waiting for a bohemian soul to bring it to life. I walked into a large room some 35 feet in length by 16 feet wide. The raftered ceiling and boarded walls were whitewashed. The western side of the room faced Sausalito and it was broken through with a ribbon strip of windows interrupted by a pair of French doors leading out to a sun deck. One more window on the north end showed me a stretch of empty beach with the steep flanks of the island to the right. I was totally overwhelmed by the whole picture and lost no time in saying, "Yes, I want to live here!" I didn't hesitate a moment, not even considering Steve's reaction to this decision. I paid them with a check deposit and left in a daze. I could hardly believe I was going to live in this most romantic, bohemian hideaway. Steve must love it too, I felt.

But the situation with him was beyond salvaging, as I was to learn shortly, and it was really time to move on. I told him I would be living at the

Wharf in Marin County whether he shared it with me or not. He accepted my decision amicably enough, no arguing ensued and he had his own love affair going anyway. We agreed that he would keep the Jones Street apartment with all the furniture we had bought together and I would drive away with the car. No lawyer was hired to wrangle with decisions. It was a trusting solution, I got the better of the deal with the new auto, but he had the guilt of having broken up the relationship with his playing around. A month or so after I left him, his new playmate had left him as well. Steve was distraught but I had no reason to trust him again and I made no move to renew the bond. He was so embittered by the turn of events that he started stalking Peter and the new lover that Peter had met. Steve would track their going out to bars and would sit opposite them and simply stare at them in a surly way — they always got up and left the bar only to be followed to their next stop. It must have been depressing for both sides and I didn't envy either of them. But I for one was finished with Steve. It was too uncertain a way of life for me.

The sundeck looking westward towards Sausalito.

Steve was distraught but I had no reason to trust him again and I made no move to renew the bond.

I felt I was starting all over again, a new home that I was already in love with and free of the uncertainty of a relationship gone sour. Although the Allen's had no immediate plans for the Wharf, I had been told that they would eventually tear down the whole complex and build expensive dockside luxury homes in its place with a shoreline road to reach them. This was a very costly project and they were looking for the investors to finance this multi-million plan. In the meantime, I could rest assured that the wharf studio was mine for a few years. I didn't have a stick of furniture, so that was my first priority. I wanted it to have a ship's cabin look — as if I was living on board an old schooner, so I began hunting through the second-hand shops and the antique shops on McAllister St. in San Francisco. I found myself six captain's chairs that were Navy surplus and scraped the

11 - Moving to Marin County—1948

ugly paint off the back spindles to reveal the handsome wood they were made of. Also, I had the good luck to run across an eight-foot long Navy mess table that had a raised lip along all its edges to keep plates from sliding off during heavy seas. Its legs were metal rods that folded up flat for storage. But the best find of all was a handsome cast-iron stove from the Victorian era that had an ornate dome-like hood to it, resembling the national capitol in Washington. To set the stove off, I became a temporary bricklayer and created a brick wall behind it and a raised hearth. There

had already been a small stove sitting there, so I didn't need to cut through the sloping eaves to have an outlet for the smoke. The stove got lots of attention from visitors and I had lots of offers to sell it if I ever wanted to. I also bought two twin beds that I had upholstered in a tomato red provincial fabric. These were placed in an L-shaped angle in front of the gleaming black stove. I hung ropes from the rafters on the Bay side of the room to hold bookshelves, beach flotsam and glass net

A friend poses by my elaborate Victorian woodstove.

At night, in this cozy small cabin, with the sound of waves lapping at the shore below me, I could drift off, soothed by the sea's rustling. It was sheer heaven and I ... was immersed in my new project to the point that I could blot out the recent break-up with Steve.

floats. At the north end of the room, by the spectacular view of the empty shoreline, I cut through a doorway, built a short staircase down to a new room that became my sleeping cabin. The double bunk was built into the wall and a simple Victorian dresser completed the maritime ambience. Oh, yes — I had found a round metal porthole so I incorporated that into the same wall facing over the beach. At night, in this cozy small cabin, with the sound of waves lapping at the shore below me, I could drift off, soothed by the sea's rustling. It was sheer heaven and I never wanted it to end. I was immersed in my new project to the point that I could blot out the recent break-up with Steve.

A talented sculptor, David Lemon and his wife had his home in the smaller building on the wharf. It must have been the quarters of the ships' crews in the early times. He had transformed it into a wood workshop where he created handsome totemic columns made of redwood and stained black. They stood on tall thin legs and somehow resembled abstract animals. I still have the one I traded with him for a painting, in my living room today.

David had planned to build himself a small catboat to sail around in but he was too immersed in his sculptural projects to ever complete his boat. I saw the shell of the hull propped against his wall and finally asked him if he had any plans for it. I really wanted to go sailing again since I was living on the edge of the Bay. I was told it was mine for a paltry sum. I began my third boat now; I was elated to think I would soon be skimming along the waves in this tiny craft. I was surprised to have Steve come help me taper the eighteen-foot long mast and the decking. We were still friends and felt no animosity, thank God. I was not willing to consider a re-union, I had learned a lesson from it and couldn't see how I could rekindle any real feelings again.

Lounging at a friend's house in Tiburon, a town nearby.

I was soon happily sailing in front of my Wharf, tacking back and forth with the gusty winds of Richardson's Bay. Across the other shore were Sausalito and its myriad collection of colorful houseboats. It was amazing to see the imagination that sea-loving denizens had used to invent wild, weird structures that floated and bobbed along the Marin Shores. Later, someone actually photographed these fantasies and printed a book to memorialize them. But the most colorful of all was the old derelict ferryboat that Jean Varda bought and turned into a studio and gallery. He was a Hungarian artist who created lovely collages out of paper and fabrics. They were unbelievably complex and colorful. He must have been quite successful because he bought a forty-foot vessel, added a blazing red sail to its wildly painted sides, and spent Sunday afternoons sailing past the docks of Sausa-

11 - Moving to Marin County—1948

lito. He always had more than enough people to sign on as crew because he provided as much cheap wine as they could take on. Sometimes, we would sit at tables on the dock of the old Municipal Pier which had been transformed into a restaurant with bar and cheer the drunks who came sailing past hanging from the rigging. It was a sight I have never forgotten.

I got in a lot of sailing as well, and on one occasion, when I was out solo, I tacked at the moment a gust hit the sail at the wrong angle and I went over — swamped. The boat lie on its port side and I was treading icy waters. Luckily for me, the Coast Guard cutter nearby saw what had happened. They keep a sharp eye out on weekends for foolhardy sailors. I was rescued along with my craft, which they towed to a dock. I was embarrassed but nothing was beyond repair.

The only drawback to this idyllic life as a wharf side bohemian, was that business of getting up and down that goat-path to the road up above. Everything had to be lugged on one's back but then I felt it was a small price to pay for the joy of living as I did. And I now had to commute into the City but even that had its compensations because I crossed over on the magnificent golden span of the Bridge that links Marin County to the rocky shores of San Francisco. I soon traded the big clunky Buick for a neat little British roadster, a Triumph model called the TR-3. It was azure blue with a white canvas hood, which I always kept folded back so I could savor the clouds and the sky.

I became the most popular destination for the weekend crowd looking for an unusual setting. I literally had to restrict who was to come over to visit because of the number of people I could accommodate. It became rather uncomfortable to realize that friends were bringing friends. I didn't

The Golden Gate Bridge enshrouded in fog. I now had to commute into the City but even that had its compensations because I crossed over the magnificent golden span of the Bridge that links Marin County to the rocky shores of San Francisco.

DEC. 4, 1949

By Chronicle Photographer Bob Campbell

This waterfront living area has a large dash of atmosphere

The Art of Living Is Demonstrated In an Old Belvedere Codfish Plant

By Alfred Kay

THE tattletale-gray buildings shown here are set in a right-angle between cliff and bay. One side is Marin county's Raccoon Strait; the other is part of the Belvedere peninsula, right where its terrain and its rents take an appreciable dip.

Inside the not promising exteriors, once a codfish plant, are eight apartments, filled with artists, sculptors, decorators and the like. And they are filled, too, with all the fine furnishings that have been dragged from the bay and/or a group of acute and gaudy imaginations.

You can see the old fish wharf if you want to take your eyes off the Waldo Grade traffic for a moment and look toward the right; or you can see it if you want to take your eyes off the preshrunk road that is wrapped around Belvedere and look straight down. And you can get a good closeup, too, if you want to wander down a steep trail, right through the signs and poison oak that collectively say: Keep Out.

The buildings look toward the west, catching the wind as it comes in the Gate and the sun as it goes out and down. And at night they catch and hold the reflection of lights on Sausalito's perimeter— shafts of light that lay flat across the water and are shattered only by an occasional small craft or an inquiring seal.

The persons in the foreground of the photographs, male and female, are highly desirable and highly talented tenants, a fact that has given rise to a rumor that only persons on speaking terms with a Muse are admitted for occupancy.

This is not true, of course, for the owners realize that even if you have no talent when you arrive, you soon will have. The view, the climate and the neighbors expect it of you.

But just as important to this area as art for a living, however, is living as an art. For, you see, these people and these buildings are bound together in a unique experiment in Bay Region life.

To explain how this evolved, it must be stated that the artists and sculptors were not the first tenants. Actually, original occupancy was divided between codfish and the men who dried, smoked and packed them. As men-

Continued on Page 8, Col. 5

11 - Moving to Marin County—1948

want to drive anyone away but it almost became embarrassing to restrict the numbers I would allow to come over. And then the San Francisco Chronicle got wind of this unusual living haven and ran a Sunday article with photos to tempt even more visitors. These three years I spent on the Codfish Wharf were to be the most romantically insane years of my life, as it turned out.

These three years I spent on the Codfish Wharf were to be the most romantically insane years of my life.

§

One of those friends who brought along a friend, was a handsome, boyish chap named Mike. He was interested in talking to me in a more private way and we found a moment or two to break away from the groups on the sundeck. It was a mutual attraction and we decided to see each other away from the crowd. We made plans for the following weekend and I suggested we would drive over the mountains to the seacoast to the west where we could be alone at Stinson Beach. That worked out beautifully and we started dating which evolved into a closer relationship. Mike and I then decided we were seriously involved. He moved in with me a month or two later and I could not have wished for a more perfect life. He was charming, witty and very talented as a photographer. He rode in to San Francisco daily with me to his job at a photographer's lab while I parked the car in North Beach and walked the last dozen blocks to my job at Roos-Atkins. We now entertained our hordes of visitors together on weekends, it was fun and we were supremely happy.

(facing page) Our Codfish Wharf living quarters was featured the in the San Francisco Chronicle in 1949. Our "Bohemian" life way actually predated the Beatniks, who began to group in SF a few years later.

Me and some of my gay buddies basking in the sun at Stinson Beach.

We devised a way of thwarting the weekend visitors by simply not being there. So we took to hopping in the little TR-3 and zipping across the flanks of Mount Tamalpais, enjoying the spiraling roads through the pine and eucalyptus clad slopes of this region. You came out of the forests to high cliffs looking out to the vast Pacific and around you the fields were colored purple from the lupine flower. Sometimes, we reversed our route and stopped on the way back as we passed through a section of the road where we knew other gay men lived. They were aptly called the Lavender Hill Mob since the lupine grew here so abundantly. Archi Bianchi, a retired Englishman, held court at his small cottage, supplying everyone with gin and tonics as you came out of his pool. Down at the Beach, we had our own special area where male couples would set-up their umbrellas and blankets. No stigma ever seemed to spoil this wonderful expanse of sea and sky; after all, Marin County had a reputation for tolerance — freedom from busybodies. We even had a roadside tavern a few blocks along the beach road where we could go to dance to a juke box while finishing off a couple of Buds. It was truly a paradise, and I relished every hour of it.

Mike and I grew closer and I even got to know his mother who lived in Alameda, next to Oakland. She was a sweet old lady, totally devoted to her son. Nothing was ever said about her son's sexual orientation although it was understood I was his partner. She seemed to accept the fact her son was happy regardless. But I began to notice something that gave me concern. Mike was writing to a dear friend who was an ensign in the Navy. I don't recall his name but he was stationed in Hawaii and the letters flowed back and forth regularly. I didn't see it as a threat to our friendship at first and hated to confront Mike about the need to write so often. A year and a half had gone by and then one evening, as we sat on the deck facing the setting sun, the phone rang. It was the Hawaiian friend who had just flown into San Francisco. Mike said he had to get over to the airport to pick him up. The TR-3 only held two passengers, so I let him go on his own as there would be luggage, of course. He seemed unusually excited and apprehensive as well. I was upset too, because I had a premonition that something was going to happen. And it did, of course. A couple of hours later, they returned and Mike started packing his bags. He was moving out! I could barely believe it was happening. He said he was sorry if I had been inconvenienced but this man was his lover from an

11 - Moving to Marin County—1948

earlier time — they called a cab as we spent an awkward half hour waiting for its arrival. I was in total shock and in my dazed mind, I even suggested it need not end, that we could work out a "ménage a trois." It was a desperate appeal that could never have worked but I was grasping at any straw. They said it wouldn't work and they were right, of course. It only works in novels or Noel Coward plays.

They hiked up the goat-path to wait for the cab and I buried my face in a pillow, too distraught to think about what had happened in the last three hours. My world had literally collapsed. I resolved that I wouldn't trust anyone, especially a gay man from this moment on. I didn't attempt to see Mike again for several years until I learned from friends that he was living with his mother in Alameda — minus the man from Hawaii. I called and asked if I could drop by and he agreed to see me. By then, I was living with someone else but I had gotten over my hurt and simply wanted to see him as an old friend. We had spent so many happy hours together. He greeted me at the door with a rather glum face and we sat and chatted for a brief half hour. I could sense he was not eager to renew a friendship gone sour and I didn't have the heart to ask him what had happened to his navy friend. Yesterday, I tried calling again, it has now been 45 years since I last saw him, and he is still listed at the same phone, his mother's, but I got the answering machine. I thought to myself, why am I doing this? Time has healed the hurt and I have moved on to a much stronger bond with someone else. But the heart doesn't forget — does it?

§

Some months later, I was offered a job at the venerable old "White House," one of San Francisco's best-known department stores. Raphael Weill, a Frenchman who arrived in the Gold Rush period when San Francisco was still called Yerba Buena, had founded it. Unlike the hordes of gold-crazed young men, who only stayed in the city long enough to provision themselves before heading east into the Sierra, Weill remained in town and set up a thriving business catering to the newly rich. It was a smart move and one that made him a wealthy man in a few months. While others impatiently sought out the golden veins in the mines and rivers, he was building a very profitable mercantile business. Now, in the 1950s, he had been long gone and his nephew Michel Weill was running the store. This elegant little

I buried my face in a pillow, too distraught to think about what had happened in the last three hours. My world had literally collapsed. I resolved that I wouldn't trust anyone, especially a gay man from this moment on.

Living Behind the Facade

(Above) "That new executive smile" as the Assistant Display Manager at the White House Department Sore.

(Below) At my designer's desk at the White House.

man still retained much of the family's French connections since he kept ties with his cousins in France and regularly flew to Paris on business and pleasure trips. The store had outgrown its limits and now occupied three adjoining buildings so that it had entrances on three streets, Post, Grant and Sutter.

I was hired as assistant display manager and was charged with doing all the designing for the windows and interiors. My boss was Lou Banks, a very talented man who also had trouble containing his wrath if things weren't going his way. He must have had the most inflated ego that I had ever had the misfortune to work under. However, I didn't know this when I came to work there, and I would soon become the object of his many tantrums. It didn't matter that I wasn't the real culprit — I was simply nearby. I endured the verbal abuse for some months because I loved the work itself.

During the Christmas season, we went to fantastic lengths to make the store as festive as possible. Since a store's financial health depends so heavily on the income generated in this six-week period, we were always competing with other stores to have the most eye-catching windows. Lou Banks came up with a definite winner, but one fraught with real risk as well. He convinced management to approve setting up a small ice-skating rink in our large corner window, which was positioned at Post and Grant. We figured that we could install a metal pan about fourteen by fourteen feet into the space. A contact with a local ice skating school was made and we had ourselves a cast of young skaters lined up to perform during the holiday period. It took some extra persuasion to get kids excused from classes as well—the busiest period for pedestrians being the noon hour, of course.

I got busy with arranging lots of snow banks, bare trees, a wintry landscape painted on the rear walls, we tied in some jingly, music with lots of bells and whistles and the children dressed in winter clothing. The look we were after was a living

11 - Moving to Marin County—1948

My display boss, Lou Banks, at the White House in an office that I designed for him. The painting, which seems to be hanging mid-air, is my work.

One of the ice skaters, a youth in his early teens, began to pay me a lot of extra attention. I soon realized that he was in the process of realizing he was gay!

Currier & Ives lithograph. It must have hit the right buttons, because people were standing three deep up against the glass as soon as they started hearing the Christmas carols being piped out to the sidewalks. We even worked out a simple little pantomime of a story to make it more endearing. But, being somewhat of a worrywart, I was preoccupied with the thought that all those skates whirling past the plate glass might not be a good idea. I talked the boss into installing a guardrail next to the glass after one week of sitting on the edge of my seat with apprehension. One of the ice skaters, a youth in his early teens, began to pay me a lot of extra attention. I soon realized that he was in the process of realizing he was gay! It became quite embarrassing to keep him at arm's length since he didn't have any idea that it was a no-no to get intimate with store personnel. He was a fantastic skater and we did-

The Christmas window ice skaters backstage at the White House.

The teen ice skater I had to keep at arm's length.

n't want to lose him. So I was advised to humor him as best I could but not encourage him. What an awkward spot I was in. And after the ice show closed, I had phone calls to deal with as well. I had never been the "object of someone's affections" in this most frustrating way before.

But Lou Banks was still a problem for me, as I endured his tirades even as I warned him to make them in the privacy of his office. But it didn't help to tell him anything; he would start shouting at me, anywhere or anytime. I decided to warn him that at the next outburst, I would simply walk out on the job. So for the next month or so, there was peace—until one day, as we were in an elevator with customers standing next to us, he suddenly couldn't control his anger about some mistake that he perceived as mine. He started in again with very embarrassing accusations about someone else's work habits. I held myself in check for a minute or two and then announced in as calm a voice as I could muster, "Okay,

11 - Moving to Marin County—1948

that's it, I am out of here for good."

Of course, I had made sure I had a safety net to land in. We had always had our carpentry jobs and painting chores done by an outside firm, the Gallagher Company. I knew that they would hire me in a minute if I were to leave the White House. And so, I marched up to the Executive offices, asked for the personnel Director and told her I had reached my limit of verbal abuse. She was very sympathetic but could hardly do more than listen. Lou Banks wasn't going to go anywhere, but I could go if I was unhappy.

The funny twist to all this was that Lou still needed a designer-draftsman since he couldn't "draw a straight line" as they always say. He couldn't wait to see who might want the job. I believe his reputation as a tyrant was getting some publicity as well. So, I was asked to still do the design work for the Display Department, but through the channels of the new job I now held with the Gallagher people. This meant that Lou Banks had to pay a premium for the same work he got out of me when he had me under his thumb. It was costing him almost double to get the same work! He tried looking around for a new assistant for a while and settled for the situation at hand. It was a supremely satisfying solution for me.

§

I now went to work for the Gallagher Company, which was a father and son operation with a team of carpenters to do all the construction. They had no designer on the premises since they were used to working on sketches submitted by the client. So now, with my arrival, they could add a new service in providing the drawings needed for the actual construction. I was to be the new cog in the machine and I enjoyed the freedom I was given to innovate. Since the father was ready to retire, the son, Ray was really running the operation. I had been working with Ray on past assignments, so we had a mutual respect for the cooperation involved. Ray was happy to have me aboard, he said, and he was well aware of the difficulty of working for Lou Banks at the White House.

§

This was a time when department stores gave the display department a much larger budget to work with because the theory seemed to indicate

(Continued on page 193)

(OVERLEAVES) CAVALCADE OF SOME OF MY MORE MEMORABLE WINDOW DISPLAYS AT THE WHITE HOUSE FROM THE EARLY 1950'S.

George Somers Display

11 - Moving to Marin County—1948

(FACING PAGE AND ABOVE)
SEVERAL OF MY AWARD WINNING WINDOWS AT THE
WHITE HOUSE THAT MADE THE COVER OF A MAGAZINE

George Somers Display

(Facing page, upper)
A Favorite Window Display of Mine,
Promoting Christian Dior Cosmetics

(Facing page, lower)
A Beachwear Window That was Much Admired

(Above)
One of My Fast Sketches Becomes A Backdrop Here

One of My Window Displays Featuring Fabric Yardage on Sale In the White House: A "Scissors Bird" Delivers Fabric to Her Chirping Babies. I Hoped It Would Catch Window-Shoppers Eyes!

George Somers Display

11 - Moving to Marin County—1948

A Window Featuring A Junior Miss Contest Winner

British Consulate General
2516 Pacific Avenue
San Francisco
California.

September 12, 1958.

Dear George,

    I enclose a set of photographs and a catalogue of the exhibits on the United Kingdom Stand at the California State Fair.

    Your design and dressage of the Stand was largely responsible for our receiving the first award and I should like to record our appreciation of your assistance. I hope that we may be able to cooperate in the future.

Yours sincerely,

P.V. Killick
H.B.M. Consul (Commercial)

Mr. George Somers
  The White House
    c/- Sutter and Grant Avenue
    San Francisco, California.

THE BRITISH CONSULATE SENDS ME A NICE CONGRATULATORY LETTER FOR A WINNING EXHIBIT I DID FOR THEM AT THE 1959 CALIFORNIA STATE FAIR. I WAS UNABLE TO LOCATE THE PHOTOS MENTIONED HERE FOR THIS BOOK.

George Somers Display

Our Old Spice window this year was setup to represent a father and son on a fishing outing. The boat and two figures were cutouts set atop a folding screen representing a cross-section of the sea. We had schools of fish impersonated by the various shapes of Old Spice bottles. Sonny has just caught a fish (or bottle) which he'll add to the string he's already caught. A large clam on the sea floor displays a varied assortment of Old Spice items. Tissue paper glued to the glass gave the illusion that you were looking thru water.
—1959 White House memo)

This is a photo of an award winning window I did for Old Spice. I never received the $500 award, which was apparently pocketed by my former boss at the White House, Lou Banks.

SHULTON, INC. • 630 FIFTH AVENUE • NEW YORK 20, NEW YORK

August 19, 1959

Mr. George Somers, Display Director
The White House
Sutter & Grant Avenue
San Francisco, California

Dear Mr. Somers:

The judges have made their final selections for the 1959 Old Spice Father's Day Display Contest. I am delighted to be able to tell you that you are once again a winner and were awarded 2nd Prize in the category of Department Stores in cities over 220,000 population.

Enclosed is your check for $500. A scroll acknowledging your achievement will be mailed at a later date. I am sure that you enjoyed excellent sales results from such a fine display of Old Spice for Men.

We are very gratified at the wide interest shown in our contest, and are particularly pleased with the outstanding quality of the entries. The judges found it difficult indeed to decide among the many hundreds of imaginative displays.

You may be interested in the enclosed list of winners in all categories.

Thank you for taking part in our contest, and I hope that we may count on having you with us again next year.

Cordially yours,

SHULTON, Inc.

Richard N. Parks
Vice President Sales

11 - Moving to Marin County—1948

(Continued from page 183)

that in order to draw customers physically into the store, you needed to entice them with very attractive windows. Display departments were a subdivision of the Advertising Department. With the arrival of shopping malls, the whole concept began to change since windows diminished in size and number. As more stores began to have branches in the malls, the budget grew smaller. Interior displays were given more attention and money but not up to the previous levels. As parking in downtown San Francisco became scarcer, and the malls proliferated out in the suburbs, there was little incentive for a housewife to shop in San Francisco. BART, our rapid transit system was built to lessen the problem but it didn't save the stores that began to close down. Only two or three giant corporations with ties to eastern chains were able to stay in business. Illustrious names like Liebes, Ransohoff's, Livingston's, J. Magnin's, Gump's, and I. Magnin's, all went out of business. Gump's, the most famous of them all, with a world-wide reputation, sold its name to a foreign company for a substantial sum and operates today in a fancier environment but doesn't live up to its fabulous beginnings as a store where you could find exquisite Oriental screens, jade and diamond necklaces or fine paintings. The store resembled a museum but here, if you had the means, you could walk out with the treasures.

§

I was still living on the Wharf, enjoying the salt air, greeting all the visitors even though Mike was no longer at my side. I missed him a lot but I wasn't going to grieve. I always felt that one had to reserve some of one's life force for the bad times. I was going through a grieving period but I kept it to myself as well as I could. There was no one to fill the nights with laughter or quiet talk. I wasn't giving up, however, life had been good and would be again, I vowed.

A new apprentice had been hired at Gallagher's at that time and I couldn't help but notice what a handsome youth he was. His name was Ray, who, at twenty-three, was in the prime moment of his life. There was something very attractive about him as he did his best to assimilate all the work habits of his mates in the carpenter crew. I was drawn to his natural elegance in the way he handled his work. Ray and I began to have conversations about art and I learned he had a very sensitive nature that he was trying to hide. I

(FACING PAGE)
A FASHION SHOW WITH PRETTY MODELS WEARING OUR GARMENTS, BUT I SEEM TO BE MORE INTERESTED IN CHATTING WITH ONE OF MY BOSSES!

wondered what else he might be trying to hide and so I started to share my lunch hours with him. We would carry our bag lunches outside to the street, sit on crates and ogle the passing shoppers. Ray was attractive enough to have swept most girls off their feet. But I began to have another sense of him that I was interested in pursuing. It was time to test his reaction to girls. So, as they would pass us, I would comment on the luscious curve of a breast or a lovely face. I noticed that his comments, if he even made one, were rather mild. He never initiated a comment on the passing parade and I began to wonder if he wasn't interested in women.

After going through the same routine a few more days, I decided it was time to take the next step. He had been hearing about my unusual living situation, and so I invited him out for the weekend. He readily accepted the invitation to come out and I was excited and apprehensive as well. I was not sure of his interest in me although by now, I was hoping he would be friendly enough.

I went through extra care with the supper: candles, flowers, a good wine (he was Italian after all). Afterwards, we sat on the sundeck, a necklace of lights strung along the Sausalito hills to the west. Finally, it was time to retire. I gave him a choice of sleeping in the living room on one of the two twin beds that formed an L-shape around the iron stove, or he could share my ship's cabin bunk. I tried to be as casual as possible, but when he said he would bunk in with me, I was thrilled. He had made the right choice.

We talked for a while, lying close to one another, barely touching the other. And when I placed my hand on his stomach, it was wet. He had exploded. I could hardly believe what had happened. This had been his first experience with another man! We began a relationship that was beautiful in all its ramifications. He had no sexual history, which was hard to believe for me when I assessed his natural sensuousness. I had a lot to teach this most willing pupil for the next few weeks and then he agreed to move in with me. Nothing was to be said at work, and his address would still be his parents' home in a nearby town.

It was to be the only time in my life that I had met and

11 - Moving to Marin County—1948

brought a man "out" not only to himself but also to the gay world. I wondered if I had done the right thing. But Ray hadn't hesitated a moment, and I felt reassured that it was right.

Ray's very Italian family had a home down the Peninsula in Redwood City. This area now is famous as Silicon Valley, the home of the electronics industry. Today, young people willing to gamble start enterprises at the drop of a hat, and who hasn't heard of the "dot comers" and their roller coaster ride to success and failure. But at the time of this story, Redwood City was still a bedroom community some twenty-five miles south of San Francisco. Ray was expected to spend the week-end at home, at least every other week and although I had mixed feelings about going down to stay there, I decided it would look strange if I didn't. I was glad I did when I was welcomed into the arms of the family very naturally. Ray only had a twin bed in his bedroom, and I was to occupy it with him whenever I came down—with no questions asked. The folks never asked any probing questions, they simply accepted what their handsome son wanted for himself. He could do no wrong, it seemed.

At Stinson Beach, age 36.

§

Life on the Wharf went smoothly for us for a couple of years. We entertained weekend guests, went sailing, sometimes took the spectacular drive over Tamalpais to Stinson beach and enjoyed just being together. We were well aware that it was too idyllic to last much longer. The Allen's mentioned often enough that sooner or later, they would raze the entire complex so that they could build their million dollar homes to sell at a huge profit. Ray and I started talking about buying a small house somewhere in the Marin hills. He started searching through the classified

ads and found some attractive offers. His parents had planned to give him several thousand dollars when he brought home a bride. It was to be a wedding present and reflected their Italian heritage. Ray expected to split the cost of the home purchase with me with this money. He was to discover that they didn't look on our love for each other as more than a dalliance, and he would need to marry a woman to claim his wedding present. I decided I would foot the bill myself when the time came to sign any deed.

Life was going along very smoothly and then I made a huge blunder. We had invited over a mutual friend who was a very attractive guy. As the catboat only held two people, it was decided that I would take the boat out with the friend and Ray would remain behind with the other guests. As the friend and I tacked back and forth across the Sausalito waterfront, I innocently flirted with him but didn't touch him sexually. I thought nothing of it at the time, but it was reported back to Ray in a blown-up version. Ray couldn't believe I had violated his trust in me. I protested how innocent it had all been but he wasn't to be placated. This was his first love affair and I had committed the unpardonable sin. In the gay world, just as in the straight world, a minor slip of this nature might be forgiven but I had forgotten that Ray was so new to the temptations of the flesh. He was so devastated that he simply decided to move out then and there. It was finished. I was very upset but felt guilty as well. I had not lost my love for Ray. He was gone in another two miserable days in spite of my pleading.

Life was going along very smoothly and then I made a huge blunder. We had invited over a mutual friend who was a very attractive guy ... I innocently flirted with him but didn't touch him sexually.

§

It was also a catastrophic moment for me in another way. It had started to be a very wet winter and the hillside we used to get down to the Wharf had begun to show ominous signs of movement. Like a slow moving glacier, the ground was beginning to give way. You couldn't see the movement, but the pilings beneath the Wharf were beginning to tilt out from the vertical. I knew we were doomed; it would probably take another two or three weeks before the collapse. Strangely enough, the Tank house was

11 - Moving to Marin County—1948

on another support system, because it must have been constructed somewhat later than the main wharf. It sat on enormous concrete pylons that could withstand earth movement. However, it would mean cutting a new path down the hill through sifting rubble and putting in a gangplank to the Tank house. The goat-path became more and more dangerous to descend, so a long length of Manila rope was draped down the entire hill and this gave one a more secure foothold on the disappearing path. I was having difficulty carrying a bag of groceries with one hand and clinging to the rope with the other.

As Ray had moved at the beginning of all this mess, I decided I should get out as well. Life on the Wharf was at an end. I was in very low spirits with my own indiscretion and with Nature's way of punishing me.

§

Ray had seen an ad for a small cottage on a hill in Larkspur, a town not more than ten miles from where I was on Belvedere. I had gone over on my own to check it out and decided I could do it on my own. It was to be my first own home, the end of renting from others and that had tremendous appeal to me. I signed the deed papers shortly.

I now had to figure how I was going to get my furniture out of the Tank house and over to Larkspur. The hill path was impossible, which left the only option of moving my stuff would be by water. I asked my neighbor, David Lemon if he had contacts in the Sausalito waterfront people. He knew an old sea dog that was eager to make a buck and he had a broken down launch big enough to haul my stuff. I sold my beautiful ship's mess table to a friend since it was too big to fit into the new house, but I kept almost everything else. The cast iron stove was my prize item and I would have gone down "a la Titanic" rather than part with it. I found a truck driver who would pick up everything on the Sausalito pier and deliver the load to the new cottage. Steve and two or three others came to my rescue for the strong-arm stuff and we got everything up the hillside on those 98 steps.

Life on the Wharf was at an end. I was in very low spirits with my own indiscretion and with Nature's way of punishing me.

12
The House In Larkspur

1955 - 1965

"One of my reasons for choosing my hillside cottage was that I had a couple of friends - girl friends - living down in this colorful community of houseboats. These two young ladies were my first lesbian friends and I adored them. They were totally unpretentious, said what was on their minds on any topic, and opened up a new world to me that I had barely known about." - GS

§

George moves from bayside to the forested hills of Marin county overlooking the Bay. I, by now, have been born and am old enough to meet my uncle. He invites me to stay once a year when I was out of school. He tells me he is gay and introduces me to his gay friends. I get my first glimpse as a 12 year old of life behind the façade. - JJ

THE HOUSE IN LARKSPUR: 1955 - 1965

Now I had the opposite task in getting to my house. Instead of going down a goat-path to my home, I had to climb those rickety steps up to my home. I vowed that I would tear them out and replace them with new sturdy ones as my first task. I also regarded the steps as my ultimate workout machine. The Stairmaster system hadn't been thought of just yet but I could have endorsed the idea if anyone had asked. I got my daily workout as I ran up those damn steps.

A gnarled old buckeye tree, straight out of a Japanese wood-block print, was directly in front of the house so that I looked through its branches festooned with apple-sized nuts, to enjoy the stunning view of the valley below. It was a flat, alluvial plain, with a meandering creek winding its way to the nearby Bay to the east. Along its banks, there were some two dozen old houseboats that would never go traveling again. They would have collapsed if anyone would have thought of moving their fragile sides. When they had first arrived, they were probably weekend retreats for San Franciscans of the early 1900s. Now, they were the weeklong homes of some very colorful folk that pre-dated the "hippies" that arrived in the late 60s.

One of my reasons for choosing my hillside cottage was that I had a couple of friends — girl friends — living down in this colorful community of houseboats. I had met Gail and Eve as friends of friends brought along on those very social Wharf side weekends. As they had bought one of these houseboats some time before I had decided to come to Larkspur, I already had a feel for the town and its atmosphere. I loved going down the rickety gangplank path to their very well-kept house tied up at the creek's edge. They had a spacious deck where we would sit and look out over the marshy waters with wild ducks and long-necked her-

> *One of my reasons for choosing my hillside cottage was that I had a couple of friends — girl friends — living down in this colorful community of houseboats.*

12 - The House In Larkspur—1955

ons stalking small fish along its shallows. It was a bit of heaven. I also had access to their rowboat if I wanted to get in some exercise. These two young ladies were my first lesbian friends and I adored them. They were totally unpretentious, said what was on their minds on any topic and opened up a new world to me that I had barely known about. Occasionally, if they or I needed an escort for some social function, we would call each other. The straight world was none the wiser, we figured, in seeing us paired that way.

A few years later, into this warm, caring friendship with them, Eve and I even discussed the idea of marriage for us. She was the most mature of the pair. We talked about it now and then but came to the conclusion that it would be tricky to pull off since there was the question of how Gail would fit into the living arrangement. Besides, it was such a denial of our true selves that we simply couldn't pull it off. We didn't like the idea of fooling people. We remained the best of friends for many years.

Along the bottom of my own hillside, bordering the road ran the old rusty railroad tracks long since abandoned. A block past my hill stairs, there was a handsome old Victorian stationhouse where the railroad ended. In the 1890s, week-enders would take the ferryboats to Sausalito, board the rail-line there to Larkspur or several other towns nearby. They would spend their weekends at cottages like mine or perhaps bring picnic baskets along for the day.

I had bought my house from an elderly couple that had grown too frail to cope with the rigors of climbing that endless staircase. They were asking

These two young ladies were my first lesbian friends and I adored them. They were totally unpretentious, said what was on their minds on any topic, and opened up a new world to me that I had barely known about.

Gay friends, Marin County, including Eve *(far left)*, the girl I almost married.

$3200 for the place and even in 1955 that was a great bargain. Of course, it wasn't a show place as it was, but I relished the idea of changing it to my taste. I also needed to immerse myself totally in a big project to keep myself from thinking of the recent breakup with Ray. I started planning with a vengeance.

Ray came over quite a few times to help me in the initial phase but although we were still friends, I didn't encourage a renewal of our bond.

The house was a tiny 850 square feet in its dimensions, but it had a living room 12 by 16 feet in size with two bedrooms, a small kitchen and bathroom. A rickety sundeck was tacked onto the front, which I soon replaced with a sturdier one. Since I was on a steep hillside, there was little room for a garden and then I began to see

> *I also needed to immerse myself totally in a big project to keep myself from thinking of the recent breakup with Ray. I started planning with a vengeance.*

At front of Larkspur house before remodeling; Ray, at left, came several times to help though I didn't encourage a renewal of our relationship.

deer along the backspaces, which I had hoped to convert into a small patio. I was warned that I would need to put up eight-foot high fences to keep them out, so I gave up on that idea. I wisely opted for the freedom of the deer to roam where they had always lived.

I started by ripping down the plaster and lathe ceiling of the living room, which eliminated the attic but gave me a soaring space of 16 feet at its apex; I kept the eight-foot ceilings in tact in the rest of the house. I had to beef up the rafters with one by six planks because the old rafters had sagged somewhat. I added a brick wall at one end, taking care to provide plenty of support under the house to handle the extra weight. I wanted my handsome Victorian stove to have a proper background. On the side of the living room facing out over the view, the original builders had placed a small three-by-three foot window totally inadequate for the

12 - The House In Larkspur—1955

magnificent view that lie there. It only proved to me that the concept of relishing a view was a contemporary idea. Victorians must have lived their lives in dark, shadowy interiors. And I was to go all the way with the idea of sunlight coming in – for I tore out the entire wall, all sixteen feet of it and replaced it with glass. The panes were six feet tall and at the bottom and top were smaller panels, which slid in tracks so that I could let in fresh air. I was aiming for a Japanese feel to remind myself of that lovely little home in Japan where I had visited the Hayasaki family. I gave the dining room area the same treatment, adding a glass corner wall there. I wanted to bring as much of the outdoors in as possible. Now I would see the deer as they fed on the hillside. It was a total transformation and I could hardly believe I hard started out with a gloomy little cottage.

The 98 steps I ran daily as my "Stair-Master" to get to my front door.

A few years later, I added a rental unit below as there was ample room to convert the useless storage space to a studio apartment. I only had to do some minor excavating to create ample headroom. I called in a plumber and an electrician to do tasks I felt unqualified to perform. As soon as I advertised the studio, I had single men eager to move in. It augmented my income nicely and was worth the effort I had expended. I made sure that my tenants were always gay men since I wanted no rude surprises to deal with in the future.

§

And so I lived on my beautiful hillside for some twelve years, meeting a lot of men, and trying to establish new relationships. Most of them were disasters and would last a few months at best.

One of them that held great promise was with a man I met on a vacation trip to visit the family in San Diego. I met Bert at La Jolla one Sunday and we were immediately attracted to one another. I only had a couple of days to know him and I learned he was living with another man that he wanted to leave. They had grown apart and Bert was eager to get as far away from him as he could. We started a correspondence that kept that promise alive for a couple of years. He came up with little more than a suitcase and moved in. It lasted a week before he returned south again. I was totally blown away by the speed that it was over and never understood him for he continued to write and say how much he loved me. I received cards at birthdays and Christmas for the next ten years, which baffled me. It seemed as if he could only love someone from a distance.

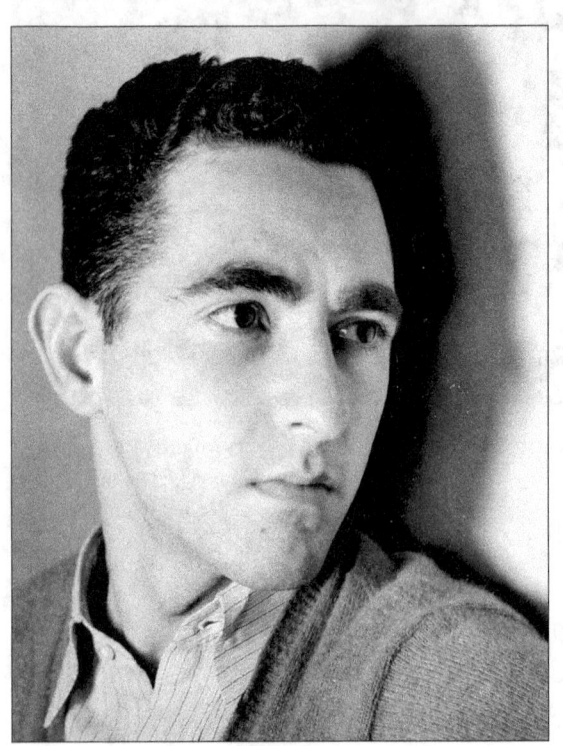

At 41

There were others who shared the house with me. One fellow I had met who also worked at the White House started out promisingly but he was so insanely jealous of anyone I knew that life became intolerable. I couldn't so much as talk to anyone without his getting upset. He was so insecure and clinging that I finally asked him to leave and that proved to be a horrendous moment. I vowed to stay away from any one that could make life so inhibiting. My own nature was to be free and inclusive, I hated having to watch my every interaction with friends. I wasn't being in the least promiscuous, so I felt as if I was bound in invisible chains. I breathed easier when he left and I came to the conclusion that I could not have loved him, perhaps it had really been a fear of being alone.

I didn't live alone for long, as it turned out. There always seemed to be friends that were looking for a place to live and my home must have had a certain appeal. It had evolved with my interests in Oriental art. I came across a magnificent six-panel screen depicting a mountain landscape in a downtown gallery in San

One fellow I had met who also worked at the White House started out promisingly but he was so insanely jealous of anyone I knew that life became intolerable ... my own nature was to be free and inclusive.

12 - The House In Larkspur—1955

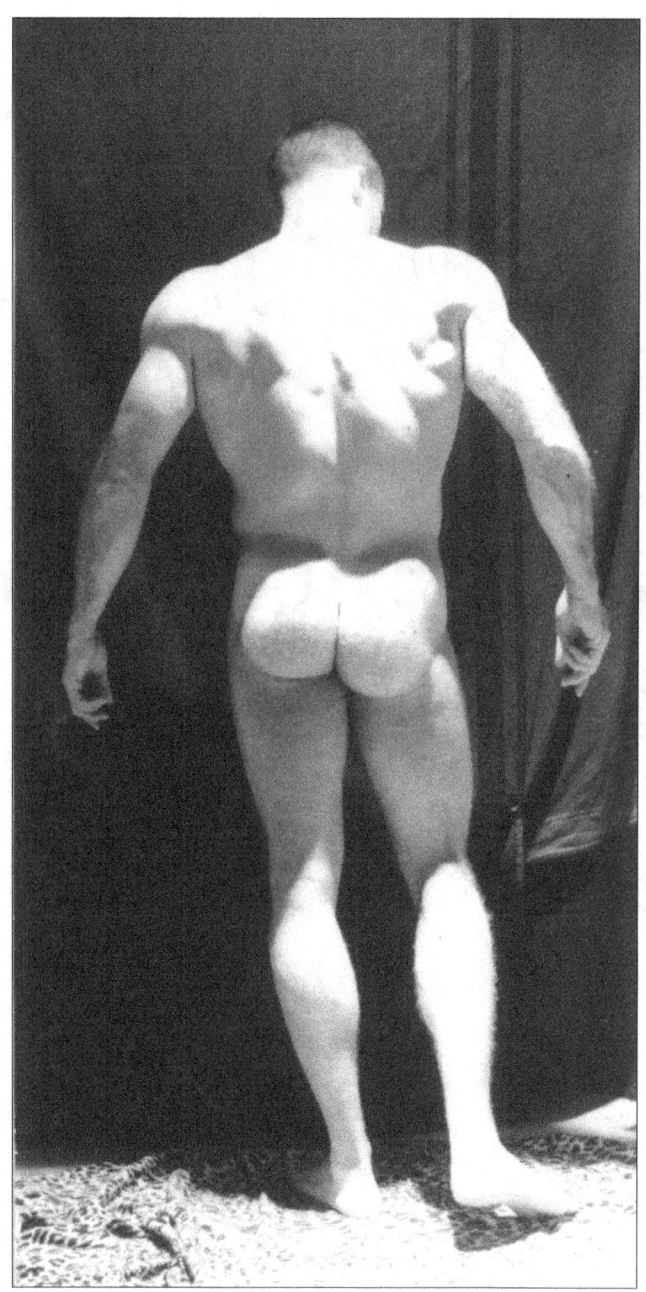

"Nude Study"   George Somers

(OVERLEAF)
THE NUDE MALE PHOTOS ON THIS AND THE FOLLOWING PAGES WERE TAKEN FOR TWO MAIN REASONS: THE MEN WHO POSED FOR ME WERE FRIENDS WHO WORKED OUT IN GYMS AND WANTED TO SEE A RECORD OF THEIR PROGRESS—
GAY MEN BEING RATHER VAIN ABOUT THEIR BODIES WHILE YOUNG. I ADMIRED THE FLUID GRACE OF THEIR PHYSIQUES AND, PERHAPS A BIT AHEAD OF THE TIMES, I WANTED TO PRESERVE THIS BEAUTY FOR POSTERITY. TODAY, THERE ARE DOZENS OF MALE PHOTO BOOKS AVAILABLE IN GAY-ORIENTED BOOKSTORES.

§

PHOTOS TAKEN 1955-1965
LARKSPUR HOUSE

"Nude Study"   George Somers

12 - The House In Larkspur—1955

"Nude Study"   George Somers

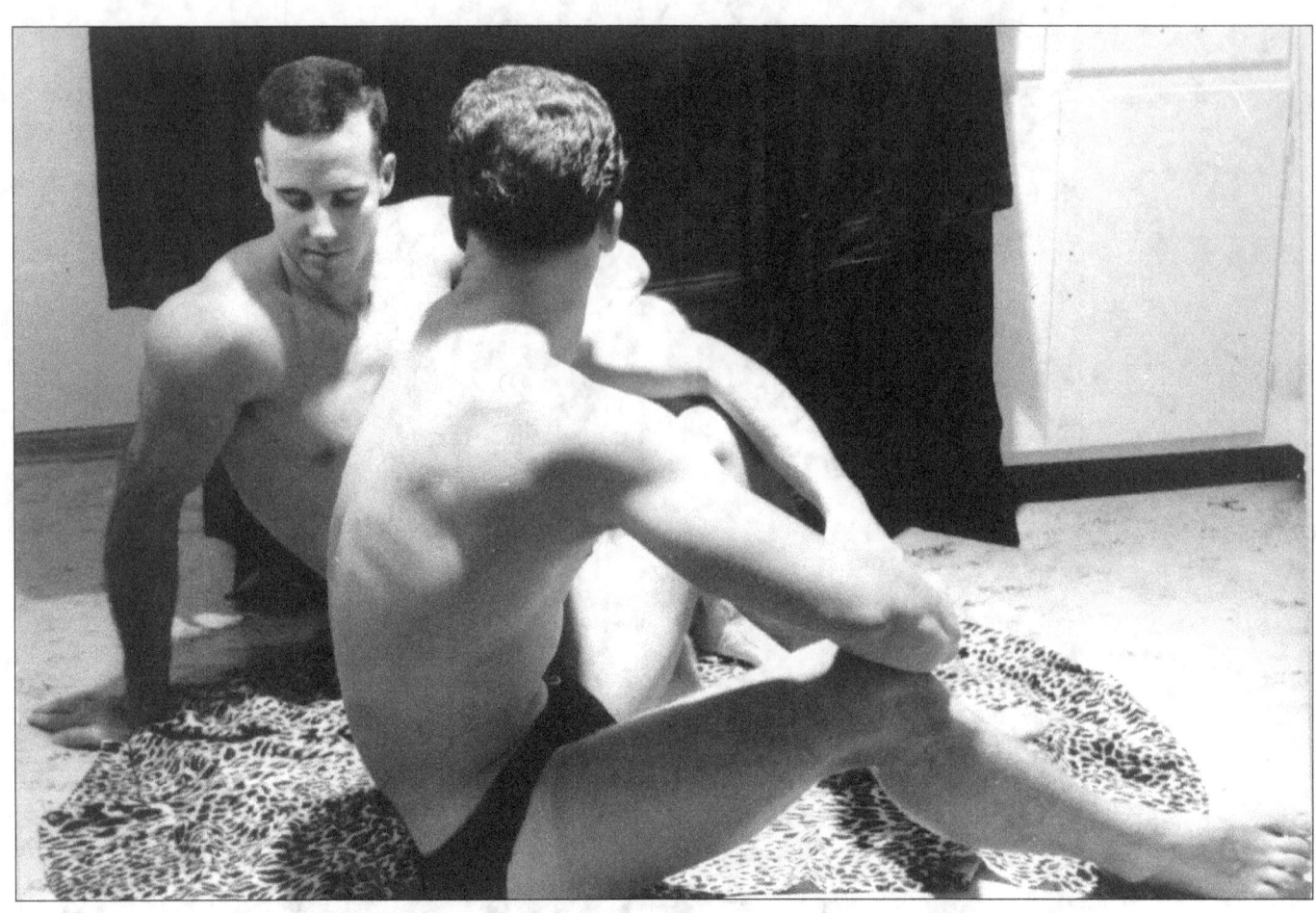
"Nude Study" George Somers

12 - The House In Larkspur—1955

Francisco. It was way beyond my financial means at the time but I felt so strongly about owning it that I went into a huddle with the store proprietor. We came to a reasonable plan where I would make payments over the next six months and I could take it home halfway through the payments. The screen was hard to pin down as to origins. The calligraphy in the upper right corner was not Japanese or Chinese, as I couldn't get acquaintances of those countries to read the text. I concluded that it was in Korean. To this day, some forty-five years later, it is the focal point of my living room's Eastern ambience. I love feeling myself entering its mountain paths and glades, past shimmering waterfalls and gnarled old pines. Down below, a long narrow boat glides along the river, creating lazy ripples as it passes a sculpted rock.

The gorgeous Oriental screen I bought before I could afford it.

I even decided I would rather build my own living room furniture than buy the junk I saw in stores. I was happier controlling the clean, simple lines I was after. Besides, it was less expensive! But I couldn't build my dining table since I wanted a table that did double duty. I wanted a Danish modern table that folded up into a card table for general use but could be opened up to three by six feet if I had several guests. It was very satisfying to say I had designed and built most of my furnishings. My walls were adorned with my own artwork as well.

§

Since I was now living on the lower slopes of Mount Tamalpais, I was spending my Sundays at Stinson Beach with friends I was making in Marin County. Tamalpais was the Indian name of a maiden in a legend told by the Pomo people who once lived here. The mountain's profile from a distance has an eerie resemblance to that of a female body's outline. She is said to be sleeping for all eternity because of some spell cast on her. It was all so romantic. And up into its beautiful winding roads, there was the Mountain amphitheater built of stone in the Greek fashion. The backdrop was the entire panorama of the Bay scintillating below. Every two years or so, the Mountain Play association would put on a spectacle of a play which fitted well with the mountain's scenic beauty [SEE FOLLOWING PAGES]. I signed up a couple of years as an extra and was transformed into one of the Kubla Khan's warriors in the Mongol court. Marco Polo came to visit this sumptuous setting. It is a shame that these extravagant productions no longer attract a big enough audience to make it profitable.

Manchurian warriors surround me at the Tamalpais Mountain Production.

But I was putting on a show of my own on a smaller scale during those Marin years. I gave three costume parties spread out over the twelve years I lived on my mountainside.

The first one had a Greek theme because I figured that borrowing a white bed sheet was so simple. The addition of sandals and a laurel headband turned you into Sophocles or Plato. Of course, those that were more daring chose to come as satyrs, which practically eliminated any costume at all. I stripped the living room of all wall décor and stretched a display paper, which comes in eight-foot wide rolls, over the entire walls. I painted black silhouettes of prancing dancers on this white expanse. I had looked at photos of Greek vases for my inspiration. Outside on the deck overlooking the view, I constructed a life-size image of a Greek athlete out of plywood. I passed the garden hose through his pubic area to create a working

But I was putting on a show of my own on a smaller scale during those Marin years. I gave three costume parties spread out over the twelve years I lived on my mountainside.

12 - The House In Larkspur—1955

My Roman party at the Larkspur House.

stream of water that cascaded down the hill. It was a hit with the crowd. I apologized that it couldn't be champagne.

Then, a few years later, I chose the 1920s, the Flapper Era for my theme. Everyone was asked to come in drag or as the Boy Friend with slicked down hair, wide bottomed pants and argyle sweaters. I drew John Held, Jr., cartoon figures on the invitations to inspire friends for their costumes. It was a great success and people even arrived with their own chrome cocktail shakers. It was all-straight out of the Great Gatsby and the Fitzgerald's world.

Everyone was asked to come in drag or as the Boy Friend with slicked down hair, wide-bottomed pants and argyle sweaters.

(Continued on page 214)

(OVERLEAF)
MT. TAMALPAIS AMPHITHEATER
§

The leading lady, a Manchurian princess from our Tamalpais Mt. Production.

The Tamalpais Amphitheater with Sausalito and San Francisco Bay in the distance.

(Continued from page 211)

The last time I gave one of these elaborate parties (*facing page*), I chose a South Pacific theme because the Musical had been in town recently and everyone was going native whenever possible. People were coming as beachcombers, sea captains, castaways or hula girls. It was a riot. In fact, I was flabbergasted to find some guests who drove up from Hollywood had brought me a birthday present — a very alive one in the shape of a blond youth who said he was mine for the evening. I could hardly turn down the gift, could I?

§

Although I was leading a very active social life at this point, I somehow couldn't seem to meet the elusive gent known as Mr. Right until the moment I met dashing Arturo. He arrived as a guest with an old friend. It always seemed that anyone I became serious about I had to meet through some friend. I was never any good at just barging up to a stranger and saying something irrational. Anyway, Arturo and I felt an instant rapport with each other. He was good-looking, tall, young, and just foreign enough to be very intriguing. He still had a pronounced accent although he had been in the U.S. for some three years. He was from the Amalfi coastline of Italy. He was fiery in temperament, and given to extremes of joy or despair: I never knew which it would be next. I seemed his opposite with my calm, laid-back way of dealing with people or problems. How could two people of such contrasting temperaments ever get along? But somehow, we did, for a couple of years, as it turned out.

Arturo had met some well-to-do family traveling in Italy and they had sponsored his coming to America, offering him employment. He had become their "go-fer" guy. He not only went on errands, but also did housework and even prepared meals. The wealthy family lived in the very posh neighborhood of Pacific Heights. You needed to have "arrived" to live in this enclave of sumptuous homes and world embassies. The family even kept a couple of horses stabled in Golden Gate Park nearby. They thought enough of Arturo to give him one of the horses, although I al-

12 - The House In Larkspur—1955

The invite to my 1920's flapper party.

"Beach combers" bash at my Larkspur house.

ways suspected he was putting me on about the gift. His horse was named Bourbon, because that was his color. In the midst of a very busy work schedule, Arturo still managed to find time to take his horse for a canter along the bridle paths of the Park. I was invited along a few times and on one occasion, when my horse was spooked by something in the path, perhaps a squirrel, he reared back violently and I tumbled off, landing hard. I lay there gasping for air for a few seconds. I had never been through such a wrenching moment trying to breathe. Somehow, my lungs had been deflated of any oxygen — and it gave me a ghastly feeling of having just been hanged from a noose in an execution. I was a bit more apprehensive about accepting these rides through the Park.

But there's always a fly in the ointment: Arturo didn't like having to come all the way out to Larkspur to be with me. I can't say that I blamed him, as it was awkward since he seldom could borrow a car from his employers and they always seemed to have endless tasks to take care of. You could say he was an indentured servant just as so many Europeans had endured the trip to the States in Colonial times. The times had changed but the idea hadn't.

Arturo, the boy from Italy who drove me crazy.

Arturo started talking about returning to Italy and my going there as well to live and work. We would open a small restaurant on the edge of the cliffs overlooking the sea, he would be the chef and I would handle the financial end. It all had such a romantic sound and I had visited Italy already on vacation trips. I had loved the ambience, the air, color and the people enough to seriously consider pulling up stakes for good. I sweated out the pros and cons of it all for some weeks before deciding it was simply too risky. I was too unfamiliar with Italian law and my rights as a new citizen there. Would I get hassled by the Mafia to be able to start a café? Too many other questions preyed on my conscience as well. What if he ended the relationship abruptly and I, as a foreigner with little grasp on the lan-

My Italian partner, Arturo, at the horse stables in Golden Gate Park.

guage, all of a sudden had to deal with the basics of life?

Then, Arturo began a new campaign, this time it was to be adopted. I was to legally declare him my son! He was some twenty years younger than I after all and it didn't seem strange to him in the least. I had always known that European gay couples were apt to evolve into these "May and December" combinations. I was talked into going down to the Immigration offices in San Francisco where we talked to a smirking executive who was determined to embarrass the two of us with prying questions about our sexual relations. I soon enough had my fill of this interview and stormed out of his office. The idea was abandoned and I never let it come up again.

But there was still the question of Arturo's reluctance to come the distance to be with me. He started a new campaign to have me move into San Francisco. As much as I loved the country life I led, I still loved the City across the bridge and was still commuting daily to my job downtown. Most of our friends were in the City, of course. And so, somewhat sadly, I began to consider the idea of selling the Larkspur house and finding a new home in San Francisco. This time, I meant to own my home rather than go back to the ridiculous paying of rent, which I had always disliked. And after some fifteen years of living in Marin in two different homes, I was ready to come back. Commuting would not be my daily problem. In those days, it wasn't the horrendous bore that it is today for the extra hundreds of thousands that daily crawl across the Golden Gate span to arrive in a metropolis that has never had adequate parking space for the hordes that arrive each day. I am deeply grateful that my working career was over before this period began. I hear about "road rage" a lot these days and it doesn't surprise me in the least. There seems to be a national apathy about finding solutions. There are just too many of us, it seems. Are we going to limit the influx of workers into cities? No — that's undemocratic. Are we going to limit the number of children born? No, again — we do not live in a fascist state.

Sometimes it crosses my mind that Nature had a way of dealing with the population problem by assigning a certain group of folks who would-

12 - The House In Larkspur—1955

n't procreate. Their job would be to create beauty: Art, Music, Literature — these works would be their children. It sounded like a great concept but I am sure someone could punch a hole in it. Still, if folks didn't try to stifle their neighbors, allowed them to be who they really were instead of insisting we all be alike, wouldn't it be a more pleasant world?

And so, I began the search for a new home in that most fascinating of cities, my San Francisco, with all its colorful neighborhoods and peoples.

13

The Bush Street House

1966 - 1968

"It was at this point, in 1966, with the Vietnam War raging, the beginning of the Hippy movement, and the widespread anger and confusion of our youth at Society, that I was to find my new home on Bush Street, one half a block off Fillmore." - GS

§

I was disappointed to learn that George gave up his quaint hillside home in Marin County. But his move into SF was otherwise an upgrade for his work and social life. It was here also that I moved in with George while going to college in the City by the Bay, and now living with gay men 24/7 before being drafted into the Army in late 1967. - JJ

THE BUSH STREET HOUSE: 1966 - 1968

I began by contacting a young gay friend who was a real estate agent as I felt he would be more apt to be honest with me. I was later to regret this naïve assumption but I will talk of that later.

Since Arturo was employed at the mansion in Pacific Heights, it made sense to look for a house near that area. I had always admired the profusion of fine old Victorians that filled the streets just a few blocks south of Pacific Heights. I wanted something more authentically pre-earthquake of 1906 than the less elegant structures that one saw in the North Beach neighborhoods. My cottage in Marin County had escalated in value after all the renovations I had made to it. You might remember I had paid $3,200 for it and now some twelve years later, I was being offered $30,000 for it. Not a bad return on one's money but then I had poured a lot of sweat equity into the place. It seemed that the lessons that I had learned from Ruth during my college days had paid off handsomely. Bless her heart, I was never to see her again, we do move on through our lives acquiring new friends and losing old ones, sadly.

I concentrated my house search to the Fillmore Street area, which bordered the posh Pacific Heights neighborhood. Fillmore had become San Francisco's main shopping street directly after the disastrous 1906 earthquake-fire, simply because it was lucky to ride unscathed through the disaster. Most of the handsome old Victorian homes were surprisingly intact. But they had sadly fallen into neglect because less affluent families had moved in. There was a great mixture of Japanese, Jewish and Black people, all working and coexisting in harmony. But the City Fathers were ashamed of the rundown ambience of the area and came up with city referendums that managed to be approved. This created a jurisdiction or board that was called the Western

I concentrated my house search to the Fillmore Street area ... there was a great mixture of Japanese, Jewish and Black people, all working and coexisting in harmony.

13 - The Bush Street House—1966

Addition Redevelopment Agency that could restructure the several dozens of blocks that centered on Fillmore Street. They started by giving out eviction notices to all the poor families but failed to provide any shelter for them. They were promised the new housing would include low-rent units but, that until these were built, they had to fend for themselves. It all seemed terribly unfair. There were countless public meetings where officials defended their stand against shouting, angry residents—but in the end, they were ousted from their homes anyway. The City used the rule of "eminent domain" to justify what it was doing. The wholesale bulldozing of acres of buildings proceeded with mounting resentment from the former tenants.

It was at this point, in 1966, with the Vietnam War raging, the beginning of the Hippy movement, and the widespread anger and confusion of our youth at Society, that I was to find my new home on Bush Street, one half a block off Fillmore. The asking price was $40,000, I offered 35,000 and was told it was mine. Since I was getting $30,000 for my Marin home, I practically owned my new home already. My gay real estate man didn't seem to think it important that I was just inside the border of the Agency's jurisdiction. If I had bought across the street, I would have been outside the borders.

The three-story home was in the Italianate Victorian style, which predated the very overly ornamented Stick Eastlake Style, the latter coming into vogue a few years later. I loved the more austere, simple façade of my building and was advised to make a call to the Water Department if I was curious to know the year it had been built. It was a matter of public record as to when the water had been turned on — mine had been turned on in 1875! On either side of me, there were identical structures separated by driveways. This is considered a great plus since it meant that the original owners were expected to have horse and buggies to park in horse barns in the rear gardens. At the end of the Row houses, there ran a little side street called a mews in England where the small cottages could take care of the servants who were employed in the six great buildings. I noticed I had a garden cottage sitting in the rear wasn't too well built but could bring in extra dollars as a rental and it was already occupied by a bachelor. Then the lowest floor, which appeared from the

It was at this point, in 1966, with the Vietnam War raging, the beginning of the Hippy movement, and the widespread anger and confusion of our youth at Society, that I was to find my new home on Bush Street, one half a block off Fillmore.

13 - The Bush Street House—1966

front to be a basement — but wasn't since the slope of the land was steep enough that it had windows on three sides — was also a rental. It had originally been the kitchen, storage rooms, and pantry and catchall area for the family upstairs. That area was also already a rental. Which meant I had income from two units on the property. That was certainly help in augmenting my income.

Arturo seemed delighted — and why shouldn't he be? — now within walking distance of his job at the mansion, he loved the faded elegance of the neighborhood and the house itself. There were three marble mantelpieces, and the ceilings on the main floor were a lofty twelve feet. The bedroom floor had ten-foot ceilings. Although the façade of the building was flat with well-proportioned window frames, the traditional San Francisco trademark, the Bay Window, was placed at the back wall looking into the rear garden. I thought this a better solution to privacy concerns anyway. The two large rooms, which were connected by ceiling high sliding doors, were the parlor and dining room, each with their own fireplace. Off the dining room rear wall, we had this handsome alcove of three bay windows. The small kitchen just outside the dining room must have been a pantry since a nearby staircase led the servants to the ample kitchen rooms below. These stairs had been sealed over since this downstairs was now a rental unit.

(FACING)
THE ITALIANATE VICTORIAN AS I BOUGHT IT IN 1966

(RIGHT)
IN THE 1990'S, 20 YEARS AFTER I SOLD IT, AND SHOWING THE GROWTH OF THE HOLLY TREE

Upstairs, on the bedroom floor, there was a master bedroom with its own bay window facing the view and its marble fireplace. The two other

Bush Street living room, 1968.

bedrooms across the front facing the street had been opened up into one large studio space, which I was delighted with. That left a very small room at the top of the staircase, which I, at first, was going to use as storage.

§

I had heard from my sister Anita that her son Jaime wanted to come up to San Francisco to attend college. I offered him this tiny room as his own bedroom study for nothing and he readily accepted. Jaime had always been a caring person with a very open, nurturing nature; he had no fear of being part of our "gay" household. When he arrived, he was asked to take care of certain house chores and we lived congenially for the time he was there, sharing meals and much talk about the problems confronting our society. He wasn't part of the Hippy culture, the anti-war movement or other "social" distractions. His main goal was to get through college and prepare for his place in the world. Arturo and I admired his single-minded determination to study and succeed. His family background had made him all the more anxious to make his life into something worthwhile. Ironically, he was drafted into the Army a year later, between semesters, and served honorably for two years, one of them overseas. That experience turned him against our country's involvement in the Viet Nam War, and for many years after, he was generally distrustful of politicians and other "establishment" types. I don't blame him. Let me state that Jaime not only encouraged me to write my memoirs, but helped me to organize my ideas and turn them into this book, which he then published at his own expense.

§

I became a brick layer again here I incorporated three wrought iron panels between the brick columns in a tribute to my love for the lace iron balconies of New Orleans.

Outside, across the front face of the building, there was a tiny square of land, perhaps twelve by sixteen feet dominated by a huge holly tree and little else. I decided to tear down the rickety wooden fencing that bordered the sidewalk and I became a bricklayer again for the moment. I had found in a junk shop, three wrought iron panels, and one foot wide by five feet long and these were incorporated horizontally between the brick columns to create a handsome border wall. It was a salute to my love for the lace iron balconies of New Orleans.

I had the exterior painted a deep hunter's green with the window trim in a blackish brown and this combination made the house stand out prominently from its five identical neighbors. No one seemed interested in painting their exteriors around me and they remained the pallid pale gray that they had been since Victorian times. I wished I could have held a block consensus on coordinating our color schemes to complement each other but I realized my neighbors weren't about to spend hard-earned money on niceties. I did have a pair of young, struggling architects who were closeted gays on one side of me, but they were anti-social souls and seldom even acknowledged the fact that they had just acquired a gay household next door. So be it, we didn't need them.

I had the roof inspected and it came through with flying colors, it wouldn't need any attention for years to come — all was well, I thought.

I was even more pleased when someone pointed out that my row house was in the handsome book, "Here Today, San Francisco's Architectural Heritage," published by the Junior League ladies. It was shown along with the other five in a row so that it wasn't singled out but part of an ensemble of buildings. I promptly went out and bought a copy of the book, which I keep on the shelf to remind me of this rather faded elegant, home I once owned.

§

A block down the street towards the south, a brand new Japantown had just been completed. This was part of the City's promise of renewal to provide more modern shopping. Very little was built in the way of housing but they erected a very well-designed shopping mall that stretched out along three blocks, connected by overpass bridges and a plaza. A multi-leveled traditional tower with swooping roofs gave this plaza a Japanese ambience. And across the street, a replica of a small town shop fronts with cobble stoned walks made you feel that you could be in Kyoto. I loved the fact I was so close to all this reminder of my wartime visit to the real Japan.

But, at the same time, there was resentment, understandably, amongst the African-Americans who felt they had been overlooked in the area's renewal. Most simply grumbled and pulled up stakes, moved to Oakland across the Bay where there was already a large Black population. The element that remained behind was the young who had little to lose. They started holding up people they met along the dark streets around me. There were some muggings, a rape or two were noted in the papers, and I

> *I did have a pair of young, struggling architects who were closeted gays on one side of me, but they were anti-social souls and seldom even acknowledged the fact that they had just acquired a gay household next door.*

(FACING)
MY NEW HOME ON BUSH STREET WAS FEATURED (2ND FROM RIGHT) IN THE JUNIOR LEAGUE'S HANDSOME BOOK, "HERE TODAY: SAN FRANCISCO'S ARCHITECTURAL HERITAGE"

grew fearful. For the first time in my life, since the War, I felt the need to own a gun. I bought myself a Smith-Wesson 35 revolver and kept it under my pillow. We avoided ever going out alone at night and even in the daylight, we had to face the sullen looks of our nearby neighbors. I never had to use it, of course, but it gave me a sense of security in sleeping safely. Arturo thought I was over-reacting, but I felt safe now. I took it to a pawnshop later when the atmosphere began to ease again.

§

The Hippy youth were the big news in all America, the papers and magazines were all writing stories about our young ones going to "pot." The younger generation was in open rebellion against the Vietnam mess we were in. Arturo and I were coming to a parting of the way because I refused to adopt him as my son or pull up stakes and move to Italy to start a restaurant. I had gotten sick of his demands and I told him to leave me in peace. He left and I can't say I was sorry to see him go back to his mansion. I, in turn, met two great friends, with whom I spent all my time. Julio and Don were lovers and they often came by to listen to classical music and chat. I grew very fond of them. Julio was matinee-idol handsome while Don was the more down at home type. I knew that Julio was sleeping around as well. With his looks, he found it hard not to accept the attention he got from everyone he met. Much as I liked looking at this beautiful Italian Adonis, I refrained from ever touching him for fear of losing the friendship of the two. How Don coped with the infidelity, I was not to learn. I simply enjoyed the two men as a couple and we remained great friends for many years until Julio's Aids-related death years later.

Because of all the excitement in the Haight-Ashbury district, I often went strolling along those sidewalks, enjoying the ambience these kids were creating. It was a carnival of sights and sounds. It seemed as if all America's youth was heading west to be here and participate in this moment. As the song was saying, "If you're going to San Francisco, be sure to wear flowers in your hair." And that was literally what young teen girls were doing. Many of them were encamped on the streets of the Haight along with their new boy friends. Drugs were everywhere and kids were over-dosing indiscriminately. The papers were full of stories of dead teens found in the streets. Golden Gate Park, on the edge of Haight Street was the scene of huge masses of young folk having "love-ins." The nights must have been incredible but I, of course, wasn't a part of this. But the days were wild enough for me. Nudes frolicked through the park's paths and the costumes were straight out of some fantasy Beaux-Arts Ball. It was all rather hard to believe that this was happening in America. What did this mean for the Gay world was my con-

13 - The Bush Street House—1966

Hare Krishna Festival, Golden Gate Park, San Francisco, in the 1966 period.

cern. It really freed the inhibitions of many and I was delighted to see people being more accepting and open, at least the youth. It seemed the start of a more liberal attitude to our gay culture and I was relieved that the world was changing its uptightness.

Down Fillmore Street, a couple of blocks, one could dance the night away at the Fillmore Auditorium which booked big name bands like the Grateful Dead, the Jefferson Airplane, and so many others I could name. The music that was being written and performed was mesmerizing, and everyone, hippy or not, was aware of the hypnotic spell songs like "White Rabbit" had on the mind. It was a heady time for San Franciscans, gay, hippy or straight — you couldn't ignore what was going on.

I myself was not the right generation to flaunt weird hair or clothing, but I was in such sympathy for the kids who were cutting the restricting ties that their elders had bound them with. I kept saying, "Let it be, let it be," a quote from those rascals, the Beatles. All this great openness was so

It was a heady time for San Franciscans, gay, hippy or straight ... you couldn't ignore what was going on.

(OVERLEAF)
SOME OF MY
FAVORITE PHOTOS OF
THE 1960'S HIPPIES

Hippy Couple At A Street Fair On Haight Street • 1968

Hippy Vendors At A "Flea Market" • 1969

Hippy Couple At An Art Fair • 1969

exciting. I admired the youngsters who weren't afraid to be themselves and to hell with anyone that stopped them. What a time to be alive, I thought. I had spent most of my life hiding behind a fake front but these brave, reckless kids wouldn't let that happen to them.

It became so intriguing to walk along Haight and take in the scene that I spent Sundays cruising along, taking it all in. The Greyhound Bus Company got into the act as well, sending a sightseeing tour every hour. Gawking out-of-towners craned out the windows with their cameras snapping away. One afternoon I saw a youngster running alongside the bus, thrusting his own camera right back at the tourists to everyone's delight.

The police were surprisingly mild in their reaction to all this, perhaps they felt overwhelmed by it all or were secretly in sympathy. Of course, San Francisco has always had a reputation for tolerance from the gold-mining days to this day anyway. The gendarmes tended to look the other way at all the little encampments, sleeping bags, tents that were scattered through the shrubbery of the Park. One worried about the toilet problem, of course, but somehow it worked out anyway, if you know what I mean.

Elaine had a voluptuous figure with the kind of curves that Rubens would have loved. Vogue would have said she was too curvaceous, but to the art student she was perfect. She had lots of gay friends, of course, since she was part and parcel of our bohemian world.

The Beatles had made Indian gurus very "in" — and so you could see files of orange robed, shaven-headed, bell-ringing devotees passing down the streets, asking for alms. The Indian crowd started staging big parades down through the main drive of the park. One float I remember vividly had enormous wooden wheels six feet in diameter. It supported a platform with a pagoda-like structure garlanded with flowers, framing live priests in its windows. It was so tall that when it arrived at an underpass, it had to be dismantled to get through. When all this chanting, flower bedecked crowd arrived at their meadow, there were food booths, oils and massage people, booklets, and musical instruments to buy and enhance one's Indian mood after you got home. It was truly amazing.

§

I soon rented the converted servants' quarters on the bottom floor to a woman I knew from evening art classes I was attending. In fact, I was used to seeing her minus clothes since she made her living nude modeling.

Elaine had a voluptuous figure with the kind of curves that Rubens would have loved. Vogue would have said she was too curvaceous, but to the art student she was perfect. She had lots of gay friends, of course, since she was part and parcel of our bohemian world. I enjoyed having her as a tenant but wondered how she could make enough money from modeling – I didn't ask.

Everything seemed to going along smoothly until her younger brother came visiting from Hawaii. He stayed in her apartment below us, as I knew

The infamous intersection of Haight-Ashbury today, 1960's Mecca for the Hippy Generation.

he would. But then, one night he had the apartment to himself as Elaine was dining out with friends. He invited a girl friend in and the heavy necking led to sex. But they must have felt they needed a more romantic setting so they lit a circle of candles on the floor around them! Evidently no plates were placed under the burning tapers. What happened next is hard to believe. They felt hungry after their exertions and left the candles burning while they went out for a burger.

Arturo was still living with me and we had retired around ten and were soundly sleeping when we heard all the frantic banging on the front door downstairs. It seems that Elaine had decided to break off her date earlier because she had this premonition that she should get home quickly. It is hard for me to believe how these things work, call it what you will, but there have been other instances in my life when something has intervened to save me from total disaster. This was one of those times. When Elaine had opened her front door, she was enveloped in acrid gray smoke billowing out to her. She had rushed around the tiny garden and up my steps to get my help in putting out the fire! I ran around to the rear garden, grabbed the hose, broke a window and aimed the water at the flames licking the living room floor. It had only just begun to burn through the floor and with the luck of our timely arrival, we contained the flames to a small circle about two feet across. It ruined her record collection nearby, but no one complained. The brother arrived shortly as we opened all the windows to let the smoke out. Our little Romeo was a bit sheepish with the crisis he had created but I was boiling mad. I didn't offer them any sleeping space, since I was too upset to even go back to sleep. I had mixed feelings about Elaine. It was her brother that caused all this near tragedy but her coming home at the precisely correct moment had saved us from burning to death in our beds.

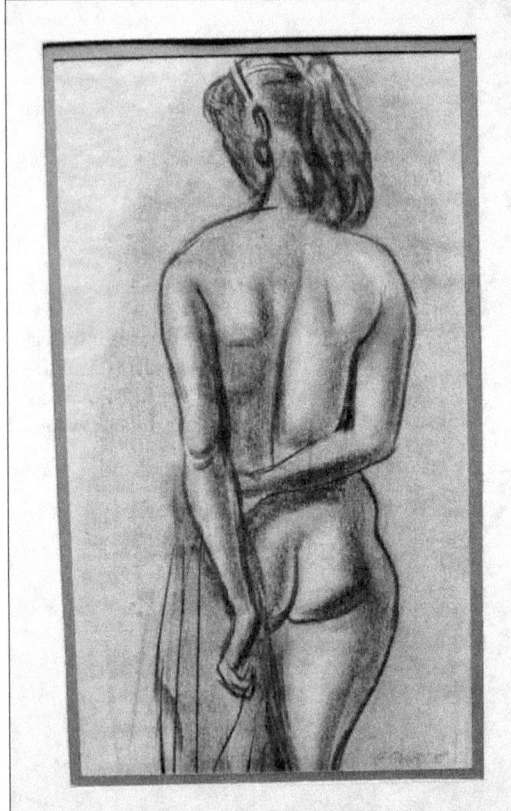

One of my life sketches rendered during the 1960's.

I didn't kick her out, of course, and the insurance people paid for the repairs and repainting of the whole apartment whose walls had been covered with a gray smudge. The teen brother stayed out of my sight for the remainder of his visit. I think I would have kicked his ass across the Pacific if he had shown himself.

§

At least at work everything was going smoothly. As the assistant display manager and designer, I was under quite a bit of pressure but I loved

ANOTHER OF MY
LIFE SKETCHES
FROM THE 1960'S

the work. We had merged with another clothing store and so now our corporate name was Roos/Atkins. A big expansion plan was under way which meant opening more stores all up and down the State. There were inspection trips, drafting drawings to show the placement of fixtures, a lot of detailed drawings to get out. I was even taken along on a few trips to the stores we were opening in the Los Angeles area. Eventually, we had 33 stores open from the original five or six we started out with. It was an exciting time to live and work.

§

At 50, in a somber mood.

At home, Arturo had moved, of course. He wasn't happy nor was I, but it was obvious neither of us was going to give in. I wasn't happy living with a very bossy person who was twenty years my junior to begin with.

Then I began to notice a very attractive, dark-haired young man with a wonderful deep voice and great presence. As part of my duties were to walk through the store every day looking for displays that had been sabotaged or changed without our say-so, I had passed this fellow a number of times at his station and he had always greeted me warmly. There had to be something there or why else was he so friendly? I decided to go a step further and ask him to lunch with me one day. He readily accepted the invitation for the next day. While we were enjoying the meal at a nearby restaurant, he hesitated a bit and then said something that struck me as very naïve. He said that he was "already taken." This struck me as a Victorian phrase and even as I instantly regretted hearing it, I wondered how far he was in the business of being a gay person. Why had he been so friendly to me? Eric, for that was his name, turned out to

Then I began to notice a very attractive, dark-haired young man with a wonderful deep voice and great presence.

13 - The Bush Street House—1966

be ten years younger than I, but then I always seemed to be attracted to people considerably younger than me. I soon learned that he was involved in his first relationship and he was anything but happy with the way it was developing. The other man was even older than me and was quite alcoholic. Eric hadn't seen him drink at first although that was how he had met him. He soon realized he was teamed with a man that spent his free hours with a bottle at his side. So, Eric was unhappy and was hoping to somehow break away and didn't know how. I felt awkward about the situation, but didn't want to walk away either. Some more lunches and chats made me realize we were getting serious and so he finally got up the nerve to confront the drunk and say he was moving out. Surprisingly, it wasn't a big scene at all; the other man simply said he wasn't surprised. He admitted he was a poor choice as a mate and wished him well on his next venture!

We dated for a month to make sure we were temperamentally suited to one another and we were quite happy to spend our evenings together. He was ready to move in and I couldn't have been more pleased. At this point, and at the urging of my nephew and publisher, Jaime, I would like to comment on the current hot political topic of same sex marriages:

> ### My Feelings about "same sex" marriages.
>
> In the gay world, since marriage vows and certificates are unheard of, it may seem we are prone to make impulsive decisions. The fact that we aren't able to marry as the straight world does has always proved to be a joke to me. We are called licentious and predatory and, yet, aren't allowed to marry and settle down. Does it make any sense to forbid same-sex marriage and then castigate people because they sleep around? What a crazy set of rules we live under. And then, we read in the papers that half of American marriages end in divorce.

Continuing — just as Ray, my last great love, had a very loving family, Eric had close ties to his own family. I liked that a lot since my own was too far away to see often. Eric's parents lived a couple of hours away in the San Joaquin Valley. Modesto was part of the great farming valley that makes up the central plain of California. I was soon to meet them, as he had no qualms about bringing me home with him. I don't think it ever occurred to him to try and explain our relationship to them. It was never brought up anyway. The family simply welcomed me with open arms. His mother had remarried and her name was now Alma R. She was born in Greece and had a wonderful, Earth Mother instinct about her. She adored her kids. Eric was her only son and then she acquired another son and daughter when she married Al. Alma loved to cook up peasant food and when Easter came around, they always ordered a slaughtered lamb for the outdoor grill. Food was always plain but so delicious. I loved to cook also and so we became buddies in the kitchen. One Christmas, Alma gave me the twelve volumes of the Women's Day Encyclopedia of Cookery because I was always reading her set. I did an acrylic painting of an amorous young couple for her, which she really loved (*facing page*).

Eric and I fell into that familiar pattern of visiting the folks on alternate weekends just as I had with Ray. It was comforting to feel a part of their world. If they ever questioned what our true relationship was, it was never voiced. Bill, the father as a barrel-chested, gruff man that had obviously spent much of his life doing hard, physical work, yet he was as docile with his family as a big shaggy St. Bernard. He worked at one of the big canneries nearby in some managerial capacity and when he got home from all the stress, he immediately plunked himself in front of the idiot box to watch sports programs. I had not caught the bug yet and didn't own or plan to own this contraption yet. In fact, it was another five or six years before I even bought a small black and white set. I was convinced that once a person owned a TV, his life was not his own — as it turned out, I was only partially right.

§

13 - The Bush Street House—1966

An acrylic painting of An amorous young couple I did for Eric's mother, Alma.

But I was facing a serious problem with the house itself and how I was going to keep it. At the time I had bought 2121 Bush St., my gay real estate man had not informed me that I was just within the borders of the Western Addition Redevelopment Agency's lands. If he had, it must have been said in such a passing remark that I made no note of it. I was now confronted with an ominous, official letter stating that I was in violation of certain building codes. It seemed that inspectors had determined that my roof might not be up to standard, but the big issue was the foundation. The Agency had the authority to demand that certain conditions be met.

I had no idea if the other five identical buildings had also been inspected but my concern was with my building. If I had bought across the street, I wouldn't have been in this mess. But I would also have been in a much less attractive building. The roof wasn't a problem because I had paid to have it inspected and could produce papers that proved it. I got down into the narrow crawl space below the lowest floor — it was only thirty inches off the ground and had a good look at the brick columns that held up the three-story structure. They seemed in fairly good shape and were spaced about every six feet. But now I began to wonder if they were adequate to bear the stress and shaking of the next big earthquake. The building had ridden through the 1906 crisis but then it was only a 31-year-old house. I wondered how stable the mortar between the bricks could be now — another 60 years later. I became quite worried and went to a couple of contractors to get bids on having the house jacked up, and the brick columns replaced with a concrete retaining wall that would run continuously around the perimeter. The cost from both of the contractors was very similar and would be roughly $25,000. That was a figure 10,000 short of what I had paid for the entire building! I was really dismayed at being saddled with such a debt. Thirty-five years ago, thanks to inflation, that was a substantial sum. Friends advised me to use delaying tactics by hiring a lawyer but I saw no future in that at all. I would have to do the work eventually and now I had the constant worry of thinking what would happen with the next quake. One doesn't have an option on whether there will be a quake or not, because one can be assured that there will be one in the future. So, it was time to sell and let the next owner deal with the problem. I was devastated.

At this same time, Eric was transferred to the Oakland Roos/Atkins store and he was unhappy about the commute. He did have a small Karman Ghia, which was made by the Volkswagen firm, so getting there wasn't a problem. I had become aware of the house next door coming up for sale and had contacted Steve, my first lover, of the availability. He promptly bought it just as I was moving out a few months later. It seemed ironic. And now, out of the sextuplets of houses, three were gay-owned. It seemed we were taking over the district. It is true that the gentrification process in most cities takes place, in part at

And now, out of the sextuplets of houses, three were gay-owned. It seemed we were taking over the district. It is true that the gentrification process in most cities takes place, in part at least, because gay men have what is referred to as "disposable income."

On the move once more, leaving my beloved San Francisco behind.

least, because gay men have what is referred to as "disposable income." Since we haven't the enormous burden of children to support, we lavish our dollars on house improvement. It works this way in most of America's cities and whole districts of shabby, neglected old homes get the face-lift they need so badly.

I was asking for $40,000 for the Victorian and didn't wait long before I had it sold, but I made sure I had a home to move into before packing up. It had been three years.

§

Jaime, my nephew, had by now been drafted into the Army and so was off to Ft. Lewis, Washington for basic infantry training in preparation for the Viet Nam War. And so, after a three-year stay in my beloved city, I was on the move again. I was going to live in Oakland, across the East Bay. This move conjures the jaded words of Gertrude Stein, a famous lesbian author from a previous generation — and a close friend of Picasso — who had been raised in Oakland (later moving to Paris), "There's no there, there." Well, I certainly didn't feel that negatively about the town, after all, Berkeley spilled right into Oakland and I had spent three happy college years there.

My nephew Jaime, at age 21 and ready for overseas duty in the Army.

14
The House In Oakland
1969 - PRESENT

"I loved the wooded ambience of the hills with their magnificent views of the City across the Bay ... the house sat just below a forest of Monterey pines, and there was easy access to it. It even harbored a herd of deer that had persisted in living in this little forest hemmed in by encroaching homes." - GS

The "House in Oakland" would be George's final home. I never lived there with him, but visited often to witness the further flourishing of his life and deeper connections to the gay and straight communities of the SF Bay Area. A direct contrast with my own chaotic life as I emerged from the military alive but a confirmed anti-war radical against the deadly debacle in Vietnam and in a deepening need of a spiritual awakening. - JJ

The House in Oakland: 1969 - Present

For the next three weekends, I was shown the exteriors of houses in all sorts of neighborhoods from the so-called "flatlands' to the wooded hilly streets. This time, having been bitten by a devious realtor, I chose a man who I had met through friends and felt confidence in. Although he was married to a lovely wife, he also dated men on the side. This may seem strange to some, but it is more widespread than one would believe.

Although he was married to a lovely wife, he also dated men on the side. This may seem strange to some, but it is more widespread than one would believe.

I loved the wooded ambience of the hills with their magnificent views of the City across the Bay. Everyone accepted the term "City" to mean San Francisco. But the problem in choosing a hillside home was that one's house would be perched on these ridiculous stilts necessary to give the house some anchorage. I simply wasn't going to worry about collapsing foundations this time. I would settle for a house dug into the hillside and some garden space. And, on the third weekend, I was shown the perfect answer to my search. We had been driving through the Oakland hills area when the realtor decided that I should look at this particular property he felt I might like. It sat at the end of a steep little cul-de-sac street not more than a half a block long. It was secluded, had easy access to stores three blocks away, church nearby and two schools within two blocks. I could send my kids there, if I ever married. I knew right away that I had found what I wanted. I would retire here — happily.

The house sat just below a forest of Monterey pines, and there was easy access to it. It even harbored a herd of deer that had persisted in living in this little forest hemmed in by encroaching homes. Since the hill was rather steep, no developers had risked placing homes on it for a change. I loved the look of the land and the house was a low-slung modern ranch

14 - The House In Oakland—1969

The front of the Thornhill house, as seen from the driveway.

house anchored to a concrete slab with a courtyard between the house and the hill's flanks. The two-car carport was a separate building a few feet away from the front door. There was lots of glass looking into the patio and side garden but the front of the house was solid planking. Built of redwood in 1955, the structure was sound with a good tar and gravel roof. It was selling for $35,000, which meant I was $5,000 below my selling price for the Bush St. house. I decided to use some of that profit to trade in my old auto and buy a brand new Mercury Cougar '69. It was a wise choice as I kept this handsome car for the next 13 years before I wrecked it in a highway accident — but more on that incident later.

The house was wall-to-wall carpeted in a shag rug that I hated and there was a long 30-foot expanse of glass looking into the courtyard hiding behind draperies. That had to go along with the shag rug. I built Japanese shojis to be easily removed during the summer. I tiled the floors with tile that could frame accent rugs if I chose. Then, since the living room didn't have a view except for the courtyard, I brought in a contractor to install skylights in the living room, kitchen and one of the three bedrooms, which became my stu-

The living room of my new Oakland home with skylight And the wonderful 6 panel Oriental screen.

dio. I was now to get a wonderful flood of light where I particularly needed it.

Since Eric didn't have a dime to spare, I became the sole owner of the house in Oakland. I wasn't too concerned nor was he. It simply put me in a more dominant position but I was used to being that anyway from past experience. It does mean that the dependent half of the couple has to worry about being sent packing if the pairing hits an impasse. But it seemed the only other choice would be to always rent apartments and I had always hated the idea of paying landlords these ridiculous amounts to live in an uncertain tenancy. One might get an announcement of a rent hike or be evicted for whatever reason. No, I was much more secure in owning my roof even if it put me in a dominant position.

§

14 - The House In Oakland—1969

But a tragedy was in the wings and I found myself ill prepared to deal with it. Back in San Diego, it was nearing the end of the year and Mother wanted to spend the Christmas weekend with her daughter, Anita, who had remarried and now lived in the Orange County area. Soli, my youngest sister was still living at home since she had never married. She was bitter about having to stay on and keep Mother company while my other two sisters had gone on with their lives and started families of their own. I always felt it was simply an excuse to avoid the reality of her orientation. I don't want to dig into any of this problem here but the family knew that I had made myself an outcast in Soli's eyes by being honest about who I was. And I had asked Soli to be as honest as well. Instead, she refused to acknowledge me as her brother. She claimed she didn't have a brother from that time on. Yet she refused the attentions of suitors, insulted any that came calling and wound up living with a female roommate from then on. I simply see it as an extreme case of self-denial but perhaps I was asking too much of someone in this time of transition.

But to resume here, Soli was not eager to make the auto trip to see her sister in Los Angeles mainly because she had had a problem with blackouts. She couldn't feel safe behind the wheel of a car and couldn't assure anyone that she wouldn't suffer a fainting on the trip. Mother was insistent that the trip be made anyway and so they started the 125-mile drive apprehensively. To this day, I simply don't understand why they didn't fly or take the Greyhound.

They left on Christmas Eve and again you see that fateful date reappear in my life. They were passing through an underpass when Soli had her blackout. She let go of the steering wheel and the car hurtled into the concrete embankment killing Mother instantly. Soli, in the driver seat and away from the wall they had hit was covered in scratches and bruises but basically unhurt. Their identity cards helped the people who had stopped to assess the situation and to get them to an ambulance. Anita was called when Soli awoke. She and her husband took care of the situation, handling the details of hospital and the morgue. Later, Dorothy was called long distance and she, in turn, called me. We talked for some time about the next step we should take. We came to the conclusion that we wouldn't go down to do anything since Anita and her husband were in charge. It was a poor decision and how we came to decide not to go has been a black mark on my conscience. We made the decision together, Dorothy and I, and I have regretted it ever since. I think it was partly the horror of knowing what we would be confronting. Soli had been driving when she had no business driving at all. We couldn't bear the thought of confronting her and she must have felt tremendously guilty. Soli, in turn, chose to accuse us of being callous and uncaring because of our decision not to come down. It was an emotional mess for all of us. I felt we were behaving badly but there we were with these very mixed feelings about blame and guilt. I never heard from Soli again to this day although she moved up to a neighboring city on the Bay. Attempts to contact have failed more than once.* Anita developed a terrible brain tumor in the next few years and she died. Her four children had moved on with their lives, two of them in tragedy and two successfully. Jaime and I always kept in touch and at one point he came up to Oakland to live for a while soon after he was honorably discharged from the Army in early 1970.

§

During the next seven years, Eric and I were to live quite contentedly as a couple. Our closest neighbors were friendly enough although we never had them over for suppers. Our friends lived in San Francisco and the twenty-minute ride over the Bay Bridge was easy enough. We usually headed to Modesto to visit Eric's parents anyway. He was developing an interest in weaving and found a second hand loom for sale. The darn thing was so huge, taking up a six by six floor space that it dominated one corner of the living room. But Eric was happy sitting there passing the shuttles through the vertical curtain of threads. His work had a very masculine, rough quality to it. They made splendid big floor pillows in earth colors and he did wall hangings with irregular outlines, which caught on with the post-hippy crowd. He

---

*In 2004 I convinced George that we try to locate Soli. Dorothy, along with my brother, joined in the effort and we found her living in an upscale nursing home along the North Bay. She was totally blind and in a wheel chair, but sound enough in mind to understand who we were. Apparently, her late female partner had planned ahead to have her taken care of here. It was a happy moment for all, and I sensed that whatever bad blood there had been, all was now forgiven. — J. Jackson

had no trouble finding buyers and we were both delighted in his success. He still kept his daytime job at Roos-Atkins, however. I began to see him acquire his own circle of friends; it was another case of needing to move on, just as Steve had done. I suppose I should have been more insistent that he stay but it has never been my nature to demand anything from a lover that he wouldn't give readily. If Eric felt it was important to leave me for someone younger, more attractive, so be it; we hadn't quarreled, but he was curious as to what laid out there in that great metropolis across the water. I had been his second boy friend. He needed to move on and I needed to let go.

If Eric felt it was important to leave me for someone younger, more attractive, so be it ... I had been his second boy friend. He needed to move on and I needed to let go.

The weekend drives to visit with Eric's family in Modesto came to an abrupt end. Neither Eric nor I got around to explaining to them why I wouldn't be coming around anymore but I am sure they guessed why. They waited for some months before trying to renew the friendship, sent Christmas cards inviting me down by myself if that was the way it was to be — I felt awkward and did send cards for the next few years. They continued to invite me down but I never returned — there was nothing they could have done to repair the breach. I had felt loved, appreciated by this simple, Valley family who saw nothing shameful in two men loving one another as fully as we had. It passed my mind that Alma's Greek ancestry might have been her reason for her acceptance of men loving men, after all, the history books are full of stories about Greek love. The Spartan Band was famous for fighting alongside their lovers to the death. Love between men was common, with one usually acting as the elder teacher and a younger one learning about his role in life as a student. Usually women were the child-bearers, important but not as important as the male lover.

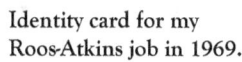

Identity card for my Roos-Atkins job in 1969.

I had felt loved, appreciated by this simple, Valley family who saw nothing shameful in two men loving one another as fully as we had.

XV

Spain and Morocco

1972

"I now went through a long period of disenchantment with the fleeting nature of gay relationships. Each of my past loves had lasted roughly seven years. Perhaps the saying "the seven-year-itch" had more truth to it than fable. I began to think of retiring in Europe." - GS

∫

I saw things somewhat differently. George's artistic, spiritual, and sense of brotherhood with gay and straights alive were on the right track. But love interests can be quite another, and George opens a new door of traveling worldwide to see what it had to offer. I got my first glimpses of the Faced on an international level. - JJ

Spain and Morocco: 1972

I now went through a long period of disenchantment with the fleeting nature of gay relationships. Each of my past loves had lasted roughly seven years. Perhaps the saying "the seven-year-itch" had more truth to it than fable. I began to think of retiring in Europe. I had always heard that European men were much more interested in mature partners and they seemed to appreciate the older lover much more than we Americans. It is even truer to say that the Gay World worships Youth passionately. Once a gay man crosses the line into his 40s, he can count on becoming invisible in a gay bar. He may have tons of friends, but lovers will become few and far between — if he has any luck.

Before Eric had left, we planned a trip to Spain, ostensibly to relax and savor the country of my mother's birth. But I was also considering the very real possibility of moving there. After all, I was quite fluent in the language and now that the tyrant Franco had finally died, Spain was on a business upswing. The whole country was waking up to the modern world. It was the moment to invest in its future, if ever.

A friend of mine had gone on a very economical jaunt through Spain just recently and he had shown me many snapshots of the southern coastline and the people he had met there. The Costa del Sol faced Africa across the Straits of Gibraltar and there was a town called Torremolinos that had made international headlines with its becoming the Mecca for the hippie and also the gay crowd. My friend also showed me snapshots of a very handsome Spaniard that had welcomed him into his parents' home there. As it turned out, the Spaniard wasn't gay but he seemed friendly enough. So I was also armed with an introduction to him. His

> *It is even truer to say that the Gay World worships Youth passionately. Once a gay man crosses the line into his 40s, he can count on becoming invisible in a gay bar. He may have tons of friends, but lovers will become few and far between — if he has any luck*

name was Aurelio Gomez-Lopez and he was indeed a looker although rather short. He was eager to have me meet his new wife. Aurelio had worked in the construction business and was actually putting up a condominium building in Torremolinos. That word stands for windmills, and sadly, only one remained along the coastal bluffs and was now a restaurant. The older section of the town was still intact, with the neat rows of fishermen's cottages lining its winding streets. There was a small bullring, since no self-respecting Spanish town would be without one, of course. But the incredible sight was the proliferation of high-rise apartment buildings that were springing up like mushrooms on the town's perimeters. It was an amazing contrast and it was obvious that there were no building codes to keep the rampant growth under some sort of control. Spain was hell-bent to catch up with the rest of the world.

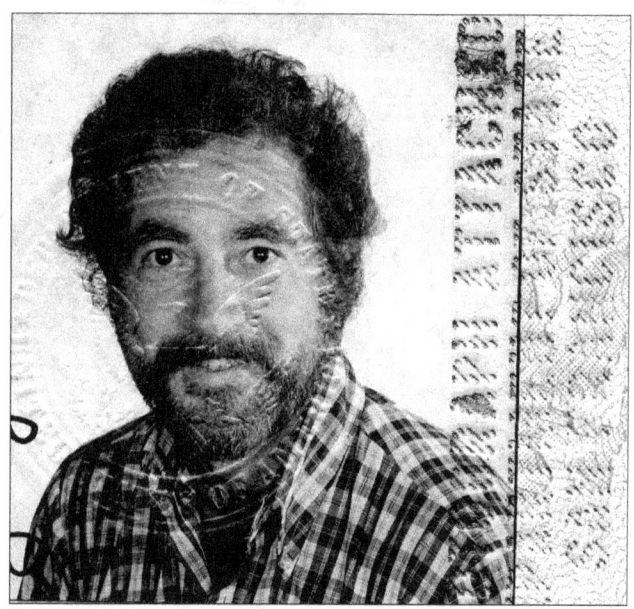
My passport image at 61.

I wasn't too interested in Aurelio's half-completed condos as they struck me as too cramped. Europeans are quite willing to live in tiny rooms but I told him if he wanted to attract retirees from America or anywhere in the New World, he would have to plan larger rooms. I promised to keep in touch with him to see what he would build next. He seemed very young to be heading up a construction company but I believe he felt he couldn't afford to wait out the times. In an odd moment of wavering, he even considered abandoning the whole works and coming to live in California if I would help him through the immigration process. I considered this for a brief period but decided I couldn't do it. I liked Aurelio but I felt he was using me as a stepping-stone to a big career in the States and I simply wasn't willing to be his means to an end.

Dorothy, my sister who lived in nearby Concord, was invited to come with us on one of these trips to Spain. Before I felt comfortable with the idea of pulling up stakes and leaving America, I was to make four visits to the land of my Mother's birth. The three of us crossed the Straits over to Morocco for a week's visit. I was much intrigued with this lovely country, so like California with its climate, yet so exotic with its people in their djellabas, the teeming, narrow alleyways through the casbahs, with piles of merchandise arranged on the cobblestones. The mosques, minarets, gardens, fountains, water-sellers — all of it seemed almost as in a dream. We ate couscous with our fingers, rode in horse-drawn carriages, watched snake charmers in the great plaza of Marrakech called Djma el Fna. I had never been in such a totally different environment, peopled everywhere by figures in long robes and sandals.

My sister Dorothy and I in a Tangiers restaurant during one of my later visits to Spain and Morocco.

Unfortunately, a terrible incident was about to happen that would ruin what would otherwise have been a perfect day of adventure and excitement in this far off land. On the tour bus, one night as we motored to our next stop, the driver ploughed into a shepherd and his flock of sheep being driven to market. It was dark and the bus' headlights didn't pick up the herd as it spread itself over the road's width. The bus didn't come to a crashing halt until a dozen creatures had been slaughtered. In the moments to follow, only two or three of us had the nerve to get out of the bus to survey the carnage and confront the wailing sheepherder. I stayed in the bus.

I did sign papers with Aurelio to buy into the next condominium building he was planning to construct in the next year. The selling price for a two bedroom, living-dining room with kitchen and bath, nice balcony overlooking the Mediterranean came to $11,500. I knew I could rent it until the time I would need it for myself. That time didn't seem too far off.

§

Unfortunately, a terrible incident was about to happen that would ruin what would otherwise have been a perfect day of adventure and excitement in this far off land

15 - Spain & Morocco—1972

On the streets of Marrakech, Morocco.

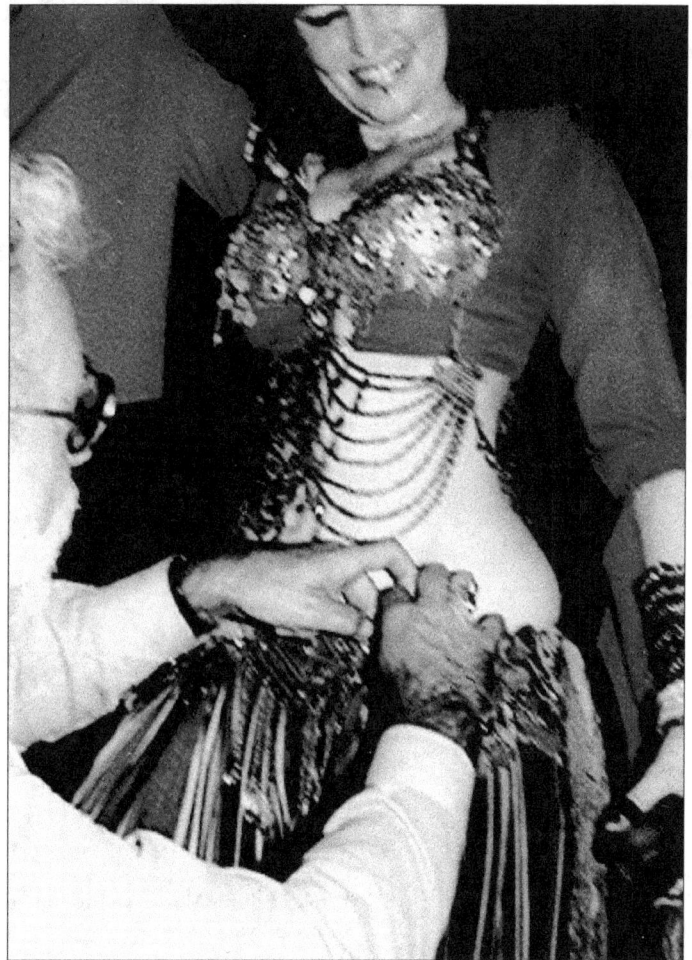

I'm tucking money in the belly dancer's girdle, Morocco.

I stole into this Moroccan Mosque to get this lovely shot of men washing up before prayers.

Veiled Moroccan women in the streets of Marrakech.

By 1975, I was alone again, Eric had met another man named Robert who was in the interior decorating trade. He seemed a decent sort and I approved of him. The irony of the situation was that Eric would now be moving back to San Francisco, and his job was still in Oakland. But now that was their problem. I had three bedrooms in the house and I decided to augment my income and rent two of them to gay bachelors. Advertising in the local Oakland paper, I soon had men calling to see the layout. I found it quite easy to settle on two congenial people. I typed up a set of rules that I expected them to abide by. The most important rule had to be the "no smoking in bed" one. After the scary incident with the circle of candles almost burning down my Victorian on Bush Street, I wasn't eager to tempt fate again.

I felt reasonably comfortable with two other men living in the house with me. At least, I had their company some of the time as they used the kitchen. They generally had boy friends dropping by and they moved on to other arrangements when they became serious about their relationships. That was the annoying feature of renting to gay men; they tended to be so transitory.

So I was often faced with running ads looking for single men. It was surprising to me that I could insert the word "gay" into the ad without a remark from the classified ad people. But then, times were a-changing — the world was becoming more forgiving. I never had anyone call and breathe threats into my phone lines.

For some unexplained reason, as a matter of fact, I have been exceptionally fortunate in my dealings with people in general. I had heard others complain about being called "faggot, queer, homo" and a few other choice terms, but I had never had that problem myself. I suppose I was lucky that I didn't look "gay" to others. The world only sees the flagrant, hip-swishing, lisping, fluttering hand types as the homosexual to be feared and reviled. But there are a huge number of us out there amongst you that you would never label as gay because we are invisible. When Kinsey and his wife did their groundbreaking research back in the '70s, he set up a scale lining up gays in a hierarchy of gayness. The degree of masculinity to femaleness was numbered from one to eight. So a man could be placed anywhere in this scale depending on his degree of femaleness. We Americans like everything to be either black or white, either you are gay or you're not — no ifs, ands or buts. The truth is quite different if one wants to admit it. There are countless men who have had homosexual contacts in their youth and then moved on to heterosexual marriage. Some marry successfully, raise children but find they need to meet men in clandestine situations. The business trips out of town, the night with the boys playing poker, and I could go on for another page. Women also find ways of connecting with other women. I am hardly exposing any secrets here, but I find it so hypocritical of Society to point the finger at the Gay world for its loose morals when the straight world is no less immoral.

I am reminded of the railing of Senator Joe McCarthy some years ago who was famous for hunting down communists in government posts. He moved on to the movie industry and its writers. In all

That was the annoying feature of renting to gay men; they tended to be so transitory. So I was often faced with running ads looking for single men ... I never had anyone call and breathe threats into my phone lines

I find it so hypocritical of Society to point the finger at the Gay world for its loose morals when the straight world is no less immoral

For some unexplained reason, I have been exceptionally fortunate in my dealings with people in general. I had heard others complain about being called "faggot, queer, homo" and a few other choice terms, but I had never had that problem myself. I suppose I was lucky that I didn't look "gay" to others

the uproar and angry shouting that ensued in Congressional hearings, the good Senator never got around to asking his assistant, Roy Cohn, whom he was sleeping with. This man reputedly died of AIDS some time later and then we learned he was a gay man who never admitted his orientation.

§

Eric's fascination with weaving and his success with selling his work got me interested in trying my hand at some similar type of work. I wasn't interested in doing the same thing but I wanted to use yarn in some creative way. The opportunity to explore this avenue miraculously presented itself very shortly. We had been rambling through a new shopping mall and had come to a craft shop that was selling hooked-rugs either finished or as kits containing jute, yarn and the ingenious patented tool needed to puncture through the fabric. I was intrigued with the concept, but wasn't about to follow the guidelines plotted out on the material. The samples were all small panels of perhaps two by three feet maximum and depicted cute animals or flowers. I was visualizing big wall hangings with semi-abstract motifs.

The tool itself was an ingenious bit of engineering and so basically simple that I wondered why no one had thought of it sooner. As you passed the yarn through the needle's eye, you could set a screw to limit the length of the loop that was made as it punctured the burlap or jute. By setting the loop length where you wanted it, you could achieve various depths and ridges. It gave the finished panel a very sculptured look, which I admired.

I built a series of wooden frames in graduated sizes. My most popular size proved to be one that gave me a finished work 40 by 60 inches. This was a size that adapted well to a wall behind a living room couch. I was soon turning out hooked panels in a variety of sizes and finding shops that would take them on consignment to sell. Eric helped by introducing me to decorator friends and I was launched in the craft. At one point, it became apparent that the State of California wanted a cut into my small enterprise. I had sold two 3 by eight-foot pieces to chic women's clothing store to be used as in-store decoration. They had listed their purchase as a tax deductible in their year's expenses so I was contacted by the State. I had to get a license now to operate. Every year for the next ten or so years, I paid an annual fee to sell my products. As I was reaching my retirement year in

He hooks his 'paintings' like a rug

By CAROL FOWLER

Remember when every home had a hooked rug spread before the fireplace, usually with a rocker at one corner and a sleeping cat at the other?

A Montclair artist and designer, George Somers, still makes hooked rugs in the old style. He will be in residence at Bernard Galleries in Walnut Creek, hooking a tapestry set in the window, through Friday.

On opening day he worked on a design based on an American colonial pattern. A boy and girl stand in straight symmetry on either side of a house. Reflecting the naive art habit of filling every space, a stylized dove and sun float in the sky. It promises to have the charm of the rugs that go with rocking chairs and cats.

However, it is Somers' abstract, modern tapestries that are the most compelling and, he allowed, the most interesting for him. Done in natural colors, the bold compositions look like great clefts in the earth's crusts. In some the looped fibers swirl with the concentric currents of the ocean. Still another has the austere patterns of a Japanese rock garden.

Somers hooks his yarns through the tapestry backing — jute — in varying lengths so the designs take on a sculpted, reliefed richness.

In objective works, he exploits the characteristic to give an illusion of depth. In a landscape tapestry that hangs in the gallery, foreground palms are done with fairly long yarn loops, the hills are rounded, almost as though sculpted, and the lake and sky are created with a flat, tight surface, indicating that they lie behind the foreground objects.

He performs other tricks with spacial illusion. The tapestry to the left of the door is not hanging in folds — the overlapping areas are shaped and hooked to look like folds!

Somers explained that his inspiration comes from many sources. The Korean art exhibit of two summers ago led to his doing two tapestries shaped as kimono, with arms bowing out and the suggestion of the garment's shape built into the pattern. Celtic designs led to another work and children's drawings to two pieces which hang in the pediatric ward of the Vallejo hospital. Two large works, 25-feet long, hang in public buildings in Oakland and Berkeley.

"This really is a second career for me," said the painter who worked in window design for Roos Atkins for several years. He picked up the mechanical "hook," which has replaced the simple instrument that our grandmother's might have used, and demonstrated the rapid in and out motion that punches the yarn, usually all-wool, through the backing material. He draws the cartoon on the back of the fabric, working from the back and turning the tapestry often to see the results. The yarn is easily pulled out if he wishes to change a color or the depth of the loop, done by a screw adjustment of the hook.

When the design is completed, liquid latex is poured on, totally saturating yarn and backing cloth. Once dry, it secures the yarn.

The method is exactly the same process used for hand-hooked rugs. Although Somers' are sturdy enough to be used as rugs, most of them are so richly decorative that it would be unthinkable to walk on them.

Asked if he felt conspicuous working in the window, he smiled, "Not at all. At Roos Atkins I spent every day working in a window."

George Somers hooks white yarn through his colonial-inspired tapestry in Bernard Galleries in Walnut Creek.

My hooked rug tapestry business was featured in a Bay Area newspaper.

1979, it was nice to have a business to augment my diminished income level. By the time I found I had saturated the market for my work and I stopped punching these works, I had produced some 250 complete panels ranging through a myriad of sizes and motifs (See OVERLEAF, "Tapestry Gallery"). I had kept meticulous records of all of them. The largest and by far the most impressive work was commissioned for the new engineering building at my old college, the University of California. The Bechtel Building's lounge area has a piece of mine, which measures 5 by 25 feet long. Its abstract lines depict a mysterious scene that seems to suggest a lake at the base of a mountainscape. It was one of several

15 - Spain & Morocco—1972

sketches I submitted for approval. Since I was placing this huge panel in the lobby-lounge of the Engineering Building, I wondered how it would make sense with the nature of the work being studied there. It would have been more in keeping to have planned a vista of bridges and vast public buildings. But they wanted a natural, organic look: Nature *before* Man appeared on the scene.

(OVERLEAF) "TAPESTRY GALLERY" A SAMPLING OF SOME OF MY 250 HOOKED RUGGED PANELS

The Bechtel tapestry titled, "The Lake", still in place at the University of California at Berkeley. 5' x 25'

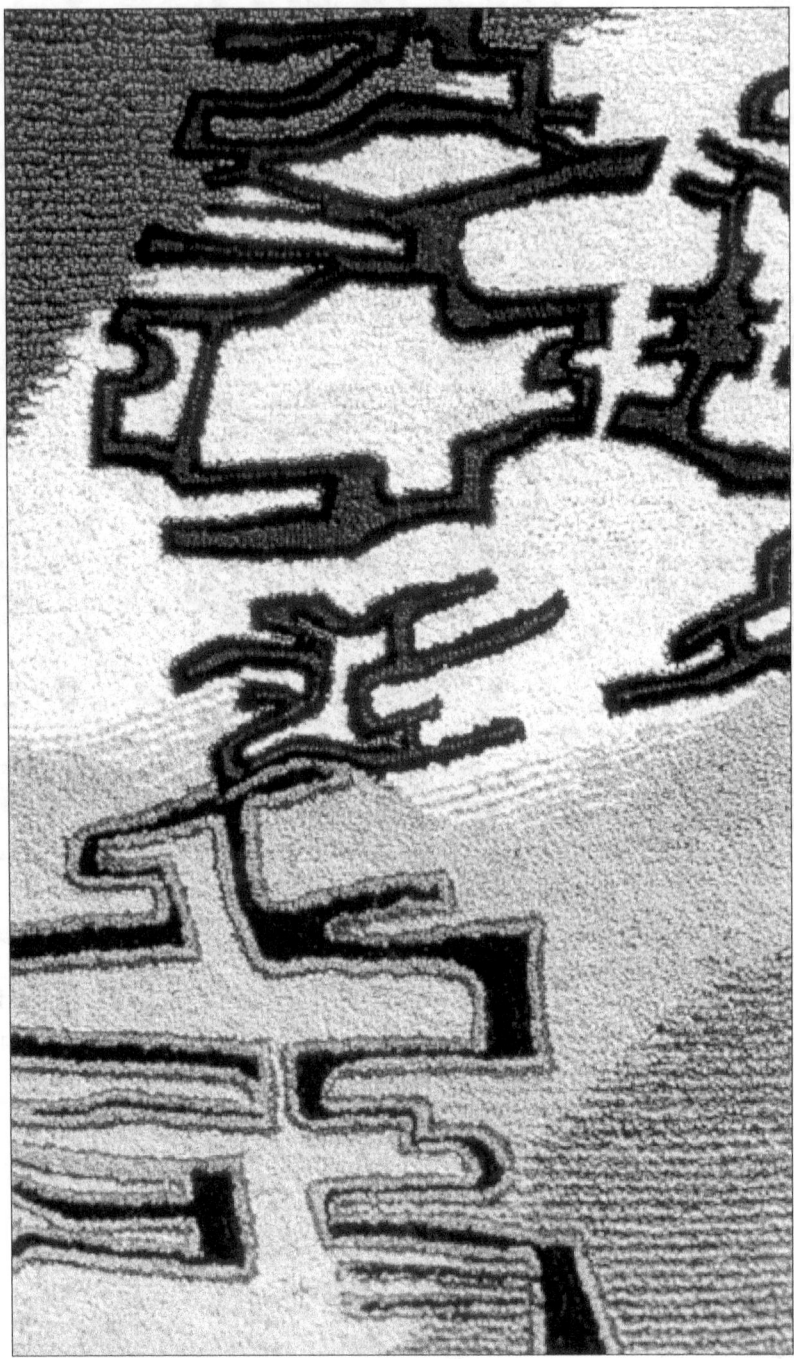

"Petroglyphs" 42" x 56". Customer unknown. A trip to Australia stirred my interest in aboriginal art. I loved the marvelous child-like scratching I saw on rock walls. This is a more abstracted interpretation of the wonderful qualities they evoke.

15 - Spain & Morocco—1972

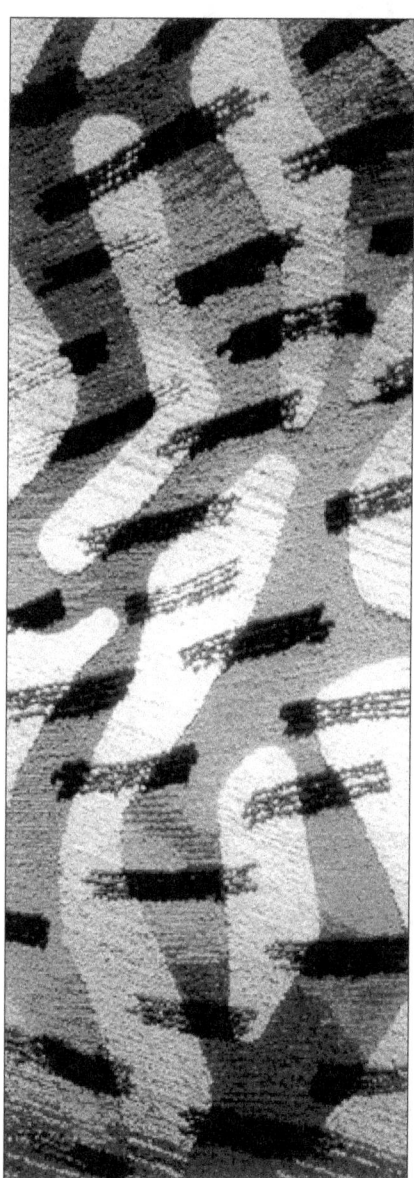

"Boomerang" 30" x 84". In the Artist's collection. This quite abstract motif suggests the "to and fro" movement of objects flying thru space.

"Flower Dance" 42" x 56". Created for three different customers. The linear flow of shapes evolving the sensual nature of flowers magnified. I was inspired by the works of Georgia O'Keefe.

16
The Right One
§
Travel Bug
1978

"I was spending my weekend nights in these bars, looking at the sea of faces, wondering if any of them might be the One. Of course, in my case, as in so many others, I tended to devalue a person because they were in a bar to begin with." - GS

§

George finds "love," or at least a lasting and stable relationship as I saw it. But he does not forsake his commitment to seeing the outer world. His "gaydar" is active, and actually becoming steadily "activist." - JJ

THE RIGHT ONE · TRAVEL BUG: 1978

Life went on. Eric had left to live with his new love, and I had started living with a series of new roommates who generally stayed for a year before they met the "love of their lives" and promptly moved out. I began to feel like a clearinghouse for lost souls what with all the transitory movement. But, I needed to have some company, someone I could chat with over Sunday morning coffee and croissant.

I was driving over to the big City — "Baghdad-by-the-Bay" — as San Francisco's favorite gossip columnist, Herb Caen, had dubbed it. The term had stuck in people's minds because it reflected the diversity of lifestyles and nationalities, which made up San Francisco. The gay scene was proliferating into a number of neighborhoods. There were now some one hundred gay bars catering to various tastes. Gay men are as different from each other as are straight men. There are the "A-gays", a haughty, snobbish set that look down their noses at the leather crowd that hangs out in the SOMA district (South of Market). There was the Polk Street crowd with their middle of the road attitude. Here along this street are the "rent boys," those kids usually in their teens who were cast out of their homes all across America by condemning parents. It is a sad fact of life that America treats its teen children with such callous disregard once they come-out to their mothers and fathers. "What did I do wrong in raising this poor child?" This was, and is, the standard query when a mother realizes she has produced a homosexual child. I wondered if Society would ever stop castigating itself for something that is part of Nature's way of stabilizing population growth. We talk about ZPG, zero population growth, in the abstract but ignore the fact that some people simply weren't meant to reproduce. They are often the segment of humanity that creates the Art of a

It is a sad fact of life that America treats its teen children with such callous disregard once they come-out to their mothers and fathers

16 - The Right One · Travel Bug—1978

civilization. If you take a look at the longish list of famous persons I have added to the end of the story (See APPENDIX: FAMOUS GAYS AND LESBIANS), you might be impressed with the names that appear there. Most of them are in the Fine Art, Music and Literature categories but there are kings, warriors, and statesmen there as well.

§

I was spending my weekend nights in these bars, looking at the sea of faces, wondering if any of them might be the One. Of course, in my case, as in so many others, I tended to devaluate a person because they were in a bar to begin with. "Not that there is anything wrong with that" — as Seinfeld, the comic put it, but still I preferred meeting a potential mate through friends. I liked the idea of getting to assess a person from their interaction with others and I wouldn't have to decide within an hour or so whether I would want to invite them home. I was lucky enough in my choosing new bedmates that none of them ever turned violent on me and stole my wallet.

One night, a friend suggested we do something different: instead of going to San Francisco to bar hop, we would instead drive in the opposite direction to a nearby town called Walnut Creek. I hadn't realized that even the smaller cities that make up the Bay Area have their discreet little hangouts for the gay crowd. Although I wasn't too impressed with what we might find in these venues, I agreed to go and see what it would be like. Stan and I jumped into my car for the twenty-minute drive to the Hub. It was so discreetly set behind another business address that I marveled how anyone could find it at all. I wondered if this was what it was like in America during prohibition days. One came up to a back alley door with a porthole window and a pair of suspicious eyes appraising the possibility you might be the police.

We walked into a lively scene with a young crowd swiveling their hips rhythmically to a jukebox full of very loud dance music. We ordered beers, avoiding Coors. That company had been blacklisted by the Gay Community for endorsing "homophobic" senators (whom I won't name here). I looked around and wasn't too thrilled by what I saw. There were a few lesbians out on the dance floor and that made the patrons a little more secure about a possible police arrival. At this time, it would seem strange that we might be raided for congregating at all but I still harbored these feelings that we could feel the wrath of a small community against the arrival of a group of people they felt were alien to their set of ethics. Feelings of this sort die hard, it seemed to me even in 1978.

After loosening up with a couple of drinks, I followed Stan out onto the floor for some hip grinding and found him inviting a nearby youth to join us. He seemed a bit tall, but very personable. I liked his looks a lot and he must have felt the same way for he joined me at the bar afterwards where we got better acquainted. I learned he had just had his twenty-first birthday and that was a setback for me. I was decades older, forty to be exact. I had no business getting interested in anyone of his age at all. Nevertheless, we exchanged phone numbers and I figured I would never hear from him again. I was completely wrong. He is still my mate today — and it is 24 years later!

Sadly, because he still deals with homophobic types on his job, I can't reveal his name here. I will have to invent a name for him, much as I resent doing it. Some of my readers will know of whom I speak as you know both of us, but the vast number of you will know of him as — Jim. Even though he shows no characteristically gay mannerisms, Jim does endure taunting from his fellow workers. He handles it by throwing a taunt right back at them. There's a huge amount of joking, backbiting and name-calling he has to deal with anyway. Some of the men think nothing of labeling each other "queer" or "fag" just to get a rise out of them. One of Jim's jibes at himself in jesting around with these brainless wonders is to declare himself a tri-sexual — "I'll try anything once!" That seems to bring them to an amused surrender. What can they top that with?

As the years have rolled by, and with a less homophobic employer to cater to, he has gained much respect. He has been put in charge of a group of straight men, and proved to be more responsible than the regulars. And in general he has gained the respect of his staff. But first, he

16 - The Right One · Travel Bug—1978

had to undergo the "trial by fire."

I don't remember who called first but within a few days, Jim or I had called to set up a second meeting at my house. It turned out that Jim could hardly expect to entertain anyone at his home since he lived in a very closeted world. There were four women in his domestic setup. First there was his mother, his grandmother and his aunt. He also had a sister who was to be married shortly. His mother tended to be rather uninterested in raising her two children and left the job to the grandmother. Jim had never known a father since that gentleman had left home as soon as he realized he had gotten his young wife pregnant for the second time. So Jim's mother had a rather cynical view of men in general. She had been asked to do fashion modeling in her twenties but by the time I had a hasty glimpse of her in those first years, she had evolved into a lethargic, overweight woman no man would have eyed with any interest. She and I were not on friendly terms. I think she always felt I had somehow seduced her son into homosexuality. He tried telling her that he was of age and was completely capable of making rational choices — but she still maintained a guarded, rather arrogant tone in her phone calls to her son after he started living with me.

At first, we spent all our weekends together and as time passed and we felt we had evolved into a stable partnership, I proposed he move to my house. It meant commuting back to Fremont where he held a job at a firm in the computer industry. He had a motorcycle for transportation and would be at his job in thirty minutes from my house. But Jim showed wisdom beyond his years when he spoke up and decided we had to know each other for one year before he would take the drastic step of pulling up stakes. I was impressed with this thinking, realizing that it was much saner than my more impulsive desire to have him living with me after only a couple of months. I agreed to the plan realizing it was more the sort of thinking that the straight world he had lived in, would see as logical. We didn't want to rush into a relationship that might sour after a few months. My other pairings, marriages, partnerships — whatever one could call them since we couldn't say, "marry," had lasted from five to seven years. But this was the riskiest venture of them all when we realized our huge difference in ages. Could it work? All we could do was to try with all our hearts. Jim

She and I were not on friendly terms. I think she always felt I had somehow seduced her son into homosexuality

had missed the important parent of his growing-up years, a father. I was to be father and lover combined in one. An odd role — but one that seemed right for us. We simply ignored the mutterings of friends who gave us a year at the most before an inevitable break-up. I was now sixty-one and forty years senior to Jim — quite a scary thought. But I had never felt my age, in any event. I was forever being taken for someone in his forties — so I had somehow lost twenty years down the line. I have always credited my health to my mother's Spanish heritage. The genes one gets from parents is the answer, I felt. And then I made a point of moderation in all the different aspects of my living. I gave up smoking early on in college, drank very moderately, joined a gym during the San Francisco period, and stayed out of the sun after I reached fifty. I never overdid the barhopping routines that are such an important part of a gay man's social life. I preferred meeting new friends at parties or friends' homes. So I felt I deserved to look better at my age with the moderation I had followed in all things.

§

Scotland

Early into our new domestic arrangement, we decided to visit Scotland, the ancestral home Jim claimed as his. Although there were other lines from the English as well, he was most interested in seeing Scotland. After buying Britrail passes that lasted a week, we toured up the eastern coastline as far as Aberdeen. I was curious to see the town that had given its name to my Army camp in Maryland during my first period of training. Then we had to back track to Glasgow to do the run up the western coastline. I was in doubt about the idea of even going to find a certain loch (as the Scots call their lakes) but Jim was insistent. When we got off the train, night had fallen and the train had made a special stop for us since no other passengers were interested in this forlorn station. One light bulb was all that lit the bare little station we had reached.

I was in a panic, what could we do now — as the train disappeared down the track? Jim discovered a rough road nearby and we lugged our bags on our shoulders for a half-mile or so before we even glimpsed a light. We walked up to a farmhouse, rapped on the door and roused a farm-wife who seemed friendly enough. Because her home was the nearest to the station, she was used to strangers showing up at all hours of the night. After a cup of tea, we were shown to a cozy bedroom upstairs. The goose down comforters and mattress on the double-bed were the deepest, most luxurious I had ever slept in. We slept soundly that night. The next day, after an incredibly great breakfast, we hiked to the lake. I was impressed with its pristine, rugged beauty, with the mountains spilling down to the lakeshores. At the water's edge near us, stood this giant column, a monument to Bonnie Prince Charles. It was the site of a great battle fought here long ago in the struggles of Scotland to free itself from the yoke of the English. We found the column had an entrance at its base, so we climbed a narrow twisting stone stairs until we came out on top for a spectacular vista of the scene. Just behind us on a base, stood the stone image of the prince himself. Later we climbed the rocky hillsides nearby to simply enjoy the area with its rugged beauty. We also made love amongst the rocks even though I protested the brazenness of the act.

At Loch Schiele, Scotland, at 64.

Later we climbed the rocky hillsides nearby to simply enjoy the area with its rugged beauty. We also made love amongst the rocks even though I protested the brazenness of the act

Glasgow was interesting with its brick and stone buildings everywhere. I would have wanted to see Charles Rennie Mackintosh's famous buildings but we were limited in time. And then we arrived in Edinburgh. We had no idea of where we would want to stay but that didn't turn out to be a problem anyway. As soon as we jumped off the train, a portly gent approached us. He asked if we were looking for lodgings. He and his wife had a B&B a mile away. We were invited to have a look. So taking him at face value, we jumped in his auto and saw his rooms. They seemed fine to us, and we stayed on. We took in the sights, walking the Royal Mile from one end to the other, ambling along the cobble-stoned mews and alleyways of this ancient thoroughfare. I bought myself a handsome Harris Tweed sport jacket and a Bothy throw blanket to snuggle under on a winter's night. Jim was interested in visiting the Tartan museum where one could check out the family tartan. His turned out to be a lovely blue, lavender and green combination that seemed so contemporary it surprised you. We walked along Princess Street, the main shopping avenue, took in the wonderful Greek temple that houses Edinburgh's art collections. I was quite impressed with the mix of classical portraits and the abstract work being done and exhibited at the time we were there. We even stumbled into a gay bar on a side street that was so discreetly gay that it almost seemed not gay — but we knew that the glances we were getting weren't those of a straight crowd. I was more interested in the stunning tiled walls that clad the interior. They were possibly over a hundred years old and depicted Victorian scenes. I would have loved to be able to pry one off the wall for a souvenir! After an ale or two, we left since we wanted to check out the Gay Information Center. We entered a door barely acknowledging its gay connections. It seemed the Scotch gay world still closeted its people then. There were a couple of youths lounging around who perked up when we entered, but we didn't like their eagerness to show us around. We simply asked where we might find a good friendly café where we could dine that evening. The one recommended turned out to be one of the best of the trip. It was a memorable meal in a charming basement room filled with paintings of the Scottish scene.

Hill House, the largest and finest of Mackintosh's domestic buildings was built from local sandstone in Scottish Baronial tradition.

We left since we wanted to check out the Gay Information Center. We entered a door barely acknowledging its gay connections. It seemed the Scotch gay world still closeted its people then

We left Scotland shortly, after regretfully thinking we could live here

16 - The Right One · Travel Bug—1978

Edinburgh skyline as seen from our hotel room.

We left Scotland shortly, after regretfully thinking we could live here in peace even with its very low-key gay presence. It had a wonderful air of having survived the centuries gracefully

in peace even with its very low-key gay presence. It had a wonderful air of having survived the centuries gracefully.

§

A few years later, we again returned to Europe but this time we came armed with Eurail-passes. These tickets, which you can only buy outside of Europe, give you almost unlimited travel through the entire Continent at bargain rates. You hop on these wonderful trains and hop off anywhere you please, taking care that the train has come to stop! We became gypsy types, starting with London. We had heard that the Earl's Court area was less expensive than other sections of the city. It was also the home of a large Indian population. But even more important, it had a few gay bars. We took a room in an Indian owned building, not anything to write home about, but it was cheap and

England

we were concerned about what we would be paying on the Continent. After some looking around, a short visit to the British Museum and some Indian curry at a small café, we sauntered to the Coleherne on old Brompton Road. We had heard that this was a really amusing gay bar. Since it didn't open until 11, we wondered if British gays bothered with getting any sleep on the nights they barhopped. When we entered, a few pairs of eyes swiveled around to take note of us. As we got more observant of the clientele, we were amused to see that the long U-shaped bar had sectors which had its own clientele. At one end were the swishy fem types, and then you had the business suits, very uptight. Then the chain and leather chaps crowd populated the rest of the bar length. It was hilarious to see the gamut of stereotypes all assembled in one bar. In the States, a bar usually attracts only one type of gay. We had a couple of beers, chatted a bit and left. There was too much to see and do to hang out in a gay club.

§

A day or two later, we took the train and ferry across the Channel to Amsterdam which was great fun. We had been given the address of a small gay-owned hotel right on one of the canals. It was a hoot managing the impossibly narrow stairs up to our room. Everything was immaculate, and the owners themselves seemed to be the bellhops, concierges, waiters, you name it. The only thing that went wrong was that we were so pleased to be in this delightful city that we wanted to stay an extra day or so but our room was already booked by the next visitors. We saw Amsterdam from the canal-boat level as we wandered down the charming waterways. We took in Rembrandt's House and walked through the famous Red-light district with its "girls" sitting in the picture windows. I was thrilled to see the Rijksmuseum where we stood before the gigantic Rembrandt, "The Night Watch." This world famous painting was to be slashed by a vandal a few years later. Today, it is surrounded by a brass rail and is covered in glass, which makes it hard to see, with all the reflections.

§

We left for Paris on our super express train shortly, wandered the Champs Élysées, did the Louvre but despaired of seeing much because of its

16 - The Right One · Travel Bug—1978

"The Night Watch", one of Rembrandt's world famous paintings, was slashed by vandals, and is now viewable only behind glass.

enormous size. A six-deep crowd surrounded the Mona Lisa. Mesmerized tourists made her inaccessible to anyone on a crowded schedule. We gave up on her and stood before the fabulous "Winged Victory" from the Greek world. I felt more in awe just standing at her feet on that grand staircase than I did with Mona. Again, we chose a very small hotel in an unfashionable part of town. We had devised a system for locating a decent, cheap hotel. It had to be within walking distance of the railroad station, and as Jim or I sat with the bags, the other would canvass the neighboring streets. It proved to work every time since there always seemed to be a rash of small hotels catering to the budget types like us.

§

We didn't really have a nailed down route to stick to at all. It just seemed like we were deciding as we went along

Then after feeling we were barely skimming the surface of what we should have seen in this elegant city, we were heading southeast to Zurich and Basel in Switzerland. We didn't really have a nailed down route to stick to at all. It just seemed like we were deciding as we went along. I remember visiting a wonderful museum in Basel that had a whimsical fountain in its front courtyard. The avant-garde sculptor Tinguely had devised several surrealist objects, which spewed streams of water from their orifices. A Medusa head with writhing snakes for locks

Switzerland

THE FABULOUS "WINGED VICTORY" FROM THE GREEK WORLD, LOUVRE, PARIS

was crying streams of water from her eyes. Inside the building, a quartet of stringed instruments played Mozart as we wandered from floor to floor. It was all so gorgeous. Music and Art together, always so complementary.

§

Spain

Then we entrained for Spain crossing through Provence but barely stopping. I had only seen southern Spain before on the earlier trips and was surprised at how French the city of Barcelona seemed. We did the famous walk along the Ramblas, that charming, tree-shaded stroll through a myriad of outdoor stalls selling anything you could name. Strolling musicians, jugglers, fire-eaters, dancers, and, of course, pickpockets. We ended up down at the harbor where we found a number of seafood cafes. The shrimp plate with Spanish beer was a hit with us. We sat and took in the boats and the hustle and bustle of a port city. The proliferation of porno magazines for straights and for gays made us realize how Spain had loosened its straightjacket that had bound it under Franco's strict regime. Spain could be honest with itself at last.

The proliferation of porno magazines for straights and for gays made us realize how Spain had loosened its straightjacket that had bound it under Franco's strict regime

Sunset Through
The Eifle Tower

Lake Lugano
Switzerland

When we boarded our train again heading down to the southern cities, we found our compartment had been taken over by a very pushy Spanish housewife type who was evidently moving her entire worldly possessions along with herself. She knew she was occupying much more rack and seat space than she was allowed. In fact, we didn't know what to do with our bags after entering the compartment. After some glaring and gesticulating, and I was pretending not to speak the language, we got a ticket agent to move her out. She went, but not quietly. And we acquired a more docile passenger to share our compartment.

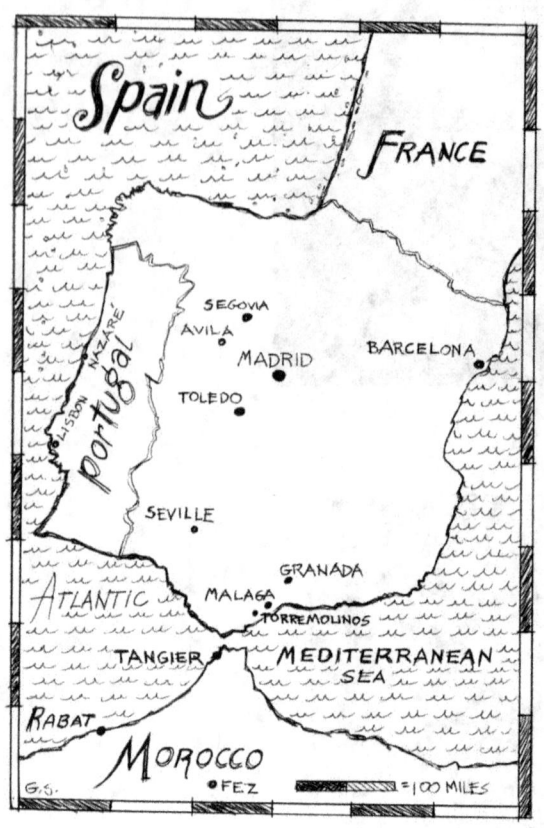

A tenant was occupying my condo so we found other accommodations in Torremolinos. It was curious to see how the town had evolved into the twentieth century. The ancient village remained in tact, with its winding streets and neat-whitewashed cottages conjoined to their next-door neighbors. On the outskirts of the town lay a smallish bullring, an important fixture in any Spanish settlement. As the town sat back away from the long stretch of beach, there was ample room from the rapid growth of 20th Century development. There were high-rises, apartment buildings sprouting all along the old highway, which now had been broadened to a four-lane speedway. It jogged off to the side of the old town to spare the inhabitants from the frantic modern pace.

My friend, Aurelio Gomez, was one of the developers busy with putting up these new towers. I marveled how they were held together since no re-enforcing metal rods seemed to be used. A type of hollow brick commonly used over all the Mediterranean was the accepted norm in building. I shuddered to think what this would mean if this building method were used in California. But when I brought it up in a conversation, Spaniards would simply say, "La suerte...su suerte esta decida," meaning, "your fate is decided." I imagine the people of Pompeii had much the same outlook as they glanced up to the slopes of the smoldering volcano, Vesuvius.

But in the present moment, Torremolinos was living it up with rampant construction, unheard of prosperity, hordes of tourists and a sizable proportion of them were gay men from every European country. Wherever they came from, it seemed the balmy, sun-drenched climate was such a contrast to their own overcast, damp skies. We counted nineteen gay bars in this small town, an amazing number for any European city. James Michener, the American author, had written "The Drifters," the story of the arrival of American hippies just after the '69 rebellion against staid morals and straight-laced attitudes. Any young American, who could afford the fare, was heading for Spain's southern coast. I imagine Hemingway's stories had much to do with the appeal of this sunny world. I likened it to my own California climate and felt much at home. But having joined forces with Jim, I no longer felt the longing to emigrate.

We took in a bullfight as almost a required item on a Spanish visit, but the spectacle of Man against Beast held no fascination for me. I have long felt that we are cruel enough to our fellow creatures, so that making a show of it is not very appealing. I had to avert my eyes when the final sword thrust was given — it was all so destined.

Village near Torremolinos, Spain.

We took in a bullfight as almost a required item on a Spanish visit, but the spectacle of Man against Beast held no fascination for me. I have long felt that we are cruel enough to our fellow creatures ... I had to avert my eyes when the final sword thrust was given

Seville Cathedral, "Door of the Conception," in the North façade.

Tomb of Christopher Columbus, Seville Cathedral. The remains are borne by kings of Castile, Leon, Aragon, and Navarre.

My real thrill was in traveling inland to Seville, which was staging Holy Week — La Semana Santa. Standing in the packed streets, seeing the hooded penitents shouldering immensely heavy religious floats. The tableaux on them were works of art, depicting stages in the life of Christ in florid detail. The carving of these lifelike figures was stunningly executed; you almost felt you were seeing a real Christ hanging on the cross. The hooded pallbearers were barefoot as a way of doing penance for their sins. They reminded me of the Ku Klux Klan's grotesque adaptation of this sinister costume.

At the great cathedral of Seville, we stood in rapt awe of the depiction of homage for Christopher Columbus. Four over life-sized, grieving pallbearers sculpted in stone held aloft his elaborate coffin. There was much evidence of the long period of Arabic rule in the handsome buildings of this city. I bought a few tiles done in blue fretwork to remind me of the beauty of this most Spanish of cities. In Malaga, only eight miles from Torremolinos, I hunted down the house where Picasso had been born. It was like a pilgrimage to him, but the only thing I could find was a plaque next to the door. No visitors allowed.

§

Returning to California, I was finishing my working career at Roos-Atkins and it was just as well. The company had misjudged its goals, had over-extended its empire of stores and was hiring a new cadre of executives to save itself from collapse. I was demoted when they decided that a New York display designer had a better sense of how to draw in customers. David Dunay was arrogant and considered San Francisco a hick town. He put me in charge of the carpentry shop across town in the warehouse district. I had a team of six workers who built fixtures for all the stores. I was happy to be out of the loop and with only another year before retirement, I could hardly object. Still, it was embarrassing to realize I no longer mattered to the company.

Return to Oakland

16 - The Right One · Travel Bug—1978

Of course, my hand-hooked tapestry business was booming so that I didn't feel useless now that I had reached sixty-five. I was busy every day and selling my work easily. I had heard of an agency that was city-and-state supported for mentally disabled youth here in Oakland. They held a yearly sale of donated art and I had started giving them a tapestry to sell to help their funding drive. Then, I was offered a job there teaching and supervising students as they made smaller hand-hooked pieces. Although the pay wasn't up at the level I had been accustomed to at my previous job, it hardly mattered since I now had my social security income to rely on.

I accepted the position, we constructed some frames and special stands to prop the works-in-progress and I was in business. At first I was apprehensive of interacting with people who were deemed "retarded." I soon found out that they made up in enthusiasm and perseverance what they might lack in "intelligence." I began to really connect with most of the dozen workers that were assigned to me. They were carefully screened for the level of proficiency necessary to produce the work. If a mistake was repeatedly made in the process of hooking, the student was removed to another type of art production. But I was impressed with the level of creativity shown by most of the group. One man, Dwight Macintosh, who dwelt in a foggy world of his imagination, would spend the whole day writing in a special script that was totally his own language. He would add rather erotic figures to embellish these pages. Eventually, a world-class museum of Outsider Art in Switzerland heard of his work and started buying whatever he produced. It didn't seem to impress Dwight that he was now a sought after, naïve artist and he continued his mysterious writing and phallic drawings. I used his work as the basis of a number of tapestries although he never got the hang of working with the tapestry hook we used.

We had an art gallery attached to the large studio, a converted auto repair shop. Here, we changed the art on the walls monthly and invited the public to openings. It was heartening to see a nice crowd come to these evening events. They actually invested their money on this charming, childlike art. I wound up with a collection of some fine work that I hang on my own walls at home. Some of these young people, who were delivered by bus from their institutional homes were afflicted with Down's Syndrome

At first I was apprehensive of interacting with people who were deemed retarded. I soon found out that they made up in enthusiasm and perseverance what they might lack in "intelligence"

and would never hold jobs in the real work-day world, others had murkier mental afflictions harder to diagnose but they all seemed to love to sit and produce art.

I began to feel a great kinship with this population of cast-off people, as I thought about my own hidden self. They seldom held back on displaying their affection for me as their mentor. But I was having a problem with the director, the head honcho of the operation. She had decided to attract national attention to the School and had submitted photos and a story to a couple of home design magazines. The hooked tapestry classes were a prominent part of the articles that were accepted and published — but nowhere was it mentioned that I was the teacher or initiator of this most successful part of the school. I felt slighted and overlooked. So I made a point of telling her I wanted to be recognized in print in any future magazine stories. It didn't register with her and a new article in an issue of House Beautiful magazine simply mentioned her role in the endeavor. I had grown somewhat tired of the job and I used this slight to hand in my resignation. I had been there for three years now but I walked away in sorrow at losing the friendship of my little coterie of students. Was I wrong in wanting a little recognition for the devotion I had expended in this job?

§

I had been giving the garden area next to the three bedrooms some serious thought. There were the steep flanks of the hillside, which made a charming view, and once in awhile, there was the added surprise of seeing a couple of deer grazing their way along the paths. Because of the danger of Lyme disease, I seldom if ever intruded into their primeval scene. It was sad enough that we suburbanites had taken almost all their land, leaving them with these last remaining few acres to exist on. My plan was to build a Japanese teahouse on the slope facing my studio so that I could feel transported to that exquisite landscape. I had never forgotten the few weeks I had spent in that sad, war-devastated country. Yet, there had been a tiny fragment of its former loveliness left for me to see when I visited with the Hayasaki family. I know that some will frown on my willingness to look past the horror of war atrocities, my own loss of my grandparents who were never heard of again. These concerns are not the stuff of day-to-day living for the millions of ordinary peoples in countries swept into the turmoil of War.

My love of Japanese Art and Culture gave me the incentive to move ahead with my idea. I first created the teahouse in a model using an inch to the foot scale so that I could visualize any problems. I went to bookstores, bought books on Japanese architecture. I studied the layout of a "cha-no-yu", which is the term for teahouse. The typical structure is four and a half tatamis (straw floor mats). So my building would be this size and it would be in a harmonious scale to the garden below it. At the time, in 1985, when this project was conceived, I had a gay friend on whom I placed my faith in getting this dream to come to life. I would have never been able to build this tea-pavilion without the help of Gene. He and I had met at San Francisco gay raps and had become good friends. He had always been a fine carpenter and when he heard of my idea, he was ready to help on weekends. He had often dreamed of building his own home in the woods, a la Thoreau of Walden fame. This would give him valuable experience and I was also going to pay him. In cash as well as two of any tapestries he would choose from my stock.

The floor dimensions had to be exacting because the tatamis had to fit snugly into the space. So I bought the mats first and measured the layout of four mats circling around a half mat in the center and this gave me an interior space of 9 by 9 feet. A verandah 2 feet wide encircled 3 sides adding to the feel of much more space. I ordered two Japanese workers to build my 7 shojis (sliding screens) at a cost of $1,600. I had hoped to build them myself, took a class in the City for it but found it much too tricky to grasp with its exacting requirements. I did the roofing myself with cedar shingles, built a tokonoma (alcove for art) on one wall, and bought futons to sit or sleep on. And the final touch — which I had almost decided was not important, but which Gene said was achievable — was the idea of having the center mat (3 ft. by 3 ft), spanning across a well into which your legs could drop. This allowed me to have the square mat as a dining table when it sat on corner posts. It quickly changed back to a floor mat by removing the corner posts. Westerners are usually too uncomfortable to sit on the floor cross-legged. So now the completed teahouse sat comfortably on its stilts and a concrete staircase led you up to the porch where you re-

Gene, my master carpenter helping me put the Tea House frame into place, 1985.

moved your shoes before entering this bit of Japan. I had spent $8600 and a bit more to bring a Japanese gardener in to do the landscaping with rocks, plants and gravel. I was amazed at how perfectly it all fitted together, and today as I write I glance out to this bit of Japan on my hillside and dream of the time spent there.

§

Spain, again

On the subject of adventures, I was to return to Spain another time when I couldn't talk Jim into going with me. He would complain of the awkwardness of fitting his extra length legs into the absurdly confined spaces airlines dole out to modern travelers.

It was the summer of '83 when I decided to go alone and also to sell the condo since it was apparent after five years that Jim and I were settled in for the long haul. We had come to an agreement that it was OK to have a little amorous adventure or two when we were off on vacations. There's no point in deluding oneself about the temptations that invariably present themselves. Jim had his "nights out" as well before I had gone vacationing so that I didn't feel I was betraying him. In the gay world, a dalliance doesn't create the crisis that the straight world suffers through. I suppose we

We had come to an agreement that it was OK to have a little amorous adventure or two when we were off on vacations ... in the gay world, a dalliance doesn't create the crisis that the straight world suffers through

(ABOVE) THE INTERIOR OF MY TEA-HOUSE. (BELOW) AS SEEN FROM THE GARDEN.

The Center Mat Spanning Across A Well Into Which Your Legs Can Drop.

16 - The Right One · Travel Bug—1978

take the fact that men, gay or straight are always testing the waters to see if their sex appeal is still there. What vain creatures we are – and this was supposed to be a feminine attribute!

I flew to Madrid, Spain, switched to a smaller plane to go the short haul to Malaga, where the airline lost my luggage. I was 8 miles from Torremolinos by commuter train and arrived with nothing but the clothes on my back. I was assured that I would have my bag within 24 hours. So I bought a toothbrush and made the best of it. I returned to the terminal the next day and was handed my missing bag. On the beaches, there were countless beautiful bodies turning bronze but I had come to the conclusion by now that skin cancer was not a pretty sight. I applied plenty of lotion, and limited the time in the sun. I made friends easily enough on the beach and was bemused by the different languages I heard. It was like the Tower of Babel. Nights I spent at my favorite tiny bar, the "Pourquoi Pas" – the "Why Not?" It had a total of 6 bar stools but most of the men sat outside at the small metal tables fronting the bar. I met any number of attractive guys here and bedded a few of them. It has always been a European custom for younger and older men to form relationships. I thought about the fact that this idea had its beginnings in Ancient Greece. Men married women to create families but turned to youth of the same sex to be truly sexual. I can imagine the protests that are coming from my readers. But, I believe that men and women are more bisexual than they readily admit.

Me as a sheikh in a photo studio at the Alhambra in Granada, Spain.

I can imagine the protests that are coming from my readers. But, I believe that men and women are more bisexual than they readily admit

But there was a rude surprise in store for me one day when I took the local bus into Malaga to do some exploring. This small city had been the site of a Moorish fort back a thousand years ago. There were still ruins, bits of walls, arches, and columns that remained. It wasn't as magnificent as Seville's Alhambra, which is not to be missed, if one visits Spain. But I wanted to see this small bit of Moorish architecture regardless. I took a few snapshots, dreamed myself into the past centuries and walked the mosaic pavements in a trance-like state. I seemed to be the only visitor at that moment and it was tempting to go into a reverie about life as it might have been then.

As I followed a trail leading up the hillside behind the ruin, there was a great wall pierced by arches every hundred feet. I suppose it had been an aqueduct to bring water down to the palace's cisterns. I knew that at the top of the hill there was a parador (inn), which I was interested in seeing. These are converted monasteries or convents that the Spanish Government has refurbished to modern day standards as inns. I expected I might want to stay in this one on some future visit. I was alone, but there were tourist couples a hundred yards ahead of me and behind. All at once, I was surrounded by three young men who said not a word but hustled me to a nearby rock, with two of them grabbing and pinning my arms down. The third youth pulled out a knife, which he jammed into my crotch while he used his free hand to divest me of my wristwatch, my camera, and my wallet. He then ripped off my tennis shoes and tossed them down the steep side of the cliff path. As a parting gesture, I was smashed on the forehead with the butt of the dagger, and I started bleeding profusely. I was in such a stunned mental state and it must have all been no more than a minute in time. It had gone so smoothly for them that it seemed rehearsed. They disappeared through the arches again as I sat like a felled ox on my rock. When I got my composure back, I crawled down the hillside to retrieve my sneakers. I wandered back down the path in a funk, cursing my luck. It was a gorgeous, sunny afternoon and my face was covered in blood. I knew that at the bottom of the hill there was a police station and I purposely left all that blood on my face for the "guardia civil" to see. I was ignored for a few minutes and I finally collared a police sergeant and told him I had just been robbed and attacked. He showed little interest, wrote out a complaint, and advised me to avoid that path, because it was known to be dangerous! When I asked why there wasn't a sign warning strollers, he simply shrugged his shoulders.

I was in the wrong, of course.

17
Bali and other Indonesian Ports of Call

1988, 1996

"In the subsequent years, I took vacations in the opposite direction, going to Bali on three separate journeys. I knew that I would find Bali very familiar in feeling and culture to my own beginnings in the Philippines." - GS

∫

This connection to his birth home and family in the Philippines opened a nostalgic door in George's life. But he never returned to the Philippines when he could have. Why go back to a time when your own father, and even your mother, simply can't or won't accept what you are as a human being? - JJ

BALI AND OTHER INDONESIAN PORTS OF CALL: 1988

*I*n the subsequent years, I took vacations in the opposite direction, going to Bali on three separate journeys. I knew that I would find Bali very familiar in feeling and culture to my own beginnings in the Philippines. Bali was south of the Equator but no more than 1,580 miles below Manila, that is, as the crow flies. I had heard much about the artistic achievements of this fascinating isle. Strangely, the Balinese had remained Hindu while the rest of Indonesia had become Muslim. The Dutch had conquered these lovely islands back when the rest of Europe was busy setting up colonial empires. The term "Spice islands" explains why this area of the world was so attractive to Europe.

Denpasar & Kuta

§

I booked myself on a two-week tour with a San Francisco travel agency, endured the tedium of long hours on the plane, before arriving in Denpasar, the capital of Bali. I was immediately immersed in a scene bursting with throngs of brown-skinned people rushing about on their errands. It brought back the distant past of my childhood so vividly that I stood there as if I was awakening from a long sleep. It was an eerie feeling, but a pleasant one at the same time. I got into a jitney taxi to the nearby suburb of Kuta where my hotel was located. Kuta is a beach town mainly known for its honky-tonk bars, dives and Australian visitors. Because Bali is only a two-hour hop from the top of Australia, it gets more visitors from that continent than any other lands. I won't go into a lot of detail here about what I did on these trips. They were wonderful experiences with some very gracious Balinese.

I was immediately immersed in a scene bursting with throngs of brown-skinned people rushing about on their errands. It brought back the distant past of my childhood so vividly that I stood there as if I was awakening from a long sleep

17 - Bali & Other Indonesian Ports of Call—1988

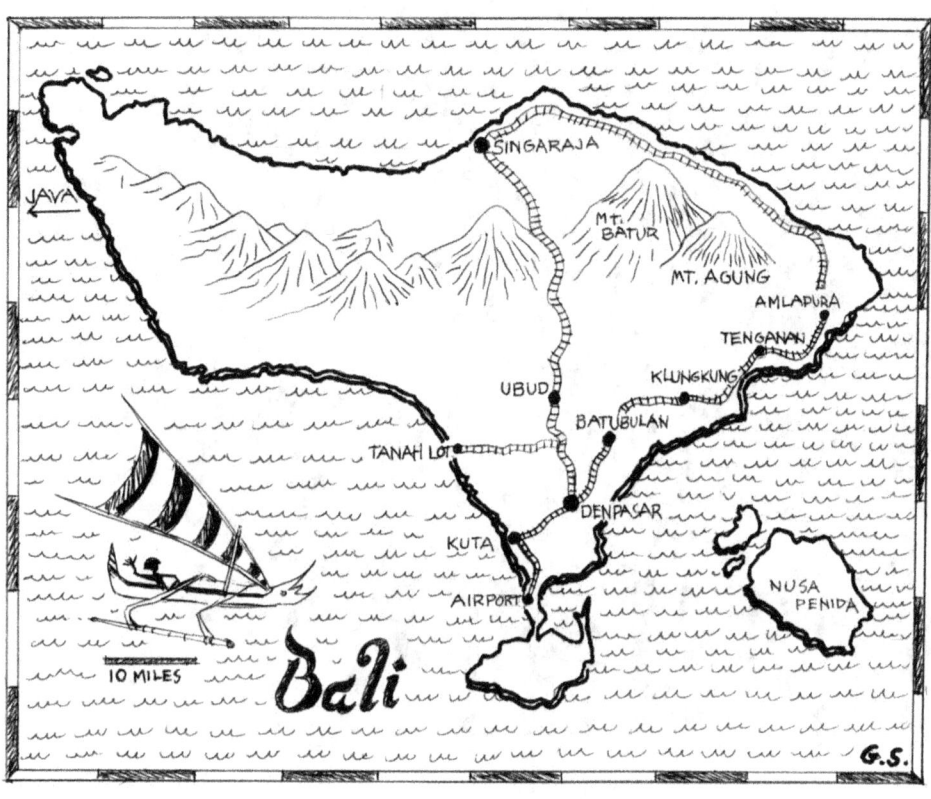

Ubud

§

A visit to Bali is not complete if you don't see Ubud. This village some sixty miles up the mountainsides, has long been know as an arts center. It is difficult to distinguish who is an artist and who isn't since almost every Balinese is one; in fact, they don't have a word for "artist" since everybody knows how to paint, carve or make beautiful things. I was in awe of the simple expression of creating that I saw all around me. One of the most appealingly was the tiny offering to the gods that you would find everywhere. This two by two-inch piece of banana leaf folded just so, containing a bit of fruit and rice was a prayer to the gods to protect the family from the demons. I was to stay in a wonderful thatched cottage overlooking a steep ravine filled with giant timber bamboo. I had never seen bamboo grow to these sixty and eighty foot heights. I saw art everywhere. The volcanic stone carvings of Hindu gods and goddesses were even placed as guardians to bridges across rivers. It was truly mind-boggling to me as an artist. As a hotel guest, I was being attended to by a Balinese youth

It is difficult to distinguish who is an artist and who isn't since almost every Balinese is one. In fact, they don't have a word for "artist" since everybody knows how to paint, carve or make beautiful things

George Somers on Indonesian Art Principles

It has often been stated that there are no words in the Indonesian language for art or artist. This is true and logical; making a beautiful offering, carving a stone temple gate, or making a mask are tasks of equal aesthetic importance and although the artist is regarded as a preferred member of the community there is no separate class of artists. A sculptor is simply a carver or figure-maker, a painter is a picture maker, a dancer is a *legong* or a *djanger*—the names of the dances they perform.

The artist is essentially a craftsman and at the same time an amateur, who uses his talent knowing that no one will care to record his name for posterity. His only aim is to serve his community, seeing to it that the work is well done when he is called to embellish the village temple or when he carves his neighbors gate in exchange for a new roof or some other similar service.

Nothing in Bali is made for posterity; the only available stone is a soft sandstone that crumbes away in a few years, so that temples and reliefs have to be constantly renewed. White ants devour the wooden figures, and humidity rots away all paper and cloth—so their arts never become fossilized. They are extremely proud of their traditions—also progressive and unconservative. When a foreign idea strikes their fancy, they adopt it with great enthusiasm as their own, but always translated in their own style and becoming Balinese in the process.

Balinese art is not in the class of the Great Arts like great Chinese painting—the conscious production of art for its own sake with an aesthetic value apart from its function. But yet it is too refined, too developed to fit into folk art. Nor is it one of the primitive arts—those subject to ritual and tribal laws which we call primitive because their aesthetics do not conform to our own.

Their art is a highly developed, although an informal Baroque folk style that combines a peasant liveliness with the refinement of the classicism of Hindu Java. The Balinese took the flowery art of Ancient Java—itself an offshoot of the aristocratic art of 7th and 8th Century India—and brought it down to earth and made it a popular art. When Bali became a colony of Java, the conquerors brought their art with them. Thus, the early classic period of Javanese art matches a classic period in Bali until Islam and political chaos severed all connections between the two islands and Hinduism took reguge in Bali.

Although at the service of religion, Balinese art is not a religious art. An artist can carve ludicrous subjects in the temples or embellish objects of daily use with religious symbols. The Balinese carve or paint to tell the only stories they know—those created by their intelllectuals, the religious teachers of former times. — G.S.

[My statement on Indonesian art principles, given before a group of travelers in Borobudur]

17 - Bali & Other Indonesian Ports of Call—1988

that was exceptionally handsome. He offered to sell me tickets to see the dancers at the Puri Saren palace in Ubud. He even offered to take me there on his motor scooter and I would be sitting scrunched up against his torso with my hands encircling his waist. Of course I couldn't refuse this delightful offer. Later, I was to be invited to meet his equally beautiful young wife and child. I became friendly enough with him to learn his name, Ketut Suwarnaya, and to keep in touch

My friend Ketut with his lovely wife and baby.

over the next few years and to be invited to his family compound. He lived with at least a dozen close relatives in a walled garden containing several buildings. They were mainly roofs over tiled platforms. There were smaller quarters attached to these for sleeping. But the main business of living was all out-of-doors since the climate was so benign. The only difference in the seasons was that it rained a lot for six months and then it was the dry season. much like the Philippines. I kept up a correspondence with Ketut, occasionally sending a money order to help them along with their next child. They were my way of feeling I had a family for a while.

I kept up a correspondence with Ketut, occasionally sending a money order to help them along with their next child. They were my way of feeling I had a family for a while

I need to confess at this point that not having a family of my own has made me seek this so important tie with the rest of humanity, by becoming an uncle of sorts in other families. It's hard to explain, and for many years I simply ignored it as a sentimental weakness. But then I see so many other gay and lesbian couples openly adopting children these days and Society has grown used to the fact that we in the gay world have the same needs they have.

The first visit to Bali made me think I might want to live there too, but I knew I would never convince Jim that he should go as well. I resolved to

I need to confess at this point that not having a family of my own has made me seek this so important tie with the rest of humanity, by becoming an uncle of sorts in other families

return again. In the meantime, I enjoyed the loveliness of the scene, visiting the ancient temples whose stones where often covered in velvety green moss, handing peanuts to the monkey troops that ruled the Monkey Forest at Ubud, buying paintings and sarong fabrics from the wayside shops. I was amazed at the daringly large figures of the monkey god, Hanuman that flanked the hotel's entrance for they sported enormous rampant phalluses. No one seemed bothered by this openness and I wondered what attitudes towards homosexuality would be. I was never to find out. I do recall as a child in the Philippines, that a "binabuy" (a drag queen), would create titters as "she" passed us on the street. I think I knew then that I must never be like that or I would be laughed at. However, in Bali, I never saw open gayness. Perhaps it was easier for the Balinese to blur the sexual differences since the men are not as distinctly masculine as they are in Western societies. It is hard to pinpoint the softer qualities that Balinese men exhibit, but they certainly do not strut about, act aggressively or shout when they want to dominate women. It is a much gentler, more feminine attitude.

§

The second time I flew to Bali for a couple of weeks, it was to be with Jim. He had actually consented to go as long as we added Australia into the deal. I agreed readily for I had always wanted to see that huge island continent. We worked out an itinerary that had us hopping to Cairns, up in the northeast corner of the country, and then taking a local plane to Darwin on the northwestern shores. From there it was an hour and a half to Bali. We would return to Darwin for a week on the way home giving us a chance to explore that region.

The flight went well, overly long, of course, since we were going such a long distance. Cairns was only to be a day's visit and we decided against spending good money on a day's excursion out to the Great Barrier Reef. Neither of us was eager to see the underwater grottoes of that much-ballyhooed attraction. We simply walked about the very touristy shopping mall and entertainment center built out over the water. We weren't that impressed by Cairns, but then we didn't go on the railroad ride everyone talked about or did the glass-bottomed boat ride that is the highlight of a visit to this sportsman's paradise.

17 - Bali & Other Indonesian Ports of Call—1988

We took our plane to Darwin early in the morning, arriving somewhere before noon, asked the taxi driver to recommend a motel and were whisked to his girl friend's lodgings on the edge of the downtown area. It was hot and humid as hell and we perspired freely just by standing still. Darwin is a small city with a history of surviving howling hurricanes. It has literally been blown off the map some four or five times and even prepared for an invasion of Japanese troops during World War II. It seems impossible to believe that Japan would attempt a take-over of this gigantic continent almost the size of the U.S. Out in the harbor, there bobbed a flotilla of ramshackle vessels from various nearby islands not a part of Australia's dominion. They were not welcome ashore and were supposedly not in contact with anyone in the town. We did a lot of walking around, took a boat tour out around the coast, seeing how tropical this part of Australia really is. We walked into the Quantas Airlines Office to check on some item of our flight and my gaydar switched on automatically. The very personable young man at the desk had returned that subtle signal which tells us that we are talking to a kindred soul. No direct words are necessary but we knew who and what we were. After a bit of desultory chatting, we were invited to meet him at the only gay bar that Darwin had. Nick — for that was his name — was partnered with another man, he told us, and they owned their home and a small yacht in a nearby suburb. So, having gotten directions to the bar, we left. It proved to be in an out-of-the downtown area. We continued our looking at the souvenir stalls. Every now and then, we would see a group of aborigines gathered in a grassy area having a quiet conversation. I was conscious of the sorry status that they seemed to be in. It reminded me of the African-American struggle for civil rights that we Americans had witnessed such a short time ago. I venture to say that the Aborigine is a few steps back in his fight for equality. Skin color seems such a deterrent to acceptance by us — the dominant white races.

We enjoyed a few Australian beers with our new friend at the ramshackle little bar, were invited to his home to meet his partner when we returned from the Bali visit and we were driven to our motel after a couple of hours.

> *We walked into the Quantas Airlines Office to check on some item of our flight and my gaydar switched on automatically. The very personable young man at the desk had returned that subtle signal which tells us that we are talking to a kindred soul*

The doors to my carport are figures from Australian aboriginal art. I am posing with two of my Russian friends

§

Jim and I found the same hotel I had stayed at on my first visit to Bali, and since it was a block from the beach, it was ideal. I found that Jim was much more interested in getting a tan than in prowling around the alleyways of Kuta. There almost seemed to be more Australians than Balinese and they were having an uninhibited ball getting very tipsy. Every other doorway along the main street seemed to be a beer bar. You were expected to order beer by the pitcher, never by the stein. But we hadn't come to Bali to see how drunk we could get. We made the decision to see more of the island by hiring a taxi driver to show us the villages bordering the sea.

Bali (*see map*) is shaped like a diamond that has been squashed at the top so that it has a longer axis going from east to west than the north-south points. It has two volcanoes that dominate its skyline from almost anywhere on the island. Mt. Agung is the sacred one and it lies to the eastern center. Mt. Batur lies to the left of Agung and it has been active as recently as 1974. We decided to stick to the coastal villages for our tour when we discovered that there was a very scenic road following the seas edge if we traveled counter-clockwise. Kuta is just outside of Denpasar and near the southern tip of the island. We had hired a very chatty driver who was elated with his good fortune in finding such a fare as we represented. He was to be our

17 - Bali & Other Indonesian Ports of Call—1988

guide for the next few days. I had brought along my new camcorder and couldn't wait to shoot all the beauty around us. Our first stop once we had passed Sanur, where there is a large group of very pricey hotels, was the Dance Exhibition hall at Batubulan. Here in this tin-roofed large shed in the rice paddy fields, we sat and watched a troupe of actor dancers telling the familiar story of the princess captured by the evil king and how Hanuman, the monkey god came to her rescue. There was a large group of musicians with their marvelous xylophone music. I managed to tape the whole performance before we left.

Batubulan

We headed on to Gianyar, where we saw dozens of sculptors working along the roads carving grotesque images out of the soft porous volcanic stone that Bali is made up of. We stopped in Klungkung, an ancient capital that still retained its governmental complex. This was a series of pavilions set in a man-made lake filled with lotus flowers and huge goldfish. You walked across to the pavilion on a stone bridge, up steep staircases to the airy open-sided room were the court sat in judgment. The sloping ceilings were completely covered with murals depicting the punishments for various crimes. It was enough to deter any Balinese from straying from the righteous path. The colorful paintings had lasted these last one hundred or more years in excellent shape.

Klungkung

We drove on another 20 miles along the coast, observing the salt-drying fields that were the main occupation of a village. Then we came into Candi Dasa, a resort-like village meant to attract the traveler. There were a number of attractive compounds here and we chose one that was right on the sea's edge. The thatched cottage had a second story, which was the bedroom with windows around three sides. The shower was nothing more than a five-foot wall surrounding one side of the downstairs room. Hanging from the eaves above me was the same carved monkey god and now his erect penis was a handy towel-rack!

Candi Dasa

I loved the ambience here, and was soon aboard a tiny sailboat with outriggers manned by a couple of brown teen-agers. Across the straits to the east, I could make out the hazy outlines of Lombok. This island neighbor has yet to be trampled by the tourist hordes but the ferry ride over to it was simply not one we could fit into our full schedule. We did walk along a small beach where fishermen were busy pushing large triangular arrangements of poles and nets that harvested hundreds of tiny

Hanging from the eaves above me was the same carved monkey god and now his erect penis was a handy towel-rack!

fish.

Tenganan

Not far from Candi Dasa, we asked our driver to show us Tenganan. This inland village is a remnant of old Bali, preserving the ancient customs very rigidly. It is surrounded by a low stone enclosure, which only keeps the forest out. There is no modern structure within its confines, with the center of the village dominated by a great covered pavilion for town meetings and dance performances. We paid an entrance fee to come into this very authentic bit of Bali and it was well worth it. I was amused at the wicker cages of gaily-colored roosters kept at doorways. Cock fighting is supposed to be banned but it persists anyway. I found an old scribe who made me a palm leaf page with my name in Balinese and in English. I bought a small book from him made by stringing together sections of palm leaf, which folded like an accordion. This was the way story telling was recorded in much of the Indonesian world for centuries, perhaps thousands of years. My "Lontar" book told an ancient story in Balinese script and pictographs. I treasure it amongst my library collection.

Tirtagangga

It was time to move on and we left sadly but anticipating the next stop we were hearing about from our talkative driver. We were going to spend the night at Tirtagangga. This had been the palatial home of an early sultan and the extensive grounds were adorned with several connected ponds surrounded by fanciful carved beasts spouting water into the pools. The sultan's residence was now a tourist hotel and we dined on his verandahs overlooking the main pool with its stone tower spouting water from many carved creatures. We ordered a sticky black pudding made of some strange jelly-like stuff and wondered when we got rather sick, what it contained. It didn't keep us abed long though.

Singaraja

Now we were rounding the coast in a northern direction and there were fewer sights to take in for the next few hours until we came to Singaraja on the most northern edges of the island. This was once the main area occupied by the Dutch when they conquered the island. There were still buildings with a definite Dutch look to them. We heard the dreadful story of the defiant stand of the Balinese Royal Court when the final moment of surrender came. The entire retinue of courtiers committed suicide by sword rather than submit to foreign rule.

We heard the dreadful story of the defiant stand of the Balinese Royal Court when the final moment of surrender came. The entire retinue of courtiers committed suicide by sword rather than submit to foreign rule.

17 - Bali & Other Indonesian Ports of Call—1988

(Facing Page)
Favorite Shot, Bali

> *The food was good but the real show was in watching the gecko lizards, which scampered along the ceilings over our tables. I recalled the childhood trauma I experienced when one of these little geckos fell into my food.*

At the beach cottages we stayed at, we met a couple of Australians who were father and son. They were quite friendly and we decided to join them for the rest of the trip back to Kuta. We dismissed our own taxi man here regretfully, but he seemed content in having earned more money than he would have competing with all the other drivers. The four of us got on well and decided to stroll down the beach to a great restaurant that was recommended by all. The food was good but the real show was in watching the gecko lizards, which scampered along the ceilings over our tables. I recalled the childhood trauma I experienced when one of these little geckos fell into my food. But that was long ago in Manila, and we were assured that it rarely happened here to anyone.

§

The next day we drove up over the winding roads that led one south across the flanks of Mt. Batur. It was drizzling most of the way as we passed through dense bamboo forests. We made a few pit stops as we hurried back to Kuta. We learned from our Australians that they were staying at an excellent hotel and they suggested we stay there too. Since ours was not much to our liking, we decided to upgrade our hotel stay. It was a gorgeous new resort hotel that was so well hidden down a side street that we would never have found it ourselves.

The Bali Padma was luxurious and as we arrived dirty and travel worn, I wondered if we would even be admitted. But they knew the Australian father and son from their previous stay and so we decided to splurge for the remaining three days of our Bali adventure.

The Australians immediately asked if we were ready for the night's pub crawl. I have never gotten much bang out of swilling beer and reciting dirty jokes all evening, so I begged off. I was tired anyway and soon hit the sack. Around two in the morning, Jim came in bleary-eyed. No sooner was he in his twin bed but there was a knock on the door. The younger Australian had been told by his father that he couldn't sleep in their room because he had a young lady in tow. How he managed all this in the brief time he had puzzled us all, but we took the teen in and assigned him to the love seat across the room. He must have been extremely uncomfortable because when daylight arrived, he was cuddled next to Jim in his twin bed. I wondered if he knew who we were, but then, it didn't really matter. Jim only

17 - Bali & Other Indonesian Ports of Call—1988

would have been interested if the youth was considerably older and then there was the fact that I lay a few feet away.

I had booked an excursion with a sightseeing group for the day, and Jim had to hustle around to be part of the sight-seeing plans for the day, when he would rather have slept it off. The youngster had the best of it — staying in bed for hours more.

When we got back to the hotel, we were amazed to find our room-key didn't work at all. Other guests were standing about puzzled about the same thing so we went back to the front desk and were handed new keys. Then I found that a gorgeous new black silk shirt I had just bought the day before was missing from the closet as well as a bit of money. The reason for the new keys became quite apparent now. The front desk people were rather vague about it, but it seemed that someone on the hotel cleaning staff having master keys to our rooms, had selected one or two items from each room and then hit the next room. I suppose they figured it wouldn't cause any hue and cry if only one item was missing from each room. I was furious in losing the handsome shirt but the staff refused to compensate me, saying I had probably left it somewhere on my travels! I don't know how they could have used the same story on others but we were quite unhappy. Then to make matters even more ridiculous, I insisted Jim and I get to the airport in a hurry only to find I had read the ticket wrong and the flight was for the next day. We returned to the hotel, and spent another day seeing the sights, but not with the Australians this time.

§

In 1996, the church I belonged to decided to do a study tour to Indonesia, which would go much further than I had gone on my two previous visits. The plan was to take the twenty-two of us down through Jakarta on Java, hop a plane up to the island of Sulawesi and then end up in Bali. We were gone for about seventeen days on our way back through Taipei, Taiwan. There were a number of human rights conference sessions at Jakarta and other stops because that was the reason for our trip. We were investigating civil rights problems, the working conditions for women and other related matters. I tended to skip out early from these meetings, feeling inadequately prepared to talk about the subject. I wasn't very impressed with Jakarta's new skyscrapers or freeway building when I saw hovels a few yards away from all the wealth. Someone was collecting a lot of cash while others

Jakarta

barely existed. Then we bussed to a college town called Salatiga in central Java for more discussions. I got to see a more balanced sort of life here. There was a lot of interest in showing us how well their Presbyterian church schools were operating. One fascinating side trip took us to a train museum where old antique locomotives and cars were lined up on tracks for us to admire. But there was much else, as well. We were taken to Yogyakarta where there was a sultan's palace to stroll through. It was like being an extra in the movie "The King and I." I loved the courtyards, pavilions, gamelan music and the turbaned men. I bought a turban but never had the nerve to wear it.

Borodbudur

Hopping on buses again, we were taken out to a world famous site, Borodbudur. This looks at first like a stone mountain sitting in grove of trees. It was actually a stair step pyramid constructed millennia ago by tens of thousands of workers. Rediscovered by the British governor of Java in 1814, it was poorly restored and required a UNESCO grant of $25 million in recent times to bring it back to its former splendor. Built on ten levels,

My church, Montclair Presbyterians on the 1996 trip to Indonesia. I'm third from left, foreground.

17 - Bali & Other Indonesian Ports of Call—1988

which you ascend as on a Buddhist heavenly journey, you pass carved walls depicting Buddha's life. There were 505 figures of Buddha enclosed in bell-shaped domes which you peered into. Half the Buddha's had lost their heads and these now reside in smart apartments all over the world. Well, one has to make a living and here was all this stone which brings in a lot of cash!

We also took in a nearby ruin called Prambanan, which consisted of strange Dali-esque stone towers covered with writhing figures. There were literally thousands of other stones scattered about the site, which were still a puzzle for anyone interested in reconstructing more towers.

Sulawesi

Now it was time to take a small commuter plane northwards to the island of Sulawesi. It used to be called Celebes on maps but with the new nationalism, it had adopted its current label. This seemed to be a new variant on the Indonesian look. We liked what we saw of the natives, they seemed friendlier, the architecture was particularly beautiful and we had never seen anything remotely like it. We planned to drive up into the mountains for a stay at a mountain retreat. The villages we passed through were arranged in neat rows of buildings that resembled ship's hulls. The rooflines were upswept at the ends and I likened them to a horse saddle as well. The walls were intricately carved with strange abstract geometry. On closer inspection, you could see that the water buffalo was the constant theme for the designs. Later, I was lucky enough to buy a model of this fascinating house concept and it sits on my coffee table today

A 3,000 year old pyramid at Borodbudur, Java, in later years (1996) with my church group.

Typical homes resembling ship's Hull In Tana Toraja Sulawesi, Indonesia.

for anyone to admire. I found out later why this style of construction was adopted. The men were ship-builders and also — centuries ago — feared pirates. They were called the Buginese and that name was the way that children were disciplined: you surely remember your mother (or grandmother) saying, "Be good or the 'bugiman' will get you!"

We traveled along steeper and more rut-filled roads, bumping over boulders and noticing the narrowness of our goat path we were supposed to call a road. Finally we arrived at the camp and were warmly greeted by four young men who had formed a 21st century touring company. They had brought up all the provisions for a five-day stay. We were to sleep in these fascinating houses here and I chose to sleep in one of the smaller ones that had been a granary for rice. I knew that I was in for a very discomfiting night when I would need to go the bathroom. The granary was easy to roll out of. But all through that first night, I kept hearing scratching sounds below me. I crept out fearing an attack from some unknown tropical beast — but nothing came of it.

All through that first night, I kept hearing scratching sounds below me. I crept out fearing an attack from some unknown tropical beast— but nothing came of it.

17 - Bali & Other Indonesian Ports of Call—1988

We toured around, visiting a strange cemetery. It consisted of a stone cliff set in a forest. Men had laboriously carved out shallow rectangular caves in the cliff walls randomly. In these openings stood wooden carved figures of their family members dressed in their finery. They reminded me of the naïve artists' work I had known when I worked at Creative Growth. It was just as well that they were high up on the cliff walls or they would have disappeared into western collections. The water buffalo was the revered creature in this culture, pampered and petted daily when it was needed to pull a plough through rice paddies. But when some ancient patriarch finally died, the buffalo was part of the funeral rites as he was slaughtered ceremonially and provided the meat for the feast', and the beasts horns might join others sacrificed to decorate the family's home.

We strolled through a great gathering of merchants set up under an immense corrugated tin roof who were selling buffaloes, pigs, chickens and all sorts of foods. I bought several lengths of stunning batik cloth. One vendor took a piece sewn into a tube arrangement and he demonstrated the dozen ways it could be tied on. You could end up sleeping in it as a blanket – or a shroud depending on your status.

Later, we drove out to a field were a picnic had been arranged while we watched a troupe of teen girls in lovely costumes performing traditional dances. I zeroed in on one particular beauty to photograph and she insisted on my sending her a copy of the shot when I got back. Her thank you letter, in very stilted, carefully scripted English words, was heart breaking and sweet.

My other souvenir from this wonderful province was a section of the boards that made up the house facades. It was handsomely carved with geometric symbols in black, white, orange and yellow.

§

It was time to leave Sulawesi and we now flew back to Bali for the last few days of this great trip. I was acting as advisor to Virginia Hadsell who was our journey leader. I recommended spending as much time as possible away from the big city of Denpasar or Kuta. I was able to steer them up to Ubud, which I knew so well and I think they truly enjoyed the ambience there. We did the Monkey Forest, visited the Elephant Cave called Goa Ga-

> *In these openings stood wooden carved figures of their family members dressed in their finery. They reminded me of the naïve artists' work I had known when I worked at Creative Growth*

Family couple in front of their Tana Toraja home decorated with sacrificed water buffalo horns.

jah, lunched at superb restaurants overlooking lotus pools, watched costumed dancing girls, bought souvenirs like mad and had a marvelous time until the last day when something terrible happened.

    I had been assigned to share my room with Jack York who wasn't in the best of health but had assured us that he could go anyway. His wife had stayed back at home. When I returned from sightseeing that day, I

Polina Sampe Rante, the dancer I thought was a beauty. She lives in the village of Tana Toraja.

found I couldn't open my hotel door. Jack had decided to rest and I knew he had to be in there, but I couldn't get him to open the door. I got the friends in the room next door to let me out through their window and I crawled along a ledge until I got to our window. When I climbed into the room, Jack was prostrate and out — on the bed. I got someone to call for an ambulance while we tried reviving him with cold compresses. He came to feebly and was rushed to a hospital. He became an invalid for the last two days as we winged up to Taiwan to change to a

The front gates to my home are from a Balinese house.

larger plane. When Jack finally reached his distraught wife, he closed his eyes forever. It was a bitter finale to our adventure but he did see his beloved wife before he went over to the other side.

18
Russia
1992

"During the nineties, I was becoming very interested in what was happening in Russia. The papers and television were full of news about the breakup of the Communist world in 1991. It was mesmerizing to me that this great ominous power that Reagan had called the "evil empire" was collapsing into nothingness ... I decided to go see for myself. I went the first time in 1992, just after Yeltsin took over the reins from Gorbachev." - GS

§

By now, George was more comfortable in relating moments in his life (I have spared the reader the many annoying battles to pull information out of him). His interest in Russian history, art, and its people are clearly laid out here, but I also pressed him on his gaydar and what gays were going through in the new Russia. - JJ

Russia: 1992

In an odd way, during the nineties, I was becoming very interested in what was happening in Russia. The papers and television were full of news about the breakup of the Communist world in 1991. It was mesmerizing to me that this great ominous power that Reagan had called the "evil empire" was collapsing into nothingness. I kept bringing up the hilarious image from the movie version of "the Wizard of Oz" where the Wicked Witch of the West dissolves into a messy puddle on the floor.

It may seem incongruous to others for me to show an interest in Russia, but with all the media attention, the hype, and the relief that the U.S. was now the only super power left, it was bound to affect me. I decided to go see for myself. I went the first time in 1992, just after Yeltsin took over the reins from Gorbachev. I had seen some tour advertising, which included a swing through Russia. The trip started in London, crossed over to Amsterdam, Copenhagen, Stockholm, Helsinki, and then into Russia via the great city of St. Petersburg. There was the train ride to Moscow that is famous in literature, then coming out of Russia through Minsk (now in Ukraine) and on to Warsaw, Berlin and back to London to fly home.

Jim and I were friendly with another gay couple that lived in Berkeley at that time, Bob and Ernie. I knew that Ernie wouldn't consider going for certain reasons but Bob would be more inclined to go for it, and so he agreed to make the journey with me. Jim had no interest whatsoever, he had done Europe with me twice and that had satisfied his interest. I felt differently about exploring this area of the world. After all, my grandparents had all been Europeans and it was somehow important, as one grows older to connect with the past, to see the cities and meet people who might have been relatives and friends if

My grandparents had all been Europeans and it was somehow important, as one grows older to connect with the past, to see the cities and meet people who might have been relatives and friends if fate had dealt a different card from the deck

18 - Russia—1992

fate had dealt a different card from the deck.

Bob came up with a great idea when he found a short letter reprinted in a local gay newspaper from a gay Russian offering to escort visitors around St. Petersburg if they happened to be in town. This very timely offer had turned up a week before our departure and almost seemed pre-destined. I immediately sent the man a letter telling him the date and hotel name where we would stay the two days we would be there. His name turned out to be Boris and he only wishes to be known that way, as he still has to remain in the Russian closet, his job would be jeopardized.

> *His name turned out to be Boris and he only wishes to be known that way, as he still has to remain in the Russian closet, his job would be jeopardized*

It was 1992 and I won't say much of anything about the other cities we visited before we entered Russia. The experiences we had were typical of this sort of trip. I had my new camcorder in hand and managed to keep a rather good record of what we saw. I must comment on the visit in Stockholm where we took a short boat ride over to an island in the harbor where the old village life of Sweden was reconstructed to give you a vivid feeling of the past. But the highlight here was the immense shed housing an ancient galleon intact. This vessel had only just been completed in the 1500s when it sank as it came down the runways at its maiden launching. The maritime shipwright who designed her must have been red in the face at the ceremony. But for posterity, it was a godsend since it was in prime condition when it was finally lifted from its watery grave. It took advanced technological know-how to resurrect it. I stood in awe of it and tried to visualize its passage through the Pacific seas as it sailed across to Acapulco. It was a dead-ringer for the Manila galleons I had seen in history books. The ship was absolutely stunning in its elaborate detailing. The stern face was a sculptor's dream of a job, heavily ornamented with mythical figures of Neptune, sea creatures and mermaids all in life-size proportions.

I also found myself in a shopping plaza beautifully enhanced with an ensemble of bronze figures dancing around Orpheus, God of Muse, plucking the strings of a lyre. The figures all seemed poised in midair as waterfalls tumbled around their feet. It was an enchanting work by my favorite sculptor, Carl Milles. We also drove out to visit Hittrask, a writers' retreat some miles out of Stockholm. This gave us a hint of the charm of living in rural Sweden as a revered poet or author. It seems that Europe pays more attention to the artistic folk that it nurtures. I compared it mentally to the neglect that America has for its creative people.

We were soon in Helsinki but so briefly that I formed no impression outside of a gigantic staircase that framed the city hall. We were now on a bus and soon crossed the Russian border at Vyborg. There seemed to be a lot of delay crossing the border with the guards making minute inspection of all the bus' undersides and interior for contraband. It all seemed in keeping with the Russian paranoia about foreign spies. We were almost afraid to look up for fear of being thought spies or terrorists. We were allowed to drive on finally and rolled through groves of white birch forestland. We had not been given a pit stop for hours and were informed we would be left to our own resources in a few minutes. We expected some rest station with properly marked doors for men and women. Instead we parked by the forest edge and the men dashed off to the nearest bushes while the women made tracks for a spot further away. It was a grim token of what to expect now that we were in Russia and we grew apprehensive. But, it wasn't to be so bad later, after all.

We rolled into St. Petersburg to find it a stunningly beautiful city of handsome Baroque buildings. Peter the Great had conceived it in 1703. It had been nothing more than marshy delta land traversed by several rivers, which emptied into the Baltic Sea. This giant of a man (he towered over other men at 6 foot, 6 inches) was so domineering and determined to give Russia a decent seaport on the Baltic that he enslaved thousands of peasants to build it from the swampy site. The Russians refer to it as the city "built on bones." Because it incorporates the river Neva and the lesser streams that flow into the Baltic Sea, it has hundreds of bridges on its main streets, giving it another appellation – "Venice of the North." Peter commissioned Italian architects to design his buildings and so they have a harmonious connection to each other. They all rose in their baroque splendor in the next few decades giving the city a consistent style seldom seen in other world capitals.

Our hotel, The Moskva, was at the end of the main thoroughfare, Nevsky Prospeckt. As our bus pulled up, a small fry armed with dishrags besieged us; he immediately began polishing the grime off the bus sides. A

It seems that Europe pays more attention to the artistic folk that it nurtures. I compared it mentally to the neglect that America has for its creative people

ragged band of men played popular Russian tunes nearby with a violin case left open with some tattered paper money in evidence. It was obvious that Russia needed any spare change we might be hoarding. As we entered the hotel, we noticed two plainclothesmen who barred any Russian from entering the lobby. They were going to be sure no exchange of any kind took place between foreigners and natives. Our room was small, with tacky wallpaper and would have been rated third class by America's standards. The TV was dead, of course, and perhaps it was meant to be merely decorative. But the dusty window looked out on the Neva River, which was spanned below us by a huge bridge.

Although it was Bob who first saw the published letter that told us of the young gay Russian who would show us around the city, it fell to me to go downstairs to the hotel entrance to meet Boris. I didn't have a clear idea who I was supposed to look for but somehow we recognized each other — gaydar working? Boris was slender, bordering on thin, quick moving, with crew cut hair and blue-eyes. He was dressed in casual slacks and a bright blue, shiny pullover with the English words "Commodore" printed across his chest. He was accompanied by another youth, also very slim, with black-hair and a more effeminate sort of bearing. Sergey didn't speak English at all and took a back seat in the ensuing conversations. But Boris was a mine of information, speaking in deliberate, well thought out sentences. I was relieved that he was fluent enough that the talk wouldn't be stilted.

I didn't have a clear idea who I was supposed to look for but somehow we recognized each other– gaydar working?

We crossed over the plaza in front of the hotel and headed though massive iron gates fronting the Alexander Nevsky Monastery and Cemetery. There were gardens and benches here and perhaps Boris chose this site to talk since any snoopers could easily be spotted if they came near enough to hear us. I had my camcorder in hand and also some copies of International Male magazine to give them. I figured that they would enjoy looking at handsome American models wearing expensive sports clothes. I had no idea if magazines of the Western men's fashions would mean anything to them but the magazines took up little luggage space in any event. They sat with their arms slung over each other's shoulders and it occurred to me that this was a brave act for them in this moment of Russian thaw. After chatting and making sightseeing plans for the next day, we said our good-

They sat with their arms slung over each other's shoulders and it occurred to me that this was a brave act for them in this moment of Russian thaw

byes. I was still tied into the Tour's plans of seeing the city from the bus windows. Bob was curious as to what I had learned from the two Russians and he said he would join us the next day even if it meant missing some of the Tour's schedule.

We visited important places like the Kazan Cathedral, the Bronze Horseman, St. Isaac's Cathedral, the Smolny Church where Lenin first set up the Bolshevik rule, Peter and Paul Fortress, where most of the Czars are entombed, the Hermitage Museum and then out to Pavlosk and the Catherine Palace. At these magnificent places, we were required to pull socks over our shoes so that we wouldn't mar the lovely inlaid marquetry floors. The Catherine Palace's main reception room was so vast that it could have enclosed a football field easily. It was amazing to know that this was all restoration work. The Nazis had turned it all into a ruin. They had used the priceless tapestries, paintings and carved decorations for target practice. One Russian woman, who headed up a group of people, had had the foresight to bundle up most of the finest pieces onto trains heading east to the mountains past the German military. She also managed to bury large statuary groups. They returned after the War to restore Pavlosk and Catherine Palace to most of its former glory. It was a heart-rending task for her since money was more desperately needed for the sick and wounded.

Boris and Sergey escorted us into the Hermitage Museum, which covers a city block. It was the creation of Catherine the Second, daughter of Peter the Great who founded the city. There are over 2,800,000 exhibited items ranging from the Neolithic Era to the Modern. There are a number of Rembrandts, Da Vinci, Rubens, Titians, and on and on. It was absolutely overwhelming. And one has to remember that there was a lot more before the Communists started selling off masterpieces, as they needed cash

I was asked if I wanted to see Boris's home and I readily accepted. Bob chose to stay with the Tour. As in most Russian cities, the central district is not where most of the people live. You take subways out to the outskirts, board buses that take you out even further. What you see are huge gray, concrete

The Catherine Palace's main reception room was so vast that it could have enclosed a football field easily. The Nazis had turned it all into a ruin. They had used the priceless tapestries, paintings and carved decorations for target practice

What you see are huge gray, concrete slabs devoid of any charm, rising 7 or 8 stories. The elevators have mostly stopped working, the hallways reek of urine and light bulbs have been stolen. It is a depressing picture and the interiors aren't much better. It is amazing that Russians can endure the cramped living that is their common lot

slabs devoid of any charm, rising 7 or 8 stories. The elevators have mostly stopped working, the hallways reek of urine and light bulbs have been stolen. It is a depressing picture and the interiors aren't much better. It is amazing that Russians can endure the cramped living that is their common lot. Of course, government officials live in another world with all the perks, but I am describing the common family. Boris's mother and father who were gracious and welcoming slept in the tiny living room whose double bed was also the sofa. A card table was the coffee table and the dining table combined. Off around a corner, Boris had contrived a little alcove where he and his brother slept. Every possible wall space was filled with shelves or posters. I would have developed claustrophobia the first week, yet they had lived this way from birth and felt it was natural.

We had a decent meal, nothing fancy, I think I remember meatballs and cabbage but even that was probably special for them on the meager diet they have had to live on. I had brought a bottle of wine.

We left St. Petersburg sadly, realizing there was so much we hadn't seen. I vowed to come back and did two more times in the following years. I talk about that later in this story.

§

Our Tour bus pulled out the next day, heading south along the two-lane highway that connects St. Petersburg to Moscow. Not too far along the route, we stopped at Novgorod. This was an ancient town before anything else even resembled a town. There was a magnificent monument here to all the Russian heroes going back to the Vikings and the Cossacks. We strolled along a park leading down through fortress walls to a river where a holiday crowd was sunning and frolicking in the water. Much of all this I was able to tape and can enjoy today: a man feeding a squirrel in his hand, a band of men tooting on their trumpets to earn a few rubles, young couples arm in arm along forested pathways, and teen-aged soldiers in ill-fitting uniforms moving about always in pairs.

Our bus stopped along the highway so that we could get a closer look at the farmhouses that dot the road. Not a one had had a coat of paint in the last decades; their shabbiness was an indication of the economy. But the window frames were always elaborately carved with an exuberance that spoke of earlier more prosperous days.

We came into the vast sprawl of Moscow's Centrum and again the drabness was the overwhelming impression. I saw that this place was a business city with no regard for civic beauty. The buildings were uniformly ugly and without any grace. We checked into the Belgrade hotel and almost immediately one of our tour members was involved in an incident. He had stepped out to the sidewalk and was soon surrounded by a mob of children who were all jabbering away while one of them started to rip his wristwatch off his arm. He managed to grab it back and bat the kid off. When these sorts of incidents occur, the usual response is, "Oh, those are the gypsies, be careful and don't go near them!"

We were soon taken to the prime sight one must see here in this world capital. Red Square is truly imposing with its cobblestone vastness. At one end sits the most amazing jumble of towers, onion domes, circus-looking building that ever came out of one man's mind. In fact, when the architect finished this bewildering ensemble of shapes, it was considered by the current Tsar to be too beautiful to ever be copied. So he had the architect blinded! At least that is the story we were told. The building was sealed so we didn't get inside. But there was a raised platform nearby with a decorative iron railing and we were told that this marked the spot for public beheadings and hangings in the past.

Also, in front of the Kremlin wall, sat the Lenin Memorial Tomb in a rust colored granite. Its simple block shapes were a striking contrast to the baroque splendor of St. Basil's onion domes. I was surprised that we were permitted to bypass the long queue that snaked across the vast plaza. I suppose it was setup to let foreign tourists through faster since they had limited time schedules. A squad of young soldiers was performing a very ritualized performance of goose-stepping as they exchanged themselves for the group that had guarded the entrance up until that moment. I taped the whole thing for my later enjoyment. We then filed into the dim interior with only a soft spotlight focused on the glass case that frames the embalmed body of Lenin. He didn't look human to me, with his waxy white features. Since he was periodically re-embalmed with fresh fluids, he has taken on a sickly pallor that is unearthly. We heard that his widow was aghast when she learned that he was going to be put on public display for the future generations. Since the time that I was there to see him, he has been removed from view and the ceremony of the guards no longer takes place.

18 - Russia—1992

We were also escorted into the Kremlin walls, walked the broad streets, saw an impressive collection of very ornate sleighs, carriages, court costumes and uniforms from the Tsarist days. We entered one of the huge cathedrals, the Annunciation, where the Tsars were crowned hundreds of years ago. The walls and columns were totally covered with frescoes of saints and kings — absolutely breath-taking. Outside, there was a huge cast-iron bell heavily decorated that must have been 20 feet tall. It was impossibly heavy to hoist into a tower and simply cracked off a piece as it was finished. You could stand in the doorway made by the crack. Another monster nearby was a gargantuan cannon that again was too cumbersome to actually work. It seemed the Russian national psyche demanded that it surpass anything yet conceived by other countries. It all seemed to make sense when one thought of the recent history of this nation, which has always felt compelled to be grander, bigger, more advanced than any other.

We felt more at home watching folk dancers, balalaika players at a small concert hall that evening. I managed to tape that as well. I almost fell in love with the handsomely bearded man who was directly in front of me on the stage as he sent his fingers racing over the steel strings of his triangular balalaika. The women were stunning in their floor length ethnic costumes, which had very high waists pushing their breasts up seductively. There was a lot of beautiful embroidery over the sleeves and upper sections. The men were simply dressed in the traditional banded neck shirt and baggy trousers.

Later we were taken down to the famous shopping street called the Arbat, which is now a pedestrian walkway. It was tempting to buy stuff but most of us held off after considering the amount of space available in our luggage. There was a very elegant version of MacDonald's at the end of the street, which we checked out but didn't patronize. Why would we come all the way to Russia to go to a MacDonald's?

What caught my eye was a man that carried a bear cub on his arm and he would take a photo of you holding it yourself. I couldn't resist this come-on and was soon trying to hang on to a very wriggly animal. After all, the bear often symbolizes Russia. I had one of our tour members take it so that I would have a better chance of seeing the print after we returned. I tipped the man, of course, since he was a "biznezman" as the Russians say.

That evening some of us were doing an optional item, which always costs extra on the tour, but you can't really skip them if you expect to see anything. We were to go to the Circus! Russians do their circus with only one ring and the audience sits around it on all sides just as Romans sat around their coliseums. But at one point, there is a grand staircase coming down from the highest seats. The performers parade down these stairs as a way of previewing what you will see. I had my camcorder going through all the first half of the show up to where the high-wire artists were doing their daring work when all of a sudden a woman usher came dashing over to me and screamed, "Nyet, nyet!" I couldn't believe it, as they had said nothing up 'til then and then I realized they hadn't seen me taping. I stopped and thank God they didn't try to confiscate my tape. I had valuable military information in my camcorder, of course!

We left Moscow the next day, driving west to Smolensk, a much smaller city but famous in World War One battles. We did a short visit to a handsome old cathedral with its myriad onion domes. A wedding had just been performed and I caught the bride and groom rushing out of the front door on my camcorder. No rice was tossed but I know that Russians are flocking back to church weddings since the Thaw. They also hike themselves to the nearest war memorial to be photographed. I didn't understand the significance of this custom, unless it was to remind them not to get into wars?

Holding a Russian cub on a Moscow street.

18 - Russia—1992

Then on to Minsk, which still had Communist heroes on their pedestals in the squares. I suppose they just hadn't gotten around to dumping them. I forgot to mention a special little trip in Moscow. We were shown a park where they had hauled some twenty or so bronze statues of disgraced leaders. Stalin was much in evidence. I got a kick out of posing as a statue here amongst the Fallen.

Communist statuary relegated to a junk sculpture park after the fall of communism.

§

Our next big stop was Warsaw and here we were put up in a very western motel with a modern flair to it. Bombing destroyed most of Warsaw, but there had been a tremendous amount of restoration done already. The ancient section was rebuilt almost perfectly because there were so many photos and architectural drawings to refer to. We toured the Chopin Monument Garden, gaped at the presidential mansion, and that evening many of us attended a piano concert in a stately old mansion. I loved the ambience here and would have stayed on but we still had a schedule to stick to.

§

Berlin was our next city and I looked forward to see this center of the Nazi world. We drove down tree-lined boulevards with monuments at several points and I looked in vain for the devastation I had expected to still see but I had forgotten what tidy souls the Germans are. They seem to hate messes and the only sign I saw of desolation was the area around the old Reichstag government building. There was a large sandy mound there and it was the site of Hitler's bunker. This was where he had hidden underground until he realized there was no hope. He married Eva Braun, his mistress, and then shot her and himself. The German public was now split on what to do with the site. Shovel it all flat and try to forget the horror of his regime or turn it into an under-

There was a large sandy mound there and it was the site of Hitler's bunker. The German public was now split on what to do with the site. Shovel it all flat and try to forget the horror of his regime or turn it into an underground museum of Nazi crimes

ground museum of Nazi crimes. I have no idea how it was to be resolved.

We were to stay at the Stadt Berlin, a skyscraper of a hotel with all the most modern amenities. And we were right on the Alexanderplatz, which is a great plaza area with a train terminal, a huge TV tower with a restaurant atop it. Next to the tower was the old civic center with its brick buildings and a handsome fountain sporting gods and goddesses playing in their watery domain. I took some great cam shots of children romping through these statues. The big public spaces were teeming with people rushing to their jobs and shoppers paused to listen to the South American pan pipers. It seemed a bit incongruous but the music was seductive.

> *We were shown the Brandenburg Gate and Checkpoint Charlie, which was the only gate into the eastern section when Berlin was rent in two by the Russians. It was only five years earlier, on June 12th, 1987, that President Reagan gave his famous Brandenburg Gate speech, "Mr. Gorbechev, tear down this wall."*

We were shown the Brandenburg Gate and Checkpoint Charlie, which was the only gate into the eastern section when Berlin was rent in two by the Russians. It was only five years earlier, on June 12th, 1987, that President Reagan gave his famous Brandenburg Gate speech, "Mr. Gorbechev, tear down this wall." There was a small museum here with some of the ingenious contraptions that the East Germans contrived to get across the forbidden zone. One marveled at the imagination it took to dupe the border guards and then there were photos of failed attempts including a photo of a youth as he was shot crossing the no man's land. We also stopped briefly at a vast cemetery to those who died in Berlin during the War. We drove past a mile of the famous Berlin Wall gaudily painted with political cartoons and I dutifully bought a fragment of the Wall from a peddler. The Pergamon Museum was off limits to camcorders much to my chagrin because this was such a stunning place. Inside was a complete Greek temple with gorgeous figures carved into the walls and a great staircase leading up to the altar. Then there was a lovely blue tiled entry gate with heraldic lions marching in procession. It was unearthed in the Arabian Peninsula at some time in the 19th Century when these priceless artifacts were being sold off for practically nothing by destitute Arabian countries.

Close by the Pergamon Museum, there was the Egyptian Museum. It was a converted mansion and here I was privileged to look at the most famous sculptural portrait of all ... the exquisite head of Nefertiti. She is so modern and stunning that she seems alive. And, I was allowed to use my

18 - Russia—1992

President Reagan at the Brandenburg Gate giving his famous "tear down this wall" speech.

camcorder here — I couldn't believe my luck!

We did the main shopping street, the Ku'Dam, and entered the fanciest department store, the Ka da We. Don't ask what that stands for, but I was open-mouthed at the goodies for sale here. Up on one of the top floors, there was a food section with the most caviar I had ever seen in one spot. It was mind-boggling and I wondered who could afford all this affluence.

We left Berlin frustrated with the thought that we had just begun to see all the beauty it held. Somehow, I had expected to see a devastated capital but outside of a handsome old cathedral which had the top of its tower blown off by bombs, there was nothing much to remind you of what it was like in 1945. In the forty or more years since that fateful date, the Germans had almost completely erased the stigma of a conquered nation.

The White House (U.S. Public Domain Images)

§

It wasn't far to the western edge of the continent. We were in Amsterdam again for a brief overnight and then rolling along past the beaches of Dunkirk, which saw so much bloody butchery of our soldiers. I felt a cold chill run up my back as I thought about the thousands of lives wasted here. One likes to think it couldn't have been in vain but do we ever learn really?

At Calais, we finally said our good-byes to our driver and the guide who had made this journey so smooth.

We could see the famous white cliffs of Dover as we neared the English coast and I thought of the armies and navies of European history as they planned attacks on this small island kingdom. Our hotel was close to Brompton Court Road and I discovered an old cemetery along its route that was like stepping into the Victorian past. The tombs and statuary here were so perfectly preserved that you expected to see hoop-skirted ladies to come by with their parasols held aloft. We toured Piccadilly Square, passed Madame Tussaud's Wax Museum, Hyde Park, Kensington. We saw the changing of the Royal Horse guards, passed the Royal Palace, and visited the Tower of London to gape at the Crown Jewels. We also toured the Covent Garden with its street entertainers and listened to public speakers get on soap-boxes to harangue the crowds about their problems with the government — free speech having its say. Now, it was time to board a plane back to the States.

19

The Army Doesn't Forget

1994, 1997

"Jack had written to get me involved with coming to the old company's reunions, which were being held annually. Every year, one of the "old boys" would volunteer to host the event at his home state ... it seemed like something very sentimental and I wondered how I could possibly fit into the camaraderie since everyone would have their wives in tow." - GS

§

Early on, I had asked George if he kept in touch with members of his Company. Had I not asked, none of it would have come up. And here again, after 50 years had gone by since leaving Japan, George confided he wasn't sure what to do. I reminded him that a number of his comrades harbored their own secret after pulling a "rape train" on a French teenage girl. - JJ

The Army doesn't Forget: 1994, 1997

A couple of years back, I received a letter from Jack Doll whom I had been friendly with in my Army Company. We weren't close friends and I had never divulged my gay self to anyone in the outfit for fear of being betrayed. I had kept any friendships on a certain level of confiding. In fact, during the 3 years, 9 months and 5 days of my Army life, I had become celibate except for the short weeks that Jerry had been training in Aberdeen. I was determined to come out of the Army with a spotless record of behavior. Of course, it seems ludicrous now that we see gays being discharged by the hundreds in the "don't ask, don't tell" era. But, it's convenient for the Army to not be particularly concerned when there's a big war raging and men are desperately needed. I never was questioned as to my sexual orientation except for the initial paper that everyone initials as you sign on. It simply asks if you are homosexual and everyone answers "no."

> *I had never divulged my gay self to anyone in the outfit for fear of being betrayed.*

1994

§

Jack had written to get me involved with coming to the old company's reunions, which were being held annually. Every year, one of the "old boys" would volunteer to host the event at his home state. He would make the arrangements for motel rooms, rent a party room, and plan an outing or two for the brief 3-day event. It seemed like something very sentimental and I wondered how I could possibly fit into the camaraderie since everyone would have their wives in tow. On top of this, they had started a little newsletter titled, "The 480th Re-Treads," which was written and published by anyone that volunteered to do it. I was soon receiving my quarterly copy of this 8-page booklet filled with stories, letters, photos, and anecdotes from the past. Jack had a vast collection of old photos of everyone and I found myself on the

> *It seemed like something very sentimental and I wondered how I could possibly fit into the camaraderie since everyone would have their wives in tow.*

19 - The Army Doesn't Forget—1994, 1997

There were now 31 men left from the original hundred or more we had comprised as a company.

pages as well. I was urged to come to the 1995 get-together, which would take place in the southeast corner of Pennsylvania, close to New York. I realized I could stick around and take a bus into the Big Apple after the 3-day hobnobbing with old friends. Jim decided he would join me in NYC when I arrived there.

There were now 31 men left from the original hundred or more we had comprised as a company. It would be interesting to see what 50 years had done to our faces and bodies. As for anyone beside myself being gay, I had no idea but I certainly wasn't going to reveal anything to them. It was interesting that no one ever asked me during the event, if I had married or why I hadn't married. I had come to the conclusion that it is understood that I was gay and there is no point in asking embarrassing questions.

Jack and I corresponded and I decided it made sense to take Amtrak from California across the continent to his home in Cincinnati, Ohio where, after a day's visit, I would join them on the fairly short drive across the state of Pennsylvania. Jack and Marian were delighted to see me and I was shown around the city briefly before we jumped into his car for the trip. As we were leaving in plenty of time, I tried to interest them in doing a small side trip to see the world famous Frank Lloyd Wright house called "Falling Water." It is probably the most celebrated piece of domestic architecture in America and we would be within 40 miles of it as we entered western Pennsylvania. I was disappointed that they felt it was important to keep moving even though we were arriving ahead of everyone else. I felt terrible at missing this singular opportunity but said nothing.

I had come to the conclusion that it is understood that I was gay and there is no point in asking embarrassing questions.

As the "old boys" started showing up, it was hard to recognize them now as old men. Sadly, I had to ask them for their names. I wondered

"George Somers attended his first reunion this year and he said he was having a great time. He volunteered to design a new newsletter cover." (excerpt from "480th Ordnance News", 1994)

what I had gotten myself into now. But everyone was gracious as wives were introduced. Some already knew each other from the last reunions. We sat and had cocktails, and snacks, and went to see our host member's house a few miles away. Chick Hiken and his wife Lucy were especially friendly as they piloted us around the countryside. Our sightseeing bus was a replica of the famous San Francisco cable cars, which I thought was hilarious. We saw bits of the Appalachian Trail, the Delaware River, and a Quaker village, which was a fake construction to entice tourists with antique shops in a charming small town. I enjoyed the chance to see them again but I saw the ravages that time had made on their faces. Was it due to the stresses of living and supporting a wife and family? I was complimented on how young I looked in spite of my white hair. At least I had hair while most of them were bald or close to it. Did being gay somehow keep me youthful? I leave it to the scientific researchers to investigate that point.

As the "old boys" started showing up, it was hard to recognize them now as old men. Sadly, I had to ask them for their names.

§

After the good-byes, I boarded a local commuter bus, which took me into Manhattan. I had reserved a room at the Pickwick Hotel on 51st Street between Second and Third Avenues, I think. It is amazingly inexpensive and was a special secret that a lady friend, Karen Callahan had revealed to me. To stay in New York City can be budget breaking but this little gem of a hotel is still in the $60 a night category or was anyway in 1996. I ate at little cafes nearby, did the scenic tour on a double-tiered bus with the open to the sky top deck which is a great way to see the lofty heights of the skyscrapers. Jim arrived a day later and we moved into a larger room. We did the Museum of Modern Art, the Metropolitan, and the Guggenheim, Central

"A True Hero of WWII," inscribed on the back of this 1994 reunion photo by Merle Murphy, an old Army buddy from the 480th Ordnance.

Did being gay somehow keep me youthful? I leave it to the scientific researchers to investigate that point.

19 - The Army Doesn't Forget—1994, 1997

Park and discovered a small gay bar called the Gray-Haired Club. It was packed every night with older gays and their admirers. It comes as a shock to realize there are young men who prefer older men and they aren't always looking for "sugar daddies" as the term implies. I had one gorgeous youngster from Argentina who was very interested but I pointed to Jim nearby to cool him off. Still, it was fun to flirt a bit. All in all, it was a delightful visit even though we didn't get to the great shows. I find them overrated and way too expensive. We flew back to California soon after.

> *We discovered a small gay bar called the Gray-Haired Club. It was packed every night with older gays and their admirers. It comes as a shock to realize there are young men who prefer older men and they aren't always looking for "sugar daddies."*

§

1997

I should have mentioned that I volunteered to host the next reunion at my own state in '97. It was heartily accepted. I knew it entailed a bit of work on my part but Oakland has developed a wonderful wharf side area called Jack London Square. This complex includes several hotels, motels, restaurants, boat berthing, souvenir shops, and historic points of interest for Jack London fans, and even has a yacht which was Franklin D. Roosevelt's. I planned for them to stay across the street from the Square at a nice motel and the banquet would be at a village restaurant with a large dining room. About eleven men and their

Hamming it up in 1994.

The remains of the 480th Tire Repair Company some 50 years after our overseas adventure at a reunion in Oakland's Jack London Square.

wives made the trip, which was quite successful. There was ferry service to San Francisco from the docks and it was a dramatic way to come across to visit the City. They particularly loved passing under the Bay Bridge as you glide into the Ferry Building. We rode the cable cars up California Street to Nob Hill to see Grace Cathedral. We took in Fisherman's Wharf, Ghirardelli Square and the Cannery Shopping complex. Had Irish coffee at the Buena Vista where they were invented. I had them out to my house for a patio lunch; they peeked into the Japanese teahouse and trooped through the handsome Oakland Museum on the way back to their motel. A lot of photos were snapped everywhere we went and I felt rewarded by the enthusiasm they showed. They were a foot-weary bunch at the end of the three-day visit.

20
Russia, again?
1995

"My fascination with Russia hadn't disappeared after the '92 trip and in 1995 I started planning to go again. After checking out several ads and travel brochures, I zeroed in on a company out of Orem, Utah. I guessed they were Mormon but I wasn't one to discriminate against any religious or ethnic group. After all I belong to a group that has had its fill of discrimination in its ugliest forms." - GS

§

I was as curious about Russia as George had been. In fact, I had taken a Russian language class in college while living at George's with the thought of going there one day myself. In this chapter, I was able to get George to cast his visits in the historical context of Russia, with which he was well-versed as it turns out. To me, this part of his memoirs is a primer to understanding Russia before and at its demise as a soviet communist state. - JJ

Russia, Again?: 1995

My fascination with Russia hadn't disappeared after the '92 trip and in 1995 I started planning to go again. After checking out several ads and travel brochures, I zeroed in on a company out of Orem, Utah. I guessed they were Mormon but I wasn't one to discriminate against any religious or ethnic group. After all I belong to a group that has had its fill of discrimination in its ugliest forms. I won't mention the firm's name here since they are mean-hearted enough to hit me with a lawsuit. I loved the general experience of this particular trip but there were times that I cursed the people who were in charge, as you will learn soon enough.

Amsterdam

§

We were traveling in May, which is the beginning of good weather for traveling after the snows have melted from Russia's long winter. The trip started in Amsterdam actually and then a short plane ride to St. Petersburg for a two-day's visit before we entrained to Moscow for the real adventure of traveling by a small ship along the waterways called the Golden Ring. The Volga does a northerly swing and then continues on eastward and south to Volgograd, which once was Stalingrad. However, our trip was to go only to Nishni Novgorod before coming back along the same waterways.

The first problem came up at Amsterdam where we found no one from the company was at the Schiphol Airport to greet us. We did-

> *I guessed they were Mormon but I wasn't one to discriminate against any religious or ethnic group. After all I belong to a group that has had its fill of discrimination in its ugliest forms.*

The gorgeous Kuekenhof Gardens near Amsterdam on our Volga River cruise.

n't know which travelers who would be our companions on this trip. We started asking anyone what we were supposed to do before we eventually went out of the airport and asked a bus driver if he was going to the Ibis Hotel. This hotel near the airport was miles from Amsterdam's center. We wound up taking a suburban train later to see the city. We still didn't see anyone connected with the travel company until we reached St. Petersburg a day or two later! This was a real gaffe for the company and, much later, we found out that the greeter had been fired earlier. Anyway, somebody was substituted the next day from some other source and we made it into Amsterdam where I led the dozen or so souls who heard I knew my way around. I led them down through the Dam, over to the Rijksmuseum, through the bordello area and back to the hotel out by the airport. We boarded a bus the next day with the half-day we had left for more sightseeing and got out to Aalsmeer to see millions of flowers being packed in a gigantic warehouse for shipping to the rest of the world. It was amazing to see how very efficiently every step of the packing was done. Conveyor belts sped cartons of flowers along to waiting trucks. Then we were taken out to the Kuekenhof Gardens where tulips are grown in the most stunning settings I had ever seen. There must have been several acres of lovingly designed formal gardens and waterways to enhance the flowers. It was a photographer's paradise of vistas.

Our plane was ready when we returned to the airport and we were soon winging to Russia for the next part of this trip. I found myself sitting next to a very sexy gent, George Kostulsky, and his charming wife. George was athletic in build, the rugged outdoorsman type and could speak Russian! We decided to try and stick together in any future rambling on this trip and I told them I had already seen a bit of the Russia we were coming into shortly. But at the moment, I was quite annoyed that we had acquired a smoker across the aisle and his fumes were wafting over to us. My frantic waving of a magazine to dispel the smoke did no good and he continued blithely to pollute the air. It seems that Europe looks the other way when it comes to health concerns with smokers.

§

St. Petersburg

We dropped down to Helsinki to let off two thirds of our passengers and then forty minutes later we had crossed the Baltic Sea to glide down into St. Petersburg's Sheremetevo airport. It was a stark contrast to the Dutch airport, which was sleek, and ultra modern. This airport had the typical careworn, shabby, dated look of most Russian public spaces. But, heck, this was Russia and you either love it or hate it. You get used to it and the people make up for it in their warm humanity.

And now, I was becoming aware that we had a "friend of Dorothy's" in our group. No, I'm not referring to my sister Dorothy but to a term used in the gay world to discreetly identify a brother in a public situation. Rather than say — oh, look, there's someone gay, we would use the term, "friend of Dorothy." We lost no time in chatting while clearing customs and it turned out that Barry wasn't in our group and was traveling solo. He was also

I was becoming aware that we had a "friend of Dorothy's" in our group. No, I'm not referring to my sister Dorothy but to a term used in the gay world to discreetly identify a brother in a public situation

going to our same hotel and asked if he could get on our same bus. Although it wasn't exactly correct, we let him sneak aboard with us since the driver didn't check off names. Barry seemed quite personable and he lived in San Francisco on Twin Peaks, which is a rather gay neighborhood. It was now 4:30 p.m. and we were driven over to the huge cathedral of St. Isaac's for a thirty-minute look-see after wading through hordes of souvenir-toting vendors. And one had to keep an eye on the pocket book, as there were thieves amongst the hustling and jostling of arms that accompanied this sort of selling. I thought it strange that we were even inspecting this landmark before being driven to our hotel to settle in.

I tried calling Boris at his parents' but he wasn't there. I was able to reach Vasya, whom I had met the last time here and he told me that he would tell Boris I had called and that they would come to the hotel, the St. Petersburg, when Boris was finished with his basketball referee duties. That turned out to be 10:30 by the time he had traveled by bus, metro and walked. We hugged each other after the three-year absence, sat and had beers in the lobby until we opted for more privacy in our rooms. Barry had come by and was urging us to go gay-bar-hopping now but the Russians felt it was too risky to do. It seemed that there were gangs of thugs out looking for innocents who hadn't been alerted to late night strolling as dangerous. We were even told that a taxi cabby could be a hold-up man — what a country!

At 4 a.m. I was wide-awake thinking about the new adventures ahead. As I lay there, I glanced over to my new roommate whom I just met. In order to save several hundred dollars, I had agreed to share my room with another single traveler of the same sex. This was something I have always grudgingly put up with since it does save considerable money. My roomie was a Latter Day Saint's guy (Mormon) and hailed from the Salt Lake City area. I had almost no contact with him through the trip as he was very distant and wasn't even friendly with the rest of the gang.

I went down to the huge dining room to greet the Kostulskys and another couples the Ashbys that I had been attracted to. By 9 a.m., I had finished and joined Barry and Vasya outside. Across the Neva River in front of us the Battleship Potemkin rode at anchor. It is a historic landmark in the Communist Revolution because the first shots were fired from its decks. It is now a revered museum holding many interesting mementos of that era.

The three of us dashed over to the metro station at the Finlandia Station to make the short hop over to the Hermitage Museum, as that was our first item. Culture before crass shopping and sightsee-

The Gray Granite — 12 foot giants at an entrance to the Hermitage, St. Petersburg, Russia.

ing. We passed along Millionaires' Street, stopping to admire the colossal black granite giants who hold up the portico of an unused entrance into the Hermitage (*above*). I later came back to shoot film of these magnificent figures of the nude slaves supporting the porch roof with their muscular arms. It amused me to see how much the male body was used in public architecture here. One saw a few female figures here and there but not in the profusion of masculinity used to promote the exuberance of Tsarist culture. The Communists had reversed this way of thinking, and their public monuments showed men in modern dress. What a contrast in thinking. The big cover-up!

It amused me to see how much the male body was used in public architecture here. One saw a few female figures here and there but not in the profusion of masculinity used to promote the exuberance of Tsarist culture.

The Griffin bridge in St. Petersburg.

Vasya hurried us to the more drab entrance around the huge pile that makes up the Hermitage. It had once been the Winter Palace of Catherine the Great and had grown into a series of adjoining structures all in the Russian baroque style. Catherine had little faith in her own native architects and imported the Italian, Rastrelli to design this and other palaces for her.

Our young guide, Vasya, tried to slip us in for the vastly cheaper admission fee of one dollar by buying the tickets himself but we were caught as we passed through the ticket gate by a sharp eyed babushka and went back to pay the tourist rate of $8. After 2 hours of ogling masterpiece after masterpiece, we were exhausted. It was like eating a gallon of rich ice cream The three of us wandered on along the Nevsky Prospeckt which is the main street bisecting the entire downtown area. We inspected the Kazan Cathedral where the tsars were crowned, and walked behind to the small footbridge that crosses a canal. The four gilt-winged lions that hold the bridge cables in their mouths are for me, the most romantically, charming spot in all St. Petersburg. Tucked away in a side street, it doesn't get the attention that the other 300 bridges have gotten. A more famous bridge on Nevsky Prospeckt shows four groupings of nude males leading rampant stal-

St. Basil's Church in Red Square, Moscow.

lions. And I was amazed to be shown a detail that would normally be ignored. Vasya led me to one corner of the bridge to view the underside of the horse's belly. And instead of the correct anatomical detail one would expect at that spot, we saw the sculpted face of Napoleon, Russia's enemy.

Down a side street along another one of St. Petersburg's numerous canals, we spotted a cathedral so similar to the world famous St. Basil's in Moscow (*above*) that I wondered if that unfortunate architect hadn't dashed off another church before he was blinded. The similarity was unnerving; you almost felt you were back in Moscow. This church called the Church of the Sacred Spilled Blood marked the spot where a tsar had been assassinated in the 1800s. We wandered through a big department store carrying very inferior merchandise, checked out a big bookstore called Dom Knigi but saw few books that we could read anyway. But with my love of books and the hundreds I own, I could hardly be expected to pass by.

By five thirty we were foot-weary and returned to the hotel to bathe and have dinner. I took the evening off and got to know my traveling companions a bit better. Vasya, our faithful guide, had gone home to rest, as he was to meet us the next day again. Boris couldn't get away

The river cruiser we lived on for Volga River trip.

from his referee duties, it seemed.

    The next morning, a Sunday, a strange mournful whistling, which had a ghostly sound to it, awakened me. On dragging myself to the window, I realized it was a crack in the windowsill that caused it. The weather outside was dismal with a thin rain enveloping the streets. I knew that Vasya was coming with a friend, Paul, to escort us (Barry, that is) out to Pushkin some fifteen miles south of the city. I wished I could have cancelled, but I didn't have the heart, knowing they had traveled some forty minutes by bus and metro to come to us. So, with umbrellas hoisted, we picked our way along rain-swept streets to get to the train station that took us out to Pushkin. Our objective was the Catherine Palace, which I had seen before but hadn't seen enough of. We tramped the last five blocks after waiting long minutes for a bus to come. As we arrived at the palace, there were groups of Army and Navy cadets also about to enter on a Sunday holiday tour and they were also soaked to the skin with no raincoats or umbrellas. I couldn't believe their officers were that negligent and imagined dozens of these teen-aged soldiers with nasty colds to deal with in the near future.

We donned the usual carpet slippers over our shoes to save the gorgeous inlaid marquetry of the floors. Room after room, each with more carved paneling and gilt detailing, made the mind reel. How could a country allow this enormously expensive décor while the serfs huddled in their miserable shacks out in the countryside? It is a wonder that the Revolution didn't happen any sooner than 1917. The hate that had been contained up until then simply burst forth in the blood bath of that year. The most unusual room of the whole palace was not to be seen but we could view the scraped walls. This was the Amber Room, of course, but the invading Nazi soldiers had wrenched the amber off and carted it back as war booty. It has never turned up in Germany since, and most probably lies in a dusty basement somewhere and the present owners are afraid to reveal its existence. Russia still pesters Germany today to return this treasure. But the bickering about what should go back and what can be kept goes on. War spoils have always been a problem for Europe's quarrels and boundary disputes.

Moscow

Three hours of gaping at aristocratic splendor had us ready to call it a day. The rain was still coming down and we got wetter in spite of our two umbrellas. I needed to get dried out and, on top of that, we were due to board the train to Moscow at 9 p.m. Boris showed up at 7:30 for a brief visit and I gave up going to the tour group's visit to a folk dancing concert to have this last bit of time with him. We said our good-byes and I joined the rest of the troops out to the train station. As is usual in Russian trains, everyone has a compartment reserved for four souls. The tour guide was handing out a special metal loop that we could slip over the sliding door's lock. It seemed that there were unscrupulous travelers — professional criminals — who made a specialty of riding these trains to ransack and hold up passengers! Our upper bunks were especially hard to sleep on with their minimum of padding. I wondered why they had to be so Spartan with their concern for our comfort. The train also had a bouncing roll, which made sleeping very trying.

§

By eight of the morning, we were rolling through Moscow's limits with its vast gray pile of drabness. Moscow is not an attractive place, it is a business city, and no effort is made to give it a handsome aspect. After the classical beauty of St. Petersburg, Moscow is terribly disappointing. And we saw little that pleased the eye along the boulevards as we headed out to the boat docks. This was actually the beginning of our river journey and we were a bit excited.

But when we pulled up to the small ship we would spend the next week on, there was utter confusion. It seemed that the previous tour group had not vacated their cabins yet and no room assignments could be passed out for an hour or so. They gave us a hasty breakfast to fill in the time and then decided we were to visit Red Square now even before we had a chance to shower or change clothes. We weren't in our cabins yet but we were being hustled out to see the sights! There was a lot of grumbling about the lack of planning, but we got back on the bus to do Red Square since we had little to say, anyway. Since I had seen this world famous square before, I wasn't too interested and spent more time walking through the gigantic shopping mall that borders Red Square called Gum. It was being refurbished with new shops and stalls to bring it up to western standards. There were carpenters and painters at work everywhere in the languid work style so much a part of the Russian work ethic. I remembered the famous rule about Russian work, "You pretend to pay us and we will pretend to work." And now I could see it in action (or better yet, in non-action). Custom dies hard here and workers were still apt to do what they had always done, work at a snail's pace for fear of finishing the job. I soon joined the Kostulsky's who were headed into a small church along the side of the vast Square to light a candle or two for their Catholic relatives. We next jumped back onto our bus for a short trip to the Lenin Hills area. This rise in the landscape around Moscow is most unusual since

I remembered the famous rule about Russian work, "You pretend to pay us and we will pretend to work."

20 - Russia, again? —1995

the city is mostly built on a vast flat plain. But here we could look out over the entire panorama of a hazy, smoke polluted city, Russia's nerve center. And now we also were meeting another sight so typical of Moscow. Stalin had decreed that seven enormous towers housing governmental offices, a university and communal apartments, were to be built. This was done over the next ten or so years of his rule. He saved millions of rubles by using the same architectural design for all seven buildings regardless of their use. So the one on Lenin Hills was the University of Moscow. It arose some thirty or more stories in a ziggurat style with lots of decorative detailing. It resembled nothing more than a Victorian architect's concept of what a skyscraper should look like. And there were six more of these buildings studding the city. The broad sidewalk flanking the view was a busy scene of vendors hawking their wares. I found a number of open stalls selling the famous lacquer boxes. I found them to be quite inexpensive and came away with three in various sizes. One had to be especially careful about the painted images on their lids. These were sometimes no more than a clever gluing on of a printed scene. I checked the work carefully to be sure I wasn't buying the bogus copies of the finer examples. The good pieces were exquisitely done with tiny brushes, which produced a line so delicate that you wondered how a human eye could have guided the line. As an artist, I was very impressed with the beauty of these small boxes almost always done on a black background. I use one today as a stamp box and it brings back memories of this moment in Russia's capitol.

But the tour members were getting restless; we still hadn't changed clothes from our train ride or seen a shower. It was incredible to think that the tour managers hadn't planned better because now we were hustled through a quick supper at five and then had to be ready to board the bus again to get to the evening performance of the Circus! No shower, no fresh clothes — we were fuming with annoyance. So we could skip the circus we were told, but few took that option. We weren't going to miss one of the great experiences of being in Russia. So most of us went along, of course. It was well worth the time with all the high wire acts, the jugglers, the performing elephants with their hula-hoops, the amazing clown, and the clever monkeys. Two exhausted hours later, and we were bussed back to the ship for our first chance at showering in a tiny, cramped stall in the cabin that could barely be called a shower. But it was heaven to us anyway. A sound sleep in a built-in bunk, and we would be ready for more Moscow sights the next day.

After a short breakfast, I was assigned to a group of 6 under the supervision of Lena, an Intourist guide with a golden smile — that is, she had gold-capped teeth. I wondered about this custom in Russia to add this entire dazzle to your mouth. Was it cosmetic or medically necessary? None of us ever had the nerve to ask.

We were hauled to Red Square again, and it seemed as if Russians were determined to cram this awesome place down our throats. We had a look at Lenin, lying there under his glass box with a soft pink spot trained on him to give him a more life-like look. You aren't allowed to stop moving along, and so it turns out to be a brief acquaintance with this infamous character who was the brains behind the Russian Revolution. All the talk we heard from Russians indicated that they were ready to give him a decent burial, just as his widow had wanted for him.

After breakfast, the horror began. About thirty of us out of the forty on the cruise, began to have stomach pains and the runs. Stalin's Revenge had been laid on us.

As we came out of the tomb, we were led along the great forty-foot high wall that forms a backdrop for the Lenin Tomb. Here we could inspect wall plaques with the names of famous Russians, if you could read Cyrillic. The most famous name was Stalin's, of course, and he rated a stone column with his bust atop. He seemed to exude evil even as a portrait bust in bronze. John Reed, the author of *The Seven Days that shook the World*, had his burial plaque on the wall, the only American to be interred here. If you ever saw the movie "Reds," you may recall him, as played by Warren Beatty.

We drove on to visit the Arbat shopping street again and I ordered a coke and a half pizza for $6 but wound up paying 8 because one of our gals didn't have any change. When we returned to the bus, we sat and waited a half-hour while one little old lady who had wandered off on her own, finally figured out where the bus would be and returned shamed-faced. The traffic on the way back to the ship terminal was as bad as any I had ever endured in the U.S — creeping along at a snail's pace. Supper at 6:30 and we were advised to repair to the Music Room for entertainment. I seemed to have sat next to a lady of indeterminate age who somehow exuded the same aura as Blanche DuBois, the main character in "A Streetcar named Desire." I didn't encourage her flirting glances, not wanting to start a shipboard romance. The music was quite good, with three men playing sax, flute and violin. Afterwards, I bought two tapes of their rendering of "Moscow Nights" and other familiar ditties. After all, it really was Moscow at night. One of the musicians, Igor, insisted I borrow his tape player so that I could lull myself to sleep. The battery lasted about five minutes before giving up the ghost!

Sometime during the night, the ship finally pulled away from the dock, but we were all sound asleep. After breakfast, the horror began. About thirty of us out of the forty on the cruise, began to have stomach pains and the runs. Stalin's Revenge had been laid on us. We fled to our cabins to be near the bathrooms and there most everyone stayed the entire day in fear of showing ourselves.

The ship was next arrived at Uglich — the first riverside town on our voyage — but only a dozen of us had the nerve to forsake the toilets. Despite its ugly name, this town, founded in 1148, had a surviving Kremlin (fortress) and a handsome old church built on the spot where they found the body of the boy tsar, Dimitri. This 9-year-old was mysteriously murdered in some political intrigue. He was the son of Ivan the Terrible, and that might explain his death. Of course, most of us could only peer out the portholes to see the vendors lining up on the dock and a bit of the town's church steeples with their familiar onion domes.

The ship did have a doctor, and this was a very plump middle-aged woman with an amazingly frizzy hairdo. But I didn't see anything of her until late afternoon when she finally knocked at my door. She brought a few pills, advising me to stick to bread and water for the next day or so. She seemed harried and anxious to move on. The word got around, as we started talking, that the water was the culprit. It was discovered that although it was filtered, it wasn't boiled. It didn't affect the Russian crew, of course, but our sensitive western stomachs were cringing from the onslaught of bacteria. We ended up calling this "Diarrhea Day" since it was a total wipeout!

§

Kostroma

Our ship sailed blithely on through the night, arriving at the next town by 8 a.m. This morning, having had a fairly decent sleep, I was determined to be ready to see things. This was the town of Kostroma, home of the noble families of the Godunov and the Romanovs. It was the young Alexei who was elected as the first tsar, to begin the long line of Romanovs who ruled Russia for centuries. We had to get into a small launch since the dock wasn't adequate to handle our larger ship. We docked by the Ipatyevsky Monastery, which was a handsome complex of ancient buildings surrounded by a Kremlin. The ancient church's interior walls were entirely covered with frescoes. I tried to imagine myself four hundred years ago, brush in hand, working up on a scaffold. It was mind-boggling to think of the artists who had spent their entire lifetimes painting these walls.

The ancient church's interior walls were entirely covered with frescoes. I tried to imagine myself four hundred years ago, brush in hand, working up on a scaffold. It was mind-boggling to think of the artists who had spent their entire lifetimes painting these walls.

A few yards away, we entered the ancestral home of the Romanovs; it had been lovingly preserved somehow. I have no idea how this had been accomplished since the Communists had such contempt for the royals. There were lots of framed photos of Nicolas the Second, who was shot to death, along with his wife, four teen-aged daughters and his son who would have inherited the throne. We returned to the dock for another landing

20 - Russia, again? —1995

at the town itself. Dominated by an incongruous Greek temple, we sauntered the streets surrounded by hordes of children pleading for coins.

§

We returned to the ship to sail a few miles further on to Plyos, an even smaller town with a lacquer box museum I visited. I was intrigued with the ambience of this town; it must have been what rural America would have looked like a hundred years ago. I got busy with the camera, photographing old babushkas sitting on their benches winding yarn or knitting. Later, after supper on the ship, twelve of them entertained us with old folk songs while they knitted or stitched small doilies. It was charming and nostalgic; I held back a tear for their simple lives in this backwater bit of old Russia. On the dock, sat a hollow-eyed, scrawny artist with a dozen very mediocre little paintings. He seemed disconsolate as no one showed any interest in his work. I thought to myself, that could have been me if Fate hadn't been kinder.

Plyos

§

In 1992, when the Russian economy was destroyed with the fall of Communism, the ruble could exchange at 5000 for one dollar. Now in 1995, it was 50,000 for the dollar and you wondered how people here would survive. But one has to remember how patient and docile the Russian people can be. They endured terrible conditions for decades before finally erupting in the blood baths that shocked the world. I thought back to another incident in Russian history little known and mostly ignored. I tell it now somewhat out of context but vital to us as an example of gay courage:

I thought back to another incident in Russian history little known and mostly ignored. I tell it now somewhat out of context but vital to us as an example of gay courage.

Everyone has heard of Rasputin, of course, but did you know that he was finally shot and killed by a gay aristocrat? Rasputin's hold on the royal couple, Nicolas and Alexandra, was so powerful that he was reputed to be the secret ruler behind the throne. Because of his ability to keep the young heir, Alexei alive, he had tremendous influ-

Rasputin, seated at left, surrounded by admiring women.

ence over the Tsarina. The teenage boy was a hemophiliac and bled dangerously at the slightest bruise. But Rasputin was hated by most everyone else; indeed, a circle of ministers had decided it was time to rid themselves of this evil man. It fell to Prince Felix Youssoupov to do the deed. The prince was an effete, spoiled royal but since no other man was willing to do the killing, he took on the job.

On a freezing December night in 1916, he managed to tempt the amoral priest to visit him at his palace where he plied him with drink and then shot him. Rasputin survived the first bullets and was finally killed when he was dragged out to the nearby canal to be drowned.[1] On my later visit to St. Petersburg in 1997, I made a point of visiting this palace and sat in the basement rooms where this all happened. It was now a café where we sat and had coffee and a biscuit and talked in whispers.

I apologize for the aside here; it just had to be told somewhere.

§

Nizhni Novgorod

We had now arrived at the port of Nizhni Novgorod. It was the furthermost we would journey on the Volga for here we were to turn

---

[1] According to investigative researchers in 2016 (a year after George passed away), the autopsy surgeon who examined Rasputin found no water in Rasputin's lungs, and reports that Rasputin had been thrown into the water alive were incorrect. — J. Jackson

around and retrace our trip. I haven't said much about the river itself but it was a rather placid stretch of water, not a fast flowing thing at all. We were surprised to come to points along its windings where we entered locks and were lifted to new levels. There were lakes to cross over to new canals that connected to other lakes. I had always thought the river was a continuous one. During the reign of Catherine the Great, she determined to inspect her domains by royal barge. The ministers knew that the peasantry was struggling to stay alive in spite of huge taxes. So Potemkin, the most powerful minister, delayed the royal passage down the river while he had carpenters erect false rooflines and cupolas along the banks to convince the Tsarina that she had a thriving nation under her rule. The term, "Potemkin villages" became a worldwide term for governmental subterfuge in many other countries afterwards, as the whole scam was exposed.

This town, Nizhni Novgorod was especially interesting because it was absolutely off-limits to foreign visitors during the Stalin years and even later because it produced military hardware. The Russians closely guarded their factories to outsiders. But we were seeing it in better times and the townspeople were as curious about seeing us as we were about seeing them. First, we visited a church near the riverbanks that was still undergoing restoration from the neglect of the Communist years. Outside under the ornate portico, we noticed a group of four young men in formal black suits and ties who began singing as we exited the dark church interiors. They sang old Russian orthodox hymns that were so solemnly lovely that I was mesmerized by their beauty. We had little time to linger but I noticed that they had set up a little stool with tape cassettes at $10 each. I didn't hesitate to buy one and am playing it as I write these lines as a way of bringing back this time in a Russian church. Another distraction right on the heels of this impromptu concert — a wedding party came streaming out of the church with a glowing bride and her groom running ahead of a laughing crowd. Russians were just beginning to use churches again instead of the drab Communist practice of

Russians were just beginning to use churches again instead of the drab Communist practice of simply applying at a government office for a license and skipping the church altogether.

Bride and groom at a church we visited on the Volga.

simply applying at a government office for a license and skipping the church altogether. It reflected the need of Russia to appeal to the soul, be sanctified by more than a scrap of paper.

We walked on into the Kremlin grounds through a massive gate and inspected the tanks and a plane set up on the lawns. This was a display of what this secret city had once produced by the hundreds for the war machine.

On the way back to the ship for our lunch, we passed a garden park where we saw four teenage girls who were Young Pioneers. They stood in rigid attention at the four corners of a marble platform which was highlighted by a central pit where an eternal flame burned for all the young men who lost their lives in Russia's wars. I felt saddened by the symbolism.

After our lunch, we bussed back to the main street, which was recently turned into a pedestrian mall. This idea seemed to be copied in several Russian towns now and is in line with Europe's old cities where the streets are often too narrow to manage auto traffic. I spotted an artist who had hung his small paintings on an iron picket fence (*facing page*). I handed him $8 for a 5 by 7-inch oil of a moody landscape of the Russian countryside. The ugly frame I asked him to remove and I took it, as is, intending to add a better frame later. We returned to the ship for a supper and music from our Russian troupe of musicians now dressed up in military uniforms from the Tsarist past. Igor Vassiliev had his teen daughter, Anya with him for his folk songs and they were in peasant costume. We sat on the open to the skies deck as the sun disappeared on the horizon and the

20 - Russia, again?—1995

Nizhni-Novgorod, where I bought a painting from this artist.

beauty of their voices lulled us into private reveries.

We still had another half day to buzz around the town, so this time I returned with the Kostulskys. We opted to ride the tram the mile and a half to the town center. It was raining lightly now; and as we got off the train, a Russian man approached us for the time. Had I been mistaken for a Russian? Our faces were no clue since we look much the same as they do. The way a Russian knows he is confronting a foreigner is by looking at his shoes. They are of a much better quality usually and a dead giveaway.

The way a Russian knows he is confronting a foreigner is by looking at his shoes. They are of a much better quality usually and a dead giveaway.

By noon we were pulling away from the dock for the return up the Volga. The afternoon was whiled away looking at the scenery gliding by or listening to a heavy-set blond woman who spoke on the history of lacquer boxes. I was personally interested in the craft and the fact that at least two Russian villages did nothing more than make these lovely keepsakes. I wondered what condition the eyes of these workers were in after spending countless hours scrunched over these miniature scenes and

The beautiful frescoes at St. Elijah's Church at Yaroslavl.

their amazing minute details. Our lecturer also invited us to a Q&A session where we could bombard her for information about the current state of affairs. Later, after another meal, and feeling like we were royals on Catherine the Great's barge, we sat enjoying our own group of musicians before going to our cabins.

§

Yaroslav

It was now Sunday morning as we pulled into the dock at Yaroslav. The city is the oldest on the Volga, and was founded by the Grand Prince Yaroslav the Wise in 1010. It stretches for some 18 miles along the river and became a great mercantile center in the 1600s. We boarded a tour bus that showed us the tree-lined streets with hardly anyone astir. The exquisite ancient frescoes of the Church of Elijah the Prophet caught my eye, of course, and I was kept busy snapping shots of all this ancient splendor. Then we drove to another part of town where we entered a Kremlin gate into what was once the stronghold of the city in time of war. The townspeople could run to this haven to evade the enemy troops

20 - Russia, again?—1995

that were ransacking the rest of the city. A young man stood by a set of bells hung from a rack and as we came up to his stand, he commenced a concert of bells. The bell, in Russia, has tremendous significance and is revered as a savior in time of war. We tipped him for his concert and wandered on to visit another symbol of Russia: a huge bear in an iron cage. He had nothing except a suspended tire in his cage to amuse him. My heart went out to the poor animal. I was told that he had been found as a cub alongside a dead mother, but I wondered how the mother happened to die. A bear symbol appears on the Yaroslav City coat-of-arms,

Then back to the ship for a late lunch and off again, passing through park-like vistas of birch forests and meadows. We were told we were going to be the entertainment this evening! We rehearsed with music sheets giving us the phonetic Russian words for "Moscow Nights" – probably the best-known song that the rest of the world recognizes as Russian. I was also in the fashion show as Jane Ashby's escort. It is hard to believe that they wanted me instead of her husband to accompany her down the center aisle. After the impromptu fashion parade that was more like a joke, the fun part began. I was quite surprised at what came next. Three young men came out dressed in ballet tutus and did a burlesque turn as the swans in "Swan Lake" and as if that wasn't campy enough, another pair came in as little old ladies (babushkas) and hammed it up. So, it gave me a laugh to see Russians doing drag, just as we do ourselves. We all stood to sing "America, the Beautiful," and another rendition of "Moscow Nights." By 11:30, after a few drinks, the older crowd toddled off to bed but it was hard to sleep with all the foot pounding we endured over our heads as the younger members of the tour danced themselves on into the night.

This was our last full day on the Volga and it was not going to be a visit to another hamlet along the riverbanks. We were passing through more parkland, and a few fishermen sat by the river like statues. We were going through a series of small lakes connected by man-made ca-

Three young men came out dressed in ballet tutus and did a burlesque turn as the swans in "Swan Lake" ... it gave me a laugh to see Russians doing drag, just as we do ourselves.

nals before we stopped at a designated pier for a barbecue lunch at 1 p.m. Some of us wanted to explore the pine forest beyond the clearing only to be attacked by ferociously large mosquitoes. The forest floor was carpeted by little groups of lily-of-the-valley flowers and I gathered a bunch to take back. I had also discovered that we had a retired opera star in the few Russians traveling on this trip. I persuaded him to sing a favorite Russian song for eight of us. He sang "Gori, gori" (little star) for us in a soft, melancholy voice way that had us close to tears.

As we waited for the meats to broil on the grill, I noticed a car had driven up to the edge of the clearing, and two men got out and immediately spread out trinkets on the hood of the car. The older guy was an ugly, pockmarked gangster type but the other, a younger man, was so handsome he could have modeled for a career. He was dressed in the shortest pair of cut-offs I was ever to see on this trip. He had the legs to show them off, of course, and I was startled to see how American he looked. I didn't buy anything from him but the rough one had a series of war medals that looked interesting. I chose one that seemed stained with old blood wondering what stories it could have told me.

The picnic lunch over, we boarded the boat again and proceeded up the waterways to make an unscheduled stop because we didn't want to arrive in Moscow too early. A tiny village of a few houses hove into view. Three babushkas stood on the docks selling bunches of lilacs while teen boys yelled at us to throw them money. When that didn't produce much response, they raced off to strip lilacs off nearby bushes and tried to sell us the flowers as we glided away from the dock. Some of us tossed them souvenir pencils.

Now that we had clearance, we entered a series of five locks that raised the ship some twenty feet in the air and down again as we progressed. Madame Gordeeva again lectured us on Russia's economic woes and our musicians regaled us with some lovely Jewish songs. The retired opera singer volunteered to sing and he dedicated his songs to

20 - Russia, again? —1995

me — calling out to me — "the collector of operatic arias." I was surprised to be named that. As I stood watching the shores pass, a young Russian girl handed me a small sketch she had made of a village tower we had passed. Evidently, she had done it earlier in her cabin since it was beautifully detailed. I was touched and I handed her a couple of photos of my own work I had with me.

§

Moscow

By mid-morning we were pulling into the Moscow terminal where we could see at least another dozen ships like ours. We were so crowded by them that we exited out to the dock through one other ship. Boarding a bus marked for us, we were driven out to an area on the edge of the city that had been transformed into a new complex of buildings dedicated to the "Great Patriotic War." The Russians prefer to call World War Two by this name, which seems more appropriate for them. Here we entered a vast building new in construction, which must have cost billions of rubles. We heard that it had taken four years to build and that a huge group of teachers, doctors and scientists had worked at half wages to supply the money to get it built. They had rushed it to completion for the May 9th, 1995 Clinton visit! There were walls lettered with the names of the war dead, and a vast dome like St. Peter's in Rome, while on the lower floor there were 6 life-sized dioramas depicting key battles from the Great War. They were so realistically rendered that you almost felt as if you were standing in the midst of the carnage itself. It was gruesome and yet very absorbing. You hoped it would be anti-war propaganda at its finest. As you walked out, you passed an enormous obelisk reminding you of the Washington monument. This one was a towering 450 feet tall. Nearby, there was a handsome small church more like a chapel that was the first new church to be built since the fall of Communism. Instead of the usual solid, fresco-painted interiors, this one was filled with light cascading down through stained-glass windows. It was a metaphor for the new Russia that was allowing the light to come through.

With the afternoon left, we were driven back to the Arbat shopping street for more chances to get rid of our rubles by posing with the bear cub, a monkey perched on the organ grinder's shoulder or with a boa constrictor draped over your neck. We also gave in and lunched in the elegant MacDonald's and I must say it wasn't a bad experience. Then, Lena, our guide with the dazzling golden smile, suggested we should really check out their subway system. Russia had lavished enormous sums to build the most elaborate metro system with stations that were more like art galleries. The bronze figures adorning the arches were very beautifully sculpted; the ceilings were adorned with elaborate chandeliers and mosaic tiles. And all this had been done under the Communist regime, which supposedly hated the opulent lifestyle of the Tsars. We rode through three stations, getting off each time to oh and ah the magnificence. It had started to drizzle now, so we chose not to get off at Gorky Park.

Bronze statuary adorning the Moscow Metro.

Back at the dock again, we were alarmed to find that our ship was gone, but were reassured it had only gone to be refueled nearby. We re-boarded for dinner at eight. We were told to stay put and enjoy our musicians again. Were the tour managers running out of ways to keep us entertained?

This was now our last day in Russia. A new guide had taken over, a gal named Natasha wearing a tall beehive arrangement of hair and a pair of red spike heels. How she managed to walk in them was a miracle. She escorted us out to a park area with exhibition buildings

The Fountain of Russian States in Moscow's Industry and Science Park.

ringing around a vast central courtyard. A Stalin dreamscape of overblown heavily decorated halls to honor Russia's achievements in Science, the Arts, Agriculture, etc. We arrived through a triumphal arch and were led past a huge fountain decorated with life-sized maidens done in gold. Each represented one of the Russian States and was dressed in their native costume. It was impressive but it wasn't gushing water at all. Like all the other buildings, it was shut down for much needed repairs. We took pictures anyway.

With the afternoon at loose ends and nothing scheduled, the guide asked us what we wanted to do or see. I suggested we go visit an art museum I had heard was just refurbished after ten years of neglect. Eleven tour members chose to come along with the guide and me while the rest just collapsed on the ship. The Tretyakov Gallery wasn't that well known by the guide and she had to ask a number of people before she figured out the route in this huge city. We rode trams and buses for a half-hour and were gawked at by ordinary Russians who generally only saw us as faces in tour bus windows. The rich merchant, Tretyakov had collected over a thousand paintings to decorate

I was particularly taken by an enormous canvas, some 20 by 24 feet in size, which depicted Christ arriving at the river's edge to be baptized by John. The figures were life-sized and the artist had spent over ten years creating this masterpiece not known in the West.

his palatial home, which had been expropriated by the communist regime in 1917. His imposing home was the building we now entered and I was awed by the magnificence of the rooms. I was particularly taken by an enormous canvas, some 20 by 24 feet in size, which depicted Christ arriving at the river's edge to be baptized by John. The figures were life-sized and the artist had spent over ten years creating this masterpiece not known in the West. As I came down one of the marble staircases, I suddenly twisted my knee and was in excruciating pain. I was so miserable I could barely walk away but was helped by one of my companions to get around and back to the ship.

§

After an early supper on board, we were driven to the airport, sat around for two and a half hours before our flight at 10 p.m. Three hours later, we were back where we started, at Amsterdam's Schiphol Airport. A five minute bus ride to the Ibis motel and we were snug in our bedrooms anticipating the long flight home.

With my very sore knee, I was in no mood to go into Amsterdam to see anything and chose to gab with others who were by now absorbed in memories to recount to each other.

§

At three thirty we were airborne and passing over the British Isles, Ireland, the southern tip of Greenland and New York City. It was now six hours later when we were saying our good-byes, promising to write and bussing into downtown Manhattan. My knee was still a problem as I checked into my favorite hotel, the Pickwick. Although the clocks said it was 9 p.m., I knew it was really 3 a.m. by Dutch time and I needed to sleep. But first I called Jim in California to let him know I was, more or less, back in one piece.

21
To Russia With Rick

1997

"One would think I had seen enough of Russia to last for a few years, but I had only been teased by the two previous visits with their hurried glimpses of intriguing streets and people ... In February of '97, I happened to be chatting on the phone with sister Dorothy and I was telling her how I wanted to return to visit Russia in a more intimate way. She mentioned that her youngest son, Rick, was talking of going there himself. Why didn't I write him and see what could be arranged?" - GS

§

This is another extraordinary commentary on Russian culture and history, including revelations about the gay rights movement in Russia in 1997. At age 83, this was also George's last visit to Russia but by no means the end of his relationship with people there, telling us at chapter's ending, "I want to add here that my interest in Russia continues currently. I am in e-mail contact with several Russian friends, all of them in various stages of learning English." - JJ

TO RUSSIA WITH RICK: 1997

One would think I had seen enough of Russia to last for a few years, but I had only been teased by the two previous visits with their hurried glimpses of intriguing streets and people. Of course, I had returned to Indonesia in '96 with the church group as you recall, so it wasn't an annual visit to this most fascinating country.

In February of '97, I happened to be chatting on the phone with sister Dorothy and I was telling her how I wanted to return to visit Russia in a more intimate way. She mentioned that her youngest son, Rick, was talking of going there himself. Why didn't I write him and see what could be arranged? I didn't have a computer yet and so by phone and snail mail, the two of us started planning a trip to be taken in May. Rick had had some unfortunate experiences in establishing a family. I won't elaborate but let's say he was ready to check out the Russian world for a wife. I was certainly sympathetic but I also felt it was such a long shot. The chances of getting to know a girl in the brief time we would be there seemed slim. However, he had been in contact with an agency that had lined up hundreds, perhaps, thousands of Russian women very ready to marry American men and immigrate to America. I had seen a TV program earlier that gave me a sense of the process of pairing American bachelors with Russian brides. It was not something I would have gone through myself and I wondered how people endured the evenings of looking each other over. It smacked of being judged at a prize winning animal show. Yet, it was no worse than standing in a pickup bar, waiting for someone to turn up that you might like. I had certainly been through that demeaning experience many times as a youth. I could hardly recommend

I had seen a TV program earlier that gave me a sense of the process of pairing American bachelors with Russian brides. It smacked of being judged at a prize winning animal show . . .

. . . yet, it was no worse than standing in a pickup bar, waiting for someone to turn up that you might like.

21 - To Russia With Rick—1997

it to anyone and many of us, gay or straight, have felt the rejection or thrill of meeting someone we could like — either for a night or a lifetime.

Rick was living in Nashville, busy with a career in the music world. He had little time to meet women but he was interested in taking the time to go with me to actually see the three young Russian women he had already made contact with through letters. It seemed like the next step and didn't commit him or the girl to anything more serious than a date or two.

So we started the ball rolling, he had to get a passport and I had to write Boris to tell him I was coming with my nephew and that we needed that all-important piece of paper, the official invitation. This was obtained through their OVIR offices and since Russia loves red tape, we sweated the weeks it took to get it and then the wait for the Russian Consulate in San Francisco to approve it. Finally, after all the writing and hassle, we had permission to visit just two weeks before we boarded our different planes. We were to meet in Frankfort, Germany since we were starting from two different U.S. cities, San Francisco for me and Nashville for Rick. He had scheduled his flight to arrive at the Frankfort airport ten hours ahead of my arrival and I felt sorry for him but it was the best we could do.

A portrait of my nephew, Rick whom I painted from a photograph of him in St. Petersburg.

I hadn't seen Rick in years in person, but I recognized him immediately when we actually joined up. He was still the handsome, outgoing young man he had always been as a teen. We gave each other a big hug after all the years we hadn't seen one another. I've never made it a point to hide my orientation as a gay uncle to any of my four nephews. It has proven to be the best route to take in any event. I hate the idea of having to hide.

And even with my meeting up with Rick in this gigantic, world airport that is the hub of air travel in Europe, we still had three hours to kill before we would do the short hop to St. Petersburg. There was a lot of catching up to do and the three hours flew by easily.

I've never made it a point to hide my orientation as a gay uncle to any of my four nephews ... I hate the idea of having to hide.

Rick lounging in our quarters in St. Petersburg.

We landed at St. Petersburg's Pulkovo airport at ten p.m. Having lost about eleven or so hours since California because of the Earth's rotation. Boris was waiting in the shabby, small airport that was a great contrast to the gleaming, sleek efficiency of the Frankfort airport. Boris's father had brought his car, thankfully and I was surprised he even owned one. Perhaps it was a borrowed one, I didn't ask. The greetings were enthusiastic, they seemed happy to see us, even though the father spoke no English, we hugged anyway.

In our letters, we had learned that Boris had arranged for our stay, as I had asked, to be in a very central area. We were to be the paying guests of Alex Kukharsky, an older friend who lived in the downtown area just a block off the main street, Nevsky Prospeckt. I was elated, knowing the hassle it is for most St. Petersburgers to get to the center of town. Boris normally took an hour or more to get downtown but we were right there. The apartment was on a small side street ending abruptly at one of the city canals and the street entrance was heavily fortified. We talked on a connecting phone to announce who was at the door before Alex released the lock and we took a rickety small elevator up to the fourth floor level, which was the entire apartment. For $25 dollars each a day, we had the spare bedroom which was quite spacious. It had a large window looking down into a back courtyard, two studio couches and a large round dining table, two armoires. Everything looked at least a hundred years old and we learned that Alex had been born

21 - To Russia With Rick—1997

Alex was a gruff, authority figure, a bit heavy, and dressed in sweatpants and pullover. Not one to put on airs, he was a mine of information. I decided to interview him later when I learned he was the president of the St. Petersburg Gay and Lesbian Association.

here himself, as had his parents and grandparents. One doesn't give up his apartment in Russia easily; it is a priceless possession and is handed down through the family regardless of the good or bad times. Alex was a gruff, authority figure, a bit heavy, and dressed in sweatpants and pullover. Not one to put on airs, he was a mine of information. I decided to interview him later when I learned he was the president of the St. Petersburg Gay and Lesbian Association, known as "Krilija."* This translates to "Wings" and is actually the name of a famous Russian story everyone seems to know. I remembered that Russians have an enormous respect for writers. I was impressed with his daring in being so openly gay in a country that has long suppressed any "deviant behavior" whether it was politically subversive or sexual. I admired the man even more when I learned he had stood in a downtown square with one or two others with placards to declare his gay self to an unsympathetic world.

*I condensed Alex's remarks from the interview at the end of this chapter. —J. Jackson

Alex had taught at a college but that had ended for undisclosed reasons. He now had a small consulting firm employing 3 or 4 women and was openly gay to his employees. What they consulted about was never discussed but he implied it was scientific data of some sort. He also had a young boy friend of 25 or so who was generally around the apartment since he preferred the more relaxed, open ambience of Alex's world. The cramped, crowded typical Russian apartment was not in evidence here at all. Alex had inherited three spacious rooms, connected by a hallway, a tiny bathroom and a kitchen. The bathroom wasn't a pleasant spot to be in for any longer than necessary, but the rest of the apartment was nicely set up and I loved the feel of being in an authentic Victorian setting that wasn't put together as a decorator's whim. Everything except for the television was old and showed the wear and tear of a hundred or more years. Alex kept an impressive library in his bedroom, read in several languages, and with two TVs going almost constantly, he was certainly in touch with current events. A giant black dog lounged on the hallway floor, and one climbed over him to get into the other rooms. He most probably had St. Bernard ancestors from the looks of him. Alex took him for two walks daily, with the evening one long after the streets were quite empty. I asked if he wasn't wary of being out at that late hour, thinking of the criminals we had heard about. But, no, he felt safe enough with this massive dog at his side. I was to walk with him and the animal several nights enjoying the beauty of the city in the long, lingering twilight of the "White Nights." But Alex was fearful enough of intruders that he had devised an elaborate system of locks on his hall door. There were hasps, locks and bolts to decipher and we never got the hang of it. One night, we were left on the sidewalk for a good hour because we had come home at an hour not agreed upon and it was a lesson to us to stick to a schedule for getting in.

Our first day of sightseeing started at ten as we waited and waited for Boris to show up to be our guide. Since he had to come for miles out in the suburbs, we were lucky to see him at midmorning. I wanted Rick to get his first view of the city from a high point, so we walked along Nevsky, down to the Admiralty Building, which borders the Neva River and is framed by a handsome park. We arrived at the huge mass of St. Isaac's cathedral and Boris led us up an obscure circular staircase to a viewing station on the flanks of the great dome. It was a breathtaking view of the entire panorama of spires, onion-domed churches and canals. I thought of all the great figures of world culture that had lived in this setting: Tchaikovsky, Tolstoy, Dostoevsky and there were so many others I could have named.

We descended to the ground level where we got a look at the interior of this vast church with its enormous, green malachite columns framing enormous paintings of saints. Stalin had enough respect for this cathedral to leave it as it was. It resembles St. Paul's in London or even our U.S. Capitol in its classical style of dome supported by Corinthian columns. A wealth of statuary adorns its ledges. Built by a French architect, Montferrand, in 1818-1858, it was the despair of a dozen previous builders who had to cope with a very mushy, sodden ground to erect this giant. The 300,000-ton building was set on 11,000 pilings sunk into the marshy land. The portico columns are 50 feet tall and weigh 114 tons apiece.

Next, we strolled behind the cathedral, through Decembrists' Square to the banks of the Neva River. An obelisk column marks the spot where a revolt against the regime of Nicolas the First took place. Led by aristocratic officers, who despised the monarchy, the mob was set upon by loyal troops. They massacred 1,271 people and captured the five officers who had plotted against the Tsar. They were hung on the gallows with signs around their necks reading "Assassins of the Tsar." When three of the ropes broke, they

The Bronze Horseman by Falconet Statue of Peter the Great, Founder of St. Petersburg in 1703.

were hung once more. Russian history is filled with such stuff.

As we walked to the River, we passed the imposing equestrian monument to Peter the Great. This famous sculpture memorialized by Pushkin in his poem, "The Bronze Horseman," was a gift to the city by Catherine the Great, Peter's daughter in the year 1765. Then, a few blocks along the River, we came to the Hermitage Museum, which was once the home of the Tsars. It was called the Winter Palace then when Catherine lived within its vast interiors. I have described it earlier so I will pass over this visit, noting only that we merely scratched the surface in our attempt to see its treasures. Boris had not come in because he was so familiar with its vast horde of priceless works of Art.

He did show up after our first supper at the apartment and we discussed our sightseeing plans for the next few days. I presented Boris and Alex with a few small gifts as is customary. We chatted about the current status of the gay world in this city and then at midnight, it was time to take the St. Bernard out for his stroll through the sleeping city. Again, as we crossed over the enormous Palace Square next to the Hermitage, we were reminded of the tragedy of "Bloody Sunday." On a bitterly cold January Sunday in 1905, a large group of demonstrators wanted to present a petition to the

Palace Square adjacent to the Winter Palace where the Russian Revolution began in 1917.

Tsar. The police misunderstood their intentions, opened fire and killed hundreds of men and women. Nicolas the Second, his German-born wife Alexandra and the evil priest, Rasputin were already the butt of much slander and this slaughter led to an unbridgeable gulf between the people and the Tsar. "Bloody Sunday" became the impetus for the 1917 Communist Revolution.

In the center of this vast space, a ninety foot granite column (*above*) is a memorial to the routing of Napoleon's armies which had been beaten back in their ill-fated invasion of Russia.

That late evening, as we crossed the Alexander Square, a lone figure with a saxophone was practicing jazz tunes at the base of the giant column. The notes bounced off the pale yellow walls of the great Army Staff headquarter buildings forming a huge semi-circle around us.

The next morning we were up early but found no one else stirring. After breakfast, there was a call from Boris to say he wouldn't be available until 1:30. We needed to convert traveler's checks to rubles and dollars since both were used in money transactions. We decided to stroll Nevsky Prospeckt and have a closer look at the Kazan Cathedral with its handsome portico of col-

21 - To Russia With Rick—1997

umns, which form a semi-circle across the facade. This was where all the Tsars were crowned after its completion in 1811. I was surprised to note that the massive bronze doors were exact copies of ones in Florence, Italy. Ghiberti had sculpted lovely miniature scenes in bas-relief. The same doors could also be seen on San Francisco's Grace Cathedral. It was amazing to me to find them here in Russia. We know that a good thing bears repeating. But the jewel for me — as I mentioned in an earlier chapter — was the charming little footbridge just behind the cathedral with the four bronze griffins with golden wings. They sit there holding the cables in their mouths and create handsome tableaux of past magnificence. I could have lingered here all day.

We found a small museum dedicated to the theater arts that interested me. The musical instruments were particularly curious since they were ancient prototypes of the modern ones. Then we decided to hail a cab across town. Ordinary cars often double as taxis since a chance to make an extra ruble is very important. In no time at all a car stopped and Boris gave him our destination point. We were a bit apprehensive since Boris had warned never to get in a car that already had a Russian passenger who could easily be a hold-up man! Or even the driver could be a criminal. But with Boris to assess the situation, we felt confident. But still we got into trouble. Later as we got out of the car in front of the Astoria Hotel, Rick's fanny-pack slipped off his waist. He didn't realize it had fallen off until a minute later, as the car sped off. We were devastated, especially since it contained all of Rick's ready cash, his passport and credit cards. We stopped at a nearby café to assess the situation. Rick mentioned that he had placed Alex's business card in the pack and that was our slim hope for retrieving the wallet.

That evening, Rick was meeting his first Russian blind date and he felt he couldn't cancel so I promised to stay in and hopefully wait for a phone call from whoever found the wallet. I loaned him money since he now had none. At 9 p.m., the phone rang with a young girl's voice saying she had found the wallet, which now only contained the passport. She had found it at the same corner where we had boarded the taxi. So we realized the driver had taken what he could easily dispose of and left the passport to be picked up by the first passerby. We called Boris's father to get him to drive us out to the suburb where the girl lived and arranged this for the next morning. Alex suggested we should reward her with a fifty-dollar bill and a nice big chocolate bar. The next day we drove out to a very depressing area of huge, gray concrete monoliths that is so typical of Russian cities. The girl was standing were she had said she would be. She had an older woman with her as a safety precaution. She was quite grateful for the money and chocolate and we were relieved it had ended as well as it could. Rick was out $100 of his trip's spending money but still had his passport.

The next bit of business on the schedule was to process the paper work for our invitation to visit Russia. A very antiquated system had been set-up to insure that Russia wasn't letting any potential spies into the country. We spent the next hours waiting in outer offices while several clerks shuffled all the necessary documents to prove who we were and who had let us come to visit. Boris was to come back two more times to finalize the documents.

Another citizen taxi driver took us across town for $6, leaving us in front of the Russian Museum for the Arts. I wanted to see the awe-inspiring icons that had been torn down off church walls when Stalin was rampaging against the churches. Lenin had declared, "Religion was the opiate of the Masses." It surprised me that we saw as many churches as we did. Many were torn down, of course, leaving only a few examples as museums of art.

Rick had another lady to look up in his search for a bride. This one, I later learned, was so desperately poor that she crawled under the turnstile when she took the subway across town to meet him. I felt the anxiety that drives young women in Russia today to do anything to find a husband. I chose to stay in and interview Professor Alex and later to promenade through the empty streets with his giant hound.

Friday dawned and we were to learn that it was Victory Day. This is rather like our American Fourth of July in spirit but celebrates the defeat of the Nazi forces and also any previous wars going back to Napoleon's defeat in 1812. There was going to be a parade of citizens with placards, flags and military retirees with chests full of medals, but no tanks or guns.

Boris arrived at 10 a.m. Then we headed a few blocks away to Palace Square to watch platoons of smartly uniformed cadets practicing drill formations. Russia had always prided itself on military show. Rain seemed to be in the offing with damp skies hanging over us and we hurried back to Nevsky

I later learned, was so desperately poor that she crawled under the turnstile when she took the subway across town to meet him. I felt the anxiety that drives young women in Russia today to do anything to find a husband.

21 - To Russia With Rick—1997

Prospeckt where we sat at an outdoor café with brilliant yellow umbrellas. We were told that around ten at night this was a great place to pick up a gay bedmate. Across the side street, we could see the Gostiny Dvor. This ancient monster of a building a half a mile long was built by the tradespeople of the city after a series of fires and lootings had destroyed earlier wooden structures. The two hundred year-old stone galleried building was the largest store in St. Petersburg, containing hundreds of small shops. Restoration work in 1965 unearthed over 300 pounds of gold hidden by long dead merchants. And now as we walked the long passages through its center, we saw international names on shop fronts like Gucci, Armani, and Chanel. Although most Russians could only gape and wish they had the money, the affluent West was making itself felt and it was rather like a kid standing in front of a candy store. There were no lines of Russians waiting to part with their scarce rubles.

Down Nevsky a few blocks, we came to the Anchikov Bridge with its magnificent male nudes and their rearing stallions. Remembering the face of Napoleon on the underbelly of one horse instead of his genitalia, I had to show it to Rick! Then we descended the stairs leading to the canal boats that cruise along the Fontanka Canal. I got all this down on my camcorder to enjoy later. The Fontanka is the main canal through the heart of the city center and we passed the Summer Gardens to come out onto the broad expanse of the Neva. Big tankers and large cruise vessels lined themselves along the industrial docks. Here a gigantic drawbridge was built to allow the sea-going vessels to come into port. It was the dream of Peter the Great's to give Russia a year-round sea port, because the only one they had had before had been at Murmansk far to the ice-bound northern shores. St. Petersburg boasts 302 bridges today to span its canals and is often called the Venice of the North.

When we returned to the apartment, the Professor announced that he had arranged with his friend, the manager of the Maly Theatre, for us to attend a performance of "Iolanthe." This was to be a Russian version of the Gilbert and Sullivan operetta. We barely had time to eat and had to run most of the way to the theatre about 6 blocks away. We had complimentary tickets it seemed, but Alex said we should look in on the young manager and treat him to cocktails and snacks during the intermission. I had supposed the Professor intended to join us at this point and was dismayed to find that

> *We hurried back to Nevsky Prospeckt where we sat at an outdoor café with brilliant yellow umbrellas. We were told that around ten at night this was a great place to pick up a gay bedmate.*

we had a language barrier. The very handsome young manager spoke no English and we resorted to sign language. We were led to the lobby bar where he ordered cognacs and little sandwiches with salmon slices. The bill was $25 and we were handed the bill soon after. I had no idea we were going to need rubles and had brought none. Waving dollars around was non-productive and I resorted to my meager Russian to assure him it would be taken care of – "zaftra" – Tomorrow! Later, I was really annoyed with the Professor for not warning us that we would be put in this embarrassing spot. I handed him the $25 and he called the manager who offered to let us return again for free.

Since performances start at 7 p.m. in Russia, we still had some light in the skies as we came out of the theater. We joined the surge of the crowds as they made their way along the broad sidewalks bordering the Neva. Fireworks were soon bursting over the waters and the crowds let out appreciative "hoorahs" as the great bursts of light colored their upturned faces. It lasted for a brief fifteen minutes since it was simply too costly to continue, as we were told later. On returning to the apartment, we found ourselves locked out at the sidewalk. The professor had never issued us a key, and so we were lucky that Sergei, the boy friend turned up to let us into the fortress.

Saturday morning we talked to the professor about the incident with the theater manager, explaining that if we had just bought tickets, we would have spent the same amount of money and would have chosen a play or musical we would have enjoyed more. He agreed that it was all a bit hasty and that we had almost been coerced into the evening but that he had no idea the manager would take us to the lobby bar or that he spoke no English. So, apologies were offered.

I have mentioned earlier that Prince Felix was homosexual, yet he of all the men who were anxious to be rid of Rasputin, was the only one with nerve enough to act on his hatred of the peasant priest.

We decided to visit Yusopov Palace, which was a handsome old mansion on the Moika Canal. This noble family was reputed to have been wealthier than the Tsar at the end of the 18th Century. And the young prince was famous as the assassin who ended Rasputin's life in 1916. I have mentioned earlier that Prince Felix was homosexual, yet he of all the men who were anxious to be rid of Rasputin, was the only one with nerve enough to act on his hatred of the peasant priest. Later, after I got home, I picked up a copy of *The Man who killed Rasputin: Prince Yusopov and the Murder that helped bring down the Russian Empire*, by Greg King. It is a fascinating account of an immensely wealthy family living at these last few years of the Russian aristocracy. There's even a rather well done film of the whole Rasputin affair, which is worth seeing if you want a more vivid account of the dissolute priest.

Anyway, I felt it important to walk the halls and salons of this opulent mansion and I wasn't in the least let down. It was rather eerie that we were the only visitors that morning, except for the usual little old guardian ladies sitting in their corners, watching to see if we touched anything. These babushkas have the most boring jobs ever imagined, but I suppose with the economy being what it is, they are luckier than most. I won't try to describe the salons, ballroom, and dining hall but our favorite room was the small theater seating perhaps a hundred. The golden balustrades, ceiling frescoes, the stage curtain were absolutely beautiful. We asked the way to the basement rooms where the murder had taken place and were surprised that this area with its vaulted ceilings had been turned into a café. No one sat at the small tables but Rick and I. We ordered tea and some cookies and tried to imagine what it must have looked like in 1916 on an icy cold December night. I stole the menu card with Rasputin's glowing red eyes gracing the cover.

And now, on foot, as usual, we headed for the Peter and Paul Fortress. This was the first structure that Peter the Great erected in this marshland with its dozens of small islands. It was 1703 when he employed the Italian architect Trezzini to design its ramparts and bastions. The rest of the city came second, as Peter needed to defend his prize. He had just won the land from the Swedes. The importance of the site was incalculable since it commanded the entrance to the mouth of the Neva River. Completely surrounded by water, it was the ideal defense position. Yet it was never to defend the growing city and instead, part of it became a famous prison.

We entered through St. John's Gate, and then a few yards further, through Peter's Gate. The tree-lined street led us to the handsome cathedral where lie the bones of most of the sovereigns of Russia. It was awesome to enter this most revered spot, which is considered the symbolic center of the Russian Empire. The last Tsar and his family, whose bones were recently discovered, will probably be interred here. I stood alongside Peter the Great's tomb and mused on his incredible achievements. His tremendous energy and magnetism had created this gorgeous city out of a swamp. The man was

Russian school children around Peter the Great's tomb.

over 6 foot 5 tall with a dynamic will that accepted no excuses. The city that rose under his direction was often called "The city built on bones" — thousands of serfs perished from the bitter winters and filthy living conditions of the time. Yet, beauty arose from this misery. We peered into some cells where Dostoevsky and Lenin's brother had languished in damp, fetid darkness.

We wandered back across the bridge and down to Gostiny Dvor, the huge shopping mall, to buy my ailing camera its new battery. Then, hungry at last, we ate a snack and decided to visit our first gay bar. Since it was too early, we didn't return home until 9 p.m. The Professor was entertaining a young gay visitor from the U.S. who was staying at the Grand Hotel where the rates were $250-300 a night. We were definitely out of his league. The gay bar visit was postponed to another night when our feet were less sore from walking all day. Rick took the opportunity to visit another young lady from his E-mail files. Feet seemed to be no hassle for him.

It was Sunday morning, and I proposed we visit the Summer Gardens. Peter had had this lovely spot placed next to the Fontanka Canal where it empties out into the broad Neva. It was lined with lime trees along its central axis and at every cross-path, he had decreed classical statuary of the Greek gods and goddesses on high pedestals. It was a favorite spot for romantic couples. I placed Rick alongside Diana, the Huntress and I was pictured at Apollo's feet. At the end of the Park stood a handsome small mansion, which had been Peter's simple home. This had none of the imperial grandeur of the Winter Palace and he retired here to live a more simple life. I was intrigued with the décor and furnishings of the rooms and took pictures of everything including a special armchair that had been carved with wooden arms and hands surrounding you.

I asked Boris to take us to Peter's first home — a little log cabin where he lived while the city was under construction. Boris had never heard of it to my surprise. Of course, few Americans have any idea where Abe Lincoln's log cabin might be, either. But we do know of Mount Vernon, Washington's home but how many have visited the place? My guidebook helped us find the street address and it turned out to be fairly close. The address was at a riverside garden with Chinese lions set facing out over the river. The rather ordinary brick house set back a way from the water actually was nothing more than a covering for the actual log cabin. We could not enter the cabin but could peer in through its windows. It had been built in three days but was surprisingly well constructed. The furniture, his desk and dining table, everything had been preserved carefully. Russians revere their famous citizens perhaps more than any other country I have visited. Household objects we would deem worthless are displayed reverently, as I was to see in so many historic sites. Even Peter's first boat, the size of my own boats, was there on display. This is considered the beginning of the Russian navy and every naval cadet comes here to stare in awe at the humble little vessel.

We soon left the log cabin and the small sail-boat which Peter had first owned, to walk a couple of blocks along the banks of the Neva to have a look at another famous ship, the battleship "Aurora." The sailors aboard this vessel fired the first shots in the Russian Revolution, from its decks. The film director, Eisenstein made a famous movie called "Potemkin" which dramatizes this critical moment in Russian history. I looked forward to go aboard and see below decks where there were many photographs, nautical gear and quarters to inspect. And across the River, sat the St. Petersburg Hotel, where I had stayed in '92 on my first visit.

I proposed we wander on across the Sampsonievsky Bridge nearby and simply see what turned up. The walk along the river, bordered with trees, was very pleasant and it became more so as we arrived at a Muslim mosque straight out of the Arab world. The Mechet Mosque had a turquoise tile dome and minarets surrounding it. There was an air of neglect as if the caretakers were losing the will to keep it in repair. I was curious about the interior and decided to venture in. Rick chose to remain outside. The interior was a huge space looking up to the dome. The floor was laid with oriental carpets but I saw only two or three men sitting on the floor in the twilight gloom. At least one of them appeared to be sleeping, but perhaps he was meditating. I reverently tiptoed out again to where Rick waited under the trees at the river's edge.

There was a small zoo nearby but I chose not to see the caged animals. I have mixed feelings about seeing the conditions most animals have to live under so that we may have a moment's amusement.

We re-crossed the bridge to walk along the streets leading us to the Military Museum in Alexandrinsky Park. There were huge guns, howitzers, cannons parked in its courtyard and I photographed them. It occurred to me that if I had been doing this a few years ago, I would be on my way to a gulag in Siberia. The sky above us was dotted with people dropping to earth in parachutes, the latest thrill for city-people with a bit of extra cash to splurge. I wondered how they had enough expertise to guide their parachutes onto the lawns instead of the surrounding river. There was a small zoo nearby but I chose not to see the caged animals. I have mixed feelings about seeing the conditions most animals have to live under so that we may have a moment's amusement.

We crossed another bridge, the Birvzevoy, which brought us, on this Sunday stroll, to Vasilievsky Island. We were passing the very handsome Rostral columns. These two rust-colored columns towering some 70 feet are adorned with ships' prows and at first, before electricity, they were lit with oil flares to guide ships into the harbor. Flanking the columns were giant statues representing the four great rivers of Russia: the Volga, Dnieper, Volkhov and Neva. It was a particularly lovely spot as you looked out over the city panorama of onion domes, spires and classical buildings. We bought ice cream from a nearby peddler and soaked in the ambience of this gorgeous city. We moved on down the street to visit the Kunstkammer. This was Peter the Great's first interest in museums, and this one was the predecessor to modern museums because it housed "curiosities." People in the 18th Century went to museums mainly to see freakish things. We inspected large jars containing two-headed calves, human babies with abnormal heads and limbs, artifacts from aboriginal tribes from all over the world, and anything odd anyone could think of. It was eye opening but not particularly pleasant. Peter even had problems getting people to come and see, so he enticed them with a free meal after the visit!

It was Monday morning; poor Alex would be doing a trip back to the OVIR offices to finish processing our invitation paperwork. We weren't expected to go with him so we walked to the Engineer Castle, a famous palace sitting along the Fontanka Canal and a handsome little park. This palace was built by Tsar Paul, son of Catherine the Great. He was not a popular ruler, made numerous enemies in the Court. So he had this formidable home built with all sorts of safety passages and escape routes. It all came to nothing when forty days after moving in, he was murdered by his palace guards. As we entered the huge brick structure, we were told that it was not possible to see anything except the souvenir shop. I bought a coffee mug with a coat-of-arms on the side and we left disappointed. The Professor had suggested we see the wax museum in the Stroganov Palace, so we headed there next. No one was sure if this was the family that invented the famous dish — Stroganov Beef — but when we arrived we realized this was a new enterprise. There were only two rooms to inspect and six historical figures. Peter the Great, of course looming up to his unusual height of six foot and five inches and a few others like Rasputin and Catherine the Great. Not the best wax figures I had seen since I had already visited Madame Tussaud's in London.

We had bought tickets to a piano recital at the Philharmonic for the evening. Rick was escorting Rita, one of his two new girl friends. Actually, both of these gals were named Rita, and this was Rita, #1! I had thought Boris would go with me but he asked me to take his mother who spoke no English. I went along with this wondering how we would communicate but we simply smiled a lot and used sign language, awkward but necessary. The all-Beethoven program was beautifully done, but I was enjoying the handsome white hall and the great glittering chandeliers. Tchaikovsky had introduced his music in this place and I was thrilled by the thought. Afterwards, I invited Boris's mother to come with us to Sadko's for a drink but she preferred to return home by Metro, so the three of us sat in this elegant spot which is inside the Grand Hotel.

On Tuesday morning, Rick got through to one of his ladies and planned to meet her at 8 p.m. I suggested we go out to visit the two lovely palaces at Pushkin, which is 15 miles south of the city. We set out for Pushkin on the suburban train that had been operating for over a hundred years. I don't think it had been modernized in that times either. Pushkin, which is named after the most famous Russian poet, evolved as a town built especially for the hundreds of servants needed to staff the two palaces which are only a couple of miles apart. Catherine the Great built the smaller palace, Pavlosk for her ungrateful son, Paul. But he rarely ever visited this elegant home in the country, preferring to stay in St. Petersburg and drill his special squadron of soldiers. He was rather peculiar in his fascination for the military life and even played with toy soldiers inventing new drill formations and planning war maneuvers. He was the chap I mentioned earlier who wound up being murdered by his guards in the Engineer's Castle.

I had failed to check my guidebook or perhaps, it was one of those off days when the Catherine Palace just wasn't open because of some obscure reason — anyway, we couldn't go in. Since I had seen it before, it wasn't heartbreaking, but it meant Rick wouldn't see the football stadium size ballroom. We spent an hour or more wandering through the beautiful grounds, past artificial lakes and airy pavilions. I was amused to find an over-life sized marble statue of Hercules, his massive muscles looking a bit exaggerated.

We left the Catherine Palace, taking a local bus to Pavlosk. In World War II, the German army had penetrated up to this area fifteen miles out of St. Petersburg. They had laid waste to everything in their path and Pavlosk was hard hit. Many of the walls had been hammered by mortar and cannon shells, the elegant rooms had been used as stables and soldiers had shot up

Hercules at the Catherine Palace grounds.

the frescoes and generally turned the interiors into a frightful ruin. When the Nazis invaded the Soviet Union in 1941, Hitler's orders were to obliterate every trace of Russian culture. German armies systematically torched and ransacked museums, libraries and other artistic treasures. During the 900-day siege of St. Petersburg, the Nazis used Pavlosk as a military headquarters, cutting down 70,000 trees for firewood from the 1800 acres, which surrounded the palace. But in a miracle of forethought, a group of Russian patriots, mostly women, determined to save what they could of the furnishings. They managed to carry off precious objects, and statuary was buried deep in the parks. Several trainloads of art objects were sent to Siberia. It was a gargantuan undertaking by dedicated citizens. And the irony of it was that these were Communists salvaging the Imperial past!

But in a miracle of forethought, a group of Russian patriots, mostly women, determined to save what they could of the furnishings ... and the irony of it was that these were Communists salvaging the Imperial past!

We were to be almost the only visitors that afternoon, and I relished walking the stately rooms as if they were my own. Only the little old babushkas, sitting in obscure corners were to be seen. And so we returned to St. Petersburg in the late afternoon, Rick for his date and I to have a long rambling talk with the Professor on the trials of living in Russia in these transitional days.

The next day was to be our Literary Day — I felt we should pay homage to two world-famous authors and consulted my map to find their homes. The Russian passion for preserving the homes of their famous was serving us well. First we headed for the apartment of Anna Akhmatova, who was alive during the Stalin Reign of Terror of the Twenties through the Forties. Hundreds of thousands perished because of his insane paranoia. But Anna somehow beat the odds and lived on to write her sublime poetry. I had made a copy of Altman's famous painting of her some months before this trip.

We entered the upstairs flat overlooking a small park to find an interior quite spartanly furnished. There were handsome Regency style chairs, desks and tables, with a shawl, a fan, a cigarette case left on a surface here and there. I was amazed that no one had made off with these treasured bits of the past. Only the one babushka stood guard. In America, everything would have to be in glass cases. A sad commentary.

Here are four short lines from her sublime poetry:

> Before me in this chamber lived
> A solitary sorceress:
> Her shadow is still visible
> On the eve of the new moon.

We left Anna's world to walk a few blocks into another era, the time of Dostoevsky. Everyone has read or at least knows of his "Crime and Punishment" and "The Brothers Karamazov". This district of the city had a different air about it. It seemed as if we had been dropped into the 19th Century. The streets were narrow, the buildings a grimy, neglected collection of dark facades. We seemed to be the only foreigners around as we jostled through the streets. The Church of Vladimir stood at the end of a short street, so we entered it to light a taper on the rack near the altar. People were streaming in and out for a quick moment of silent contemplation. Churches had never really been wiped off the Russian landscape, in spite of Stalin's years of persecution. This was evident to us as we looked at these devout faces.

Across the street was a small restaurant, very untouristy, and so we entered a room with pale apple green walls and oilcloth covered tables. I ordered "pelmeni" for us, a favorite Russian pasta. Then it was time to visit Dostoevsky and so we ambled down a few blocks to an old 19th Century business building on a corner. It was some kind of a store on the ground floor, but a back staircase led us up to the third floor landing. It was 1878 at that moment since nothing had been changed. Even the wall-clock had been

21 - To Russia With Rick—1997

stopped at the moment of the author's death. Dostoevsky's wife had had the presence of mind to have the entire flat photographed so those restorers could recreate the feel of the rooms. It was eerie as we walked around the small rooms and you almost felt he could have been in the next room ready to greet you. His tall stovepipe hat sat under a glass bell in the hall. His desk was strewn with working manuscripts.

Another famous author, Josef Brodsky had been memorialized across the hallway, although he was of another time. Since I wasn't familiar with his writing, we only glanced at the displays of his books and posters for his readings. I think he wrote in the 1930s or 40s.

Walking back to Nevsky, we were passing a new symbol of Russian freedom, the Sex Shop. The sign outside in French, called it the "Intime." Rick politely declined to enter but I had to have a look. It wasn't a gay establishment at all, but seemed a general appeal sort of place with racks of sex toys stocking the shelves. A pretty young lady sat at the cashier's counter while a giant dildo floated from the ceiling. A bit much in the way of the New Freedom, I concluded as I exited out to my waiting friend.

Dostoevsky's hat under a glass bell at his historic apartment.

Rick had his date to get ready for and the Professor and I were scheduled to go to the Maly Hall to watch the "Swan Lake" ballet. I was advised to wear a tie, but since I hadn't brought one, I borrowed one while Alex struggled into a suit he no longer fitted into. Swan Lake is an old war-horse of a ballet but it was still fun seeing it in its original setting. We had ice creams during the intermission, as Russians adore ice cream as much as

Americans, perhaps more.

Since the performance was over by 9:30, we decided it was time for me to see a gay bar. But we needed to change clothes as the Professor assured me we had to be more casually dressed to fit into the scene properly. We walked a few blocks to the same shabby pink building from a bygone era that Alex had indicated a few days ago. But now it was later in the evening and the proper time to be there. There must have been a dozen young men sitting around at small tables mostly drinking an orange drink from bottles. I wondered about this until I realized it was what they could afford. I was surprised how quiet it was as I was used to the deafening speakers blaring rock music in the States. But here it was almost as if people were afraid that the police would raid the place at any moment. I ordered Tuborg, the Danish brew for the two of us. The rather small room was mainly decorated by strobe lights, which darted across the walls haphazardly from a hidden source. Then, one at a time, a young guy would come over to our table for a brief chat, which I couldn't understand, of course. It turned out that the Professor was holding court: dispensing advice to people with financial or emotional problems. I remembered that the Professor was the president of the Gay and Lesbian Association and that as a mentor for the troubled gay youth of St. Petersburg, he had advice to give to these questioning boys. He was a true father figure for the young gays of this city.

As we arrived at the sidewalk gate to the apartment, we found Rick lounging there since he had no key. He had also developed a very sore shin from walking so much, so I gave him a soothing foot massage.

A new day, Thursday and I was interested in visiting the Marble Palace, which sits on Millionaire's Row appropriately enough. This imposing residence has a handsome courtyard across its façade, dominated by a bronze equestrian warrior. This imposing sculpture had languished in a forgotten corner of a warehouse for years, banished by the Communists for some reason or other. But our Professor had learned of it one day and gone to the City fathers about restoring it to its rightful place. He convinced them to bring it out again and let the world see this proud figure on horseback, in its original site. Catherine the Great had built the palace for her favorite lover, Count Orlov. Unhappily, he died before it was completed and now it was a

> *We decided it was time for me to see a gay bar . . . I was surprised how quiet it was as I was used to the deafening speakers blaring rock music in the States. But here it was almost as if people were afraid that the police would raid the place at any moment.*

museum for traveling art exhibitions. Since it was a block from the Hermitage Museum, it made a lot of sense to be near by. I discovered a favorite painting of mine in one of the galleries, Claudio Bravo's Madonna and Child. I was particularly impressed with the enormous crystal chandeliers and the high ceilings. One room had walls covered in 27 different varieties of marbles from around the world. I marveled at the utter disregard that the nobility had for the peasant masses that were living in abject poverty a few miles away in their mud and thatch huts.

Of course, a visit to St. Petersburg would be incomplete without a stop at Pushkin's apartment which was nearby. We walked up to the second floor to see his carefully preserved 4,000 book library and study. This favorite Russian poet had fought a pistol duel with his wife's lover and died from his wounds. The opera written by Tchaikovsky, called "Eugene Onegin", tells the dramatic story. We left around noon to stop in at a very plush little restaurant catering to the new, very affluent "biznesmen" now appearing in Russia's economic scene. The menu was a bit expensive but we couldn't resist the blinis filled with caviar. Again, we felt the stark contrast of a posh dining spot with the general shabbiness of the streets. This was even more evident as we walked on to nearby Palace Square. This immense expanse of courtyard, dominated by the 90 foot Alexander Column, was at the moment, being turned into a very commercial venue for advertising the Lego and Smitherol Companies. Colorful balloons and big signs over booths were set up around the Column. And yet this was the same spot that had witnessed the slaughter of hundreds of innocent men and women who had only petitioned the Tsar for better working conditions on that infamous day in 1905 known as "Bloody Sunday."

We passed through the great arch, which empties out into Nevsky Prospeckt and wandered about looking for a bank to do a money exchange. Rick was changing a $20 bill into 114,000 rubles and it seemed a bit ridiculous to us. We stopped at another famous address, the Café Literatura for an ice cream. The place was empty but we knew that the evenings used to be filled with the intelligentsia arguing about the Arts and the state of Culture.

Again, the Professor and I attended the opera as guests of that young manager. I didn't ask what favor was being paid off by this free admission and sat back and enjoyed "Boris Goudunov." The lavish production of this historic opera was resplendent with scenes of the old Imperial Russia, giving

Myself at Tchaikovsky's grave.

I immediately recognized the Tchaikovsky stone ... it was lovingly surrounded by two guardian angels ... sad to think that this man had spent his life denying he was gay, even going to the extreme of marrying a nymphomaniac.

me a sense of what it must have been like to live in those distant times. As we came out onto the streets at 10:30, it was still daylight for the city was enjoying its "White Nights." Rick returned from his evening with a young Russian lady and I massaged his sore shin while he told me the story of his son's battle with cystic fibrosis and his sad death at the age of 20.

Friday morning — Rick's painful ankle will keep him from doing much walking today, but when Boris arrived from the suburbs at ten, we took the Metro across town to the Alexander Nevsky Square station which is next to the first hotel I stayed at on my first trip to Russia. Across the Square were the Church, Monastery and Cemetery where I had my first meeting with Alex and his boy friend. I hadn't known then that the Cemetery held the remains of almost all of Russia's greatest musicians and writers. They were all in the same section, which had a Victorian air with its tree-shaded lanes and very ornately carved stone monuments. It was difficult to read the Russian lettering but I immediately recognized the Tchaikovsky stone because of his portrait bust. It was lovingly surrounded by

21 - To Russia With Rick—1997

two guardian angels; one holding a cross behind his head while the other pensively studied a musical score. Sad to think that this man had spent his life denying he was gay, even going to the extreme of marrying a nymphomaniac. The marriage was never consummated, however, and he lived apart from her. She ended up in a mental ward, where she later died. He, on the other hand, met a death that has ever since been shrouded in mystery. Did he really die from drinking tainted water or was it true that a committee of his musician colleagues voted that he was to take poison to avoid scandal that was building up around his illustrious name? We also know that another woman, the Countess Von Meck, who admired his music passionately, subsidized his work so that he never had to worry for funds, yet she stipulated that they were never to face one another in person. What a bizarre relationship!

We rode the Metro back to our own neighborhood and spent time admiring the walls of the Church of the Spilled Blood, where a Tsar had been assassinated some hundred years ago. The façade was ornately covered with mosaic portraits of saints and martyrs. It was uncanny how closely the whole structure echoed the same look as St. Basil's in Moscow. Nearby, a side street was filled with cheap souvenir stalls, including "Matroyshka Dolls" in limitless profusion. These are the fat little figures that open up to reveal another smaller doll, which hides yet another doll, ad infinitum. One doesn't leave Russia without one or two of these! The new gimmick seemed to be to paint Yeltsin's figure on the outermost one, then Gorbachev inside that and going all the way back to the last Tsar. There were usually six or more progressively smaller dolls inside. I bought one, of course. But I really needed a blank cassette to record my proposed interview with the Professor.

When we returned to the apartment, we asked him to reveal the intricate system for unlocking his apartment door. I never did grasp the concept at all, nor did Rick, who later paid the price of not knowing by being left out on the landing for 30 minutes until the Professor returned from an errand. I was on the inside but couldn't solve the riddle of letting down the portcullis to enter the castle.

It was Saturday and we planned to board a local train west for 20 miles to visit Petrodvorets. This is often referred to as the Russian Versailles because of its opulence. Covering 2,500 acres of manicured gardens and pavilions, it faces out to the Gulf of Finland. In its heyday, courtiers arrived by boat or barge and walked a long avenue decorated with fountains every hundred yards. The façade we now saw was framed by a series of stair-stepped waterfalls culminating in the golden statue of Samson battling a lion. Other golden figures lined the steps down to the garden level creating a magnificent ensemble. More fountains placed throughout the extravagant gardens played tricks on you like turning on as you crossed over them. The sheer playfulness of this should give you an idea of court life in the early 18th Century. I should have mentioned that we were accompanied on this outing by Vasya, a young friend of Boris's who constantly had a grin on his face. He spoke a dozen words of English but made up for it in his happy face. I was to learn that he was later inducted into the Army, sent to Chechnya and returned alive. He was evidently bisexual and I heard he married and fathered a little girl.

When we left the train terminus, we still needed to board a bus to arrive at the Palace gates. Walking across a half mile of graveled walks through clipped hedges and flowerbeds, we passed an imposing Neptune fountain before coming around the vast building to the side facing out over the Baltic Sea. On this grand esplanade, we noticed a number of elegantly costumed actors chatting with tourists: 18th Century aristocrats mingling with 20th Century citizens!

Boris and Vasya had no interest in walking through the Palace, so Rick and I entered to do our own tour. We ascended to the second level and started down a corridor that was the length of the entire Palace. As you glanced down, each door beyond the next diminished in size so that the last one was tiny. It must have been a thousand feet to the last room. We gaped at the Throne Room, with its four enormous paintings of the Battle of Chesme, and made sure we had slipped on the "tapocki' (the bedroom slippers donned to save the gorgeous marquetry floors). The White Dining hall was set for a formal dinner for a hundred guests. I loved the Chinese Room on either side of the Portrait hall. Every room had a color theme and was handsomely furnished with lovely antiques. It was the finest example of opulent interiors we were to see. The irony of it all was that this was a restoration since the German Army had also laid waste to

> *We were accompanied on this outing by Vasya, a young friend of Boris's who constantly had a grin on his face ... I was to learn that he was later inducted into the Army, sent to Chechnya and returned alive. He was evidently bisexual and I heard he married and fathered a little girl.*

21 - To Russia With Rick—1997

this Palace. Photographic records and architectural records had allowed the Russian people to restore most of it. Amazing that the Communist regime had permitted this recreation of the Tsarist past. I bought a picture book of this entire splendor.

We returned to our Russian friends and strolled the long avenue leading down to the boat docks, enjoying the sea air. A hydrofoil launch was just arriving with a group of foreign tourists. And it was time to head back now. Soon after exiting the royal gardens, we passed an ancient church just as a wedding entourage was arriving adding a festive air to the solemn beauty of the golden onion-domed church walls.

At 7 p.m. we felt energized enough again to buy tickets to a performance of folk dancing at the Belozersky Palace on Nevsky Prospeckt. The costumes were a riot of color as the dancers whirled through intricate steps. I was in awe of the tremendous energy of this young troupe. We stopped for Russian pizza on the way back to the apartment but I must say that they haven't perfected the art of making a pizza, as it should be constructed. We Americans come a bit closer to the perfect pizza.

Rick had another date with his new group of lady friends. I chose to stay in, a bit tired from a busy day, and simply enjoyed reliving the day's scenes.

It was Sunday morning, the weather was balmy and we decided to stroll to the Decembrists' Square to get a closer look at the Bronze Horseman. A woman under the direction of the French sculptor, Falconet, created this magnificent equestrian figure of Peter the Great in the center of a green meadow. He had won the competition arranged by Catherine the Second. Finished in 1778, it represents the Tsar ascending a rock and trampling a serpent, which symbolizes the Swedes. Pushkin based his most famous poetry on this imposing memorial. At the moment we were admiring its heroic outlines, a workman aloft a cherry-picker crane was hovering over its surface as he lovingly washed off the grime. It was an amusing juxtaposition of modern technology serving history.

Boris suggested we have a look at an address he was familiar with. Down a side street, we came to Mayak House, a palatial residence long since in a closed state but recently resurrected as a gay disco. The huge ballroom was ideal for modern Russian gay youth to dance the night away in.

Down a side street, we came to Mayak House, a palatial residence long since in a closed state but recently resurrected as a gay disco. The huge ballroom was ideal for modern Russian gay youth to dance the night away in.

The ornate plaster carving on walls and ceilings, crystal chandeliers must have made a stark contrast to the pulsating rock music bouncing off the plaster cupids and floral garlands decorating the ceilings and walls.

We were passing the St. Petersburg History Museum, so we entered, paying a small entrance fee. Its main focus seemed to be on the terrible 900-day siege that the city endured in World War Two. Over 650,000 people perished from starvation and the cold. Bodies were left on the sidewalks for days before they were hauled away on children's sleds. Cannibalism was even reported. It was a ghastly experience for the miserable survivors. The city was never taken by the Nazis because of the heroic resistance by the Russian Army. A babushka collared us and gave us a 5-minute lecture in Russian, ignoring the fact that we only understood two words of Russian. We returned to our neighborhood street, Bolshaya Konyushennaya, feeling terribly depressed and decided that food might revive our spirits. The little restaurant at the end of the block had recently undergone a facelift and sparkled under the new fixtures and paint. Most eating establishments in Russia are so drab, but this one seemed so inviting that we had to enter. Rick noticed the very pretty blonde who waited on us and returned the flirting glances she threw at him.

But we still had a good bit of the afternoon to spend so we headed over to the Ethnographical Museum. This vast building (everything in Russia is vast, it seemed) was particularly interesting with the Arts and Crafts of all the Russian States. We could peer into typical homes from the faraway corners of Siberia, Kazakhstan, and many other states. It was eye opening to realize how extremely diverse the Russian Empire had been. How did all these nationalities ever fit into one unified whole? One wondered that it lasted as long as it did.

After having a bite to eat at Minutka ("a little minute"), we returned to the apartment, Rick to keep another date with an Olga and I to run over the list of questions for the Interview with the professor. We then stepped out with the giant dog to take a late night stroll through the sleeping city. As we passed a building on Nevsky Prospeckt, I was shown a famous sign on a wall warning citizens to stay on the opposite side of the street to avoid the German shells that were devastating the city. It has never been removed.

Today, a Monday, was our last day in this handsome city that Peter the Great dreamed into reality. We were at a loss on how to fill the day, so

Bust of Peter the Great at the Moscow Train Terminal.

much that we hadn't seen but what to choose to see. We wound up simply walking along Nevsky, visiting a couple of small commercial art galleries with prices set ridiculously high, even for tourists. But I did find a couple of small etchings of city scenes that I was willing to buy. Then Boris mentioned it was worthwhile to saunter down to the Moscow Train Terminal to view the imposing bust of Peter the Great on a marble pedestal some 8 feet high. It was worth the walk, a thought provoking character study of this colossus of a man who fathered this great city. I took a good photo of it. Boris also mentioned that one night, a group of Lenin admirers had actually spirited the bust away and replaced it with their own god. No one talked of the switch the next day, the news media and radio were silent but then Peter was restored to his pedestal. We revisited the huge sprawling shoppers' mall called "Gostinny Dvor" where I admired two round birch boxes with intricately carved sides. I bought them as my last purchase here. Then it was time to bid Boris good-bye and we talked about his plan to visit me in California in time to see the Gay Pride Parade down Market Street. It seemed that he would be able to afford this trip as the referee for a basketball team that he often worked with. They were scheduled for a visit to a Long Beach sports event and that southern California city wasn't that far from my area. I promised to facilitate the lodging and bus ticket parts of the trip to visit me in Oakland.

§

On Tuesday morning, very early, we had a taxi ordered from the night before, purring at the sidewalk to haul us to Pulkovo Airport. I assured the professor that I would try to get his Interview published in some gay newspaper. At 7 a.m. we were winging our way to Frankfort where Rick and I parted — he to Atlanta and then on to Nashville; I to San Francisco arriving at 1 p.m. the same day, having gained back the 11 hours that I had lost.

§

I feel it would be of interest to my readers to learn a bit about the Gay and Lesbian world in Russia at the moment of the Communist collapse. On the following pages are answers to questions I put to Alex Kukharsky, the president of the first officially registered Gay and Lesbian Association. The abbreviated title for this group is "Krilija", which translates to "Wings". This, in turn, comes from the name of a famous Russian story. Alex works out of his apartment for his correspondence on gay issues and I have kept his e-mail address in my files if anyone wants to contact him.* He also provides a nice room, which can be rented, for a small fee. Since he is in the center of the City, it is ideal for anyone who hates being stuck a mile or two out in the suburbs with transportation hassles to surmount.

§

I want to add here that my interest in Russia continues currently. I am in e-mail contact with several Russian friends, all of them in various stages of learning English. A young "straight" couple living about 60 mile east of Moscow at Kolomna are especially friendly and when I came "out" to them in my second letter, they took it in stride and continued to be interested in writing. I am invited to come visit at any time. I find the husband less willing to write, but the wife, Svetlana is full of questions and gives me a realistic picture of what it is like to be a Russian at this particular moment in history.

On the Civil Rights of Gays and Lesbians in Russia
Interview with Alex Kukharsky, PhD
[Professor Kukharsky is the President of Krilija, Russia's first Gay and Lesbian Our gay and lesbian public organization, officially registered on October 9, 1991]

Alex Kukharsky, center, President of "Wings" Holding a Vigil at the Catherine Monument.

How did Krilija come into being? It was formed in the summer of 1990 when 10 men and 2 women met at my apartment. At that time, there existed a paragraph in Article 121, which dealt with consensual anal sex between men. It had not been used in some years but remained in the law books. We got resistance from the authorities that used various pretexts to block the registration of our group. We addressed the various levels of courts and after a year of struggling, Krilija was finally registered in October 1991. It was indeed a historic moment for the Russian gay movement since nothing close to this had ever existed before. Another St. Petersburg group also registered, a month later but we never learned if any group in Moscow ever became officially registered.

What position do you hold as a college professor? I am a doctor of mathematical and physical sciences, but at present I am a free, private businessman providing scientific consulting. It does not pay much but enough to live, enjoy life and travel abroad once or twice a year.

Was your sexual identity known at college? I am no longer associated with the college and this does certainly not bother my employees, who are women.

Does Krilija meet on a regular basis? Yes, from the moment of our official registration as "Wings", we began round table meetings every month and attracted from 100 to 150 young men. We rented a hall to discuss our current problems. At first, we received about 10,000 letters and 20 volunteers were answering these letters. Only 30 of these letters were anonymous threats, mostly from women who thought we were taking the best men away from them. Some letters came from men who wanted to meet lesbians. We are still getting mail from gays who live in remote areas such as Siberia who have much difficulty in meeting each other. (I would venture to suggest this problem has been somewhat lessened by the chat rooms of the Internet but we also know how entrapment can make e-pen pals quite wary of giving out too much information.)

Do you celebrate Gay Pride Day in Russia? No, we don't have a Parade but our group did send a delegation to the 25th New York Stonewall Parade. Some gay businessmen tried to use this day here for commercial purposes, renting a swimming pool for a disco evening and calling it the St. Christopher Street Celebration. Also, we had a Candlelight memorial for the first time 4 years ago. We gathered around the Catherine the Great Monument on Nevsky Prospeckt where we answered people's questions about our group. We have done this several

(Continued on page 390)

(Continued from page 389) years now.

Can you tell us how you developed as a gay person? My first gay adventure was at 12 with a schoolmate. Then, at 18, I was at a sport camp where bicyclists where training and I had more experiences. On my 20th birthday, a girl happened to mention the cruising area around the Catherine Monument of which I was ignorant. The very next day, I went there and my eyes were opened. My gay life began from there.

How large an organization is Krilija now? At first, about 500 people joined and were given tickets for a small fee to support us. Now, the group is about 50 people. Each year on the last Saturday of October, we hold a conference to discuss current problems. One example was the situation of an 18-year old Russian accused of killing his American lover. He had not committed this crime and we investigated it ourselves, finding new evidence. His case was reviewed and he is now waiting for a new court date. Another young man was falsely accused of robbery, but due to our efforts, he was found not guilty. Another of our activities is to visit AIDS patients in a local hospital. They end up here from all over Russia. We bring them little gifts and talk about the latest treatments; also we get letters from gay men who are considering suicide. We try to help them see other solutions.

Are there more men than women in Krilija? Yes, there are more men, so that 90 % of our members are men. Women tend to drop out and then later rejoin.

How can we be of help to Krilija? We are not a commercial group and almost all our financial resources go to AIDS people. We would be very grateful if some U.S. group would make a gift of a fax machine. We do have a computer address, so you are all welcome to communicate with us and will receive a prompt reply.

How has AIDS changed your lives? It is a great sorrow, but it has not changed our lives as we have very few cases. About 13 persons have died so far, half of them women out of a population of 5 million in the St. Petersburg area. About 150 people are currently listed as HIV Positive. We distribute condoms and lubricants at gay discos and warn young men not to have sex without condoms. We have given interviews on the local media, but sad to say, most of the boys are having sex without condoms. When I visited Paris recently, it was the same. They think this virus will only attack others. What to do? We do try to change their habits.

Are you interested in contacting American gays or groups? Yes, of course, we are greatly interested and we took part in the 14th International Gay and Lesbian Association Conference, New York 1994. Our success was mostly with private individuals, however.

What future plans to you have as an organization? Now that Article 121 has been repealed, our main problem is the registration of same sex couples and to continue to help people with AIDS.

We were surprised how soon Article 121 was repealed, so how did this happen? This Article has a long story: after the Bolshevik coup d'etat in 1917, homosexuality was persecuted for about 17 years Then, in 1933, by the personal order of the tyrant Stalin, Article 121 was installed in the law books. This immediately caused the suicides of many Moscow and St. Petersburg intellectuals, as they preferred death to Stalin's gulags. As the other tyrant, Hitler, came to power in 1933, we don't think this was merely a coincidence. It was simply another way of gaining power over the lives of men. Female sex or lesbians were never mentioned in the criminal code. I would emphasize that Article 121 was only about anal sex. Several hundred men went to prison each year due to this article. We started sending letters to Mr. Yeltsin, to the Prosecutor's Office, to the Supreme Soviet and always got the same answer, "You shouldn't bother, there is no such article in the new criminal code which will be put in force, wait a little and everything will be all right". But we still didn't want to wait; life is so short. In the spring of 1993, in a government newspaper, there was an announcement that

Article 121 was abolished. We now consider that this is one of the best examples of the criminal code. The age of consent is lowered to 14-16 years depending on the type of assault, before the new code can be used. Also there is no difference in punishment for rape or seducing a minor, no matter who the victims are, male female, heterosexual or homosexual. This is a very great victory for the Gay movement and Democracy. It is one of the best criminal codes in the world.

Are Russian scientists working now on an AIDS cure? Well, yes, but I don't know the details. However, the Republican hospital here is a very good one, so that each Aids patient has his own room and can bring his own TV and magnetophone. He can usually spend a month here while being treated. The food is rather nice and we saw that the patients had access to the gardens when we last visited. They can go to a nearby subway station to go into the city. The only restriction being that if they bring in alcohol, it must be consumed in their rooms and not make a scandal with the staff. In cases like that they would be immediately expelled from the hospital. Every large city has an AIDS center. Most of the doctors are very kind men or women and don't have a prejudicial attitude toward us.

Do you have a message for us? Oh yes, to be sure. The problems of gay life are practically the same the world over. I have lived in many European countries and America. I find that one of the main problems is that in the rural areas, it is very difficult for gays to find partners. Also, that now it is not cheap to travel as it was in the evil Communist times. Then no one ever mentioned the word, homosexuality, or discussed the problems until the 80s. Now it is very fashionable. The subculture is developing very quickly and we have our own nightclubs, saunas, restaurants, beaches and cruising areas. (I am writing this information in 2001 and have just verified on the Internet that St. Petersburg has at least 35 gay venues at this time).

— G.S. (1997)

22
Boris Comes to America

1997

Boris was simply bowled over by what gay Americans were able to do now. The openness was so startling to him. The joy at being yourself with few inhibitions." - GS

§

I had heard about the Gay and Lesbian Pride parades and related celebrations, but had never seen one. Boris, George's Russian friend arrived in the U.S. and off they went to experience those festivities. But Boris's real reason for coming turned out to be a real shocker, alienating other gays in George's circles. But George was forgiving, and the story picks up in this chapter. - JJ

Boris Comes to America: 1997

My trip to St. Petersburg in 1997 was followed the next month by a visit from Boris. I was amazed that he could pay for this trip, but didn't inquire into the arrangements he had made. I did know that he was going to Long Beach, which is close to Los Angeles. He had been supporting himself as a basketball referee. It seemed an odd way to make a living to me but I hadn't a clue as to how this job was regarded in Russia. It evidently meant that the airfare was handled by the team's budget. But I was asked to find a place for him to stay while at the Basketball Conference in Long Beach. Through my contacts at the Pacific Center for Human Growth in Berkeley, I was able to call the Long Beach Gay Center. They posted a notice up and, in no time, we had a person willing to put him up for the 3 or 4 days he was there. He was even given a chance to visit the Universal Studios Magic Tour. Then, I paid for his bus trip up to San Francisco to visit me for ten days.

The big drawing card, of course, was the huge annual Gay Pride Celebration, which was to take place in a few days. This event draws over half a million people who line up along the Market Street route. It starts down near the Ferry Building and winds up in front of the Civic center some ten long blocks west. Boris was simply bowled over by what gay Americans were able to do now. The openness was so startling to him, and the joy at being yourself with few inhibitions. The Parade always starts with a contingent of lesbians, the famous "Dykes on Bikes" who bare their breasts to the world. It is an eye-opening experience to see them as they roar by usually with their partners clinging to their waists. Then come groups of people bearing flags, signs whatever. There are floats, marching bands, cable cars and limousines. Even the Mayor of San

22 - Boris Comes to America—1997

(OVERLEAF)
*COLLAGE OF IMAGES
FROM LONG BEACH,
PALM SPRINGS,
AND SAN FRANCISCO
GAY PRIDE PARADES

Francisco has to be in the Parade, along with a number of other politicians who are currying the power of the gay vote.* The whole afternoon is an absolute mind-blowing experience not to be missed by any gay person living within several hundred miles of the city. And it now rates as the largest parade that is held in San Francisco, outdoing the Chinese New Year's Parade in sheer numbers. The City reaps substantial profits from the influx of out-of-town tourists and everyone is happy, it would seem. I have marched a couple of times, myself, as a member of the Presbyterian More Light group. This is a fairly new group of churches that are advocating the ordination of gays and lesbians as ministers. Every year at the National Assembly of Presbyterian delegates, the issue is brought up. But up through the year 2002, it has been rejected. However, it is now more seriously considered. A victory for the hard work of overcoming prejudices in the Presbyterian hierarchy. In the San Francisco area, we now have 6 Presbyterian churches that belong to the More Light Group. Rainbow flags fly in front of these churches to attract gay people.

I have marched a couple of times, myself, as a member of the Presbyterian More Light group. This is a fairly new group of churches that are advocating the ordination of gays and lesbians as ministers.

Getting back to Boris, I managed to show him the local sights. Leaving him in a gay bar in San Francisco as he requested, to see what would happen. I warned him that if he stayed out past 7 p.m., he wouldn't have a local bus to bring him back to my door. He bravely ignored this warning and later found himself stranded at a bus stop some two miles from my house. Somehow, he managed to walk it by following the bus signs along the route, but at one point falling over a free-

Bare breasted "Dykes on Bikes" in San Francisco Gay Pride Parade. Over half the riders go topless!

(Continued on page 400)

Arm-in-Arm, male couples parade through the streets of San Francisco.

Gay candidate for the mayor of Palm Springs. A friend just informed me (2003) that Palm Springs just elected their first gay black mayor! That shows you the power of the gay vote in that southern city now 40% or so gay.

22 - Boris Comes to America—1997

Gay veterans display a banner supporting gay rights in the military.

The all-male West Hollywood Cheerleaders.

Even presidential candidates like to get in on the act.

Same sex marriage?

Float commemorating the Long Beach Lesbian and Gay Coalition's 20th Anniversary. This is the organization that helped me find Boris a place to stay while he was in Southern California.

How about the highway patrol?

(Continued from page 395)

way entrance wall and gashing his hand. I bound up his hand when he arrived and the visit went well after this unfortunate incident.

§

This all happened in June of 1997 and I was totally astonished to learn that Boris was returning to the Bay Area in December of the same year. How he managed to finance this was a total mystery to me but I decided not to inquire. I knew that he had another correspondent in Tennessee, a professor at some college there and I wondered if that was how he financed the trip. This visit was the last he could make on his passport's expiring date. But what he had signed up for was very revealing of his desperation. Boris was anxious to emigrate from Russia and an organization in Marin County was part of a movement to offer gays a chance to give up the "lifestyle" and revert to heterosexuality. I won't mention their name, since it might be libelous, but it is not the only group sponsored by right-wing conservatives around trying to convert gays. Of course, it is a hopeless goal, as most gays would agree. Can you imagine a similar endeavor to convert straights to become gay? I know that many heterosexuals think that we gays are anxious to turn them into gays but the truth is quite different. I have never heard gay friends talk of a need to add to the roster. There are enough homosexual persons out there already. What we do ask for is the same respect and understanding that everyone else gets — no special rights, just the same ones everyone else has!

Boris didn't last long at the ministry in Marin County. He was very restricted in his movements. Not allowed going out of the home except in the company of two other inmates that were picked out for him. He somehow managed to phone me on several occa-

My Russian visitor Boris, at the San Francisco Gay Pride festivities.

An organization in Marin County was part of a movement to offer gays a chance to give up the "lifestyle" and revert to heterosexuality ... it is not the only group sponsored by right-wing conservatives around trying to convert gays ... a hopeless goal, as most gays would agree.

22 - Boris Comes to America—1997

Me at a San Francisco Gay Pride Parade.

sions, complaining of the inhibiting atmosphere of the place but somehow hoping for release eventually. I think he expected to fool them into thinking he had changed his identity, and somehow marrying an American girl who might accept him and his problem. I saw it as a last desperate attempt to get out of Russia before his passport expired. I didn't see him at all on this latest journey and soon heard from him that he had somehow wangled his return flight. Most of our gay friends were appalled at his actions and censured him for what he had done. I felt his desperation and forgave him. He was still one of my Russian friends and we kept in touch.

I know that many heterosexuals think that we gays are anxious to turn them into gays but the truth is quite different. There are enough homosexual persons out there already.

23

Tripping Through Eastern Europe

1998

"I became intrigued with the idea of seeing more of the rest of Europe that I had ignored up until this time ... my fascination with the Old World hadn't diminished one iota. So it was off again, rather like Dorothy and her pals tripping down the yellow brick road on the way to the Land of Oz. What lie ahead to intrigue me?" - GS

§

George and his traveling companions covered 3800 kilometers (1,775 miles), passing through Germany, Poland, Hungary, Austria, and the Czech Republic. Again, George lays down his travels through an historical lens that even boggles the inquisitive mind, but is worth digging deeper into. - JJ

TRIPPING THROUGH EASTERN EUROPE: 1998

I became intrigued with the idea of seeing more of the rest of Europe that I had ignored up until this time, but I was nervous about being in a language situation where I wouldn't be able to cope. So, my answer to this was to sign up with a tour offered by the Trafalgar people. I had traveled with them before and felt confident that they would be a great way to see the cities I was interested in seeing. These cities were to be Frankfort, Berlin, Poznan, Warsaw, Krakow, Budapest, Gyor, Lednice, Prague, Pilsen, Nuremberg, Munich, and Rothenberg before returning to our starting point, Frankfort. Of course, I was well aware of the brief time I would be in any of these cities, but that didn't bother me. I figured that with the language barriers I would have to cope with, I was lucky to see these cities at all. Although one can say that English is spoken almost anywhere these days because of the Internet and the necessity to use a common language, it still is a matter of national pride to keep one's heritage alive.

So it was off again, rather like Dorothy and her pals tripping down the yellow brick road on the way to the Land of Oz. What lie ahead to intrigue me?

Although I was set on making this trip, I still felt the thrill of not knowing what I was letting myself in for. Would I encounter some disaster, get mugged as I did in Spain, meet some wonderful friends, and get sick from tainted food as I did in Russia? All of this weighed on my mind, of course, but in the end, it was just ridiculous to not go and miss any of it. I wished that Jim would go with me but I had learned long ago that he simply had no further interest in seeing Europe. My fascination with the Old World hadn't diminished one iota. So it was off again, rather like Dorothy and her pals tripping down the yellow brick road on the way to the Land of Oz. What lie ahead to intrigue me?

Jim drove me over to the San Francisco airport, where we met the usual delays in getting off the ground, causing me to arrive at Chicago's O'Hare with minutes to spare to catch my connecting flight to Frankfort.

23 - Tripping Through Eastern Europe—1998

Germany

§

A little over eleven hours later, I was scurrying down through this enormous airport, getting my passport stamped, looking for "Halle B" and something labeled "Trefpunkt." I began to notice people with the same blue bag I was carrying which was sort of an identification symbol. I started talking with a man and his wife from South Africa who would be in the group. Then I heard Spanish words coming from three older ladies who looked quite grim. I suppose they were on edge from the uncertainty of their situation and their lack of understanding. I tried to reassure them that they were in the right place but I didn't want to saddle myself with the job of being their interpreter from here on. I dubbed them the "Spanish Army" and kept myself somewhat distant from there on as a precaution. At 9:30 a.m., our guide, a Janusz Izdebski showed up and we piled onto our bus for a short run to a nearby town called Eschborn. We were driving through green countryside and skirting past the tall towers of downtown Frankfort. It really looked much like any American city you might see in the middle of America. Frankfort is Germany's banking center and the wealth of the country seems centered here. Our motel was typically like any you might encounter anywhere in the U.S. I now learned that I wouldn't have to

Me at age 84 (1998)

share my room with anyone else and I was relieved. I could have ended up with some heavy snoring type. The usual extra charge of 600-800 dollars for traveling alone has always bothered me but in this case, I didn't have to pay it since I was to be the only traveler that wasn't in a couples situation.

Outside, nearby was a warehouse to which people were flocking. I found it was an electronic discount outlet with every imaginable gadget one could dream up, on sale. Rather like our Good Guys or Fry's in the U.S. But I had no interest in crowding my one small bag with any cell phone bargains.

Most of our touring companions were in the over 50 category, but there was one young married couple that might have been on their honeymoon. Since I was single, I was to share my pair of seats with a young Filipino woman who was living in Toronto, Canada. She was in a group of 3 women traveling together. I learned her name was Lena soon enough. Her short plump build was garbed in sports sweat pants and jacket ensemble printed in orange, red and yellow colors depicting Marilyn Monroe's face.

Looking at dozens of Marilyn faces was a dizzying thought for me and I hoped she would have other clothes that were less demanding of attention. Lena giggled a lot and spent long minutes riffling through her enormous handbag for some little elusive bag of mints or whatever. Her plastic bags were a real source of annoyance since she was never sure where anything was and constantly searched for things she thought she might have left at home. It drove me nuts until I finally accepted my fate.

At four in the afternoon, we were driven over to Frankfort's Romerplatz, which was once an ancient town square but what we were seeing was a reconstruction of what had been here. During World War II, this had all been pulverized by Allied bombs. It had a real charm and it was hard to believe it was only 40 years ago that this was a rubble heap. There was an organ grinder and a man with a pair of scissors cutting out your silhouette out of black paper. Over in one corner of the cobblestoned plaza, there was a group of medieval stone saints that had toppled down from a church's walls during the bombing. I bought myself a "Schokoschalle" (a

23 - Tripping Through Eastern Europe—1998

chocolate sundae), as I wasn't hungry enough to order dinner. I had decided I didn't want to join any groups as yet. I wasn't sure who I would want to team up with and had decided I would let time tell me whom I would be comfortable with. It certainly wasn't going to be with my seatmate, Lena!

A passageway nearby looked inviting, and led me out to a river bank where sight-seeing boats were loading up, but I knew that we had little time for any river excursion. I returned to the square and found myself in front of the local Kunsthalle (art museum). There was an admission fee and fearing the time I had left, I simply bought 3 Chagall postcards in the lobby and then stood in the courtyard listening to a babble of voices coming from a group of stainless steel columns standing in a pool. It was intriguing and mysterious as you tried to make out words. By seven, we rounded up our wandering group and returned to the motel to watch German TV, read the American Herald Tribune and finally sleep.

We were expected to get off to an early start, so our breakfast was ready at 6:45 precisely. One remembers that Germans are a most punctual people, and since I — myself am half-German — it pleased me to see things done in an orderly manner. It was a veritable feast, buffet style with many choices. In fact it was rather standard through the whole trip to be given a substantial breakfast.

We were off through very well cared for green fields, and immaculate highways with not a single billboard to mar the landscape — America take note. Our route to Berlin was to the northeast and I thought about my grandparents who had lived here in this land. But they were from Bavaria to the south of us and I would have to travel independently to visit the small village of Pfalz to see their bit of Germany.

By lunchtime, we had reached a handsome roadside restaurant that was quite elaborate in its choices of foods. The terraces around the building were inviting, as we sat under umbrellas to munch our sandwiches and enjoy the nearby river view. We soon were on our way again for hours of driving on to our destination in Berlin. As it happened, our hotel was the same one that I had stayed in some years earlier. The Stadt Berlin sits on the Alexanderplatz and is a skyscraper of a hotel. I was on the 8th floor but there must have been 20 or more stories. At 6:30 we were on our way to a restaurant, Ziko's, in a residential neighborhood. It had an old-fashioned ambience about it. Walls tiled up partway, lots of framed views of rural Ger-

I thought about my grandparents who had lived here in this land. But they were from Bavaria to the south of us and I would have to travel independently to visit the small village of Pfalz to see their bit of Germany.

many. The tables were crowded together with little room left to pass through. Ziko's served a typical German supper, heavy on the meat course, a tiny salad and an ice cream filled pancake for the dessert course. A musician banged away on an upright piano over in a corner and everyone, as they finished, started forming a conga line which snaked itself out onto the sidewalk! I joined in, of course, wondering what the neighbors must think of this crazy bunch of tourists from the English-speaking world. After supper, we drove along Berlin's boulevards, the Unter Den Linden and others, marveling that this also was all destroyed and rebuilt in a mere 40 years. Berlin had made a triumphant comeback from a sad past. It was indeed a beautiful city closely rivaling, but not surpassing, Paris. That would be an impossible task. But Berlin was shaking off its grim history.

> *A musician banged away on an upright piano over in a corner and everyone started forming a conga line which snaked itself out onto the sidewalk! I joined in, of course, wondering what the neighbors must think of this crazy bunch of tourists from the English-speaking world.*

It was Monday now — and also Whitmonday to boot. This meant that the stores would be closed. We headed for the famed Berlin Wall, which once divided the City like an angry scar on its face. Our first stop was at "Checkpoint Charlie." This was the gate into or out of the Communist sector and it restricted movement of any citizens wishing to visit friends or relatives trapped behind the Wall. There are plenty of horror stories of people trying to cross through this no-man's land to reach freedom in the American sector. There was a sample area of the barbed wire, the metal spikes protruding from the earth and other devices for thwarting passage across. It made you shudder to realize how determined the Russians were to keep their section of Berlin from emptying out. Nearby, in a converted office building, a small museum had been set up on several floors. There were photographs, posters, memorabilia of all sorts, and most poignant of all — small Volkswagen type cars specially fitted out with false bottoms or compartments where a person could hide to make their escape to the West. A series of photographs showed the digging of a tunnel under the barricades, which took years to build and proved successful for a group of desperate people. I was amazed to see that a small balloon had also been tried as an escape vehicle. One would expect this to be a desperate plan but perhaps it was used at night. About a mile of the Wall had been left up along an industrial area, so that tourists could get an idea of its immensity. I bought a couple of fragments with graffiti still smeared on their surfaces and I later incorporated the pieces into a paperweight.

23 - Tripping Through Eastern Europe—1998

Driving on, we now passed a huge construction area with tall cranes hoisting girders around to new positions in an area that would be a civic center. A bright red "box" sat in the middle of all this new construction and one could go up into it to get a panorama of the entire work. The box was like a giant alphabet block that kids learn from and looked incongruous in all the welter of materials. As we past the Brandenburg Gate, another famous landmark I described in an earlier chapter, we noticed a circus-sized white tent erected in front of the Gate. Some big civic event was scheduled for the evening, making it impossible to photograph this all-important Gate that Hitler had loved to use for Victory parades.

Downtown, we stopped briefly at the ruin of the Kaiser Wilhelm Cathedral, which was partially destroyed by Allied bombing, with its spire pared down to a stub, and most of the nave missing. The small side entry to the Cathedral still stood and there were gorgeous mosaic panels of historic figures riddled with bullet holes for us to see. But next door, Berlin had built a modern cathedral in an octagon shape and here the walls were almost entirely blue stained glass. The atmosphere was one of standing in another twilight world serene and mystical. The glass used was in four inch thick slabs that varied just enough in their blueness to create a lovely ambience. I was really captivated and stayed longer than I should have with our limited time.

We next headed out of town to visit Potsdam in the outskirts. This was where Churchill, Stalin and Roosevelt met to sign the treaty that would carve up Germany amongst them.* We trooped through the meeting rooms, the quarters where each leader stayed. The place had the air of a country lodge and I was reminded of Ahwnanee Lodge at Yosemite with its emphasis on rustic architecture.

Also, on this outing, we included a stop at Sans Souci. This elegant small version of France's Versailles, was once the home of Frederick the Great. I was particularly interested because I knew that this important German King of Prussia (1712-86) was a gay man. There is plenty of evi-

> *Sans Souci ... this elegant small version of France's Versailles, was once the home of Frederick the Great. I was particularly interested because I knew that this important German King of Prussia (1712-86) was a gay man.*

---

*In July of 1945, following Germany's unconditional surrender on May 8th, Communist Party General Secretary Joseph Stalin, Prime Ministers Winston Churchill and Clement Attlee, and President Harry S. Truman (replacing President Franklin D. Roosevelt who had died while in office during April of that year), met in Yalta to decide how to administer post-war Germany. Five months earlier (February/1945), anticipating the end of the war, President Franklin D. Roosevelt, Prime Minister Winston Churchill and Premier Joseph Stalin convened near Yalta in Crimea, Soviet Union to discuss the re-establishment of the nations of war-torn Europe. — J. Jackson

dence to support this fact but I can't elaborate on it here except to say that he was an admirer of Voltaire who had his own apartment in this stunning palace designed and decorated in Louis Quinze style. Although Frederick was forced to marry, he never allowed women to enter this luxurious home. We wandered about the rooms and gardens, wondering what the 18th Century had been like. An authentic Dutch windmill in a corner of the gardens had us puzzled until we realized it made sense — wind power, just as we are rediscovering it today.

Back at the great plaza behind our hotel, a wine festival was spread out over the pavements, and we went around sipping wine from merchants to our hearts' content until we were slightly tipsy. Two Australians that I had grown fond of, Vince and Jen accompanied me. Though at times I could barely cut through their accents, we began to form a bond.

§

We were up early, 6:30 and heading directly east to the Polish border, passing without stopping at the other Frankfort, this one with a "Von Oder" attached to its name. Arriving in time for lunch, we were on our own here. I bought a dozen postcards from a handsome teen boy as I exited the bus, then we all scattered around looking for a fast food shop. As we passed across the Town Square, hundreds of school children were counting down to twelve and staring up at two carved goats on the façade of the town hall. It seemed a tradition here to watch as the noon bells rang and the goats kissed! We found a Polish version of MacDonald's packed with people, finally managed an order and fled outside to munch our burgers. I ruined a roll of film here because of a dead battery and lost the shot of the kissing goats.

We were driving through lovely green farmlands, well cared for and then at 5 p.m. we were in Warsaw. Our hotel was a *Forum* hotel, 36 stories of sleek modern glass in contrast to the wedding cake monster that Stalin had given Poland as a gift. Again, this is the same architectural plan that was used for the six identical buildings in Moscow. The district we were in was very ugly and commercial with block upon block of shops vying with each other for your attention. There seemed to be nothing to do but tramp

Jen and Vince from Australia, my two traveling pals.

Poland

23 - Tripping Through Eastern Europe—1998

along with the throngs hurrying home. I was handed a small card with a voluptuous girl holding her overblown breasts and giving me a soulful look. The card advertised "fantastic entertainment, beautiful girls, good-looking men" — call us and be our client — the maximum for the realization of your orders is ten minutes! I pocketed the orange slip of paper for my scrapbook. Along the side of the hotel, a brick wall memorialized 36 freedom fighters that were lined up and shot by the Nazi regime.

Warsaw went through hell in the chaos of World War Two, losing 85 per cent of its infrastructure and 700,000 people dead. This city has seen devastation repeatedly through the centuries and one wonders at the determination of its citizens to rise up again and rebuild.

Warsaw went through hell in the chaos of World War II, losing 85 per cent of its infrastructure and 700,000 people dead. This city has seen devastation repeatedly through the centuries and one wonders at the determination of its citizens to rise up again and rebuild.

This morning I had to choose between two destinations for the evening: either the Chopin piano recital at a palatial residence, or, the Willanow Palace. I chose Willanow since I had attended the Chopin concert in '92. But for the morning excursion, we were driven over to the Chopin Memorial Gardens, which I had seen before on the previous visit but this time we lined up all 40 of our tour group (*next page*). Behind us loomed the very handsome bronze of Chopin sitting under a windswept tree being inspired to create another lovely melody. The setting itself was an inspiration with the round lake and roses blooming in profusion. It was fitting that the Polish nation revered this giant in the musician's world. Right behind the Chopin memorial, there was another reminder of Poland's tragic past, the Jewish Holocaust Memorial with beautifully sculpted figures looking defiantly undefeated.

This little scrap of paper was handed to me while I strolled the streets of Warsaw that evening.

Then on to the old town Castle Square where I spotted a hunk of a young man displaying a pair of magnificent legs in very short shorts. I think he was counting on his limbs to bring in customers. He was succeeding as I noticed women glancing quickly at his bare, well-tanned legs and a provocative tattoo near the hip. But I strolled on to buy a charming blue

The Chopin monument at Warsaw (*above, below*). I'm stationed at center just below the sculpture.

coffee mug in a nearby shop.

Returning to the hotel for lunch and then the visit to the Willanow Palace: a royal residence with sumptuous rooms in a baroque style, surrounded by lovely gardens bordering a canal so that guests could arrive by boat. My camera balked at this point and I left, frustrated that I couldn't record it. The Australians were with me as we strolled down the main streets, stopping for a drink at a sidewalk café and a splendid view of Stalin's souvenir to Po-

(*Left*) The Jasna Góra Monastery at Czestochcwa near Kracow, location of the revered Black Madonna icon (*below*).

land — the florid, gargantuan skyscraper meant to outdo America's towers.

In the morning, after a huge breakfast, I made a sandwich since I didn't intend to go for the optional $49 lunch with folk-dancing entertainers. That, along with several other options seemed a bit overpriced to me. It's one of the irritating features of this type of touring, having to give up something on the agenda because of its cost.

Our bus was now heading southwest towards Czestochowa and the great monastery of Jasna Gora. Its tall spire was visible for miles before we arrived at what looked like a fortified castle on a vast plain. The attraction here was the "Black Madonna," but I didn't learn much about her as I walked around separately from the guide's wordy lecturing. I think I heard something about miracle cures of people who kissed the image. Hundreds of school children were running around the grounds, frantically it seemed. In a gift shop attached to the convent, I bought a silver encased replica of the famous Madonna for 20 zlotys ($6.50). As we resumed our journey, the guide decided to test our IQs on how many famous Poles we could name. I did quite poorly, while a Chinese woman in our group scored 35 personalities with the aid of her hidden guidebook. She got away with it and received a CD of Chopin melodies. Some of us thought this was outrageous.

As we entered Kracow, we dropped off the 6 who had splurged and decided to go for the $49 lunch with folk dancing. We were treated to a sightseeing tour of the city as we drove in to our ultra-modern Forum Hotel on the banks of the Vistula River. It was a very upscale hotel setting in manicured gardens overlooking a panorama of the old city skyline. At 4 p.m. we were escorted down to the old City Square where we were to listen to a bugler sounding his horn from a high perch up in a cathedral tower. It seemed that this was a recreation of a sad event from medieval history. The original bugler had been killed with a well-aimed arrow as he warned the city of an attack. In the center of the large town-square, we visited a cloth-hall now transformed into souvenir shops. Later, we drove up to Wawel Castle on the hilltop, passing under a portcullis with huge spikes aimed at intruders. Back at the hotel, we dined and I did nothing more exciting than watching Polish TV even though I understood nothing being said.

In the morning, it was time for our gypsy caravan to hit the road once more and now we were heading straight south through Slovakia. We were scheduled to stop at Wieliczka, a famous salt mine. It sounded quite boring but was anything but boring. We had no idea of the strange beauty we were about to see. The mine was somewhere out in the countryside and had been in production for hundreds of years. One has to remember that before refrigeration, the only way to preserve meats and other perishables was by adding salt layers over the food. I hate to think what food must have tasted like to our modern day palates with all the excessive salt added, but perhaps there was a way to compensate for this.

A fabulous salt sculpture at Wieliczka, Poland.

We descended in a rather ordinary, work-style elevator platform holding a dozen people and then at some unspecified depth, switched to staircases that spiraled around a central airshaft. We began to see huge walls of dusty white salt scarred with pickaxe grooves. Then we arrived at a great hall the size of most modern basketball courts. The ceiling must have been some four stories up and an eerie light seemed to come from the niches carved into the walls. We seemed to be in an ancient cathedral with statuary set into the paneled walls. Chandeliers made of rock salt crystals hung from the ceiling. The religious figures were glowing from within because lighting had been set into their backs. It was a weird effect, almost suggest-

23 - Tripping Through Eastern Europe—1998

Salt sculpture at Wieliczka, Poland.

ing alabaster and I wondered how the sculptors had achieved so much detail. There were passages surrounding this main hall with more figures including a tableau of the medieval miners carving out a salt statue. I had never realized you could make anything artistic out of such humble material.

Back on the bus, we were exiting Poland and ascending into mountainous country, with cows grazing in the lush meadows. It was the Czech Republic's ski country and we stopped for lunch at a winter resort restaurant that was operating with a small staff since the crowds were gone until the next ski season but tour busses still came through. The ski lifts hung forlornly in mid-air simply waiting.

§

Mid-afternoon and we were crossing into Hungary. At the border, our guide, Janusz found that the border guards wanted to detain us for some obscure reason until 3 six-packs of Coca-Cola were handed over. Our bus promptly took off then at six, rolling into Budapest and out the other side for 6 miles to reach our hotel, The Forte Agip. We had a 7:30 supper, and everyone simply wanted to collapse on his or her bed and watch TV. I was amazed to see Jay Leno poking fun at his usual victims on the television screen!

We started the morning sightseeing by driving up to Castle Hill, which was entirely built up with churches and business buildings, no open ground. But from the Fishermen's Bastion outlook, we had a splendid panoramic view of the two halves of the city — Buda and Pest. A majestic

Hungary

river divided the two halves with bridges crossing every half mile or so. After savoring the view, we entered the cathedral of St. Mathias and also inspected the handsome equestrian sculpture of the king outside. Driving across town, we came to a great plaza called the Heroes' Square. Here was a ring of handsome statuaries atop colonnades of marble surrounding a gigantic column topped by a Victory angel. The plaza could easily hold several thousands and must have been used for celebrations. It made me feel I was standing in a movie version of Imperial Rome. I expected Elizabeth Taylor as Cleopatra, to arrive on her huge triumphal float. Hollywood could have saved a bundle if they had used this square. And out in the countryside, later we were passing the ruins of a Roman highway.

But our next stop was to see the great parliament building with its massive dome, which reminded me of our own Capitol in Washington, D.C. We got to sit in the empty chambers where legislators would carry out their lengthy discussions on new laws. Something I had never experienced in the U.S.

It was time to head out of town for the village of St. Andrew, which was once the Roman town of Aquincum. Along the modern highway laid the stones of an old Roman viaduct. We parked in a small forest and walked for three blocks, passing a lot of vendors of Russian military uniforms and gear. It really brought home the downfall of the Russian Empire to see the bits and pieces of its once vaunted past now reduced to cheap souvenirs. I bought nothing. The village had an air of a Disney creation; it was almost too quaint. It was obvious that, with its abundance of lace-work and crystal, dolls and dinnerware, and so forth, it existed solely for the tourist hordes that descended every day during the summer. Our goal was a restaurant, where we crowded into a small courtyard. We were served soup out of strange little kettles that hung over a small flame. The gimmick was contrived as a metal branch that arched over the bowl and was the table centerpiece. The food was mediocre, too dependent on the meat course, but we didn't care. The wandering musicians came to our tables to serenade us with melodies from our various countries. Later, while some of the other members of our group were buying crystal cats and etched eggs, I slipped into a shop to buy a packet of Hungarian postage stamps that were a tiny art gallery of religious images for $2.

When we returned to the hotel, most of us showered and changed

23 - Tripping Through Eastern Europe—1998

clothes since it had been a very warm afternoon. Then we were taken down to the famous Danube River for a dinner cruise. A lavish buffet was spread out for us as we joined our little cliques. I ate with the two young Australians, Vince and Jennie. She vowed to resist the luscious desserts, asking me if I thought she was getting too plump. I told her there was just more of her to love. It pays to play the diplomat and before the tour was over she was inviting me to visit them in Australia and she promised she wouldn't charge me. The Ladies from Manila, which included my seatmate, I had grown to avoid at all costs. They were having a giggling fit and I could hear them through the walls as they became very silly.

It was Sunday morning as we left Budapest and now we were turning westward toward Vienna. We had left at 7 am, and by 10 we were at a small city called Gyor. It was almost empty of people and we walked through its deserted streets wondering when the inhabitants got up on Sundays. I spotted a doorway into a church, which was now a museum. It was surprising to have it open and I toured its various rooms to inspect the furnishings. It was set up rather like a wealthy man's home and I was trailed by a youth on duty that evidently was meant to keep me from walking off with anything not tied down. As he was quite attractive, I was enjoying the little game of watching each other furtively.

Outside again, I ran into friends from the Tour group and we popped into a nearby McDonalds's (seems they exist in any city in the world) for a milkshake as our lunch. We also discovered another museum in an upstairs setting. This place had spacious halls filled with collage work and large abstract paintings. But what caught my eye were the open windows and the billowing white gauzy curtains that formed interesting patterns across the polished floors. I wished I had had my camcorder along. We made one other stop at a handsome yellow church on the edge of town before zipping on to Vienna.

§

Austria

Another border crossing but we didn't have to bribe any guard to enter Austria. We were delivered to our hotel, the Park Hotel as soon as we arrived. It must have been named from the fact that it was across the street from a huge area of tree-lined promenades leading up to the Schonbrunn Palace. My room was very small and airless this time and I vowed to spend as little time in it as possible. I walked around the neighborhood shops, bought batteries for my ailing camera, and took a photo of a very homoerotic poster in a shop window. I was surprised to see the openness of this depiction of a very sexy youth wearing only a pair of sox, which was the merchandise he was advertising. However, I lost this entire roll of film as the camera malfunctioned. A car passed me as I stood rather lost on the street and I spotted an elderly woman sitting next to a driver with both of her breasts exposed! I couldn't believe my eyes. I had decided against the option of attending the "Waltz Concert" for the evening and found myself $41 richer but also very alone. Everyone else had bought tickets!

We had our breakfast in the hotel's huge ballroom dating from the early 1900s and I tried to imagine the waltzing couples whirling to Strauss tunes in those heady times. Then it was off to visit the Schönbrunn Palace nearby. I had visited it before on an earlier trip so I was familiar with the vastness of this most famous of Viennese sights. I still marveled at the opulence of the salons and décor of this regal residence even though I had no knowledge of its history. The vast gardens were dotted with marble statuary framed by clipped hedges some 20 feet high. The great fountains with Roman gods and goddesses languishing in the sprays of water made me long to jump in with them.

Driving into the heart of the city, we parked at the Albertina Platz and were turned loose for a couple of hours. I chose to go it alone and inspected the Holocaust memorial with muscular bodies half-emerging from rough blocks of marble. They seemed to be trying to free themselves. I walked into a coffee shop, ordered a torte and enjoyed the fragrance of coffee, Viennese style. They certainly had a way with this beverage. I went a few blocks further to get a look at St. Stephen's Cathedral with its marvelous shingle patterns on its roof. Horse-drawn carriages were lined up outside to take us on very expensive jaunts around the City. I found my way back to the gorgeous oval fountain in a city square with bronze figures lounging around its edges and took pictures. Then I spotted Sacher's coffeehouse close by — across the street from the Opera house. I couldn't leave Vienna and say I hadn't tasted their world-famous Chocolate torte and coffee, so I was really coffee satiated by now, but happy. The rest of the gang had met in front of the Opera House to inspect its interiors. Nothing was going on, of course, as we toured through four huge foyers decorated with modern mosaic walls. We got to sit in orchestra seats, watching stagehands assembling sets for the night's production.

We returned to our hotel to rest, shower and dress for a supper out in the wine district of Heurigen, where a guitarist and an accordionist entertained us as we had a country supper in a village inn. When they finally got around to playing "Edelweiss," we were all so taken by the melody that I spotted a tear or two. Was it the handsome waiter in lederhosen that was turning the ladies on? Afterwards, we drove through the Prater Park where the giant Ferris wheel can be found. I was familiar with the film "The Third Man," a four star British movie from 1949 that had Orson Wells playing the mysterious Harry Lime. In a climactic scene, Wells almost pushes Joseph Cotton off a Ferris wheel cabin as it revolves slowly. The scene builds up to an unbearable tension seldom equaled in more recent movies. And we were riding the same gondolas now, so there was much joking about whether anyone was missing. Even the drizzling rain added to the scene. One got a spectacular view of the city of Vienna from its highest point some 200 feet above the ground. They say that if you haven't been on the "Wiener Risenrad", you really haven't been to Vienna. A British engineer constructed the original wheel in 1896. He also built similar wheels in London, Blackpool and Paris, all of which were dismantled shortly after their use in fairs. The Viennese loved their wheel and refused to tear it down. The Nazis did it for them with fire and bombs in the last days of the War. But the City lovingly reconstructed it in 1947 so that the one we rode was only 51 years old. And its interesting to note that modern day London has also gotten around to rebuilding a Ferris wheel on the Thames. The fascination of the wheel is still there.

§

We were up early, as usual, to continue our journey, leaving this lovely old city behind. We entered the Czech Republic now and an hour later we were in Brno for lunch. Most of us hadn't the correct money — crowns — to buy lunch, so there was a scramble to change traveler's checks into the right currency. Someone has discovered a bank office and we hurriedly lined up along the sidewalk. Lena, whom I have mentioned before as my seat partner with the clownish costume, realized she hadn't been quick enough to secure a good spot in the line. She had acquired an umbrella

Czech Republic

She used her umbrella to poke into me! I put up with it for a minute or two and then, exasperated, I simply grabbed her offending umbrella and tried to snap it shut. We had a tug-of-war with it as she started screaming bloody murder.

somewhere and she began to inch her way up past all of us as she starts chatting with those in line. This is a cardinal sin in the art of queuing up in a line, as we all know. I can't believe she was brazen enough to do it. And to make matters worse, when she was finally just behind me, she used her umbrella to poke into me! I put up with it for a minute or two and then, exasperated, I simply grabbed her offending umbrella and tried to snap it shut. We had a tug-of-war with it as she started screaming bloody murder. I warned her to behave and get back in the proper place in line and she retreated sullenly. I think it amused everyone else but I never spoke to her again on the trip, which, thank God was in its last days anyway. I simply couldn't bear rude women or men, and I had to be saddled with one as a seatmate. No one was interested in trading places with me since they were all in pairs to begin with.

We drove on the rest of the afternoon, arriving in Prague in time to have supper at 6 at our hotel. Prague spans the River Vltava at its center. This is typical of medieval cities when river barges were the best way of transporting goods. The Charles Bridge was the showstopper with its baroque sculptured figures adorning its edges. But we were not really to see much until the next day. We did assemble at a square in the Hradcany Castle area for a Disney-like choo-choo train ride down to the main square along cobble-stoned streets unchanged in a thousand years. Prague was lucky to have been spared the bombs and shelling of the last war. It survives today as a prime example of the medieval past. I joined my two Australian buddies, Vince and Jen who were young enough to be my grown children. We had formed a sort of bond and often stuck together on the outings. They wound up at the end, inviting me to visit them in Australia, if I ever made it again. At the moment,

Hradcany Castle area in Prague.

23 - Tripping Through Eastern Europe—1998

we spotted a Pilsner bar on a side street where we simply sat back and listened to an accordion-player for an hour or so before taking a bus back to our lodgings.

In the morning, we were delivered up to Hradcany Castle where the chief amusement seemed to be to try to make the sentries at the gates, smile. They were impervious to our funny-face making, having to endure this every day from stupid tourists. We were told that the same designer who worked on the famous "Amadeus" movie, which was filmed here a few years back, conceived their gorgeous uniforms. Vienna was not ancient enough though for some particular scenes.

We passed under a huge archway and were directly in front of the St. Vitus Cathedral. I had always known that there was something called the St. Vitus dance but I didn't know that he had a cathedral named after him. The stained glass windows were breath taking and Alphonse Mucha, the Art Nouveau master who had done dozens of posters I was familiar with, designed my favorite. We left the lofty-ceilinged cathedral to wander down a cobbled staircase lined with souvenir merchants. Crossing the Vltava River at the Checuvo Bridge, we entering the old city quarter. The main street here was the Parizka named after the most famous French City. Expensive women's shops lined this street and we could gape at the jewels and perfumes displayed in elegant windows. Gucci and Chanel were some of the names we saw emblazoned over haughty establishments. A bit further along on this route, we came to the main town square, with its Janusz monument to Czech heroes. It seemed to remind me a great deal of Rodin's way with sculpture — craggy, rough surfaces and stoical poses. And the Tyn church occupied the square like a huge royal personage. Everyone was scurrying around to the edge nearest the Charles Bridge where the Clock Tower was about to do its thing. Most of us have seen miniature Swiss or German clocks with their little processions of figures that pass in and out of windows. But here it was done on a life-sized scale and much more elaborately. A turntable fitted with ornately garbed figures was issuing forth from the stone façade to bells and whistles. The skeleton apparition of Death clanked along after these figures, reminding us all of our mortality. This tableau was some 30 or 40 feet up on the Tower's façade and is probably the most famous sight in Prague. No one should miss it. I had to console myself with humbler souvenirs, a tiny chicken attached to a string that emitted squawks as you pulled the string between your fingers and everyone was buying them at the moment. Then I bought a black T-shirt with the Prague medieval skyline printed on it. But I found two of my Canadian friends, Sandy and Carol, buying a much more interesting item, charming hand-held puppets depicting storybook characters. I picked a hobo doll dressed in rags for myself. He hangs by my computer desk as I type these lines. I bought an ice cream cone with the gals as we wandered through these old streets.

All of a sudden, I had a strange feeling that I had lost my airline tickets. I did a hasty search of my bag to no avail. I rushed back to the hotel and emptying all my pockets, they fell out from the accordion pleats of a postcard collection. I returned to the great square with the little time I have left and saw a ragged looking hippie type of youth rummaging through trash cans for something to eat. I couldn't believe this was going on at this time. I had known that Prague was the favorite destination for the post-Beat Generation but I hardly expected to see anyone still living that life.

After a 7 p.m. supper at the hotel, Jen, my Australian girl friend talked me into doing a pen sketch of her while her boy-friend bought us a round of drinks. Carol and Sandy joined us for "berozkas", a brandy and fruit juice combination, not bad. Our collection of puppets was on the table as we got better acquainted with each other. I was invited to visit Sandy who lived in Canadian Toronto. I have always meant to visit Montreal and Quebec some day but somehow have put that trip on the back shelf—why, I don't know.

§

Germany, again

In the morning, it's off again for our gypsy band, with Nuremberg as our next stop. We enjoyed stunningly beautiful countryside with picture-book villages dotting the landscape. There is such a satisfying aspect to the neat fields, nary a billboard to mar the scene, thank God. The tallest thing is always a church spire. Nuremberg's town square is decorated with an ornately decorated Gothic monument ablaze with gold leaf. It's where young women leave a token to catch a husband. Nuremberg has a dark past tied to Adolph Hitler but we aren't to see that, of course. Only time for a quick burger before heading on to Munich. We arrived at 4:30 in drizzle. I was in a T-shirt and got cold in this damp weather but made a dash to see another parade of effigies gliding out of a tall medieval tower. The room assignments over, we dashed back to a downtown Hofbrauhaus for a typical German evening of

The Husband Catcher Monument at Nuremburg. About 30 ft. tall.

beer and supper in this huge restaurant filled with carousing Germans. I tried to envision myself in its heyday with the Hitler gang getting tipsy. It was all so innocent looking. I simply couldn't relate these jovial souls to the evil that we all know started in these halls. I refused to think about it, perhaps much as the average German did in the '30s. It was simply incomprehensible to me. As a descendant of German people, I wanted to believe there had to be something good to be said of the German psyche. After all, when one reflects on the towering genius of men like Brahms, Beethoven, Bach, Mann, Goethe, what can one say about the dark aberration of that short period in recent history? We are made up of good and evil, it would seem.

We left the beer hall and its noisy revelers to dine at a quieter spot nearby — Donisl's and as I passed the kitchen doorway, a very handsome dark-haired German shot me a meaningful glance. I made sure to pass more slowly on the way out and again, he and I exchanged a look. It was back to the hotel and an empty bed for me. This was now the last day of see-

As a descendant of German people, I wanted to believe there had to be something good to be said of the German psyche.

We ate here at Hofbräuhaus am Platzl, Munich – Hitler's old hangout.

ing Germany, as tomorrow my flight home was the reality. We boarded our trusty bus once more for a look through the windows. We were told that most of what we were seeing was restoration since Munich had been hard hit by Allied bombing. We passed the Olympic Stadium for the 1972 games and noted how the whole concept had been designed, with a tent-like structure hung from enormous poles. A shiny silvery material set the whole thing glittering. Then a bit further along an elegant shopping street, we passed a gigantic white alien figure some 60 feet tall that strode over Lilliputian shoppers as if hurrying off to his spacecraft. We made it through crowded streets out to the countryside where we pulled in at a very attractive restaurant complex with gardens around it. Germany likes to make the rest stops as appealing as possible and it certainly works. The place was well patronized by tourists and Germans alike. There were rows of counters with glass fronts displaying a feast of choices in smorgasbord fashion. One could get very fat living here if self-control was a problem.

Our next stop was also our last look at German history. We had arrived at Rothenburg, a small town that looked as if time had stopped in the middle of the 13th Century. Once surrounded by thick walls, it now was the

The Giant (60 ft.) Alien striding the streets of Munich.

prize example of what it was like to live in that distant time. Everywhere were handsome old brick and stucco buildings with timbered framing, cobbled streets and towers. Possibly the quaintest town we saw on the whole trip.

Then it started drizzling, but I had my trusty umbrella to cover myself, but not the two Australians who hadn't foreseen rain. We stood under an arched doorway to stare up at a pair of windows as everybody said to expect something unusual. A mechanical figure of a burgher came out of one window, lifted a tankard of beer and downed it while gliding into the adjacent window. It was an enactment of a fateful moment in this town's history. Once in the distant past, Rothenburg was on the verge of being destroyed by

Quaint Rothenburg's main street.

a conquering army but was spared by the warlord if the town could find someone to drink down an enormous stein of beer. A man was found to doff the ale and save the town. In gratitude, the town erected this mechanical figure that drank down the tankard everyday at 2 p.m.

I found that the other most popular attraction was the Criminal Museum. We walked a block further to enter a basement converted to the display of torture instruments form medieval times. It was a macabre display and one wondered at the minds that had devised these horrendous instruments. I don't think I want to describe them here but I will tell you about the masks that people were forced to wear on the city streets if they were being mildly punished. These grotesque iron contraptions locked on around the neck and made the victim look as if he had sprouted donkey ears or had a mouth like a hyena. The shame was supposed to cure one of misbehavior. Outside, in the courtyard, there dangled a ducking stool and an iron maiden was ready for its next victim. We shuddered at the evil genius that had dreamed up

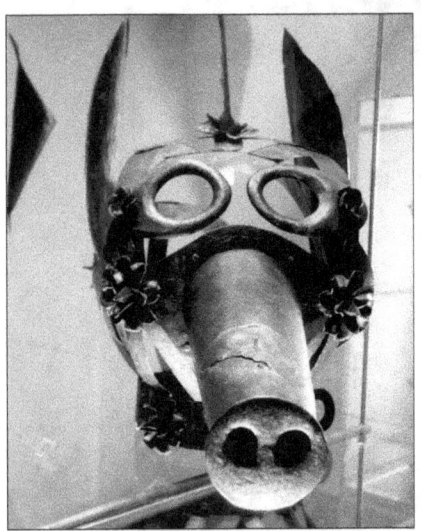

"Masks of shame" for women at the Criminal Museum.

A Rothenburg street much as it stayed from Medieval times.

Entry to the Criminal Museum. Note ducking stool in front.

Getting ready for the long flight home with my traveling buddies.

these tortures. On a more pleasant note, we entered a shop dedicated to Christmas the year round. Everyone knows how lovingly the Germans observe this holiday and the shop contained thousands of decorative items ready to hang on your next tree. I bought a tiny silver beer stein for Jim, which might hold a thimble-full of beer.

Back in the bus, it was time to guess how many kilometers we had covered altogether on the trip. I missed by a mile, not taking into account the differences between the two systems. We had traveled 3800 kilometers or about 1,775 miles total. A lady won the prize, a doll from Hungary. We returned to our first hotel, in Eschborn, close to the airport. Those of us who had formed friendships, gathered at tables in the hotel's bar to reminisce and swore to keep in touch — but this is simply wishful thinking I knew.

§

The next morning, at 10:40, my plane lifted up over the European landscape and started the long flight homewards. A pair of young Germans sat next to me; they were on their way to a Panasonic seminar to be held in

23 - Tripping Through Eastern Europe—1998

Silicon Valley, the new center of the Cyber World at that time. But I was looking forward to seeing Jim standing in the waiting room at the San Francisco airport.

24
Parting Thoughts

2004

"I pray that soon we will finally learn to accept one another as fully human and that we can love the diversity of humankind as normal." - GS

§

My collaboration with George, now in his 90th year, ends catastrophically in 2004. Although I don't bring it up in this chapter, I decided to tell "the rest of the story" in a postscript that follows. For now, it's George's coda — a summary of the story he had all along wanted to tell — as he had conveyed to me at the very start. - JJ

PARTING THOUGHTS: 2004

I am lucky that I chose to live my life at a less hectic pace than others ... but I still came close to death's door in two serious auto accidents.

In another aspect of my life, I have been fortunate to come through the AIDS tragedy unscathed. It has decimated so many of my friends that I hate to dwell on it, but, at one point, I know I lost 14 friends and acquaintances from 1985 through to 1990. I am lucky that I chose to live my life at a less hectic pace than others.

But I still came close to death's door in two serious auto accidents. I think it was in 1985 that I was returning home from Marin County in the late afternoon and as I merged onto the main highway, a large truck swerved into my incoming lane and I spun my wheels frantically to avoid the collision that was certain to come. My car then crashed into the concrete barrier that formed the road's edge and I went into a rollover and skidded upside down for a hundred yards. The truck never stopped, of course, and I was still in my seat belt and unhurt but I couldn't pry the door open. Someone pulled up behind me and pulled me out – I had feared the car would burst into flames. I was shaken, of course, but the Cougar was a total loss and was hauled to the junkyard. I had driven it for 16 years with no accidents!

Then I decided on buying a diesel engine Ford pickup which I drove to my Creative Growth job in downtown Oakland – only to end up in another accident a few years later. I had left the job and was crossing a street after having come to a proper stop. But since the street curved off, I couldn't see all the way up. A delivery truck driven by a teen-ager came barreling around the curve as I was two thirds of the way across the street. He smashed into the truck's bed directly behind my seat and the two wheels on the far side were ripped off and they rolled down the street as my glasses were also tossed out onto the pavement for cars to smash. I was again totally unhurt and amazed that I was alive. The teen stopped and assessed the damage – he had a crumpled fender! My truck went to the wrecking yard with the alignment too damaged to make it repairable. The insurance people handed me a couple of thousand and I went home marveling that I was alive.

I thought about the strange twists that we are dealt in life. Why did I survive this and the earlier accident? Was something or someone looking out for me? Did I have some unfinished work to accomplish? Were there really Guardian Angels for each of us?

Almost directly across the street from my house was a lovely modern church — Presbyterian, but I hadn't given it much thought. I figured I wouldn't be welcome as a gay man anyway. But I did come in and checked pamphlets I found in the vestibule. And to my surprise, it stated that this was a More Light church, welcoming all peoples regardless of their sexual orientation! I went to see the minister shortly afterwards and he was pleased to see me. So, in 1994 I became a regular member and even took the opportunity one Sunday, to explain to the congregation how I happened to have become convinced that I was being saved for the specific purpose of serving the church through my art.

I have never regretted my choice in becoming active with these wonderful people and had never hidden my sexual orientation. I have made trips to Indonesia and Santa Fe with them, held art shows in the Family Room, headed up the 40 or more people who are interested in Art and do monthly visits to art venues nearby or as far as the Mendocino Coast or the wine country or Carmel. I took part in a play that was about the anguish of being gay in a hostile world and we even took it to Albuquerque, New Mexico for the annual conference of church elders. The church is still debating whether to ordain gays to be ministers and each year it comes up on the agenda; although it hasn't made it so far, we keep trying.*

---

*The Presbyterian Church (USA) voted to allow same-gender marriages on 19 June 2014 during its 221st General Assembly, making it one of the largest Christian denominations in the world to openly accept same-sex unions. This vote effectively lifted a previous ban and allows pastors to perform marriages in jurisdictions where it is legal. Additionally, the Assembly voted to send out a proposed amendment to the Book of Order that would change the definition of marriage from "between a man and a woman" to "between two people, traditionally between a man and a woman." This amendment needed to be approved by a majority of the 171 Presbyteries to take effect. It was approved by a majority of the 171 Presbyteries in March 2015, and so it was included in the church's Book of Order, taking effect on June 21, 2015. [Cited in: Pulliam, Sarah (2015-03-13). "Presbyterian Church (USA) changes its constitution to include gay marriage". The Washington Post. Retrieved 2015-03-18.] — J. Jackson

THE FLYER
ADVERTISING OUR
TRAVELING PLAY
ABOUT GAY
FAMILY ISSUES

A TRAVELING RECONCILIATION PLAY
STORIES OF STRUGGLE AND AFFIRMATION
LOVE AND SPIRITUAL AWAKENING

Saturday February 25, 1995 7:30 p.m.

First Presbyterian Church of San Rafael - 1510 Fifth Avenue - San Rafael

A TRAVELING RECONCILIATION PLAY is a collage of stories drawn from the life experiences of members of Bay Area Presbyterian Churches written and told in order to further the dialogue in our churches on Lesbian and Gay issues.

A TRAVELING RECONCILIATION PLAY is a project of Witness For Reconciliation. WFR works with local Presbyterian congregations as they develop a process for dialogue concerning the ordination of Lesbian and Gay Presbyterians.

For more information call Lisa Larges, WFR director, (415) 648-0547

WITNESS FOR RECONCILIATION

24 - Parting Thoughts—2004

Also, in the last few years, I had become a front desk volunteer at the Pacific Center for Human Growth, which is a house in Berkeley close to my old campus. I dealt with phone calls from anxious parents or young gays in trouble. Typically, I would have a gay teenager asking for advice on where to find shelter because their parents had just thrown them out.

I read about the school shootings and the muggings and wonder what sort of a society we really are. The Jerry Falwells, Jesse Helms, Dr. Lauras and Pat Robertsons like to talk about family values and preach that gays are evil. We were even blamed by Falwell for the terrorist attack on the New York towers! Shouldn't he be talking about the gun lobbyists, the cigarette tycoons, and the Washington politicos who deal in graft and pay-offs? And lately we have corporate heads that make millions while their workers are bilked of their investment funds. It's a topsy-turvy world indeed.

ME IN MY 87TH YEAR

I sit here at the computer, in my 87th year on the planet and simply hope that a better world is in the making — because we were here to love and help one another.

§

It's a couple of years later now — I'm sitting in my sunny patio behind the house in the Oakland Hills and I am befuddled and amused at all the attention on the gay world. I honestly don't think there's been a time like today for our exposure in the media, politics, religion and education. We're everywhere you look if your eyes are open.

On the negative side, the newspapers have had a field day with the Catholic priests' outrageous behavior with children and I certainly deplore this sordidness. But what could you expect from a religious system that forbids its priests from any sexual outlet beyond masturbation? And why did these victims of abuse wait some twenty or thirty years before coming forward with accusations and lawsuits?

My own Presbyterian church is a "More Light" church, which simply means that we welcome the gay community as members, but will not allow them to become ministers. Our "More Light" committee holds meetings once a month and is peopled with more straight members than gay members. This is partly explained by the fact that many of our straight members

My own Presbyterian church is a "More Light" church, which simply means that we welcome the gay community as members.

have gay children or relatives and are more sympathetic to our concerns. We plan and participate in the huge annual Gay Pride March in San Francisco which is seen by half a million people lining the sidewalks. My contribution to this is to decorate and paint the signs that cover our float carrying a brass band. We also host a booth at Oakland's Gay Pride event where we pass out brochures about our churches' activities.

The Episcopalians have just elected their first gay bishop in New Hampshire, while in England, the first gay canon, Jeffrey John, and has been elected.

On June 17, 2003 Canada became the first country in the Americas to grant equal marriage rights to gays. Consequently, American gays have flocked across the border to tie the marital knot. The Ontario declaration states, "Exclusion perpetuates the view that same-sex relationships are less worthy of recognition than opposite-sex relationships." So Canada now becomes the third nation to take this bold step along with the Netherlands and Belgium.

However, Canadian marriage licenses will mean little here in the U.S. because 37 states and the Federal Government have enacted laws forbidding recognition of same-sex marriages.* Strangely enough, three states, Alaska, Hawaii and Vermont, permit civil-unions to take place. I have wondered why the U.S. frowns on our getting married and loves to point out how immoral we gays are, at same time it legally sanctions prostitution of young women in three U.S. states (Nevada being the closet to my home state)?** And with a population that now sees half of straight marriages ending in divorce, isn't that rather ironic too?***

In the entertainment world, almost anything goes now. On television,

---

*Same-sex marriage in the United States expanded from one state in 2004 (at the time George wrote this) to all fifty states in 2015 through various state court rulings, state legislation, direct popular votes, and federal court rulings. — J. Jackson

**Nevada is the only U.S. jurisdiction to allow some legal prostitution. Currently eight counties in Nevada have active brothels (these are all rural counties); as of February 2018, there are 21 brothels in Nevada. Prostitution outside the licensed brothels is illegal throughout Nevada. Prostitution is illegal in the major metropolitan areas of Las Vegas, Reno, and Carson City, where most of the population lives; more than 90% of Nevada citizens live in a county where prostitution is illegal. Prostitution in Rhode Island was outlawed in 2009. Prostitution was legal in Rhode Island between 1980 and 2009 because there was no specific statute to define the act and outlaw it, although associated activities such as street solicitation, running a brothel and pimping were illegal. A 2012 report by Fondation Scelles indicated that there were an estimated 1 million prostitutes in the U.S. — J. Jackson

***PolitiFact.com estimated in 2012 that the lifelong probability of a marriage ending in divorce is 40%-50% — J. Jackson

24 - Parting Thoughts—2004

"Will & Grace" is enormously popular with both gays and straights. HBO has featured three very successful series, "Queer As Folk," "Six Feet Under," and "Queer Eye for the Straight Guy." In the fall of 2003, on HBO, we can see "Two and a Half Men" and "Alexander the Great" who was thought to have dallied with both sexes.

In the so-called "reality" TV shows that have become so popular, we just saw "The Amazing Race" which wound up awarding a million dollars to a pair of very macho gay men who had no qualms in displaying their love for each other. They even labeled themselves as "married." I was curious enough to read the next day's newspaper to see how this epic moment was noted but there was nothing. *Zero*. I also remember a few years back, a gay man winning the first "Survivor" series, and subsequently setting up a charitable trust fund to benefit poor children.

And in the political world, a new book has just appeared on the stands about Bayard Rustin, whom few would recognize. He happened to be Martin Luther King Jr.'s right hand man. Rustin was an African-American civil rights activist, who, although openly gay (a matter downplayed by his colleagues), organized the 1963 March on Washington.

The numbers of gay men and women in Washington and state legislatures today is beyond enumerating and I won't attempt to list them.

In education, New York City now has the first fully accredited public high school for GLBT students (gay, lesbian, bisexual, transgender) students. On this issue of separating questioning gay youth from their classmates, I find myself doubting its value. While decrying the harassment and ridicule that kids endure in school, where calling another student a "fag" is the ultimate insult, I feel that learning to deal with the abuse is simply part of growing up gay. Not a very pleasant prospect for a youngster.

§

I pray that soon we will finally learn to accept one another as fully human and that we can love the diversity of humankind as normal.

George Somers
Oakland, CA/2004

> *On this issue of separating questioning gay youth from their classmates, I find myself doubting its value . . . I feel that learning to deal with the abuse is simply part of growing up gay. Not a very pleasant prospect for a youngster.*

Postscript: 2023

Midway into 2004, I prepared a bound rough draft copy that we would discuss and make final decisions on revisions, layout and cover. We met at his home in Oakland, and after reviewing what I had assembled, George, in a fit of rage and paranoia — reinforced by his equally paranoid partner — decided he no longer wanted anything to do with it. There was no way I could reason with him to change his mind, which seemed irrational. If it were to be published, it would have to wait as I explained in my commentary at the front of this book.

Eleven years later (2015), I learned in an obituary posted in his More Light Presbyterian Church, that George had died from pneumonia at the age of 101. I had written him several times in the interim, but with no response. I concluded his mind had withered further than when I first noticed its decline around 2002.

Still believing it was an important work, and having invested much time, energy, and travel expense in seeing the project through to a reasonable draft, I decided to finish and publish it myself posthumously. In 2019, I began reorganizing my transcriptions of his narrative; organizing his documents, maps and photographs; editing and re-editing parts of the text; adding in new sections on gay liberation he refused to include; finalizing a text layout; designing a cover; and eventually putting it into print as the publisher. Whatever he may have thought or contested to the contrary about bringing it to fruition, I decided it was more important to see it through regardless. The project was my idea to begin with, and those I have shared it with since agree it was the right decision. More about that decision in a bit.

§

It is 2023, and 26 years have now gone by since George and I began discussing his personal past. Many favorable changes in attitudes and in the law towards homosexuality have occurred in our American culture since then, and certainly during his youth and early adulthood. But some would argue that it is more about tolerance today than acceptance of gayness. Even tolerance is questionable, as many continue to live fearfully behind the ironclad façade that George and others have had to endure for a lifetime, long before current notions of "Gay Liberation" were openly touted in public. Gays are still the targets of violent homophobiacs — harassed, assaulted and even murdered for nothing more than being what nature assigned to them from birth. I can point to countless cases of violence against the LGBT community since George died. But such homophobic miscreants are their own worst enemy, insecure cowards by nature and in action, and an extreme minority in a vast sea of decent human beings who are not in the least bit sympathetic with their psychopathic and criminal tendencies and behaviors towards gays and others. Nevertheless, as of 2019, at least 13 Christian and Muslim legal jurisdictions around the world still provide for capital punishment for acts of homosexuality, including death by stoning. That list is expanded considerably by extrajudicial killings where homosexuals are not protected by law. So, if you are gay, and living and/or traveling in those countries today, your life is potentially at risk.*

Here in the U.S., I have shared this book with a number of "straight" acquaintances with varying economic backgrounds, political affiliations, and both religious and atheistic beliefs, and not one expressed anything but admiration for George and his story. The few gays I've teased with it are anxious to get their own copies for good and inspirational reading! So, we've come a long way since 1873 when the last anti-homosexuality law providing for the death penalty was removed from South Carolina's state statutes.

As for me? I've learned a lot about my own family — my purpose in going to George in the first place as you may recall. But as I read further into his memoirs, I was drawn into what was truly a very interesting and inspirational story about the meaning of gayness in our society. I learned far more than I thought I knew even after living for several years as a student guest in his home during society's turbulent 1960s. But having helped George forge his memoirs from the beginning of the project, it was clear to me that it was also a learning journey for George, one of self-awareness. As I pressed him again and again to be forthcoming about life "behind the façade," he was compelled to think back across his life experiences and see them for what they were — not what he might want others to think as viewed and inter-

*Afghanistan
Brunei
Iran
Mauritania
Nigeria
Pakistan
Qatar
Saudi Arabia
Somalia
United Arab Emirates
Yemen
North Korea
Uganda

preted from the other side of the façade. I think his book is very revealing of this.

    I also questioned my own motives more than once in doing this. Should I respectfully leave his shared hidden life with other gays alone behind the façade? Or bring it into the light of day to parley with the widespread ignorant and smug opinions of "straights" who have no idea what they are talking about? Or simply to educate, as George would have it, to promote awareness and acceptance of our specie's diversity? To kill the project, or move it forward? With George gone, the decision became one I had to face and decide upon alone. *Living Behind the Façade* is that decision.

Jaime Jackson
England/2023

Glossary of Gay Terms
(Adapted from the National Lesbian and Gay Journalists Association)*

AIDS: Acquired Immune Deficiency Syndrome, a medical condition that compromises the human immune system, leaving the body defenseless against opportunistic infections. Some medical treatments can slow the rate at which the immune system is weakened. Do not use the term "full-blown AIDS." Individuals may be HIV-positive but not have AIDS. Avoid "AIDS sufferer" and "AIDS victim." Use "people with AIDS" or, if the context is medical, "AIDS patients."

Bisexual: As a noun, an individual who may be attracted to either sex. As an adjective, of or relating to sexual and affectional attraction to either sex. Does not presume non-monogamy.

Civil union: The state of Vermont began this formal recognition of lesbian and gay relationships in July 2000. A civil union provides same-sex couples some rights available to married couples in areas such as state taxes, medical decisions and estate planning.

Closeted, in the closet: Refers to a person who wishes to keep secret his or her sexual orientation or gender identity.

Coming out: Short for "coming out of the closet." Accepting and letting others know of one's previously hidden sexual orientation or gender identity.

Commitment ceremony: A formal, marriage-like gathering that recognizes the declaration of members of the same sex to each other. Same-sex marriages are not legally recognized in the United States. (In April 2001, The Netherlands became the first nation to offer legal marriage to same-sex couples who are citizens or legal residents.)

Domestic partner: Unmarried partners who live together. Domestic partners may be of opposite sexes or the same sex. They may register in some counties, municipalities and states and receive some of the same benefits accorded married couples. The term is typically used in connection with legal and insurance matters.

Don't ask, don't tell: Shorthand for "Don't Ask, Don't Tell, Don't Pursue," the military policy on gay men, lesbians and bisexuals. Under the policy, instituted in 1993, the military is not to ask service members about their sexual orientation, service members are not to tell others about their orientation, and the military is not to pursue rumors about members' sexual orientation.

Drag: Attire of the opposite sex.

Dyke: Originally a pejorative term for a lesbian, it is now being reclaimed by some lesbians. Caution: still extremely offensive when used as an epithet.

Fag, faggot: Originally a pejorative term for a gay male, it is now being reclaimed by some gay men. Caution: still extremely offensive when used as an epithet.

Gay: An adjective that has largely replaced "homosexual" in referring to men who are sexually and affectionately attracted to other men. Avoid using as a singular noun. For women, "lesbian" is preferred. To include both, use "gay

(Continued on page 442)

---

*This glossary was sourced and prepared by George in 2004. However, as a reasonably definitive lexicon of definitions and vocabulary of the LGBTQ community, it is likely already — and always will be – dated and deficient, reflecting the evolutionary and often discordant character of the gay civil rights movement one can readily glean from George's memoirs and other sources. But rather than delete it, I will leave it to George's diverse audience to decide for themselves what is current and what is not. — J. Jackson

men and lesbians." In headlines where space is an issue, "gays" is acceptable to describe both.

Gay/lesbian relationships: Gay, lesbian and bisexual people use various terms to describe their commitments. Ask the individual what term he or she prefers, if possible. If not, "partner" is generally acceptable.

HIV: Human immunodeficiency virus. The virus that causes AIDS. "HIV virus" is redundant. "HIV-positive" means being infected with HIV but not necessarily having AIDS. AIDS doctors and researchers are using the term "HIV disease" more because there are other types of acquired immune deficiencies caused by toxins and rare but deadly diseases that are unrelated to what we now call AIDS.

Homo: Pejorative term for homosexual. Avoid.

Homophobia: Fear, hatred or dislike of homosexuality, gay men and lesbians.

Homosexual: As a noun, a person who is attracted to members of the same sex. As an adjective, of or relating to sexual and affectionate attraction to a member of the same sex. Use only if heterosexual would be used in parallel constructions, such as in medical contexts.

Lesbian: Preferred term, both as a noun and as an adjective, for women who are sexually and affectionately attracted to other women. Some women prefer to be called "gay" rather than "lesbian"; when possible, ask the subject what term she prefers.

Lifestyle: An inaccurate term sometimes used to describe the lives of gays, lesbians, bisexuals and transgender people. Avoid.

Lover: a gay, lesbian, bisexual or heterosexual person's sexual partner. "Partner" is generally acceptable.

Openly gay/lesbian: As a modifier, "openly" is usually not relevant; its use should be restricted to instances in which the public awareness of an individual's sexual orientation is germane. Examples: Harvey Milk was the first openly gay San Francisco supervisor. "Ellen" was the first sitcom to feature an openly lesbian lead character. "Openly" is preferred over "avowed," "admitted," "confessed" or "practicing."

Outing: (from "out of the closet") Publicly revealing the sexual orientation or gender identity of an individual who has chosen to keep that information private. Also a verb: "The magazine *outed* the senator in a front-page story."

Pink triangle: Now a gay pride symbol, it was the symbol gay men were required to wear in Nazi concentration camps during World War II. Lesbians sometimes also use a black triangle.

Pride (Day and/or March): Short for gay/lesbian pride, this term is commonly used to indicate the celebrations commemorating the Stonewall Inn riots June 28, 1969. Pride events typically take place in June.

Queen: Originally a pejorative term for an effeminate gay man. Still considered offensive when used as an epithet.

Queer: Originally a pejorative term for gay, now being reclaimed by some gay men, lesbians, bisexuals and transgender people as a self-affirming umbrella term. Still extremely offensive when used as an epithet.

Rainbow flag: A flag of six equal horizontal stripes (red, orange, yellow, green, blue, and violet) signifying the diversity of the lesbian, gay, bisexual and transgender communities.

Sexual orientation: Innate sexual attraction. Use this term instead of "sexual preference."

Sexual preference: Avoid.

Sodomy: Collective term for various

sexual acts that some states have deemed illegal. Not synonymous with homosexuality or gay sex. The legal definition of sodomy is different from state to state; in some states, sodomy laws have applied to sexual acts practiced by heterosexuals. The U.S. Supreme Court decided in June 2003 that state sodomy laws targeting private, consensual sex between adult same-sex or opposite-sex partners violate the U.S. Constitution's Due Process Clause.

Special rights: Politically charged term used by opponents of civil rights for gay people. Avoid. "Gay civil rights," "equal rights" or "gay rights" are alternatives.

Stonewall: The Stonewall Inn tavern in New York City's Greenwich Village was the site of several nights of raucous protests after a police raid on June 28, 1969. Although not the nation's first gay civil rights demonstration, Stonewall is now regarded as the birth of the modern gay civil rights movement.

Straight: Heterosexual; a person whose sexual and affectional attraction is to someone of the opposite sex.

Attributions

[Note: With the exception of the images attributed on this page, all imageries in the text and on the cover were originals provided by George Somers and Jaime Jackson.]

Cover
- Rainbow flag: dique©www.123rf.com

P. 21-23
- Cindy Sullivan

P. 26
- U.S. National Archives

P. 82
- Virtual Museum of San Francisco

P. 85
- https://commons.wikimedia.org/wiki/File:Coittower1.jpg

P. 90
- Public Domain.

P. 93
- https://commons.wikimedia.org/wiki/File:Ghirardelli_Square_1.jpg

P. 119
- Public domain: prisoners in Sachsenhausen. December 1938, National Archives: 242-HLB-3609-25.
- Public domain: Ravensbrück concentration camp (unknown source).

P. 120
- (*Above*) United States Holocaust Memorial Museum.
- (*Below*) Gedenkstätte und Museum Sachsenhausen, Oranienburg/USHMM.

P. 121
- Nederlands Instituut voor Oorlogsdocumentatie/USHMM.

P. 138
- The WebMuseum, Paris.

P. 142
- https://en.wikipedia.org/wiki/Notre-Dame_de_la_Garde#/media/File:La_basilique_Notre-Dame-de-la-Garde_(Marseille)_(14245234112).jpg

P. 145
- https://en.wikipedia.org/wiki/Atomic_bombings_of_Hiroshima_and_Nagasaki#/media/File:Atomic_bombing_of_Japan.jpg

P. 277
- https://en.wikipedia.org/wiki/The_Night_Watch#/media/File:La_ronda_de_noche,_por_Rembrandt_van_Rijn.jpg

P. 282
- https://en.wikipedia.org/wiki/Christopher_Columbus#/media/File:Tumba_de_Colon-Sevilla.jpg

P. 323
- https://en.wikipedia.org/wiki/Brandenburg_Gate#/media/File:ReaganBerlinWall.jpg

P. 337
- https://en.wikipedia.org/wiki/Hermitage_Museum#/media/File:Atlantes-Saint_Petersburg-6.jpg

P. 348
- https://en.wikipedia.org/wiki/Grigori_Rasputin#/media/File:Rasputindaughtercropped.jpg

P. 365
- https://upload.wikimedia.org/wikipedia/commons/4/48/The_Bronze_Horseman_%28St._Petersburg%2C_Russia%29.jpg

P. 414
- https://en.wikipedia.org/wiki/Wieliczka_Salt_Mine#/media/File:Poland-01618_-_Saint_John_Paul_II_(31547503070)_(2).jpg

P. 420
- https://en.wikipedia.org/wiki/Hrad%C4%8Dany#/media/File:Hradcany2.jpg

P. 423
- https://en.wikipedia.org/wiki/Nuremberg#/media/File:Christkindlesmarkt_nuernberg.jpg

P. 424
- https://en.wikipedia.org/wiki/Hofbr%C3%A4uhaus_am_Platzl#/media/File:HB-Gastraum.1.JPG

P. 426
- (*Left*) https://en.wikipedia.org/wiki/Badge_of_shame#/media/File:Mask_of_shame.jpg
- (*Right*) https://en.wikipedia.org/wiki/Scold%27s_bridle#/media/File:17XX_Schandmaske_anagoria.JPG

P. 427
- (*Above*) https://en.wikipedia.org/wiki/Rothenburg_ob_der_Tauber#/media/File:Rothenburg_BW_4.JPG
- (*Below*) https://en.wikipedia.org/wiki/Rothenburg_ob_der_Tauber#/media/File:RodT_Kriminalmuseum_7033.jpg

P. 445
- Jill Willis

About Jaime Jackson

I've always been a maverick thinker and doer, and this is reflected in my writings and changing lifestyles over the years. My books are non-fictional works (so far) dealing with a range of diverse subjects that I have spent years investigating: natural horse care based on my research of America's wild horses, the plight of wild animals living in zoos, the ancient craft of natural hide tanning (including Cheyenne Indian bison hide tanning), natural dental care, a political and economic model for democratic egalitarianism, the paranormal and mysticism, and, of course, this biography of my late gay uncle, George who died in 2015 at the age of 101.

www.ingramcontent.com/pod-product-compliance
Lightning Source LLC
Chambersburg PA
CBHW051358070526
44584CB00023B/3209